CULTURALLY RESPONSIVE STRATEGIES FOR REFORMING STEM HIGHER EDUCATION

CULTURALLY RESPONSIVE STRATEGIES FOR REFORMING STEM HIGHER EDUCATION: TURNING THE TIDES ON INEQUITY

EDITED BY

KELLY M. MACK
Association of American Colleges and Universities, USA

KATE WINTER
Independent Consultant and Evaluator, USA

MELISSA SOTO
University of California, USA

United Kingdom – North America – Japan – India – Malaysia – China

Emerald Publishing Limited
Howard House, Wagon Lane, Bingley BD16 1WA, UK

First edition 2019

Copyright © 2019 Emerald Publishing Limited

Reprints and permissions service
Contact: permissions@emeraldinsight.com

No part of this book may be reproduced, stored in a retrieval system, transmitted in any form or by any means electronic, mechanical, photocopying, recording or otherwise without either the prior written permission of the publisher or a licence permitting restricted copying issued in the UK by The Copyright Licensing Agency and in the USA by The Copyright Clearance Center. Any opinions expressed in the chapters are those of the authors. Whilst Emerald makes every effort to ensure the quality and accuracy of its content, Emerald makes no representation implied or otherwise, as to the chapters' suitability and application and disclaims any warranties, express or implied, to their use.

British Library Cataloguing in Publication Data
A catalogue record for this book is available from the British Library

ISBN: 978-1-78743-406-6 (Print)
ISBN: 978-1-78743-405-9 (Online)
ISBN: 978-1-78769-953-3 (Epub)
ISBN: 978-1-78769-954-0 (Pbk.)

INVESTOR IN PEOPLE

This book is dedicated to all of the undergraduate computer/information science students who were ever made to feel as if they didn't belong. You do.

Acknowledgments

The authors of this book wish to acknowledge the following individuals:

Our institution coaches for their help in pushing us into our institutional and personal greatness with culturally responsiveness (in alphabetical order): Dr Beverly Bickel, Dr Goldie Byrd, Dr Kristine Garza, Dr Lethia Jackson, Dr Patricia Lowry, Dr Patrice McDermott, Dr John Matsui, Dr Robert Megginson, Dr Sumun Pendakur, Dr Orlando Taylor. Our presenters, workshop leaders, and facilitators for guiding us through the journey, especially the difficult parts (in order of appearance): Dr Brian Nosek, Project Implicit; Dr Etta Hollins, University of Missouri-Kansas City; Dr Erika Camacho, Arizona State University; Dr Nathan Klingbeil, Wright State University; Dr Dorinda Carter-Andrews, Michigan State University; Dr David Truscello, Community College of Baltimore County; Dr Larry Coleman, Community College of Baltimore County; Dr Tammy Elser, Insight Educational Services, Inc.; Dr Adriana Medina, University of Maryland Baltimore County; Eva Piera Escriva, University of Maryland Baltimore county; Dr David Leonard, Washington State University; Ms Stephanie Briggs, Community College of Baltimore County; Dr Judith Katz, Kaleel Jamison Consulting Group, Inc.; Dr Kamau Bobb, Georgia Tech University; Dr Diana Kardia, Kardia Group, LLC; Dr Tom Wolff, Tom Wolff & Associates. Our editors for guiding us toward our full writing potential (in alphabetical order): Dr Elizabeth Child, Dr Judith Keen, Dr Katie McGraw, and Dr Christa Washington. Our advisory board for holding us accountable to ourselves (in alphabetical order): Dr Jamie Bracey, Dr Melvin Hall, and Dr Eileen Parsons. Our program officers for believing in our work and our potential to do better: Dr Sue Cui and Dr Ryan Kelsey. The AAC&U Staff of the Office of Undergraduate STEM Education, especially Mr Sean Penny for sharing his expertise, wisdom, and passion for equity. The Helmsley Charitable Trust for their generous funding and for partnering with us in the reform of STEM higher education.

Contents

Foreword
Ryan Kelsey and Sue Cui — xi

Chapter 1 That None Shall Perish
Kelly M. Mack and Kate Winter — 1

Chapter 2 Theoretical Underpinnings of TIDES: Priorities, Processes, and Promise
Melvin Hall, Jamie Bracey, Eileen Parsons and Tykeia Robinson — 15

Chapter 3 Cybernetic Girls Can Be Pinky: Strategies to Recruit and Retain Latinas into STEM in the Context of Faculty-to-student Empowerment
Lilliam Casillas-Martinez and Wilson Gonzalez-Espada — 33

Chapter 4 Changing Faculty Culture to Promote Diversity, Equity, and Inclusion in STEM Education
Jennifer Speed, Donald L. Pair, Mehdi Zargham, Zhongmei Yao and Suzanne Franco — 53

Chapter 5 In Search of Hidden but Accessible Truths: Coding for All at Queens College
Eva M. Fernández and Christopher Vickery — 73

Chapter 6 Fostering an Environment for All Students to Succeed in Computer Science: Integrating Culturally Responsive Pedagogies with Curricula Redesign
Kiron Sharma, Laila Khreisat, Diana Cvitan and Gurjot Singh — 97

Chapter 7 Culturally Responsive Strategies for Addressing Recruitment and Retention of Women in STEM: Online Modules for Building STEM Majors' Computational Skills
Mark Matlin, Elizabeth McCormack, Douglas Blank and Jennifer Spohrer — 115

Chapter 8 Culturally Responsive Computational Science through Research Experience in Core-curriculum Courses
Lior Shamir, Franco Delogu, Melinda Weinstein and Hsiao-Ping Moore — 135

Chapter 9 A Journey of Discovery
Alla Webb, Raymond Gonzales and Monica Parrish Trent — 153

Chapter 10 Equity through Access to Computer Science Learning at a Small Liberal Arts College
Kathleen Purvis-Roberts and Thomas Poon — 173

Chapter 11 Challenging Us to Change
Helen H. Hu, Patricia B. Campbell, Jessica C. Johnston, Brian Avery, Greg Gagne and Julie Stewart — 187

Chapter 12 The Rising TIDE of Wright State University: Context, Connections, and Consequences
Travis Doom, John Gallagher, Michael Raymer and Kathleen Timmerman — 201

Chapter 13 Music as the Icebreaker for Learning to Code
Ani Nahapetian, Virginia Huynh, Omar Ruvalcaba, Ric Alviso and Gloria Melara — 217

Chapter 14 Interventions Addressing Recruitment and Retention of Underrepresented Minority Groups in Undergraduate STEM Disciplines
Cleo Hughes Darden, Roni M. Ellington, Jigish Zaveri, Sanjay Bapna, Linda Akli, Stella Hargett, Prabir Bhattacharya, Ali Emdad and Asamoah Nkwanta — 229

Chapter 15 Strengthening Computer and Mathematical Sciences Engagement and Learning
Sambit Bhattacharya, Daniel Okunbor, Chekad Sarami, Perry Gillespie and Radoslav Nickolov — 249

Chapter 16 Measurement and Assessment
Kate Winter and Gabriele Haynes — 259

Index — 273

Foreword

What you are about to embark on in reading this book is a grantmaking team's dream scenario.

After months of dialogue and analysis, strategy, and negotiation, a foundation places a big bet on a recognized champion of higher education to tackle a complex challenge facing our country. That champion takes the bet but does not simply carry out a project or initiative. Instead, she initiates something much bolder — something akin to a *movement* — a new and different community that has the potential to grow and sustain in the lives of college communities to the point where it becomes a kind of *new normal*.

This book is a further step in the building of that *new normal*. It was not conceived of in any grant proposal — it arose from the work organically. And as with any potential movement that has sustaining power, it has been carried out as a true collaborative effort, built from the field by the field for the field of higher education.

If you have picked up this book, you may already know the United States is no longer positioned to be the long-term global leader in science, technology, engineering, and mathematics (STEM). This is in part because the United States has more or less stood in place, encouraging only our so-called "best and brightest" to proceed into these professions, while other countries have been racing to catch up. If this story is news to you, not to worry, you will be caught up by the end of the first chapter.

Given the power of technology, this stagnation cannot be allowed to stand if our country is to remain competitive in the global economy. More importantly, as has become readily apparent with our recent politics, this stagnation cannot stand because nothing less than our democracy is at stake. To foster a more equitable world, it is our collective responsibility to provide opportunity to all learners no matter their racial or ethnic background, gender, sexual orientation, or place of birth, so that those who will lead us into the next frontiers of science and technology will be representative of the population they are serving.

So what to do? Well, there are many steps to be taken, but among them is catalyzing a focus on creating a more inclusive and equitable culture on our campuses. TIDES chose to begin in introductory computer science classrooms across a diverse group of colleges and universities. Why computer science? Because at the time this work was initiated, it was *the one* discipline shown to be getting *less* diverse (particularly in terms of gender) at our colleges despite our school admissions seeing a surge in diversity. And its faculty are also among the least diverse of any field. So the determination was to start where the problem was particularly acute and connect to other disciplines through faculty collaboration.

The idea of collaboration was included intentionally because faculty are at the center of the change we seek in higher education. Together, they create the culture on our college campuses, and to use a computer science metaphor, faculty are our primary *interface* with our future: the students. And as you will come to learn, the future is bright because the vast majority of faculty are committed to student success.

This work takes place against the backdrop of important developments in US higher education. College quality, affordability, and worth becomes even more critical as a postsecondary credential becomes indispensable for upward social mobility and a career that will exist well into the future. Inclusivity, representation, and belonging of diverse people, backgrounds, needs, and philosophies are actively negotiated as a new college-going demographic arrives to class. Other shifts are manifesting in more invisible ways, in the hearts and minds of college faculty and staff, as they examine their responsibilities as educators of the citizens, innovators, and leaders of tomorrow.

The accounts in this book will demonstrate how faculty can, indeed, lead our institutions of higher education into a more inclusive and promising future for all. You will read about departments examining and changing their teaching to better attract students from underrepresented groups. There are models for discussing personal identities among colleagues and students so that our differences can be positioned as classroom assets. These chapters also reveal what it took for some colleges to integrate new elements into existing infrastructure at the classroom, department, and institution levels. This book is rich with examples of good teaching in the computational sciences, including uses of project-based learning, classroom participation tools, peer mentors, and learning communities. Lastly, the authors offer deeply personal reflections on how they came to recognize their considerable impact on individual student achievement, and as a result, how they have changed as faculty.

Because these faculty persisted over several years through courageous conversations, reflected on their identities as teachers, mentors and collaborators, and changed their approach to teaching – and then importantly – shared their experiences with others on their campuses, the work of TIDES will impact thousands of students year after year for decades.

This approach to sustained change is consequential because it is only with a diverse STEM workforce that we can hope to achieve breakthroughs that will lead us to a more equitable world. And it is only a representative STEM workforce that can be counted on to ensure that technology contributes to leveling the playing field rather than continuing to exacerbate our differences.

As grantmakers, our aim was to create the conditions for change by providing space and time for tough conversations, to respect the people and institutions who choose to do this work, and to cheer them on through the wins and struggles alike. Whether you work in academia or are an external stakeholder, we hope that these lessons can inspire you, as they have for us, to play a role in the *movement* that has begun. It has been a privilege to witness the journey of TIDES and its champions. For that, we are grateful as grantmakers, but more so as citizens of our interconnected, colorful, and hopeful world.

Ryan Kelsey & Sue Cui

Chapter 1

That None Shall Perish

Kelly M. Mack and Kate Winter

> *Don't try to fix the students.*
> *Fix ourselves first.*
>
> — Marva Collins, circa 1975

Reflection

There were only eight of us in the class. Being so few in number meant that we all sat in the front row of the classroom. An upper level, honors class for Biology majors. Of this elite eight, only one of us was white, the rest were African American like me. Not an odd situation for a Historically Black Institution. Our professor was white. Also not odd for an institution like this.

Every other day of the week — Monday, Wednesday, and Friday — for 50 minutes at a time, we pored over our notebooks to write down as much of what he said as we possibly could. He talked fast. And because it was the 1980s, there were no natural breaks or pauses between sentences for him to change slides or, Heaven forbid, write on the chalkboard (as most professors did back then). He just talked.

At the surface, this would have appeared to be "normal." But, if you looked just a bit more closely, you would have noticed one ever-so-slight subtlety that would forever change how I viewed students of color in STEM classrooms. You would have noticed that even though he was teaching, he was only teaching to one of us, for the entire 50 minutes. Guess which one. For 50 minutes, with feet planted firmly on the floor and pointed in our direction, his upper body was contorted in such a way that everything from the waist up faced in the direction of the one white student in the room, who sat at the far left end of our row. The rest of us were invisible; our learning was insignificant. There was essentially no way for him to know by the looks on our faces if we were puzzled about the material. There was no way for him to sense – as all good educators do – whether or not we were connecting with the lesson, drawing the right conclusions, or mastering the concepts being discussed at us. There was practically no way for him to know when any of us even raised our hands to ask a question. In those 50 minutes on every Monday, Wednesday, and Friday of the semester, the learning experience of one white student was generalized to an entire class of students of color. And, for him (and maybe that one white student), that was alright. But, for us, there was an undeniable and unspoken element of stolen opportunity in that class that, even today, is painful to explain.

It has been decades since I completed that course. I earned an A, but I suspect it was despite the way I was taught, not because of it. It is unfortunate that while much has changed in US undergraduate STEM classrooms since then, much has also remained the same. Students of color continue to report feelings of isolation, lack of belongingness, marginalization, and invisibility. And we, as educators, continue to search for new ways of ameliorating these feelings – many of which are focused on "fixing" the student. For the life of me, though, I cannot understand what about the me back then would have needed to be fixed in an Honors Biology class that I had earned the right (and privilege) to be in. I had a strong GPA. I was thriving in the discipline. I felt like I belonged at the institution. I had a community of friends. I was fully assimilated into the culture of the institution. I was applying to graduate schools, and getting acceptances. I had not one, but several summer research internships under my belt. According to modern STEM higher education beliefs, I was "fixed." But, was he?

Organizational Context

The Association of American Colleges and Universities (AAC&U), founded in 1915, has long been recognized and respected as a national leader in promoting liberal education at the postsecondary level. Contemporary views about liberal education, though, have been fueled by common misunderstandings that: (1) far-too-narrowly limit it to the arts and humanities only; (2) selectively dismiss the medieval origins of the liberal arts, which included both mathematics and the sciences; or (3) both. The result is a contemporary interpretation of education – liberal or not – that, as Steve Jobs noted, does not "make our hearts sing."

Through its dual, century-old commitments to liberal education and inclusive excellence, AAC&U is uniquely positioned to not only correct these misperceptions, but also ensure that all students – regardless of gender, race, socioeconomic status, or sexual orientation – have equitable access to a liberal education that affords them opportunities to meaningfully contribute to the US STEM workforce in ways that will position them for decision-making authority and maximal impact.

However, according to Chris Carter, "the teaching of any science, for purposes of liberal education, without linking it with social progress and teaching its social significance, is a crime against the student mind." Indeed, if we are to prepare a generation of scientists who are both competitively trained *and* liberally educated to solve the most complex problems of our day, our teaching strategies cannot rely so heavily upon the one I endured or any facsimile thereof. Nor can they rely upon our merely gaining a deeper understanding of "what works" in undergraduate STEM teaching and learning. In other words, the teaching of the sciences must extend far beyond teaching core scientific principles. Today, our teaching must also demonstrate both the practicality of applying those principles to real-world problems as they unfold in real time and the necessity of including diverse worldviews for prioritization of those problems and their solutions.

To better position itself for impact in the sciences, in 2010, AAC&U expanded its mission-level commitments to liberal education and inclusive excellence through a strategic merger with Project Kaleidoscope (PKAL) – a leading national alliance for the reform of STEM higher education. Since its founding in 1989, PKAL has provided high-impact professional development opportunities for STEM faculty to gain mastery in implementing advanced pedagogies, transformative leadership strategies, and interdisciplinary analyses of educational outcomes. Today, PKAL exists as both a vibrant network of nearly 10,000 STEM academicians and an epicenter for promoting the deeper understanding of not only "what works" in undergraduate STEM education, but also "for whom it works" and "under what conditions it works best."

Background and Significance

Arguably, not since World War II has there been a greater clarion call for scientific discovery and innovation than now, especially in the computer/information science disciplines. In fact, by the end of this decade, the US economy will annually create over 120,000 new jobs requiring at least a bachelor's degree in computer science to satisfy the workforce demand for emerging fields like cloud architecture, forensic investigation, and geospatial technology (Evans, Mckenna, & Schulte, 2013). However, currently, only approximately 56,000 computer science baccalaureates are produced each year (NSF, 2017). This dilemma is further complicated by a shifting sociopolitical landscape that has created and now perpetuates the systemic marginalization of the "new majority" of undergraduates in US higher education – women, students of color, and those from low socioeconomic backgrounds (Schneider, 2014) – who represent not only rich sources of untapped talent, but also the diversity of perspectives and worldviews that are essential for addressing the most vexing computer/information science problems of our day.

For decades, much attention to and support for broadening the participation of new majority students in STEM oftentimes has amounted to no more than vigorously addressing perceived academic and social deficiencies within undergraduate students themselves (Valencia, 2010). On the other hand, others – with whom we wholeheartedly agree – have identified comprehensive pedagogical reform as one of the most advanced mechanisms for redressing the systemic marginalization of new majority students in STEM disciplines (Tsui, 2007). However, mastery of the pedagogy – *particularly culturally responsive pedagogy* – commonly poses a substantial challenge for STEM faculty who oftentimes lack the substantive knowledge of and proficiency in teaching strategies that would enable *all* students to master STEM content (Froyd, Fowler, Layne, & Simpson, 2005). Further, the traditional approaches to faculty professional development, far too often either: (1) overlook the collective wisdom of faculty (Wolff, 2016); (2) fail to holistically consider the root causes of faculty indifference to pedagogical reform (Fairweather, 2008); (3) are designed primarily as isolated attempts that are nearly impossible to export, adapt, or bring to scale (Kania & Kramer, 2011); or (4) pay far too little attention to the racial and structural inequities that persist within the culture of higher education, at large, and the computer/information sciences, more specifically (Williams & Marxer, 2014).

To that end, the AAC&U Teaching to Increase Diversity and Equity in STEM (TIDES) was introduced to the US undergraduate STEM reform community in 2014 as a different approach to professional development for STEM faculty – one that could eliminate the deficiencies named above and, ultimately, turn the tide on inequity. Its goal was to touch, either directly or indirectly, at least 100,000 students, primarily those from historically underrepresented groups.

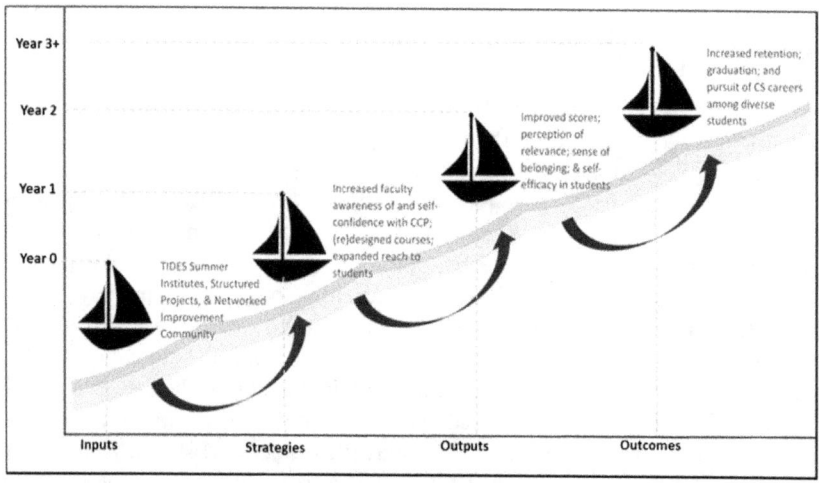

At its core, TIDES offered a re-conceptualization of the STEM faculty professional development domain in ways that reject conformity to centuries-old beliefs about the sovereignty of the STEM professoriate in deciding who deserves to thrive in the undergraduate STEM classroom. It also represented a strong pivot toward equity and justice as core essential elements for immediate and widespread change in undergraduate STEM teaching.

Implementation

A National Competition

With generous funding from the Helmsley Charitable Trust, AAC&U launched a national competition. Nearly 200 institutions of higher education responded to a call for proposals that solicited innovative ideas and strategic plans for retaining diverse students in the computer/information sciences through the implementation of culturally responsive pedagogies. Two interdisciplinary review panels selected fifteen finalist and four honorable mention institutions (Figure 1) to receive funding and/or participate in the TIDES professional development intervention for STEM faculty. Each finalist institution was awarded up to $300,000 over three years to implement course design and/or redesign of a core STEM course, particularly in the computer and information science disciplines, in ways that were culturally responsive to the lived experiences of their diverse student populations. Honorable mention institutions received no TIDES institutional funding, but were supported by TIDES for their participation in its professional development activities.

Each institution developed a set of campus-level objectives based on the context of their local realities and motivations for broadening the participation of new majority students in STEM, which could then be mapped onto TIDES program-level objectives and grounded in national STEM workforce needs. Figure 2 shows the relative frequency of each TIDES-level objective across the fourteen finalist institutions, which were fully funded.

Direct goals were identified as specific domains that TIDES institutions intended to directly impact through their project activities, while indirect goals were those that were likely to be impacted if the direct goals were achieved. For example, increasing student graduation in STEM (a direct goal) is a likely outcome of increasing STEM student retention, which can result from improving

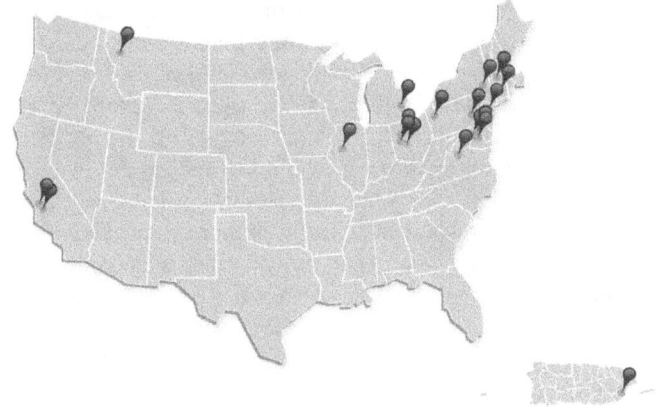

Figure 1: Map of TIDES Institutions.

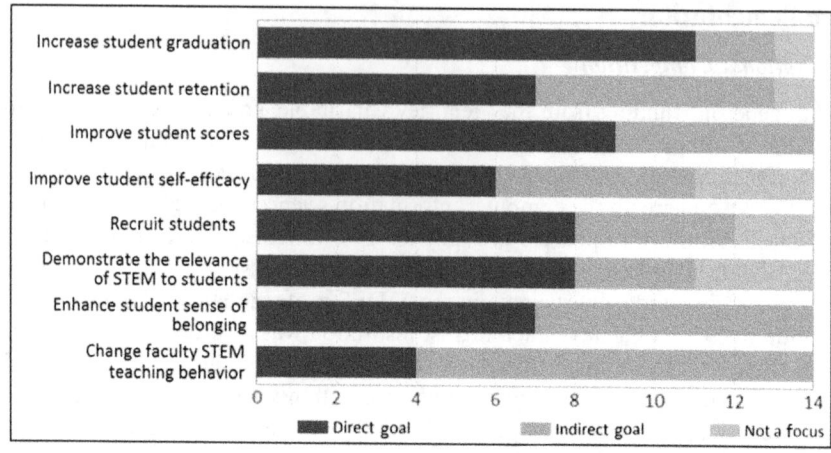

Figure 2: TIDES Institution-level Objectives Mapped to TIDES Program-level Objectives.

students' scores in STEM and demonstrating its relevance to their career aspirations and daily lives (an indirect goal).

Professional Development Program

At the outset, it is important to note that in every aspect of the TIDES professional development program, representatives from all institutions were exposed to the same intervention, regardless of whether they were fully funded finalists or honorably mentioned. As a result, what we discovered was something that we had suspected all along. There is not always a direct correlation between the degree to which an institution can change and the level of investment made in changing that institution. In some striking cases, our honorable mention institutions were equally, if not more, successful than our fully funded institutions. This is not to say that investment is not important. Rather, it is to note that careful attention must be paid to determining the level of readiness that an institution presents at the time of proposal submission. It cannot be emphasized enough that even more careful attention must be paid to the institutional environment to which a level of readiness is attributed. Indeed, no two college campuses are alike. What appears as a lack of readiness in one institution can, and sometimes is, readiness for another. Thus, it is more than the combination of institutional readiness and institutional context that is needed for predicting impact. It is also the ability to discern whether the level or type of readiness is appropriate for any given institutional context.

TIDES is rooted in an understanding that a key component of institutional readiness includes deep and critical introspection of ourselves as educators. Therefore, superimposed upon the objectives of individual TIDES institutions was a three-year-long professional development program, which, from the very beginning, sought to unmask the complexities of our personal implicit biases. Coupled with this reflection was an intentional focus on increasing our self-efficacy in implementing culturally responsive teaching strategies in the classroom. Many scholars have noted that self-efficacy is a strong determinant of behavioral change (Bandura, 1977; DeChenne, Enochs, & Needham, 2012; Mohamadi & Asadzadeh, 2012). Indeed, infusion of its core elements – performance accomplishment, vicarious experiences, verbal persuasions, and psychological states – into the professional development activities of STEM faculty not only promotes the kind of sustained behavioral changes required for culturally responsive teaching, but also positively impacts undergraduate STEM student learning even in the face of institutional barriers (DeChenne et al., 2012; Mohamadi & Asadzadeh, 2012).

Year 1 | *Journey Into the Unknown*

In every year of our TIDES professional development program, three representatives from each of the nineteen TIDES institutions were recruited as a team to participate in annual institutes and workshops. In many cases, the same representatives participated in professional development activities for the duration of the program. In other cases, the institution made the decision to rotate representatives as institutional needs and faculty schedules dictated. These interdisciplinary teams included one computer/information scientist, one administrator with decision-making authority over STEM curricular changes, and another faculty member from any other academic discipline engaged in the campus' TIDES-related activities.

In Year 1, these TIDES institution teams were immersed in the social science literature that undergirds cultural responsiveness, including elements of implicit bias, the intersections between gender and other social identities such as race and socioeconomic class, and the need for self-reflection regarding assumptions about students' abilities based on their appearances or backgrounds. It cannot be overlooked that immersion in the literature, alone, was insufficient to guarantee our success.

As a community, there were three agreements to which we had to be fully committed. The first agreement was based on a private conviction and public assertion that new majority students cannot and should not be blamed for their underrepresentation in STEM. The second agreement was grounded in our declaration that the power and privilege afforded to every STEM faculty member plays a critical role in the academic success of underrepresented students – both in and outside of the classroom.

Reaching these first two agreements was, of course, no easy task. The ease and speed with which we arrived at them was facilitated by the presence of "credible experts" (Gass & Seiter, 2016; Hovland, Janis, & Kelley, 1953) who were responsible for exposing TIDES faculty to the foundational theories and literature underpinning the underrepresentation of women and students of color in STEM. For our carefully designed institutes and workshops, our "experts" served as facilitators, plenary presenters, small-group discussion leaders, and informal advisors. Beyond their disciplinary expertise, each adroitly displayed extreme patience in responding to characteristic scientific skepticism, as well as compassion for our resistance to the intense emotions that are often evoked with difficult dialogues and a congenial disposition that fostered open and candid conversation. Collectively, this combination of expertise and empathy displayed by our credible experts contributed to an overall climate that was non-threatening – maximizing the likelihood their messages would be not only heard, but also internalized.

Beyond the didactic components of the TIDES institutes and workshops, institution teams utilized the rest of their time together engaged in meaningful small-group interactions where personal and professional tensions around cultural diversity could be more fully explored and resolutions made more relevant to a specific institutional context. To avoid having faculty revert to their default behaviors and beliefs associated with culture-less undergraduate STEM teaching strategies, all TIDES participants were paired with an institution coach. In keeping with Kotter's model (2012) for organizational change, our institution coaches served as a formidable guiding coalition. Kotter notes that individuals most ideal to comprise this body are those with strong position and broad expertise (Kotter, 2012). To that end, institution coaches were carefully selected and paired with TIDES institution teams based on the potential for full alignment between their expertise and the project's focus, and their appreciation for what more the project could accomplish if pushed to do so.

The nature of pushing a TIDES institution team toward bigger accomplishment, admittedly, meant that the relationship between institution coach and team was, at times, strained. Specifically, it was our institution coaches who were responsible for reinforcing messages gleaned from the didactic programming of TIDES Institutes, preventing faculty from reverting to old habits of mind, and challenging them to embrace completely new mindsets that could foster innovation – all while holding them accountable for operationalizing cultural responsiveness into core STEM course design and delivery. Thus, our third, and the most significant, agreement was to remain fully present and in community with each other, no matter the difficulty or uncomfortableness. With this third agreement established, together, institution coaches and their assigned TIDES institution teams powered through their work in interpreting, understanding, *and* integrating the key concepts, lessons, and motivations for culturally responsive pedagogical reform that addressed unique institutional contexts and dictated how STEM, especially computer/information science, courses were to be designed or redesigned as part of their TIDES projects.

Undoubtedly, the careful infusion of external influences – be it through credible experts or institution coaches – contributed to the development of a "safe, brave space" (Ali, 2017) for TIDES faculty. However, the penultimate influence on this environment stemmed from the community of TIDES faculty themselves. In many Institute and Workshop settings, it is often the case that there are moments of clarity – when that which was confusing to one becomes clear, or when that which was held to be true by one is proven false. It is also often the case that these moments are done privately within our own thoughts. For

TIDES, though, the strength of these moments was fortified each time they were done out loud, in open community, and without fear or apprehension. Whether in the Institute or Workshop, it was virtually impossible to predict which brave soul would emerge as the first to allow the community to witness his/her individual moment of clarity. Getting to these sometimes painful, yet vital moments of individual introspection or community co-learning was achieved with an intentional focus on creating and maintaining a symbolic and physical space that could safely foster challenging thought and dialogue while also relying on the very inhabitants of that space to protect it from the influence of undue judgment (Ali, 2017). As a result, persistently prodding and critically challenging the beliefs and values we hold dear to us became the hallmark of the TIDES institutes and workshops, where individual moments of enlightenment were expanded into community "breakthroughs."

Year 2 | *Journey into the Deep*

Numerous addiction programs understand that the first step to recovery is admitting there is a problem, and that the problem lies within you. TIDES, while absent any focus on addiction, is not an exception. However, strategically positioning this kind of training in the second year of TIDES' existence – as opposed to the first – was a departure from traditional norms. It was only after a full calendar year of coming to terms with our own implicit biases, and the role that they played in determining how we were showing up in the classroom, that we were ready to take on the next phase of reform – understanding cultural difference.

To that end, the entire second year of TIDES was dedicated to cultural competency training. As a community, we examined the entire gamut of relevant concepts – from the role of STEM in perpetuating the slave trade, to white fragility and cultural humility, to indigenous populations. As such, TIDES sought to scaffold the knowledge gained and internalized in Year 1 with specific hands-on practice with and immersion into cultures that represented those of students who have been historically excluded from the STEM disciplines. TIDES institution teams participated in a range of activities that, initially, did nothing more than reveal our complicity with the systems and structures of STEM higher education that have advantaged us as STEM academicians, yet also historically marginalized women and students of color. The major emotional "breakthrough" of the community that occurred in Year 2 resulted in our needing to abandon our planned agenda in search for one that could heal old hurts and restore deep mistrust. Abandoning a planned agenda is never the ideal situation, but in the case of our second TIDES Institute, it was necessary – especially if we were to grow as a community that could actually make a difference in reforming STEM higher education.

What followed was an intense, tearful, gut-wrenching, sometimes embarrassing, yet deeply honest dialogue among scholars from a broad range of academic disciplines, social identities, age groups, religious beliefs, and familial upbringings. In that moment, we were all sisters and brothers – supporting each other through a "rough patch," as only family can. The criticality of this turnaround moment cannot be overemphasized, though we may never be able to fully describe it in words. What is quite clear is that it is out of the pain of this moment that a networked improvement community emerged. However, unlike how it is described in the literature, this community was networked for more than a solitary goal that focused on reform, it was networked by *and* through its commitment to social justice and social change. We became strong, as a community, in the very place where we had identified our weakness. All that was left was to determine how to harness our newfound collective energy in positive ways as we looked toward the end of our TIDES professional development program and the beginning of our evangelization of the value of culturally responsive pedagogy in STEM.

Year 3 | *Journey into the World*

After two years of intense professional development, the question of how to bring resolution to our new understanding of ourselves was perplexing and, on some levels, frightening. The desire to avoid relapse was prominent for everyone involved, and was almost as significant as the desire to convince others to take this journey. What made this even more difficult was that our new understanding convinced us that there was no magical "list" of actions that we could create and disseminate to our colleagues that would somehow make them culturally responsive, no matter how committed to it they were. Nor would there ever be such a list. As rewarding as it would have been, we understood, without equivocation, that producing and promulgating such a list would do grave injustice to the entire undergraduate STEM reform movement.

Instead, we needed a new way of showing up in the classroom and a new way of being in the world. After having come to terms, even if at times under great duress, with our implicit biases and openly holding each other accountable for how they showed up in our TIDES space and with our students, our new way of being had to meet certain requirements. It had to extend beyond a "to-do" item and reach the core of who we were not as faculty, but as human beings. It had to evoke positivity. And it had to be effortless. If this was a new way of being in the world, it could not under any circumstances be burdensome. Most importantly, it had to be transferable across every possible lived experience that comes from our race/ethnicities, cultures, institutions, disciplines, genders, and sexual orientations.

We turned to mindfulness, the art of being fully present in the moment, as a way of transitioning ourselves from being subconsciously reliant on our biases when interacting with students to being fully aware of the whole student, moment by moment, regardless of their social identities. It has been linked to faculty well-being and, as such, associated with increased student success (Jeffries, Spagna, & Behring, 2017). However, its utilization has almost entirely been limited to improving the learning outcomes for students and their overall well-being.

For TIDES, our mindfulness work led us to the practice of loving kindness. Estrada, Eroy-Reveles, and Matsui (2018) summarize kindness as a unique quality that conveys respect for the dignity of another person. It is this quality, which they rightfully argue, affirms students of their presence at that moment and in that space (Estrada et al., 2018), whether it is in or outside of the STEM classroom.

As you conclude this chapter and continue with reading the ones that follow, we want to share with you a small excerpt from our loving kindness practice. It is our hope that this mantra not only informs you of the deeply personal and provocative work that characterizes the TIDES professional development experience, but also offers to you an expression of our authentic loving kindness toward you, the journey toward cultural responsiveness that you have embarked upon, and the valuable outcomes of your work that will result. It is also our hope that you will join us in sharing loving kindness at institutions of higher education across the country, with your students, your colleagues, and, most of all, with yourself.

Just as we wish to, may you be safe.
May you be healthy.
May you be free from harm.
May you live with ease and happiness.

Conclusion

The TIDES approach, unlike many others, offers a different course of action that looks beyond numbers and fabricated gradations of inclusion. This initiative wholly embraced the beauty and complexity of the human experience, as well as its myriad influences on the professional experience of STEM faculty and the educational experiences of the underrepresented students that they serve. But how?

Noted Pulitzer Prize winner, Maya Angelou, once said that "*...every journey begins with a single step.*" TIDES was our first step. Collectively, we didn't originate from the same place, and we didn't always take steps forward at the same pace. Regardless of the rate, range, direction, or force of change along the journey, the interactions that comprised our TIDES institutes and workshops caused a community – and the individuals within it – to flourish in acknowledging and addressing the cultural and historical elements causing and perpetuating the systematic marginalization of women, people of color, and those from low socioeconomic backgrounds. What will become apparent in the subsequent chapters is that TIDES made it "normal" to share challenging or uncomfortable beliefs in the spirit of learning and furthering the learning of others.

TIDES was also critical in shepherding a cadre of STEM faculty, primarily from the computer/information sciences, toward deeper introspection, a more crystallized awareness of societal inequities and their role in perpetuating disparities in undergraduate STEM education, and a more informed consciousness about what we, as educators in STEM higher education, should focus on changing and what we actually have the capacity to change. Only then could TIDES faculty make available to their students what they really need from us – effective, culturally responsive facilitation of their learning and mastering core STEM content, and advocacy for their well-being while doing so.

Later, we will recount how data were collected and analyzed through external evaluation, and how it was determined that TIDES was a resounding success – having a dramatic positive impact on faculty who, in turn, had a significant positive impact in their classrooms and departments. Here, though, it is important to identify what is perhaps the single most critical element that contributed to the success of TIDES. Arguably, it is the most valuable commodity for any faculty member – it is time. For TIDES, it is estimated that no less than 12 hours of face-to-face didactic instruction on social science theories was provided over the course of one year. We also estimate that an additional 3 hours were spent in the initial TIDES Workshop, 48 more hours in TIDES Institutes beyond Year 1, and a cumulative 152 hours were spent in follow-up faculty development workshops on individual TIDES campuses throughout the entire professional development program. Additionally, through our STEM Central online portal, TIDES faculty gained access to a series of online discussions, as well as traditional and extremist literature on justice and equity that ranged in topic from implicit bias to white fragility, and everything in between. Collectively, our TIDES faculty amassed more face-to-face "classroom" time and immersion with the theories and practices of cultural responsiveness than many traditional college courses of study!

In the end, only after three years, TIDES was able to touch nearly 300,000 students, over 60% of whom were from underrepresented groups in STEM! This far exceeded our original goal. To say that these results are exciting for us would be an incredible understatement. We are now left with no less than a durable framework for providing state-of-the-art professional development for STEM faculty. This pioneering model for professional development has also left us with a clear direction toward ensuring that "none shall perish" in undergraduate STEM education.

Yet and still, the most important thing to note about TIDES is not *what* was done by these faculties and administrators. Rather, what was most important about TIDES – which we hope you will agree – was *how* these faculty came to know what needed to be done to broaden the participation of their underrepresented students.

References

Ali, D. (2017). Safe spaces and brave spaces. *NASPA Research and Policy Institute*, 2, 1–13.

Bandura, A. (1977). Self-efficacy: Toward a unifying theory of behavioral change. *Psychological Review*, 84(2), 191–215. doi:10.1037/0033-295X.84.2.191

DeChenne, S., Enochs, L., & Needham, M. (2012). Science, technology, engineering, and mathematics graduate teaching assistants teaching self-efficacy. *Journal of the Scholarship of Teaching and Learning*, 12(4), 102–123. Retrieved from http://files.eric.ed.gov/fulltext/EJ992130.pdf

Estrada, M., Eroy-Reveles, A., & Matsui, J. (2018). The influence of affirming kindness and community on broadening participation in STEM career pathways. *Social Issues and Policy Review, 12*(1), 258–297. doi:10.1111/sipr.12046

Evans, C., Mckenna, M., & Schulte, B. (2013). Closing the gap: Addressing STEM workforce challenges. *EDUCAUSE Review, 48*(3).

Fairweather, J. (2008). *Linking Evidence and Promising Practices in STEM Undergraduate Education*. Washington, DC: Board of Science Education, National Research Council, The National Academies.

Froyd, J., Fowler, D., Layne, J., & Simpson, N. (2005). Frameworks for Faculty Development. In *Proceedings Frontiers in Education 35th Annual Conference* (pp. S3E-23–S3E-28). IEEE. Retrieved from https://doi.org/10.1109/FIE.2005.1612277

Gass, R. H., & Seiter, J. S. (Eds.). (2016). *Persuasion, social influence, and compliance gaining* (5th ed.). New York, NY: Routledge.

Hovland, C., Janis, I. L., & Kelley, H. H. (1953). *Communication and persuasion psychological studies of opinion change*. New Haven, CT: Yale University Press. Retrieved from http://www.worldcat.org/title/communication-and-persuasion-psychological-studies-of-opinion-change/oclc/187639

Jeffries, C., Spagna, M., & Behring, S. T. (2017, August). Toward a culture of self-care. *Inside HigherEd.Com*. Retrieved from https://www.insidehighered.com/views/2017/08/18/value-self-care-programs-campuses-essay

Kania, J., & Kramer, M. (2011). Collective Impact. *Stanford Social Innovation Review, Winter*, 36–41.

Kotter, J. P. (2012). *Leading change*. Cambridge, MA: Harvard Business Review Press.

Mohamadi, F. S., & Asadzadeh, H. (2012). Testing the mediating role of teachers' self-efficacy beliefs in the relationship between sources of efficacy information and students achievement. *Asia Pacific Education Review, 13*(3), 427–433. doi:10.1007/s12564-011-9203-8

NSF. (2017). Women, Minorities, and Persons with Disabilities in Science and Engineering: 2017 Report. *Women, Minorities, and Persons With Disabilities in Science and Engineering*, 1–21. Retrieved from https://doi.org/SpecialReport NSF 17-310.

Schneider, C. G. (2014). Making excellence inclusive liberal education and America's promise. *Liberal Education, 100*(4), 46–53.

Tsui, L. (2007). Effective strategies to increase diversity in stem fields: A review of the research literature. *Journal of Negro Education, 76*(4), 555–581. doi:10.1080/07351698809533738

Valencia, R. R. (2010). *Dismantling contemporary deficit thinking: Educational thought and practice*. New York, NY: Routledge.

Williams, J., & Marxer, S. (2014). *Bringing an Equity Lens to Collective Impact*. Retrieved from www.urbanstrategies.org

Wolff, T. (2016). Ten places where collective impact gets it wrong. *Global Journal of Community Psychology Practice, 7*(1), 1–13. Retrieved from http://www.gjcpp.org/en/resource.php?issue=21&resource=200

Chapter 2

Theoretical Underpinnings of TIDES: Priorities, Processes, and Promise

Melvin Hall, Jamie Bracey, Eileen Parsons and Tykeia Robinson

Teaching to increase diversity and equity in STEM (TIDES) is a project designed to increase the self-efficacy of STEM faculty in implementing culturally relevant pedagogies. This central element of STEM reform was packaged with other important innovations and campus-based objectives allowing for a conceptually broad and creative project. Critical in this endeavor was the existence of an unwavering core belief in the power of faculty to bring about fundamental change in the effectiveness of programs serving the needs of all students previously underrepresented in the STEM disciplines, particularly the computer and information science disciplines. Understanding the essential core elements that drove the project is an important backdrop against which to understand more fully the experiences and accomplishments of each institutional-based project. In particular, TIDES chose to centralize culture as an important consideration in educational practice and to recognize that culture as an element of context creates the conditions that greatly affect success in any transformation effort.

Culture and Education Practice in the US Historical and Contemporary Contexts

Contemporary US educational strategies still reflect early American adoption of the eighteenth-century Prussian education model, developed in Eastern Europe (modern-day Germany) as a tax-funded, government-run compulsory education system for children of the lower and middle classes (Soysal & Strang, 1989). Early thought leaders like Horace Mann, John Griscom, and other nineteenth-century American education leaders visited Prussia and made note of the system's focus on advancing a cultural framework or "way of being" that included teacher training to proselytize that culture. Mann advanced the Prussian system in America and led its implementation in

Massachusetts and New York (Mann, 1849). He advocated this uniform approach to learning as a policy to support America's early stages of nation-building and "liberty" indoctrination. A counterargument, offered by other scholars but generally ignored, held that the Prussian model would create American teachers and students more versed in conformity than in liberty (Alexander, 1919). Ultimately, this important philosophical debate did not deter the advocates, likely because the Prussian model offered a solution to standardizing the public's commitment to the ideals of the new nation.

The aligning of American educational systems with shared values, ideals, and history – grounded primarily in Eurocentric philosophies – was the critical source of cultural congruence facilitating nation-building. Early Americans effectively replicated the cultural best practices of European nationalism, but marketed public education within an idealistic framework of meritocracy managed by local, state, and the federal government. The framework implemented was responsive to and shaped by white Americans, since for nonwhites, it was not until 1954 that the US Supreme Court upheld access to a common shared education system as a legal right. However, this decision did not call for or anticipate adjustments to the curriculum to support the integration now required by law.

Despite the 1954 Supreme Court action, contemporary American education practices that sort and distribute American children into strata highly correlated with wealth, race, and class (Gatto, 2001) – disproportionately advantaging children who align with normed cultural values and priorities, effectively continuing defacto educational segregation. The American education system has been built upon a culture of denied access and socialization to dominant norms that presumed an emergent social primacy led by Eurocentric cultural mores and thoughts, from primary to secondary to higher education and throughout academe.

The traditional American education system reflects a culture of orchestrated differential access and socialization to support and justify the gaps in educational access and outcomes. The system's functional role in identifying and labeling stratified levels of talent within the contemporary nation-state still exists but is unsustainable from an economic perspective. In the twenty-first century, teaching and learning in the United States takes place in the most multicultural, multiethnic, and multigendered America the nation has ever known. The very real complexity of education in America reflects changing demographics. With these demographic changes, have also come cultural changes both nuanced and extreme.

With these demographic changes have also come tremendously challenging cultural changes and dynamic tension between what America was (its desire to be like Europe, but not be led by Europeans), what America is (a nation struggling to maintain dominant competitiveness in the global knowledge economy), and what America could be (an experiment in democracy that reflects an asset-driven approach to achieve a diverse and STEM-literate citizenry).

The pedagogy that has operated since the inception of the American education system is consistent with the persistent goals to ensure white children could compete with their European counterparts. American education practitioners are predominantly white, and inheritors of a framework designed to maintain white cultural and social superiority. TIDES employed culturally responsive pedagogies and practices to build American educators' efficacy through accessing richer cultural content and experimenting with ways to cognitively advantage a broader cross-section of students. Higher education faculty often enjoy the freedom to create and implement classroom innovation that their K-12 peers do not, and through TIDES, STEM faculty felt empowered to take a leadership role in engaging college students in computer science through a variety of culturally responsive paths.

With the discrepancies built into its social rhetoric and structures, America struggles to fix a system that was never designed to foster an egalitarian society. Instead, America's founding fathers adopted a cultural hegemony consistent with the culture most knew and admired – the British empire – but without the throne. It can be no surprise that the colonial war for independence against their view of England's tyranny was never a rejection of the extant elements of cultural and social superiority, but more easily understood as an intense within-group rivalry competing for primacy. Cultural hegemony within a society is operationalized within its institutions and has core attributes that benefit those who assimilate to the system, and either rejects or isolates those who do not. It bears repeating that the Prussian education system was adopted within America to advance the fledgling nation's competitive position in the world, especially against other European-descended adherents to Greco-Roman philosophy.

A challenge for contemporary education is to transform in ways that broaden the participation of nonwhites who now make up nearly half the nation's K-12 population and are slated to be the leaders of democracy and liberty within two generations. Thus, in considering the cultural foundation of the nation, culturally responsive and culturally reflective tactics will have value if the practices are in support of the vision of continued American competitiveness in a global innovation economy. Higher education certainly has a leadership role. There is optimism that pivoting the role of education from class-restricted pathways into a broader opportunity will allow America to remain one of the preeminent countries in the world.

The creators of US public education devised a system that supported a stratified society, which valued a culture of racially structured socioeconomic supremacy, even among white immigrants. The utilitarian aims of public education reproduced and reified societal inequalities and inequities. Youth born into low-income conditions received one kind of education whereas youth born into wealthier circumstances received another type of education. Similarly, individuals racially classified as white and ethnically Western European had greater access to higher quality educational experiences than those categorized otherwise.

Like pre-college education, higher education played a role in sorting, selecting, and preparing different groups for various stations in life. Although changes have occurred since the founding of public education and higher education in the United States, the exclusivity, inequality, and inequity built into the structure of the US educational system persist today. Because of its structural foundation, intentional and continuous action over a long period of time to transform the policies and regulations, both formal and informal, are required to alleviate the exclusion, inequality, and inequity that are hallmarks of US education. In the meantime, those involved and concerned about a high-quality education for all have employed efforts to change what occurs at the classroom level to achieve inclusivity, a stated goal in STEM education for several decades. Although elusive in nature, individuals within institutions with some form of institutional support have used approaches with an emphasis on culture in pursuit of inclusivity.

TIDES confronts the twenty-first-century reality that America's traditional educational tribalism poses a threat to the nation's innovation economy. Education institutions must respond to the most multicultural, multiethnic American in the most technologically interconnected economic framework the world has ever seen. Left unchecked, the traditional and dominant approach to education serves some learners well, but at the expense of its service to others. Culturally responsive pedagogy, then, is best thought of as a strategy more consistent with democratic access to educational excellence, as it seeks to respond to all learners rather than limiting that access to those most aligned with a selective cultural framework and affiliation.

The common core element across all campus-based projects in TIDES was the effort to employ culturally responsive teaching and pedagogy to encourage and support broader participation in the computer/information sciences. Within the context of teacher strategies intended to positively impact the student's mastery of computer/information science content knowledge, culturally responsive and culturally relevant teaching represents a break from traditional educational approaches aligned with the nation's Eurocentric epistemology for teaching and learning. It also marks a recognition that the content itself is not culturally and contextually neutral, so even content-focused teaching strategies perpetuate biases distinct from those derived from the Eurocentric pedagogical traditions. In other words, culturally responsive teaching alters the points of reference from which instructional strategies arise, re-centering them to align with the full array of learners' epistemological frameworks, cultural and linguistic backgrounds, and prior learning. In implementing this change in perspective, traditional content hierarchies are also challenged – giving faculty the freedom to alter when content is delivered and in what curricular packages it is provided.

The centuries-long investment in promoting European cultural dominance, while diminishing and ignoring the innovation and ingenuity of long-established Native American, African, Indigenous, Latino, and Asian cultures was used as justification for forcing low-level economic participation (denuded of their native cultural norms). The structural learning paradigm is yielding diminishing returns in a twenty-first-century America already at a risk of losing its global position as a beacon of democracy, and economic innovation. The gauntlet thrown to America's struggling public education industry is to produce thinkers, doers, and innovators from a population of American children and communities that are diverse and disconnected from pathways to success. The challenge requires faculty and administrative leaders who cull global anthropology, history, psychological and economic research to identify cultural assets that accelerate the cognitive and noncognitive development of contemporary American children, using every tool available to reflect on the content and delivery strategies utilized.

Culturally Responsive Teaching and Pedagogy Defined, Per TIDES

The common core element across all campus-based projects in TIDES was the effort to employ culturally responsive teaching and pedagogy. Against today's compelling realities, culturally responsive pedagogy is contextualized as a theoretical model for responding to social and economic transformation. If we presume the poor educational outcomes of nonwhite American students in STEM domains is a result of limited opportunities to learn (or inherit prior knowledge), then culturally responsive pedagogy also has the responsibility to explicate the culture of these aspirational domains.

TIDES is then a reflection of culturally responsive pedagogy theories, operationalized as disruptive strategies used in higher education to widen the array of students given access to the culture of computer/information science as novices, and future contributors to the field. The challenge of culturally responsive pedagogy is to not only add diverse materials to curriculum, but also respect where and how to penetrate the discipline's culture as transmitted, creating a shift toward inclusivity as a valued cultural norm within learning contexts. The culture of most American STEM domains is exclusionary given the paucity of representation of women and cultural or linguistic minorities. But the paucity alone does not provide insight into the attitudes, behaviors, and valued outputs that reflect the culture of the discipline. TIDES intentionally engaged faculty to become translators of the existing culture into a new and more inclusive computer science discipline, conveying a new code of behavior in their classes and to their colleagues.

Overall, culturally responsive (Gay, 2010) and culturally relevant (Ladson-Billings, 1994, 1995a, 1995b) pedagogies challenge traditional views about teaching and learning that are obstacles to inclusivity. If culture comprises beliefs, values, ideas, assumptions, and behaviors, it provides its members with ways to interpret reality and determine how to live their lives interacting with others (Nobles, 1980). The presumption that education is separate from culture fails to recognize learning as a process primarily responsible for transmitting culturally valued intellectual development and skills acquisition required to be a productive citizen in society. To that end, many educators fail to recognize the inherently cultural nature of US education and its alignment with European and middle-class values. These European, middle-class cultural values are replete in US education from the hierarchical and authoritative arrangement in how the system functions (e.g., teachers are accountable to numerous authorities) to communication patterns in the classroom (e.g., teacher initiates and students respond). These cultural values permeate the contexts in which teaching and learning occur and can enhance or inhibit learning.

For example, research shows that when concepts are couched in contexts that are alien to their lived experiences (an instructional decision influenced by cultural values), the students' resources are strained and are diverted away from learning the concepts to making the unfamiliar less alien, often resulting in underperformance (Song & Bruning, 2016). Traditional perspectives on education posit what the students lack or cannot do as primary explanations for the underperformance of students whose cultures are distinct from the ones embedded and celebrated in the teaching and learning contexts. In lieu of the traditional perceptions of education, culturally responsive and culturally relevant pedagogy explicitly and intentionally position education as an inherently cultural act in which only some groups' cultural values constitute educative processes. Culturally responsive and culturally relevant pedagogies do for students traditionally underserved by the US education system what the systems have done for white, European middle-class students since its founding. These pedagogies do so in the most multicultural, multiethnic, and multiracial America the world has ever seen, and elevate the cultural identities of the marginalized in teaching and learning in rigorous domains like computer science that may be more impactful when it "teaches to and through their personal and cultural strengths, intellectual capabilities, and prior accomplishments" (Gay, 2010, p. 25). Even though culturally responsive and culturally relevant pedagogy shares common premises, each has a distinctive scope and focus.

Culturally responsive pedagogy centers learners' identities – linguistic, ethnic, racial, and cultural – in teaching and learning and addresses them through aspects essential to teaching and learning, particularly instruction and curriculum. It calls for the critique and transformation of the curriculum, learning context, classroom climate, student–teacher relationships, instructional strategies, and evaluation mechanisms.

Several characteristics distinguish culturally responsive pedagogy. First, it deems the cultural heritages of racial and ethnic groups as worthy of incorporation into the educative process. It does not advocate the inclusion of all aspects of groups' cultures but promotes responsiveness to those elements of cultural socialization that most directly impact learning. Who is elevated as important in the curriculum and conversely who is not is an aspect of cultural socialization warranting attention when addressing inclusivity. Harding (1991) provided an example:

> What has been ascribed to the European tradition has been shown on closer examination to have been done elsewhere by others earlier. Although Harvey is credited with discovering the circulation of blood, Ibn al-Nafis studied the human body and beat William Harvey by three and half centuries. Ancient Iraqi schools taught algebra and geometry, knew the Pythagorean Theorem as early as 1700 BCE and knew the value of pi. (p. 308)

Second, culturally responsive pedagogy requires: (1) acknowledging the influence of cultural heritage on who students are and how they engage psychologically, socially, and emotionally with learning; and (2) linking learning to students' lived realities. Lave and Wenger (1991), and anthropologist and computer scientist, respectively, theorized learning in situated contexts as a function of everyday social processes. In fact, they argued convincingly that the witnessing and participation in socially constructed learning was mandatory for fuller, richer concept building. Thus, contextualizing a chemistry curriculum around the water crisis in Flint, Michigan, introduces both science and the sociopolitical issues available as relevant topics students may want to persist to understand.

Third, if the desired outcome is to accommodate the culturally influenced and diverse ways students learn, culturally responsive pedagogy provides the framework for critiquing the transformative potential of curricula rich in multicultural content, perspectives, resources, and instructional techniques. For instance, undergraduate students pursuing STEM disciplines, whose cultural experiences esteem social collaboration over competition, may value learning for altruistic purposes as equal to or more important than individual personal gain. As a result, their socialization can be translated to a cognitive asset that is reflected in learning contexts and cultures that foster facilitated instruction (flipped classrooms), project-based methods, and assessment based on community impact. One example would be to have undergraduates who express a preference for "real-world impact" devise a sensor system to monitor urban farm water usage. Or perhaps an instructional opportunity using project-based teaching that culminates in group projects to create age-appropriate forms of storybooks about genetics would be an appropriate mode of instruction and evaluation, respectively. In sum, culturally responsive pedagogy does not emerge organically; others must develop and cultivate it.

While situated learning theorists suggest social learning is an organic process, culturally responsive pedagogy does not emerge organically; faculty must develop competencies to cultivate it. And in the realm of STEM, expertise is particularly aligned with the behaviors, mores, and heuristic "tricks of the trade" that are transmitted to novices. Learning to code in pairs or to develop algorithms is valued inside the domain, while learning to debug open source code, or program sensors for an urban farmer may be more valued outside the formal classroom. The power of culturally responsive pedagogy is that it simultaneously provides an opportunity for mutually satisfying outcomes for faculty and students, as well as relevant knowledge acquisition in the domain and relevant problem solving that can support student motivation to persist. The ability of TIDES faculty to teach in mutually reinforcing contexts sets the stage for actualizing two levels of cultural relevance – learning outcomes valued by the domain and cultural relevance valued by their students.

With respect to the culturally responsive pedagogy, faculty serve three major roles (Gay, 2010): cultural organizers, cultural mediators, and cultural orchestrators. As *organizers*, they must be aware of how culture operates in teaching and learning and create an environment and climate that welcome and leverage diverse cultural heritages to enhance student performance. Teachers must continually work to devise spaces for expression in whatever form it may take (e.g., voice, ways of interacting, ways of knowing) and ensure mechanisms to validate and affirm are ever present. As *mediators*, faculty help students critically examine what is professed and enacted. That is, faculty assist students in identifying inconsistencies and contradictions in what society declares to exist (e.g., equality for all) and what actually exists (e.g., inequality for certain groups). Additionally, teachers scaffold constructive and productive dialogue for individuals to clarify their own understandings of their own and others' identities. Such scaffolding builds a community that honors difference, positions difference as an asset rather than a deficit, and nurtures a sense of common purpose and desire for mutual success among its members. Finally, as *orchestrators*, instructors work to make teaching and learning compatible with the cultural frames of reference of traditionally underserved students and to guide them in translating and using their cultural identities as invaluable resources.

Faculty as cultural mediators is of specific importance to TIDES. That is, faculty assisted STEM students in navigating the culture of their specific domain, ideally through the lens of what's important and valued in the domain and through the cultural lens of their students. Through its cultivation, culturally responsive pedagogy creates the opportunity to know, celebrate, and cherish the diversity of cultural heritage contemporarily possible in the domain. These opportunities become transformative when they support learners' ability to identify inconsistencies and contradictions in what society declares to exist (e.g., equality for all) and what exists (e.g., inequality for certain groups).

Like culturally responsive pedagogy, culturally relevant pedagogy foregrounds the identities of diverse learners in the educative process. It does so with a specific focus on faculty. With respect to faculty, culturally relevant pedagogy diverges from its predecessors: it unpacks and promotes a different foundation from which faculty practice, in lieu of emphasizing practices in isolation. Culturally relevant pedagogy is based not just on what faculty do, but on how teachers think about "the social contexts, about the students, about the curriculum, and about instruction" (Ladson-Billings, 2006, p. 30).

The first aim related to students is academic achievement, premised on high academic expectations for students. Academic achievement extends beyond the traditional conceptualizations of high-grade point averages and includes the development of skills, competencies, and capital (material, social, and cultural) necessary for navigating and excelling in STEM. Like culturally responsive pedagogy, culturally relevant pedagogy posits identity as a foundation for this achievement.

Through the curriculum, student–faculty relationships, learning environments, and instructional strategies, the cultural competence of learners is fostered, which is the second student-focused aim of culturally relevant pedagogy. That is, learners develop an understanding of, appreciation for, and the value of their own cultures. Some of the research in STEM indicates that students from traditionally underrepresented groups perceive they must choose either success in STEM or their identities. They receive messages that success in STEM requires assimilation, the adoption of norms and values dictated by STEM disciplines while simultaneously forgoing those associated with significant others and communities with whom they identify. Learners see a dichotomous choice: to give up and deny pieces of themselves or succeed in STEM. Culturally relevant pedagogy advances an alternative: students can excel and not only retain, but also affirm their identities.

High-achieving, culturally competent learners are equipped to pursue the last student-centered goal of culturally relevant pedagogy: critical consciousness. Critically conscious learners are able to recognize, comprehend, deconstruct, and interrogate injustices and inequities and use their understandings of STEM and STEM content for a constructive and productive change. Rather than providing learners the necessary skills, competencies, and various forms of capital (material, social, cultural) to simply succeed in dominant institutions, the critical consciousness aspect of culturally relevant pedagogy calls for learners to actively critique and contest injustices and inequities such that the United States progresses toward its valued democratic ideals.

Culturally relevant pedagogy pushes faculty members to examine how they view themselves and others. Culturally relevant pedagogues have a strong sense of self, a strong sense of community, see teaching as a way to give back to and build community, and view learners as experts with important knowledge and invaluable experience, who are capable of reaching high expectations. Culturally relevant pedagogues also view knowledge critically, as constructions of humans who are influenced by their imperfections and the imperfect surroundings in which they construct knowledge; this knowledge is adopted and validated by a select community that gives primacy to some values over others. Additionally, culturally relevant pedagogues believe in creating fluid student–teacher relationships that are equitable, empowering, and reciprocal, and act on a continuous basis to fortify them. These culturally relevant pedagogues then foster the development of students who achieve academically, are culturally competent, and who are critically conscious.

Pedagogical Practices Responsive to the Broadest Range of Contemporary Learners

Research has shown that culturally linked strategies can serve to remove or neutralize barriers to learning. Identifying which culturally linked strategies stakeholders can use most effectively is highly dependent upon contexts.

For some of the TIDES projects, institutional and departmental contexts made it more fruitful to employ strategies within the culturally responsive tradition. These projects worked to make the curriculum more gender-inclusive and multicultural, while other projects altered practices to elicit and honor student's voice and other forms of expression in planning and implementing courses. For other institutions and departments, culturally relevant approaches were most appropriate. These TIDES projects focused on changing the thinking of instructors and administrators about knowledge, students, and certain issues by engaging them in institutes, workshops, and coaching. Yet, other TIDES projects utilized a culturally congruent approach by incorporating into curricula, instruction, and learning environments different cultural values and practices nurtured by various communities in how to see and to interact with the world. Wade Boykin (Boykin, 1982, 1994; Boykin & Allen, 1988, 1999, 2000; Boykin, Allen, Davis, & Senior, 1997; Boykin, Tyler, & Miller, 2005) at Howard University has conducted several decades of work on cultural values in many African American communities and their influences on learning and engagement when those cultural values are woven into classroom practices. His work, and that of others who have continued the line of research, have identified nine dimensions (Cole & Boykin, 2008; Coleman, Bruce, White, Boykin, & Tyler, 2016). These dimensions include spirituality, affect, harmony, orality, social perspective of time, expressive individualism, verve communalism, and rhythmic-movement expressiveness. Other scholars have identified similar cultural values and practices (e.g., collectivism) for other groups traditionally underrepresented in STEM.

Cultural approaches to undergraduate education in computer/information science can span a wide range and differ in scope and emphases. Some approaches feature specific actions individuals can engage to make STEM more inclusive whereas others promote a way of thinking coupled with action. Efforts explicitly advancing action without an overt focus on a fundamental shift in understanding include funds of knowledge, and instructional and cultural congruency. Funds of knowledge (Moll, Amanti, Neff, & Gonzalez, 1992), a prevalent cultural approach, foreground the expertise of diverse communities by using them as scaffolds to connect learners' personal lives to STEM. Instructional congruency (Lee & Fradd, 1998) focuses on aligning discourses in STEM with the discourses of diverse communities. Cultural congruency (Au & Kawakami, 1994) advocates the incorporation of practices (e.g., ways of interacting) of diverse communities into the norms prevalent in the STEM. Other approaches are more comprehensive; they emphasize and foreground transformed thinking and action in concert for achieving inclusivity. Culturally responsive teaching and culturally relevant pedagogy are comprehensive models that are popular among practitioners.

An additional consideration in transitioning higher education curricula in STEM – integrated versus individualized cultural framework balancing – reflects a strategy for building first upon cultural values and practices (collectivism) and then balancing these strategies with those that favor individualized cultural orientations. Chavez and Longerbeam (2016) describe this consideration as engaging both the culturally based and individually oriented learner needs into a comprehensively responsive and balanced teaching pedagogy.

Whether the institution's TIDES approach was culturally responsive, culturally relevant, or culturally congruent, each project served to challenge the message "you do not belong here" conveyed by the absence of diverse cultural representations in the computer/information science disciplines.

How Context Considerations Shaped TIDES Underlying Assumptions, Strategies, Milestones, and Lessons Learned

With attention to the needs of learners from varied cultural and linguistic backgrounds, higher education must also attend to the context in which the learning is to occur. Postsecondary students do not have the luxury of unfettered access to learning resources, and lead lives peppered with factors that become impediments to taking advantage of learning resources that may be available. Equally problematic are classrooms or learning environments that contain institutionalized or systemic factors that become barriers for some students more than others, typically along gender, ethnic, and intersectional lines. In many instances, the TIDES projects fixed their gaze on reducing or removing these (whether temporal, emotional, structural, or simply perceived) barriers.

Attention to the ways in which context matters is prominently part of all aspects of TIDES, including the TIDES campus projects and the TIDES

Institutes. The fact that context matters and is omnipresent does not mean that it is uniformly understood or consistently identified and named, hence the need for focused inquiry and discussion of contextual issues and resolution.

TIDES faculty teams, understandably, brought a sense of context with them as a part of their collective gestalt of their campus or institution. This led to comparisons and modifications of understanding as assumptions and experiences were reviewed and compared. The varied contexts of the institutions further substantiated the often-tacit understanding that culturally responsive pedagogies must be localized and tailored to the milieu in which teaching and learning occur.

In localizing culturally responsive pedagogies, some TIDES projects leveraged orality – creative, rich, affect-inducing expression – and verve – preference for intense, vibrant stimulation that is variable. Other TIDES projects created spaces for: (1) communalism, a mode of interaction that elevates the interdependence and connectedness with people, as well as (2) social responsibility for individual privileges, and (3) rhythmic-movement expressiveness, a way of being that infuses rhythm associated with music and dance into everyday life. Projects utilizing a culturally congruent approach used instruction and evaluation as vehicles. Others deliberately altered context by structurally changing when and where computer science experiences were offered. For example, by placing coding experiences in general education courses, the context was effectively altered by extending the boundaries of the computer science offerings to potentially recruit students who previously would not have considered enrolling in a course.

Being articulate about contextual variables is a key to promoting the understanding of what TIDES interventions did. Responding to important contextual features requires knowing well the institution to be changed, and which features of the institution comprise change targets. At the same time, these institutions are the places where the effects of change efforts unfold. Without attending to the context, the work has no meaning or clear reference point.

Culture (in its many forms) is a key element of context. When you attempt to change something at your institution, the institutional, departmental, discipline, and classroom cultures are all elements of context. Therefore, the strength of TIDES comes from the fact that different types of institutions and instructional contexts are represented so that our pooled understandings create shared and defensible generalizable knowledge. Once shared, the experiences and insights of one campus project could, through the TIDES institute mechanism, come to the attention and possible adoption of others. None of the TIDES projects could tell the whole story of possibilities. The true "lift" for the TIDES community comes from the combined experiences across all projects. Typically, when one institution notes what is occurring on their campus, the information is interesting, but may not rise to the level necessary to promote serious attention and related reforms. However, when combined TIDES institutions form a microcosm of the entire range of institutions in the United States, common understandings, by definition, are a contribution to state-of-the-art knowledge. Whatever individual project results yield, they are context specific. Only through the TIDES collective, can discussions and new understandings authoritatively assert the conditions necessary to alter computer science instruction nationally.

Systems Thinking and Project Conceptualization

In general, project goals seek changes in contextual features that connote an altered organizational status. Specifically, right-sized interventions produce these altered contextual features, which when well designed, meet the challenges associated with the nature of the change intended. Conversely, results from an off-the-shelf strategy, while successful at one institution are certain to disappoint with differing contextual variables of another institution. It was with this in mind that TIDES faculty were provided access to experienced change agents that served as institutional coaches, providing an important sound check on perceptions, plans, and resource links.

Like many national STEM reform projects, TIDES projects had embedded assumptions about the institutional systems they sought to change. Keys to these assumptions were the salient contextual features (i.e., graduation rates, student demographics, and student retention) that were identified as targets to which "treatments" were intended to promote changes in contextual features. The reason behind the belief that this change was probable was the theory of change or logic model of the project – whether labeled as such or not. The theory of change is a belief about what it takes to make a change based on how we believe things work. The logic model is an operational definition of that theory of change, expressed in terms specific to the intervention planned. For TIDES, its treatments, or interventions, were in and of themselves mini systems embedded in other systems. Anything less than a stable systematic influence such as this could only hope to produce one-time, transient results. Indeed, no one would expect random or uncoordinated efforts to produce a regular change. Therefore, it is the integrity and fidelity of the intervention as a system that is critical and dependent upon the strength of the logic behind the intervention.

All systems operationally define important constructs, and these definitions create the boundaries of project influence. Unsuccessful projects often have failed to pay attention to how the actual boundaries of their intervention may be different than the project plan requires. It would not make sense, for example, to expect the graduation rates for athletes on a football team to go up if the only thing the coach did differently was to make the first-year players go to study hall. To have any chance of influencing graduation rates, such an intervention would have to include all team members. This is the boundary question, central to any intervention. Is the intervention right-sized and appropriately tailored to produce the needed results? Good conceptualization occurs when the scope of desired change matches the logic model, and similar congruence exists with the power of the intervention.

The TIDES projects intentionally considered culturally responsive pedagogies in the conceptualization and implementation of their interventions. They considered the learners, their contexts, and the boundaries most relevant to their interventions. The goals and strategies of each project were rationalized strategies within the context of the institution, defining institutional change accordingly. Theory of change and logic models brought a tangible quality to contextual considerations and the projects brought together strategically different campus actors important as allies in the success of their projects.

Range of Campus Initiative Goals and Boundaries

As noted, TIDES project sought to implement strategies consistent with the elements of culturally responsive pedagogy and cultural practices that cognitively advantaged traditionally underrepresented groups in STEM. Specific project details, provided later in this volume, contain a summary of those strategies; however, a brief list of illustrative examples reflecting attention to culturally responsive pedagogy follow:

- Engagement in efforts to change the thinking of faculty and administrators about knowledge, students, and certain issues: Westminster College, Morgan State University, and Montgomery College. These institutional efforts more closely aligned with culturally relevant pedagogy.
- Action to elicit and create space for student's voice and other forms of expressiveness: Lawrence Technological University and Fayetteville State University. These efforts more closely corresponded with culturally responsive pedagogy.
- Implementation of curriculum changes to be more multicultural and gender friendly: Bryn Mawr College, University of Puerto Rico Humacao, and Fairleigh Dickinson University. These institutions also implemented measures that reflected culturally responsive pedagogy.
- Implementation of curriculum changes to be more active and more collaborative: California State University Northridge, Pitzer College, University of Dayton, Queens College, and Wright State University. These initiatives enacted culturally congruent instruction with respect to the learners served by the respective institution.

The above illustrations provide a point of reference for the two questions paramount in any institutional transformation effort. Does the evidence suggest that the intervention was implemented as planned (with fidelity); and does the evidence suggest that it was the right intervention to install? Both questions are necessary for tandem, since it is possible to have strong evidence to support a theory that does not match the organization and therefore cannot lead to change in it. Similarly, inadequate conceptualization can produce nonsense results if the context was poorly understood and the wrong intervention chosen.

Building TIDES as a Community of Practice for Support and Critique

Institutional change, or altering the traditional, is slow, tedious, and considered to be a difficult task — especially if actions attempt to transform culture. Often, institutional change fails to overcome inertia, fizzling out as would-be change agents lose momentum over time. Purposeful institutional change efforts must, therefore, plan for ways to sustain momentum and focus. Nationwide change, like that of the TIDES initiative, is, arguably, more challenging, as it must balance changes at local institutions with a presence large enough to be deemed significant. To that end, TIDES augmented the individual institutional contexts of its participating institutions by creating a community of practice (Wenger, 1998; Wenger, McDermott, & Snyder, 2002; Wenger & Wenger-Trayner, 2015), adding an additional national context in which TIDES institutions functioned and were reinforced for culturally responsive strategy deployment.

The TIDES community of practice facilitated change in various aspects of institutional culture with tandem efforts on several campuses across the country. As such, TIDES intentionally and systematically provided professional development designed to allow STEM faculty opportunity to interact in an environment that was both stimulating and challenging while also supportive and nurturing (Austin, 2011; Bernstein-Sierra & Kezar, 2017; Gehrke & Kezar, 2017; Kezar & Gehrke, 2017). Embedded within this design is the understanding of the TIDES developers of the importance of creating a community to increase not only the impact, but also the likelihood that that impact would continue despite the expected resistance that typically occurs with change.

It is in the TIDES community of practice that knowledge production, dissemination, and learning created the tide that raised "the boat" of each institutional project. TIDES institutional teams brought this strategy to life and potency both through their institutional projects and contributions to the community itself. Collectively, these institutions formed knowledge claims that now define for them new ways of thinking about undergraduate computer science instruction. As such, the claims of knowing – along with the national sample of TIDES projects from which those claims originate – become the mechanism for transforming how other institutions can organize and define computer science instruction for themselves.

To build the efficacy of its community of practice, TIDES promoted a shared understanding of its overall goals, connoting a common vocabulary for topics related to institutional change, cultural responsiveness, transformation, and evaluation. Such vocabulary was used to facilitate discussion and share learning outcomes. Further, TIDES promoted the concept that it would support and learn from each other's efforts. TIDES naturally focused on academic STEM practitioners who shared a common domain of interest and a strong allegiance to the national-level TIDES community. As a result, the identity for this community of practice was defined at two levels – one at the level of unique campus environments and the other at the level of being a collective and national exemplar.

A major part of becoming a united community of practice was creating a safe space, but not one that was so comfortable as to promote self-reinforcing satisfaction. An important way that TIDES formed a community was to encourage teams to promote the discovery and interrogation of generalizable lessons in institutional change through sharing recognizance from their own work with the other TIDES teams. This paved the way for TIDES teams to experience and witness numerous "aha" moments, some more dramatic than the others. Such epiphanies stretched the capacity of individuals and revealed the dual nature of the TIDES work where they became more aware of their own positionalities and perspectives as they related to cultural responsiveness.

In order to deepen the commitment of TIDES and strengthen the community, at the end of the first year of conceptualization and implementation, the second TIDES Institute became a time to test whether institutional team plans and their implementation were solid. Each project team was expected to present a synopsis of the work conducted during the academic year. Based upon these presentations, teams received a dose of community feedback and tough love in the form of the "TIDES Tribunal."

A tribunal is understood in many cultures to represent a council of quasi-judges. This unique feature of the TIDES institutes included the empaneling of a team of three culturally responsive experts, also authors of this chapter, to provide formative evaluations of TIDES institution progress. The TIDES Tribunal heard presentations and made pronouncements in an open forum, relying heavily on culturally derived analogies to pronounce levels of project progress based on the presentations. Also, the Tribunal model afforded this community of practice an opportunity to take its own temperature in advancing TIDES as a collective mission across the institutions. Anecdotal feedback from TIDES project teams confirmed interrater reliability among the TIDES judges, and was deemed sufficiently consistent enough to allow the TIDES community to build on recommended strategies for culturally responsive pedagogical improvements.

The team presentations were rated by both the Tribunal judges and the entire community in real time. The judges reviewed project progress notes and team presentations, and rated them for the extent to which there was evidence of fidelity in the implementation of the planned intervention; and whether early outcome data were consistent with the implied logic model or theory of change, connoting a positive prognosis for continued success. Elaborations on the ratings provided by the Tribunal provided a nice opportunity to further coach each on issues related to what they were doing and, additionally, what they planned to accomplish by the end of the project.

Praise substantiated by examples from the projects and areas in need of improvements primarily constituted the critiques provided during the tribunals. Feedback, informed by a systems theory perspective, offered guidance in addressing gaps and missed opportunities, posed questions that teams could entertain in their own discussions and their work with their coaches, and evaluated the teams' efforts in terms of prospective impact.

Conclusion

Efforts to transform traditional structures intentionally devised at their inception to exclude traditionally underrepresented groups in STEM not only require the investment of our heads (learning new constructs and acquiring unfamiliar ways to see and interact with the world), but also necessitate the investment of our hearts. It takes more than our mental attention and cognitive "know-how" to address the systemic exclusion that occurs in STEM; it takes a commitment to a cause that withstands any resistance levied to keep current conditions the same. TIDES provides a blueprint for future initiatives in higher education to address the head *and* the heart. The institutes and workshops informed the TIDES participants about the aspects of cultural responsiveness that they did not know, and the discussions and debates prodded them to rethink what they thought they knew. Coaching provided throughout the experience helped TIDES participants to reflect and revamp, where needed, and the TIDES Institute helped to develop and cement a community who toiled together, cried together, and laughed together – while lifting each other up in order to produce an example that may help other institutions in their journeys to be more inclusive.

References

Alexander, T. (1919). *The Prussian elementary schools*. New York, NY: McMillan Publishers.
Au, K. H., & Kawakami, A. J. (1994). Cultural congruence in instruction.In E. R. Hollins, J. E. King, & W. C. Hayman (Eds.), *Teaching diverse populations: Formulating aknowledge base* (pp. 6–23). Chicago, IL: SUNY Press.
Austin, A. (2011). *Promoting evidence based change in undergraduate science education*. Washington, DC: National Academies.
Bernstein-Sierra, S., & Kezar, A. (2017). Identifying and overcoming challenges in STEM reform: A study of four national STEM reform communities of practice. *Innovative Higher Education, 42*, 407–420.
Boykin, A. (1982). Task variability and the performance of black and white schoolchildren. *Journal of Black Studies, 12*, 469–486.
Boykin, A. (1994). Harvesting talent and culture: African American children and educational reform. In R. J. Rossi (Ed.), *Schools and students at risk: Context and framework for positive change* (pp. 116–138). New York, NY: Teachers College Press.
Boykin, A., & Allen, B. (1988). Rhythmic-movement facilitation of learning in working-class Afro-American children. *Journal of Genetic Psychology, 149*, 335–348.
Boykin, A., & Allen, B. (1999). Enhancing African American's children's learning and motivation: Evolution of the verve and movement expressiveness paradigms. In R. Jones (Ed.), *African American children, youth and parenting* (pp. 115–152). Hampton, VA: Cobb & Henry Publishers.
Boykin, A., & Allen, B. (2000). Beyond deficit and difference: Psychological integrity in developmental research. In C. C. Yeakey & E. W. Gordon (Eds.), *Producing knowledge, pursuing understanding* (pp. 135–142). Stamford, CT: JAI Press.
Boykin, A. W., Allen, B. A., Davis, L. H., & Senior, A. (1997). Task performance of black and white children across levels of presentation variability. *Journal of Black Psychology, 23*, 427–437.
Boykin, A. W., Tyler, K., & Miller, O. (2005). In search of cultural themes and their expressions in the dynamics of classroom life. *Urban Education, 40*(5), 521–549.
Chavez, A., & Longerbeam, S. (2016). *Teaching across cultural strengths: A guide to balancing integrated and individuated cultural frameworks in college teaching*. Sterling, VA: Stylus Publishing, LLC.

Cole, J., & Boykin, A. W. (2008). Examining culturally structured learning environments with different types of music-linked movement opportunity. *Journal of Black Psychology*, *34*(3), 331–355.

Coleman, S. T., Bruce, A. W., White, L. J., Boykin, A. W., & Tyler, K. (2016). Communal and individual learning contexts as they relate to mathematics achievement under simulated classroom conditions. *Journal of Black Psychology*, *43*(6), 543–564.

Gatto, J. T. (2001). *The underground history of american education: An intimate investigation into the prison of modern schooling*. Oxford, NY: The Oxford Village Press.

Gay, G. (2010).*Culturally responsive teaching: Theory, research, and practice* (2nd ed.). NewYork, NY: Teachers College Press.

Gehrke, S., & Kezar, A. (2017, October). The roles of STEM faculty communities of practice in institutional and departmental reform in higher education. *American Educational Research Journal*, *54*(5), 803–833.

Harding, S. G. (1991). *Whose science? Whose knowledge?: Thinking from women's lives*. New York, NY: Cornell University Press.

Kezar, A., & Gehrke, S. (2017). Sustaining communities of practice focused on STEM reform. *The Journal of Higher Education*, *88*(3), 323–349.

Ladson-Billings, G. (1994). *The dreamkeepers: Successful teaching for African American students*. San Francisco, CA: Jossey-Bass.

Ladson-Billings, G. (1995a). Butthat's just good teaching! The case for culturally relevant pedagogy. *Theory into Practice*, *34*, 159–165.

Ladson-Billings, G. (1995b). Toward a theory of culturally relevant pedagogy. *American Educational Research Journal*, *32*, 465–491.

Ladson-Billings, G. (2006). Yes, but how do we do it? Practicing culturally relevant pedagogy. In J. Landsman & C. W. Lewis (Eds.), *White teachers/diverse classrooms: A guide to building inclusive schools, promoting high expectations and eliminating racism* (pp. 29–42). Sterling, VA: Stylus Publishers.

Lave, J., & Wenger, E. (1991). *Situated learning: Legitimate peripheral participation*. Cambridge: Cambridge University Press.

Lee, O., & Fradd, S. H. (1998). Science for all, including students from non-English-language backgrounds. *Educational Researcher*, *27*(4), 12–21.

Mann, H. (1849). Twelfth Annual Report for 1848 of the Secretary of the Board of Education of Massachusetts (pp. 116, 177, 121, 122).

Moll, L. C., Amanti, C., Neff, D., & Gonzalez, N. (1992). Funds of knowledge for teaching: Using a qualitative approach to connect homes and classrooms. *Theory into Practice*, *31*(2), 132–141.

Nobles, W. (1980). African philosophy: Foundations for Black psychology. In R. Jones (Ed.), *Black psychology* (pp. 23–36). New York, NY: Harper and Row.

Song, M., & Bruning, R. (2016). Exploring effects of background context familiarity and signaling on comprehension, recall and cognitive load. *Educational Psychology*, *36*(4), 691–718. doi:10.1080/01443410.2015.1072133

Soysal, Y. N., & Strang, D. (1989). Construction of the first mass education systems in nineteenth-century Europe. *Sociology of Education*, *62*(4), 277–288.

Wenger, E. (1998). Communities of practice: Learning as a social system. *The Systems Thinker*, *9*(5). Retrieved from thesystemsthinker.com/communitiesof-practice-learning-as-a-socialsystem/

Wenger, E., McDermott, R., & Snyder, W. (2002). *Cultivating communities of practice: A guide to managing knowledge.* Boston, MA: Harvard Business School Press.

Wenger, E., & Wenger-Trayner, B. (2015). *Communities of practice: A brief introduction – V.* Retrieved from http://wenger-trayner.com/introduction-to-communities-of-practice/

Chapter 3

Cybernetic Girls Can Be Pinky: Strategies to Recruit and Retain Latinas into STEM in the Context of Faculty-to-student Empowerment

Lilliam Casillas-Martinez and Wilson Gonzalez-Espada

Lilliam's Reflection

Attending the first Teaching to Increase Diversity and Equity (TIDES) Institute was an event that changed me forever and redefined my future. I joined the program from the perspective of a successful researcher at the University of Puerto Rico in Humacao (UPRH) and a Latina faculty who mentored over 100 LatinX, mainly females, to enter STEM fields. In addition to my publications and grants, my main accomplishment was that 40% of my students were accepted into a graduate program. The training at the TIDES institutes taught me that I was not empowering my students, but training "conformists" informed by my experiences in graduate school.

See, I attended a primarily white institution (PWI) where faculty, staff, and students were so different from me! I had no idea how to study, how to speak perfect English, or how to culturally blend in. I was determined to dress, speak, and behave like the Latina I am. However, my "attitude," as perceived by my first advisor, was "wrong," and he told me that I was not good enough and needed to go back to Puerto Rico. After changing advisors and publishing five peer-reviewed articles in three years, I proved him wrong. Yet, as I was still marked by my earlier negative experiences, I decided that I would not have my students suffer like me.

My advice to my students was as follows: (1) to assimilate and not to "rock the (cultural) boat," (2) to dress in a certain way for them to convey "success," (3) to avoid speaking Spanish, (4) to not wear high heels, and (5) to not display the Puerto Rican flag. I told them that our precious cultural symbols were trinkets, or "Latino stuff," and that they needed to be sensitive to the American culture by putting their own culture second. This advice was my perfect plan to "fit in." Because of my experiences with the TIDES movement, I now recognize that I was wrong. I learned from TIDES that there was much more I could do to truly empower my students in their future journey to graduate school. I just needed the proper training in culturally responsive pedagogies and how to adopt those strategies in the STEM classroom.

Something else I learned from the TIDES Institutes related to my perception of homogeneousness within the Puerto Rican ethnicity. When I was asked to describe how our university's proposal would help establish equity for Black Puerto Ricans, I naively hid under the comfortable blanket of overgeneralization and answered: "All Puerto Ricans are the same." Upon reflection, I now recognize that my behavior was a polite and expected response, one deeply ingrained in the minds of many Puerto Ricans by school lessons that emphasize our mutual mixture of Taíno, Europeans, and Africans. I never bothered to question my assumption that, since none of us were genetically "pure," none of us could be discriminated against due to our looks. The last thing I expected was an equity warrior to refute me by saying: "You said that because you look white."

I was speechless at this response and a flood of confusion overcame me. Those words, "you look white," still resonate in my mind because, for the first time in my life, I realized that I have a privileged position compared to dark-skinned Puerto Ricans. When I finally recovered my composure, I replied that my previous response was wrong and I challenged him to help me find strategies to help Black Puerto Ricans. There and then, I joined the TIDES militia of educational warriors to improve the way I would train new generations of students. Of course, coming from a STEM background, I knew I needed scientific evidence to convince others, and myself, about disparities between light- and dark-skinned Puerto Ricans. Upon my return to Puerto Rico, I looked for social scientists to help me, but practically all of them told me no one had ever published data on the lack of Black Puerto Ricans in STEM. The result of my inquiry was a collaborative study, described later in the chapter.

I also accept that I am part of many underrepresented groups in STEM, those of women, people of color, and first-generation STEM graduates. This acceptance is the result of a long but interesting path of discovery that, simultaneously, helped me to heal from my past. I embrace the fact that STEM educators should be sensitive and respectful to cultural differences, and that these differences should be respected, used, and integrated into the classroom to contextualize content knowledge.

Through TIDES, I learned a completely new language, consisting of important ideas such as impostor syndrome, implicit bias, white privilege, white fragility, micro- and macro-aggressions, and horizontal aggressions. As I started learning this new language, in a way, I felt liberated by the realization that there was nothing wrong with me, my language, the way I dressed or behaved, my flag, or my determination to stay close to my culture and values. For example, I remembered how distressed I felt by just learning about micro- and macro-aggressions. In addition, before I learned what impostor syndrome means,

I used to think that I never deserved the accomplishments I obtained with my hard work and that they were given to me just because I was the only Latina.

In my scientific talks, I now incorporate what I learned through TIDES. I use words like impostor syndrome to make sure all LatinX students learn about this concept, and stop thinking they do not deserve the right to be a scientist. I explain to the audience that even though racial and ethnic groups seem to be different, we have many more things in common; and whatever differences do exist, they must be embraced and accepted. I emphasize that we speak in Spanish because it is easier to convey subtle ideas with precise language, not because we have a secret code that we use to talk negatively of non-Spanish speakers and get away with it. I speak of the value of our flag as a unifying symbol. I stress that for Latinas it might be important to be feminine, but that it is not inversely proportional to being smart. In summary, learning this new language empowered me to finally vocalize and share with my students many years of insecurities, and then to use my experience as a springboard for my students to share theirs.

TIDES is a community of people where I now feel secure to confidently express my #MeToo moments without any fear of rejection or, worse, the cold and silent looks of colleagues who think: "You are right, but in science we do not talk about that. Scientists are not humanitarians, we just concentrate on science." I really hope that these new TIDES of equity, inclusion, and culturally responsive teachings do reach all Hispanic Serving Institutions (HSI), in particular the thousands of Latina students who attend them, and who may think that having vaginas somehow disqualifies them for scientific careers. The opposite is true; if Latinas want to enter careers that are perceived to be "highly masculine," it is our right to do so. I also hope that this chapter will help college faculty and students to implement specific strategies to achieve gender and ethnic equity in their STEM classrooms. I must do my best to help change the shameful statistic that less than 5% of Latinas enter into US STEM graduate programs every year.

Institutional Context

Puerto Ricans comprise 25% of all Hispanic doctorates employed in disciplines associated with science and engineering (S&E) and 23% of recent Hispanic S&E PhDs (National Science Board, 2014; National Science Foundation, 2015; Snyder, de Brey, & Dillow, 2016). Many of these professionals attended the University of Puerto Rico (UPR) system, which consists of 11 campuses and accounts for 11.5% of all US Latinos entering STEM graduate programs in the nation. UPRH is one of eleven campuses in the system, and it is the main public four-year HSI in Southeastern Puerto Rico. It has an enrollment of about 3,900 undergraduate students, 95% of whom are ethnically Latino and racially mixed (Taíno/European/African), and 18% of whom are first-generation students. About one in four students are pursuing STEM degrees, and about one in three of them come from households earning less than $20,000 a year. A total of 64% of UPRH students are female. Of these, 62% are first-generation and 65% come from low-income households (University of Puerto Rico, Institutional Research Office, http://www.upr.edu/humacao/opaii/).

Undergraduate STEM programs in Puerto Rico are designed mainly to supply professionals to the pharmaceutical and biotechnology companies established on the Island. Consequently, most STEM faculty at UPRH concentrate their efforts on teaching scientific knowledge and skills, with very little focus on assessing their own teaching or implementing the latest instructional strategies. Concepts associated with integrating inclusion in the classroom, understanding how students feel as novice members of a scientific community, and interacting with students with diverse backgrounds, life circumstances, and ways to learn, are not within the expertise of most STEM faculty. Some STEM faculty might even think that all of their students are more or less the same. The few STEM professors that do engage in educational strategies in their classrooms might not formally document and disseminate their findings through educational journals.

TIDES helped UPRH to tackle some of these challenges by funding the Cybernetic Girls can be Pinky (CGP) project. Laboratory experiences were enhanced with easily implementable strategies that promoted critical thinking and encouraged research in the classroom. STEM faculty were able to receive essential and updated training through the establishment of Project Kaleidoscope Regional Network meetings, which empowered faculty to integrate inclusive strategies into their instructional practices (Mack & Winter, 2015). These changes are now institutionalized across UPRH, serving as a model for other HSIs. Thanks to CGP, the implemented activities strengthened the pipeline of Latinas interested in STEM degrees, particularly in life science applications of computational sciences (CS).

Introduction

With 64% of Latino/as educated in nearly 500 HSIs (Excelencia in Education, 2017; Santiago, 2016), these institutions are essential to the education of Latinos. Studies have found that underrepresented students majoring in STEM disciplines at HSIs, are more likely to persist than their underrepresented minority peers at non-HSI institutions (Byars-Winston et al., 2016). While the percentage of Hispanic students graduating with STEM degrees increased from 7 to 10 between 2000 and 2011 (Asai & Bauerle, 2016; Eagan, Hurtado, & Chang, 2010), this percentage remains lower than their demographic representation, which was 16% of US residents in 2010 (US Census Bureau, 2011). Further, census data (US Census Bureau, 2011) shows that in 2010, only 14% of Hispanics aged 25 or older had a baccalaureate degree in any discipline.

For Latinas, the statistics are worse, with less than 5% female participation in STEM doctorates. The proportion of Latinas in technology and technological fields, including CS, is minimal (US Bureau of Labor Statistics, 2017), even though jobs in CS are a good fit for Latino/as due to the high salaries and work–life flexibility they provide (Scott, Aist, & Zhang, 2014; Stoilescu & Egodawate, 2010). However, most Latinas do not apply for CS jobs, partly because they do not relate to them. The main reason for this is the lack of CS programs where race, gender, and social class interests are actively taken into consideration (Mack, Soto, Casillas-Martinez, & McCormack, 2015).

Our TIDES project, Cybernetic Girls Can Be Pinky (CGP) is a pedagogical reform implemented at UPRH to overcome stereotypes of females, particularly Latinas, in computational fields. The program familiarized faculty with critical gender theories and raised faculty awareness of implicit bias, with an emphasis on how these theories and biases affect the experiences of Latinas in STEM classrooms. Indeed, much acculturation is needed for Latinas to counter the self-perception that their gender is a hindrance in the predominantly masculine environments encountered in computational fields, and to strategically challenge male perceptions that could create hostile work environments. Culturally sensitive approaches in CS are needed more than ever if real change is to happen.

Implementation/Methodology

CGP was successfully implemented at UPRH with the goal to better understand how to attract, retain, and graduate more biologists into computational fields. In order to achieve this goal, a series of integrated activities were designed to enhance and strengthen a middle-school-to-graduate-school STEM pipeline that focused on biological and computational sciences (see Figure 1). Special emphasis was placed on female students coming from low-income households.

Our focus at UPRH was the revision and updating of six courses with the implementation of research experiences such as the Tiny Earth at core labs. For these courses, we prepared pre- and post-tests. We also trained biology and

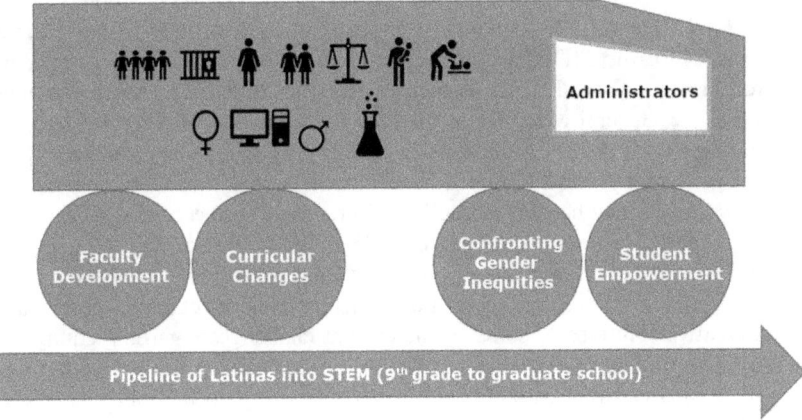

Figure 1: Summary of CGP activities that accelerated equity and inclusivity in the classroom. The dynamic "pipeline" of Latinas into computational areas requires well-trained and engaged faculty and curricular changes to core courses, as well as committed administrators who can lead initiatives like TIDES that support faculty and personnel engaged in creating STEM classroom equity.

chemistry students in programming on Python and R languages to introduce them to basic coding. Furthermore, we offered a survey on gender inequities in science to more than 200 students (see Appendix 1). The findings from this survey helped us design and implement a series of gender construction seminars to clarify many misconceptions about gender differences in STEM and how to best overcome them. In addition, a pilot course named "Women and Science" was designed and taught to STEM majors, where topics on the civil rights of women in Puerto Rico and successful Latinas in STEM were discussed (see Appendix 2).

CGP included an outreach component to middle- and high-school Latinas, mainly by collaborating with Amgen Pharmaceuticals and enticing Latino girls (ninth grade) to follow a STEM career through the Seeds of Triumph initiative. The outreach also supported Robotics Clubs in rural high schools across eastern Puerto Rico to buy kits and enter into regional competitions. Consequently, a pipeline of Latinas was established, where they would enter into the UPRH after high school and then persevere into graduate STEM programs.

CGP provided professional development training in culturally responsive strategies for faculty in collaboration with Project Kaleidoscope (PKAL). As a result of the collaboration, we have established a PKAL Regional Network in Puerto Rico (PKAL-RNPR). To date, more than 300 faculty have participated in training opportunities associated with PKAL-RNPR, attending two meetings on the Island. In the last meeting, more than 120 distinguished Latino lecturers from 47 different HSIs assembled to discuss successful outcomes-based teaching and research initiatives that improved the retention and graduation rates of undergraduate Latinos. Special interest was placed on the cultural sensitivity of these initiatives. More than 30 undergraduate students joined the conference as well, playing an active role in the discussions and participating in a networking lunch focused on how to overcome gender and educational barriers in STEM classrooms.

For CGP, the role of faculty was critical. Faculty at UPRH were active ambassadors for the TIDES initiatives. In addition to presenting their respective research projects, they also shared their educational findings in national conferences, like the General Meetings of the American Society for Microbiology, the Ecology Society of America, the American Chemical Society, and the Society for Toxicology. Faculty presentation of these initiatives was a new and empowering experience, since they had never considered presenting projects related to education in the past. Students and faculty from HSIs within Puerto Rico interacted in a 24-hr Hackathon, an event in which computer programmers collaborate intensively to design a software project. In our version of the Hackathon, participants found creative solutions to some of the current challenges regarding equity and inclusiveness in STEM disciplines. Participants indicated in the evaluation they wanted to interact more with other HSIs. Consequently, in the following PKAL meeting, faculty from 47 different HSIs united to discuss strategies for increasing the retention and graduation rates of Latinos, especially in STEM disciplines.

In addition to the yearly PKAL Regional Network meetings, faculty from other universities were invited to give seminars regarding their research projects, particularly in the field of computational biology. Speakers explained the relevance that programming and coding have in their professional development, and recommended books, courses, and training programs to enhance the computational skills of the students. Most invited speakers were female researchers that were engaged in research in Puerto Rico. In addition, UPRH administrators established awards that fostered educational projects, for example, the Active-learning Day and a Yearly Research Excellence Awards.

Although initially intended to help students enter into graduate programs, CGP rapidly evolved into a movement where Latinas expressed their needs for equal rights. For instance, students received gender construction workshops, which grew into a formal course named '*Women and Science*', where they learned about the civil rights movement of women in Puerto Rico. As the final exam in the course, students presented research results addressing a current challenge of Latinas in science, and how they will solve it. Students also received programming workshops in R and Python languages, directed to non-math majors, which were initially taught by a professor. Eventually, the workshops were taken over by students of the Mathematics Students Association, an evident empowering act. The workshops were assessed by newly designed rubrics. Students conducting research with TIDES-program-trained faculty were empowered to continue graduate programs, especially in CS fields. Focus groups and exit surveys were also conducted.

Results

Main Outcomes from the Curricular Revamping of Courses

Pre- and post-tests for quantitative analysis and critical thinking: As previously stated, two different rubrics were prepared to assess the theoretical knowledge acquired and development of computational skills during the revamped core course or lab practice. Revamping of the courses resulted in an increase in knowledge acquired according to both rubrics. In the Ecology course, students were tested on how to make specific quantitative and qualitative measurements, creating and interpreting graphs, and population analyses with up to 100% in Hake knowledge gains when students' pre- and post-tests were compared.

Science interests and perceptions survey: Students positively changed their perception about fundamental aspects related to computational biology and gender once trained. After the interventions, more male students thought that women needed the support of their male and female peers in order to be more successful in their future careers in the field. Both male and female students agreed that salaries of men and women performing the same kind of job are not the same in computational careers. There was a reduction in the number of male students who thought that females should not study computational careers to stay feminine; and that the basic responsibility of a woman is to raise her children. The number of females that thought that males have more of a natural advantage in computational biology careers was reduced. Students from both genders reduced their belief that there is an equal playing field for males and females in science.

Interestingly, in the pre-survey, most females were not aware of common gender inequities, for example, regarding salaries.

Other misperceptions were much strongly held by students and did not vary significantly. Regarding leadership capabilities, more male students thought that they should fill important positions in science and technology and not their female peers. In addition, males did not change their perception of males having more natural talent for quantitative analysis than females. This is something that we are evaluating to address in the future by incorporating in the courses more examples of successful women in positions of leadership in STEM.

Evaluations of the Women in Science undergraduate course: Students learned more about women's civil rights and felt empowered by other successful Latinas. It was noted that the two male students registered in the course dropped out, possibly showing the need for a more supporting environment for male students.

Courses were supplemented with programming workshops in two different languages, R and Python: The first group was trained by faculty from the Biology and Mathematics departments using a book manual. Those students completed a pre- and post-test each week and an evaluation form. The second group was trained by students from the Mathematics Department, supervised by a Mathematics professor, and only filled out the evaluation form. Overall, evaluations indicated a slight preference toward the faculty in their organization and how to make the topic relevant to the students. All other aspects were similarly positive.

Curriculum revamping: The revamped version of the lecture portion of the course, "Computational Methods Applied to Biology," included the addition of topics on empirical models, discrete models, matrix population, using R, continuous and system models, differential equations systems, computational tools (Stella, Vensim, InsightMaker, and Netlogo), agent-based models, and spatially explicit models. Another course that was updated was "Ecology." In the lecture and lab portions, the main activities implemented included: (1) graph analysis of meteorological and population data, (2) image analysis using ImageJ (3) descriptive statistics, (4) hypothesis testing, (5) building data matrices, (6) searching databases, (7) using measured tree data to perform graphical and statistical analyses, (8) population spatial analysis using polar coordinates (azimuth and distance), (9) modeling and analysis of population growth using Populus, (10) geolocation and coordinates transformation using GPS and GoogleEarth, and (11) principles of geographical information systems (GIS). In the "Molecular and Cell Biology" laboratory, the Tiny Earth initiative (previously named Small World Initiative), was implemented (Caruso, Israel, Rowland, Lovelace, & Saunders, 2016). This is a well-recognized discovery-based program initially designed by Jo Handelsman and collaborators that allowed students to conduct a research project while taking a core course. UPRH students translated all the manuals of the experience into Spanish to make it more accessible. Also, a five-day version of the experience was designed and successfully implemented. Two faculty-training workshops on how to implement it at other HSIs were conducted. Due to the incorporation of new instructional materials, two additional courses from the Mathematics Department were redesigned, a new section on programming was added to the "Computer Literacy" course, and a section of the course "Calculus" with biological applications was added.

Main Outcomes from the Faculty Development Activities

Findings of the program resulted in four educational and two scientific publications. Team members and students of the program shared their research results in 15 poster or oral presentations, including international meetings in England and Mexico (Bravo et al., 2016; Marvasi, Casillas-Santiago, Henríquez, & Casillas-Martinez, 2016; Perito, Casillas, & Marvasi, 2018; Sills, 2017; Sterling et al., 2016). The CGP activities were nationalized by the creation of the Puerto Rico PKAL Regional Network, where faculty discussed specific educational approaches they used in the STEM classroom to increase equity and diversity in their classrooms. In the last PKAL meeting, 120 faculty from 47 different HSIs discussed the need for better strategies to increase the graduation and retention rates of Latinos nationwide.

An electronic questionnaire was created to quantify perceptions related to discrimination of Black Puerto Ricans in STEM. Scientists were asked to participate either by completing a paper-based form, or electronically through the cybernetic platform CienciaPR. CienciaPR is a bilingual cybernetic portal that facilitates interactions among over 8,000 scientists and students located at more than 400 institutions of higher education across 49 US states and PR, and represented all major areas of STEM. Some 1,345 individuals accessed the survey, but only 332 completed it. After using a guide to classify their physical characteristics based on race, about 32% of them identified as White and 5% identified as Black. The rest of the participants identified themselves along a mixed-race spectrum, including "afrodescendiente" (3%), "trigueño" (34%), "mulato" (13%), "indio" (5%), and "evidently black" (2%). To further understand the experiences of Puerto Rican scientists with respect to color, the survey also included a scale with 10 hands of different skin tones, from "1" being the lightest to "10" being the darkest. The weighted average of the participants' selection was 3.3, with only 7% of the participants selecting darker-skin tones in the 6–10 range. The phenomenon of preferring lighter skin tones is known as colorism and might be a form of within-group racial discrimination commonly used to deny and minimize those Latinos with darker-skin tones.

When scientists were asked specifically about discrimination and negative comments caused by race and skin color, 42% of the participants reported experiencing it "occasionally or frequently" in places like college campuses (27%), K-12 school settings (24%), at meetings with peers or colleagues (23%), and places of employment (15%). These results were consistent with prior research from Chavez-Dueñas, Adames, and Organista (2014) that has shown that frequent comments within a racial group also connote a clear understanding of a skin-color hierarchy, with a persistent preference for lighter skin tones. Participants were asked if they had ever heard, thought, or used several negative statements about race and ethnicity in their workplace, such as "blue eyes are prettier," "bad (curly) hair is hard to comb and it looks ugly," and "she is Black, but pretty." Most scientists indicated that they had heard negative comments, but alleged they did not use them.

The participants' conscious racist practices, widely accepted but minimized, are far from unique. Many Latino groups use similar tactics to avoid experiencing the uncomfortable feelings of having discussions of privilege, while denying responsibility for the status of non-White individuals (Chavez-Dueñas et al., 2014). The four main strategies used to justify or deny contemporary racial inequality include: (1) minimization (color-blind racial attitudes), (2) deflection (ignoring evidence of widespread systematic racism), (3) rationalization (racial phenomena are explained as natural occurrences, "that is life"), and (4) victimization (the myth of reverse discrimination). Unfortunately, these practices do have a consequence in terms of the careers of Black STEM professionals in Puerto Rico. The survey asked participants about their degrees of interaction with Black scientists, and participants reported that their interactions were scarce, particularly at high-level positions.

Main Outcomes of the Student Empowering Program

To date, CGP resulted in 11 students entering into a PhD program, two students into Master degrees, two students into post-bacs programs, three students were in the application process, and 12 students attended different summer internship programs. Most of these students, over 65%, are female and are now empowered to enter into computational fields after only three years of training. This is an increase of 10% compared to the years prior to the implementation of CGP. Regarding the outreach program, we impacted more than 2,000 high school students via open houses and visits to schools. Two initiatives were conducted to attract students in ninth-grade science: the Seeds for Success Workshops and Robotic Clubs.

Feedback from a focus group session conducted by undergraduate students who participated in TIDES-related activities at UPRH favored these curricular changes and perceived their benefit, but further quantitative studies are required to more broadly assess the impact of these interventions. This is a summary of the statements from the undergraduate students interviewed in the focus group. Pseudonyms were used to protect the students' confidentiality.

> "Emilia", a female senior, reported having no regrets about joining TIDES because she learned about a field in biology that she knew little about, computational modeling in biology. Even though R is a bit complicated and not very "user-friendly," knowing how to use it is very important when applying for employment opportunities. Emilia would like to go to graduate school, but she is short on cash and has several debts. She would like to get a job first and then apply to graduate school. If she had the financial resources, she would like to study forest ecology or taxonomy. Studying computational biology is still intimidating

for her, she confesses that math is her weakness and it intimidates her, but less than before. She sees it as something accessible and that can be learned.

"Iris" is a female sophomore, a Biology major, knew programming and was familiar with computers. Students all helped each other, after completing Ecology, she felt more comfortable using computers and numbers. Iris provided tutoring in mathematics; she loves computers and numbers. Iris felt that this CGP program has prepared her well. She was part of the math program, most of them were males, but she felt that the professors treated all female students equally. There are many professors in the math program that are "pro-female" and very supportive of our goals. Iris would like to attend graduate school to study dentistry. But now she is into archaeology, so she might study both things.

"Marcos" was a male Biology major that completed the Methods in Computational Biology course. He described the class as a way to use different software programs to make models and explain biological events, such as predator/prey relationships. After completing the course, Marcos used his newly acquired knowledge about modeling in an industry internship at MacNeil Pharmaceutical where he created granulation models and optimization. Marcos thought that women can do science, he sees no objection for this. He said that in science women should be treated just like their male counterparts.

"Ofelia" is a female who participated in three workshops. The one Ofelia remembered the most was one led by a female professor who was doing research in caves. The professor explained how she collected data and used computers in her research. It was excellent, too. Ofelia learned about computational tools, the speaker described how she collaborated with a programming colleague because some of the software was much elaborated.

"Quintana" was a biologist female attending a summer internship. She said that "numbers are not her preference" but that numbers are needed in biology. She felt comfortable using GIS because she can see the maps and compare data from different geographical locations. Quintana has not felt any discrimination at the university, has heard no demeaning comments due to her gender. Quintana said that professors treat her like other students. Professors are pro-women, pro-equity; tell all students about workshops and encourage students to complete research internships. In 2014, Quintana completed an internship at the

Museum of Natural History in NY with a paleontologist modeling craniums to research diet and force comparisons with a software, to create better genealogical trees. Quintana used computers, numerical modeling and software a lot during the internship. It was very interesting.

"Uriel" was a male Math major who participated in a "science and gender" workshop. A social science professor led it. Uriel was very open about females being equal and did not consider himself as "machista" but he was surprised to see a large number of female students interested in science areas. Uriel thought science was mostly for males, but it is not like that for real. Uriel really liked the part about [females] are here [in the sciences], pay attention to us, treat us the same way, he thought it was already like that, but he was wrong! To collide with the reality of gender discrimination was shocking. Uriel thought society was much further ahead than that. Professors have been supportive in his goals. Uriel was out of the university for six years, but when he came back, he saw the support faculty provided.

Conclusion

Attracting Latinas from fields such as biology is an alternative to increase the number of professionals in CS fields. It is imperative to start at the curricular level, revamping undergraduate courses and retraining faculty. When Latinas are empowered and prepared with the needed computational skills to succeed, they will indeed respond positively. CGP clearly demonstrated that these initiatives could be successfully implemented. However, for the interventions to be effective they require administrators and faculty who understand the relevance of cultural constructs in the LatinX student development. Castellanos and Gloria (2007) have shown that college persistence among LatinX undergraduate students highly depends on three dimensions: (1) psychological, (2) social, and (3) cultural. A recent study by Chun, Marin, Schwartz, Pham, and Castro-Olivo (2016) indicated a correlation between specific cultural constructs such as ethnic identity, cultural congruity, and low acculturation on the emotional well-being and academic success of LatinX students. There is still a strong need for more studies that will incorporate these cultural constructs and study them specifically in STEM classrooms (Devos & Cruz, 2007; Witham, Malcom-Piqueux, Dowd, & Bensimon, 2015). Consequently, future steps would include strengthening current educational strategies and collaborations of faculty at Hispanic Serving Institutions.

The Last Word

Equity and inclusion have become important after hurricane Maria struck Puerto Rico in 2017. The first days after Maria, all Puerto Ricans became equal, all had the same basic needs for water, food, shelter, and gasoline. We learned the value of surviving as a united community and the university was not an exception. I was challenged to teach Molecular and Cell Biology with a chalkboard under a tent, since my classroom had been destroyed. Students had to study with candles, make hand written reports, read "real" books, and adapt to life without a cell phone for months. Everyone – students, professors under contract and tenured, non-faculty, and administrators – we were all one big group of survivors. There was no gender, color, or title.

Unfortunately, as time passes, we are now becoming segregated again, particularly due to the economic sanctions imposed on the University of Puerto Rico. However, the experience of TIDES has shown me that even the most diverse group of people can come together and find a consensus if we have the common goal of a better education. Thanks to TIDES, I do have a hope of a better future for the education in Puerto Rico and all over the world.

TIDES Resources

1. Web page for the Cybernetic Girls Can Be Pinky https://tidesuprh.wordpress.com/
2. Itineraries for faculty development through the Puerto Rican PKAL regional meetings https://www.aacu.org/meetings/pkal/PuertoRico/2016, http://www.upr.edu/2017-project-kaleidoscope-pkal-regional-meeting/
3. Link to a questionnaire about possible discrimination to Afro-descendants in STEM in Puerto Rico. Retrieved from https://docs.google.com/forms/d/e/1FAIpQLSeQktXcl051aeQtjucxC3wEP_7XQZFzT4ggXrVXDQp9b0XLJQ/viewform

Acknowledgments

We want to thank the following faculty members from UPRH who were key to implementing the different activities of the proposal: (1) Biology Department – Esther Vega, Denny Fernández, Aramis Villafañe, Edna Gautier, and Raymond Tremblay; (2) Chemistry Department – Zuleika Medina and Ileana Rodriguez; (3) Mathematics Department – Idalyn Ríos Díaz and Joaquín Rivera Cruz; and (4) Social Science Department – María D. Mulero Díaz and Viviana Macdougall. We also thank all of the administrators involved in the project, especially Maricelis Lebrón, Ileana Garcia, and Sonia Piñero. Ultimately, we thank our undergraduate students, who were the most important element of the proposal.

References

Asai, D. J., & Bauerle, C. (2016). From HHMI: Doubling down on diversity. *CBE Life Science Education, 15*(3), fe6, 3.

Bravo, A., Porzecanski, A., Sterling, E., Bynum, N., Cawthorn, M., Fernández, D. S., ... Volger, D. (2016). Teaching for higher levels of thinking: Developing quantitative and analytical skills in environmental science courses. *Ecosphere, 7*(4).

Byars-Winston, A., Rogers, J., Branchaw, J., Pribbenow, C., Hanke, R., & Pfund, C. (2016). New measures assessing predictors of academic persistence for historically underrepresented racial/ethnic undergraduates in science. *CBE Life Sciences Education, 15*(3), ar32.

Caruso, J. P., Israel, N., Rowland, K., Lovelace, M. J., & Saunders, M. J. (2016). Citizen science: The Small World Initiative improved lecture grades and California critical thinking skills test scores of nonscience major students at Florida Atlantic University. *Journal of Microbiology & Biology Education, 17*(1), 156–162. doi:10.1128/jmbe.v17i1.1011

Castellanos, J., & Gloria, A. M. (2007). Research considerations and theoretical application for best practices in higher education: Latina/os achieving success. *Journal of Hispanic Higher Education, 6*(4), 378–396.

Chavez-Dueñas, N. Y., Adames, H. Y., & Organista, K. C. (2014). Skin-color prejudice and within-group racial discrimination: Historical and current impact on Latino/a populations. *Hispanic Journal of Behavioral Sciences, 36*(1), 3–26.

Chun, H., Marin, M. R., Schwartz, J. P., Pham, A., & Castro-Olivo, S. M. (2016). Psychosociocultural structural model of college success among Latina/o students in Hispanic-serving institutions. *Journal of Diversity in Higher Education, 9*(4), 385–400.

Devos, T., & Cruz, T. (2007). Implicit identification with academic achievement among Latino college students: The role of ethnic identity. *Basic Applied Social Psychology, 29*(3), 293–310.

Eagan, K., Hurtado, S., & Chang, M. (2010, October). What matters in STEM: Institutional contexts that influence STEM bachelor's degree completion. Paper presented at meeting of the Association for the Study of Higher Education, Indianapolis, IN.

Excelencia in Education. (2017). *Hispanic-serving institutions (HSIs): 2015–2016*. Washington, DC: Author.

Gokhale, A., Brauchle, P., & Machina, K. (2009). Development and validation of a scale to measure attitudes toward science and technology. *Journal of College Science Teaching, 38*(5), 66–75.

Mack, K., Soto, M., Casillas-Martinez, L., & McCormack, E. F. (2015). Women in computing: The imperative of critical pedagogical reform. *Diversity & Democracy, 18*(2), 8–10. Retrieved from https://www.aacu.org/diversitydemocracy/2015/spring/mack

Mack, K., & Winter, K. (2015). Teaching to increase diversity and equity in STEM (TIDES): STEM faculty professional development for self-efficacy. In G. C. Weaver, W. D. Burgess, A. L. Childress, & L. Slakey (Eds.), *Transforming institutions: Undergraduate STEM education for the 21st century* (pp. 338–353). West Lafeyette, IN: Purdue University Press.

Marvasi, M., Casillas-Santiago, L. M., Henríquez, T., & Casillas-Martinez, L. (2016). Involvement of *etfA* gene during $CaCO_3$ precipitation in *Bacillus subtilis* biofilm. *Geomicrobiology Journal, 34*(8), 722–728. doi:10.1080/01490451.2016.1248254

National Science Board. (2014). Higher education in science and engineering. In *Science and engineering indicators 2014*. Arlington, VA: National Science

Foundation. Retrieved from https://www.nsf.gov/statistics/seind14/index.cfm/front/f3.htm

National Science Foundation. (2015). *Women, minorities, and persons with disabilities in science and engineering*. Retrieved from http://www.nsf.gov/statistics/2015/nsf15311/

Owen, S. V., Toepperwein, A., Pruski, L. A., Blalock, C. L., Liu, Y., Marshall, C. E., & Lichtenstein, M. J. (2007). Psychometric reevaluation of the Women in Science Scale (WiSS). *Journal of Research in Science Teaching, 44*(10), 1461–1478.

Perito, B., Casillas, L., & Marvasi, M. (2018). Factors affecting formation of large calcite crystals (≥1 mm) in *Bacillus subtilis* 168 biofilm. *Geomicrobiology Journal, 35*(5), 385–391. doi:10.1080/01490451.2017.1377788

Santiago, D. A. (2016). *What works for Latino students in higher education compendium*. Washington, DC: Excelencia in Education. Retrieved from https://www.edexcelencia.org/research/publications/2016-what-works-latino-students-higher-education

Scott, K., Aist, G., & Zhang, X. (2014). Designing a culturally responsive computing curriculum for girls. *International Journal of Gender, Science, and Technology, 6*(2), 264–276.

Sills, J. (Ed.). (2017). Prejudgment call. *Science, 355*(6320), 22–23. doi:10.1126/science.355.6320.22

Snyder, T. D., de Brey, C., & Dillow, S. A. (2016). *Digest of Education Statistics* (NCES 2016-014). National Center for Education Statistics, Institute of Education Sciences, U.S. Department of Education. Washington, DC. Retrieved from https://nces.ed.gov/programs/digest/d15/ch_3.asp

Sterling, E., Bravo, A., Porzecanski, A. L., Burks, R. L., Linder, J., Langen, T. … Bynum, N. (2016). Think before (and after) you speak: Practice and self-reflection bolster oral communication skills. *Journal of College Science Teaching, 45*(6), 87–99.

Stoilescu, D., & Egodawate, G. (2010). Gender differences in the use of computers, programming, and peer interactions in computer science classrooms. *Computer Science Education, 20*(4), 283–300.

US Bureau of Labor Statistics. (2017). Computer and information technology occupations. *Occupational Outlook Handbook*. Retrieved from http://www.bls.gov/ooh/computer-and-informationtechnology/home.htm

US Census Bureau, Public Information Office. (2011, August 26). Hispanic heritage month 2011: Sept. 15 – Oct. 15 (CB11-FF.18). *Profile America facts for Features*. Retrieved from https://www.census.gov/newsroom/releases/archives/facts_for_features_special_editions/cb11-ff18.html

Witham, K., Malcom-Piqueux, L. E., Dowd, A. C., & Bensimon, E. M. (2015). *America's unmet promise: The imperative for equity in higher education*. Washington, DC: Association of American Colleges & Universities.

Appendix 1: Hake Comparisons on the Pre- and Post-survey on Interests in Computational Biology and Gender Inequities Provided to STEM Undergraduate Students at a Hispanic Serving Institution

Statements on the Survey on Interests in Computational Biology and Gender Inequities ($n = 455$, 65% Females, 35% Males)	Pre-test Males	Pre-test Females	Hake % Difference
I know what computational biology is and their applications in different areas.	2.63	2.41	−9.28
I know the programs that are used in a computational biology study.	2.07	1.94	−4.44
Given their analytical capabilities, males have more of an advantage in careers like computational biology, compared with females.	1.86	1.76	−3.18
I am familiar with different types of quantitative analyses that apply in my area of study.	2.90	2.58	−15.24
I understand that I have enough skills to perform quantitative analysis.	3.13	2.90	−12.30
Given their leadership capabilities, it is preferable for males, rather than females, to fill important positions in science and technology.	1.58	1.14	−12.87
By incorporating computational skills and quantitative analysis, you will have better opportunities in the future.	4.40	4.21	−31.67
Women would be more successful in quantitative analysis and computational biology if they had the support of their male peers.	3.30	3.38	4.71
Women would be more successful in quantitative analysis and computational biology if they had the support of their female peers.	3.36	3.56	12.20
Males have more natural talent for quantitative analysis compared with females.	1.89	1.43	−14.79
Males and females experience the same work environment in careers related to quantitative analysis and computational biology.	2.80	2.75	−2.27

(Continued)

Statements on the Survey on Interests in Computational Biology and Gender Inequities ($n = 455$, 65% Females, 35% Males)	Pre-test Males	Pre-test Females	Hake % Difference
Males and females receive the same salary in careers that require skills in quantitative analysis and computational biology.	2.66	2.44	−9.40
Males and females have the same opportunities to be successful in careers that require skills in quantitative analysis and computational biology.	3.65	3.37	−20.74
To keep their femininity, it is better for females to study careers in areas that do not require computational and mathematical skills.	1.21	1.14	−1.85
One of the basic responsibilities of a professional woman is to raise her children.	2.36	2.43	2.65
A woman that works in careers related to computational sciences will always have obstacles to her professional growth.	2.15	2.07	−2.81

Source: Survey adapted from Gokhale, Brauchle, and Machina (2009).
Note: Scale: 1 = strongly agree, 2 = agree, 3 = neutral, 4 = disagree, 5 = strongly disagree.

Appendix 2: Hake Comparisons on the Pre- and Post-survey Provided to STEM Undergraduate Students Enrolled in the Women and Science Course

Statements on the Survey Provided to STEM Undergraduate Students Enrolled in the Women and Science Course ($n = 15$, 87% Females, 13% Males)	Average Pre-survey Score	Average Post-survey Score	Hake Gain %
1. Men and women have always had the same constitutional and civil rights.	4.79	5	4.48
2. Men have better mathematical, mechanical, and spatial abilities compared with women.	4.86	5	2.94
3. Women are biologically weaker compared with men.	3.54	4.5	23.81
4. Domestic chores, like ironing, washing clothes and cooking, belong to women.	4.79	5	4.48
5. Chores like discarding trash or washing windows belong to men.	4.79	5	4.48
6. When men do domestic chores, they are invading the women's domain.	4.86	5	2.94
7. Biologically, taking care of children corresponds to women.	4.43	5	12.90
8. In our society, men and woman receive an equal salary for equal work.	4.14	4.9	17.85
9. Gender discrimination in the job does not exist.	4.29	5	16.67
10. In this day, men and women have the same opportunities to study the career they want.	2.43	3.8	37.80
11. Biologically, men are smarter than women, but women can become smarter because they are more dedicated and studious.	4.50	4.8	6.38
12. Biologically, women belong in the house and men belong in the street.	4.57	5	9.38
13. At home, men should have more authority than women so that it runs adequately.	4.86	5	2.94

(Continued)

Statements on the Survey Provided to STEM Undergraduate Students Enrolled in the Women and Science Course ($n = 15$, 87% Females, 13% Males)	Average Pre-survey Score	Average Post-survey Score	Hake Gain %
14. There is a positive correlation between the number of women with a college degree and job positions in the workforce.	2.43	4.6	76.77
15. Sex and gender are the same things.	4.36	5	14.75
16. Biologically, women are more emotional and men are more rational.	3.86	4.5	14.75

Source: Survey adapted from Owen et al. (2007).
Note: Scale: 1 = strongly agree, 2 = agree, 3 = neutral, 4 = disagree, 5 = strongly disagree.

Chapter 4

Changing Faculty Culture to Promote Diversity, Equity, and Inclusion in STEM Education

Jennifer Speed, Donald L. Pair, Mehdi Zargham, Zhongmei Yao and Suzanne Franco

Reflection

The TIDES team from the University of Dayton (UD) started from a point of skeptical optimism. We were confident in our ability to make meaningful improvements in measures of student success because our faculty, staff, and administrators were deeply invested in student success, but we remained concerned that a limitation imposed by TIDES would hinder the project from the outset. Namely, TIDES demanded that we start our efforts from the time that students matriculated, and not before. The project could involve neither recruiting nor bridge programs, which are shown to have an impact on student success. Instead, we had to focus on the students right in front of us. In the end, though, the TIDES' expectation to focus on what happened in the classroom resonated with something we already knew: the classroom learning environment is ultimately the most important factor in student success and degree progression. When students are served by educators who are genuinely responsive to both their academic and cultural gifts, institutions of higher learning can genuinely create the conditions for success. Certainly, other factors come into play, such as social integration or maturity or finances, but the learning environment really does matter most.

We also began the project with some concern about a lack of the faculty's willingness to change pedagogy with regard to cultural responsiveness. It is not easy to challenge a faculty member's professional identity. To be sure, not all faculty have embraced culturally responsive teaching and curricular reforms to the same extent, but we can confidently say that the tide has turned in our entire computer science department. With the exception of the department chair, UD's computer science faculty started the project with no familiarity with the language of culturally responsive teaching, and they were largely uninformed about the ways in which each and every faculty member's classroom environment played a role in student success across their own department, in STEM fields, and at UD in general.

By combining three equally important messages – the need for change; the critical role played by individual faculty members in the success of every student; and the university's investment in and support of faculty development and pedagogy – we believe that we were able to create the conditions that fostered faculty engagement in the project. Our belief in that approach was validated by a common theme that emerged from the end-of-project faculty focus group. Faculty affirmed that UD had elevated conversations around the importance of teaching and learning and had committed resources to support a new emphasis on student success. Had it not been for the occasion of the TIDES call for proposals, we might never have attempted to change pedagogy in an entire STEM department at UD, much less in such a short period of time. We launched headlong into the project with a strong game plan, but also a good game face: we were trying out something new and uncertain and had no idea whether or not it would work. Based upon UD's experience, though, we encourage other institutions of higher learning to take that chance, too.

Institutional Context

UD is a Midwestern, comprehensive university that is the largest private institution of higher learning in Ohio. Our student body comprises nearly 11,000 students (8,500 undergraduates, 2,400 graduate students) from the United States and around the world, although the majority of students come from the Midwest. Our undergraduate curriculum combines liberal education with professional preparation in a distinctive Common Academic Program that all majors, regardless of school affiliation, complete. Faculty and students alike benefit from UD's teacher–scholar model, which makes classroom engagement and innovation inseparable from research, scholarship, creative activity, and community engagement.

Mission and Catholic Identity

The project itself grew out of UD's mission-driven understanding of inclusive excellence; thus our institutional history and culture is highly relevant for our iteration of the TIDES project. UD was founded in 1850 by members of the Society of Mary, known as the Marianists, a Catholic religious order from France. In the mid-nineteenth century, a handful of US bishops independently recruited small teams of Marianist brothers and priests to come from France and establish schools in Ohio, Texas, and elsewhere. They brought with them a readiness to meet people where they are, education-wise, and to offer solutions that were relevant for a given context. In this case, the Marianists arrived in a relatively young, but rapidly growing, urban center with a demand for education that outstripped capacity. Then, as now, the city of Dayton was not predominantly Catholic.

The Marianist focus on education and young people was not an accident. Instead, it emerged out of the experiences of the Marianists' founder, Father William Joseph Chaminade, who had suffered in the chaos and anti-religious sentiments of the French Revolution. After spending time in exile in Spain after the Revolution, he returned to France to form several apostolic communities of women and men. Education soon emerged as the focus of their ministry because Father Chaminade understood education to be a vehicle for building authentic community, repairing social fractures, and re-establishing the role of faith and religious practice in French society (Chaminade, 2006; Habjan, 2007).

The school that the Marianists founded here in Dayton, known for much of its history as the St. Mary's Institute, formed the core of what would become our contemporary university. UD has changed, since its foundation as a school for boys, into a complex, post-secondary comprehensive institution of higher learning. What has not changed is a focus on academic excellence, a concern for the whole person, shaping the education of heart and mind, relationships of care, and a concern for those at the margins of society. Whereas UD has always declared its religious identity, it has simultaneously welcomed students from every faith, as well as those without any religious identity. We emphasize this facet of our history because we think it is worth underscoring the reality that the Marianists have carried out their work in pluralist contexts – including those that have been unfriendly to faith-based groups in general or Catholic organizations in particular. For this reason, educational pursuits at Marianist schools has long appealed to educators, staff, and students from all backgrounds (Pérez-Peña, 2012).

Our commitment to diversity and inclusion, however, does not necessarily mean that UD has always been able to achieve it. High tuition rates have often meant that the University has not been an option for students with limited means, a factor that has had a disproportionate impact on the recruitment and retention of minority students. Moreover, a predominantly white student population has tended to perpetuate itself through a mistaken notion that minority students, and even non-Catholics, were unwelcome. Even as UD has provided generous base funding for targeted programs to support students from diverse backgrounds, the University has seldom undertaken the rigorous evaluation needed to know which programs are successful (or not) at promoting student success and why.

Our Catholic cultural expectation, then, has demanded that we engage in dialogue and self-reflection to understand better how we can live out our educational mission and make inclusive excellence a reality. With regard to our demographics, UD's institutional leaders, including the president, provost, and deans, over the last decade had become increasingly concerned about limited undergraduate diversity and the role that financial accessibility has played in perpetuating it. Even as enrollment among international students had grown, especially from China and Saudi Arabia, the domestic student population had remained predominantly white.

Student Success: Institutional Challenges and Responses

Given the disparity between the University's stated commitment to a diverse and inclusive campus community and indicators showing that our institution was not, in fact, a very diverse and inclusive campus, we needed to take action at all levels. UD's leaders, including the Provost and Vice President of Enrollment Management, chose to focus on student retention and persistence as a way of addressing this disparity, in part because there were significant differences between minority and non-minority students with regard to measures of student success. To that end, in the spring of 2011, the provost sponsored nine faculty and staff members to attend a professional conference focused on retention. That group became the foundation for the Student Success and Persistence Team (SSPT), which reports to the provost. Its role is not to improve retention and student success, *per se*. Instead, the SSPT is charged with recommending and promoting strategies to increase undergraduate student success and persistence, especially with regard to two measures: the first-to-second-year retention rate and the six-year graduation rate.

The early work of the SSPT centered on infrastructure building and the consideration of three problems at UD that are common to many universities. First, initiatives to promote student success are not always well-scaffolded for maximum impact across campus. Second, such initiatives are not always well-documented. Lastly, there is limited information sharing among different offices about factors affecting student success. At UD, this meant that we did not know what was working and what was not. Thus, the work of the SSPT in its first year was directed toward answering the question: "what do we know about student success and retention at UD?"

Guided by the research undertaken by Susan Sexton, UD's Director of Institutional Reporting, the SSPT was able to drill down to specific areas of concern. For example, her report identified undeclared majors at UD as having much lower first-to-second-year retention rates than the rest of their cohort, the majority of which had declared a major upon matriculation. In response, a team within the College of Arts and Sciences developed and implemented changes for the newly renamed "Discover Arts" major that started in 2012 and included: a substantially revised first-year seminar experience, major improvements to the entire advising process, and the expansion of the role of peer mentors, now known as "student teaching assistants." Thanks to these efforts, UD has seen a dramatic improvement in retention rates among Discover Arts students, the first-to-second year retention rate rising from 79% (2007–2011) to 86.7% (2012–2015) (Witherspoon, Poe, & Sexton, 2017).

Another area of concern that emerged from the work of the SSPT during the 2012–2013 academic year was the prevalence of D/F/W grades in introductory STEM courses, especially in introductory chemistry, mathematics, and computer science courses. It is widely known that D/F/W grades are all too high in foundational STEM courses nationwide, and that those grades are symptomatic of a number of individual and institutional barriers to student success. Moreover, observations offered by UD's Assistant Deans suggest that low grades in introductory STEM courses have a disproportionately negative effect on retention. UD had never delved into the data to better understand *which* courses posed the greatest barriers for students, let alone *why* those courses posed the greatest barriers. This preliminary inquiry into D/F/W grades by the SSPT would come to shape the TIDES project (see section "Background and Significance").

In order to set the tone for making student success and diversity a University priority, UD's president opened the 2013–2014 academic year with a charge to each academic unit to create formal plans for recruiting and retaining more underrepresented students. Since then, UD's administration has launched a number of initiatives to broaden participation among underrepresented students, including those who enter college through nontraditional pathways. Efforts, to date, include an articulation agreement with Sinclair Community College that allows for dual admission to UD and Sinclair, success in reaching and matriculating more veterans and their family members, and financial aid that better supports students beyond those who are traditional first-time students enrolling in higher education immediately after high school.

At the same time that UD's institutional leadership grew increasingly concerned about limited diversity, the Office of Enrollment Management and its campus partners began to examine demographic data and trends in order to respond to changes among the US college-bound population in the coming decades. By working to understand regional and national trends related to ethnicity, growth in certain career fields, perceptions about the appropriateness of certain majors, family backgrounds, and other factors that shape college choices, UD has been able to recruit a more diverse student population and is poised to expand upon that success in the coming decade. As is well known, though, recruiting a more diverse population is only part of the challenge for a truly diverse student population. Universities also need to create and sustain the conditions for an inclusive community.

In STEM fields at UD, the responsibility for recruiting and retaining more underrepresented students falls primarily to the College of Arts and Sciences and the School of Engineering. Both of these academic units have the responsibility and the flexibility to develop initiatives both inside and outside of the classroom that can advance unit-based and campus-wide goals for student engagement. At the time of the TIDES proposal submission in the spring of 2014, the deans of the College and Engineering, as well the provost, gave their unqualified support to the project because they saw in it the potential to attract and retain underrepresented students.

Specifically, UD's leadership understood that the transformation of computer science-related curricula would enhance student interest and retention and would improve student competency in STEM majors that required computer science.[1] Finally, they saw that the project would advance the efforts of the university-wide SSPT. The SSPT had members in common with the TIDES project team and comprised faculty and staff from across the campus.[2] All of these institutional factors informed the development of the project.

At the time of the project's development, computer science enrollment had been trending downward for several years. There were almost no underrepresented students among those majors. The few women and minorities who did matriculate as computer science majors tended to transfer to other disciplines by the end of their first year. The majority of males who transferred out of computer science elected majors within the School of Business. Campus wide, minority students who matriculated in all majors had much lower retention rates than their non-minority peers, with Latino and African American male students having the lowest such rates. Attrition rates among minority students were highest in STEM disciplines at UD. The same was (and often still is) true at colleges and universities nationwide (Chen, 2013). Similarly, many women who matriculated in STEM fields remained at UD, but transferred to non-STEM disciplines within their first two years.

Background and Significance

The TIDES' call for proposals could not have been more timely. The project that emerged was the result of three institutional initiatives that were already underway, all of which aligned with the TIDES program goals for improved student engagement and diversity. The first involved the implementation of an entirely new curriculum at UD; the second, an effort to invigorate the computer science department; and the third, inquiries into the D/F/W rates in STEM courses. As to the first, the goals and objectives of the TIDES project grew out of the complete renovation of UD's undergraduate curriculum, known as the Common Academic Program (CAP). The new curriculum reflects UD's commitment to diversity and inclusion as inseparable from student learning outcomes. Importantly, CAP has never been static. Instead, it continues to grow to reflect greater interdisciplinarity in learning, teaching, and research, as well as to

---

[1] Within the College of Arts and Sciences, the following majors required computer science courses: Computer Science, Computer Information Science, Mathematics, Applied Mathematical Economics, and Physics and Computer Science. Within the School of Engineering, the following majors require computer science courses: Computer Engineering and Electrical Engineering. In addition, students from other majors can elect to take a computer science course to satisfy one of the required courses for the CAP natural sciences component.

[2] Members are drawn from: the College of Arts and Sciences; Schools of Engineering; School of Business Administration; School of Education and Health Sciences; Student Development; Enrollment Management; Office of the Provost; and Institutional Research and Reporting.

incorporate a broader range of experiential and community-engaged learning opportunities.

As staff and faculty from other institutions of higher learning know well, the pace of cultural and institutional change can be maddeningly slow. Universities and colleges tend to be inherently conservative in their approach to wholesale cultural change, and the possibility of curricular change can bring to the surface longstanding frictions that may be only tangentially related to teaching and learning (Louvel, 2013). These changes might, for example, relate to concerns about workload policies or even space allocations for classes. Changes to required or foundational courses have implications for staffing and tenure lines and faculty can tend to focus on departmental stature instead of the entire learning environment. Sometimes, the larger the institution, the slower the pace. The upside of careful and deliberate change, though, especially at a school as decentralized and highly relational as UD, is that a slower pace allows for the cultivation of authentic partnerships and the consultation of a broad base of stakeholders. Moreover, that same slow pace can set the stage for truly sustainable change. This slow-but-steady pace has been the case at UD, in part because our culture values deliberation and consultation at all levels.

The preparatory work for major curriculum changes at UD had begun nearly a decade earlier, in 2005, with a campus-wide discussion about the purposes of and substance of a Marianist education.[3] That discussion extended to how the "common academic program (CAP) for undergraduates should express the ideals of university education in the Catholic and Marianist traditions" (Chaminade University of Honolulu, St. Mary's University, University of Dayton, 2006). In 2006, the Marianist working group issued a report developed from those discussions that identified key goals for a Marianist education at UD, a mission statement, and seven student learning outcomes.[4] Those learning outcomes relate to: (1) scholarship, (2) faith traditions, (3) diversity, (4) community, (5) practical wisdom, (6) critical evaluation of our times, and (7) vocation. A year later, UD adopted a University assessment plan that included these seven learning outcomes as the guidelines for the new curricula and student learning as part of the new CAP. The revised CAP framework was approved in 2010, and the work toward the development of CAP began. Whereas our TIDES project's goals and objectives are related to all of the CAP learning outcomes, the focus for our computer science courses is related to only those outcomes connected to scholarship, diversity, and vocation.

The 2013–2014 academic year marked both the first stage of CAP's implementation and the development of the TIDES project. As CAP continues, curricula in academic units are continually revised to advance CAP objectives and

---

[3]There are three Marianist universities: the University of Dayton; St. Mary's University in San Antonio, Texas; and Chaminade University, in Honolulu, Hawaii.
[4]As of Fall 2017, in connection with university-wide activities, the original student learning outcomes were reconceived as *institutional* learning outcomes. https://udayton.edu/finadmin/administrative/ir/assessment/learning_outcomes.php

to reflect changing needs.[5] For example, the chemistry department is undertaking major curricular changes to improve learning outcomes for first- and second-year students. The School of Engineering, as part of the KEEN network, has introduced curriculum and pedagogy that stress creativity and entrepreneurial thinking. Also, faculty working in formal and informal teams are working across traditional disciplinary boundaries to develop more interdisciplinary courses and experiential learning models.

As to the second major initiative, the same year that UD began its phased implementation of CAP, the Department of Computer Science welcomed Dr Mehdi Zargham as a new senior faculty member and as its new chair. In recruiting a departmental leader from outside of the University, one who could engage both new faculty and experienced teacher-scholars, UD sought to reenergize its computer science department after several years of declining enrollments and concerns about low morale among faculty. Dr Zargham launched headlong into the redesign of key computer sciences courses to ensure alignment with CAP, but he brought to the table something more: a desire to drastically improve the landscape of computer science education. A seasoned educator and innovator, Dr Zargham was keenly aware of both the potential for computer science education and the national problem of a narrowing pool of students who were being drawn into, and retained by, the field. Gender imbalance is only one challenge to which one faculty member was particularly sensitive: "there's this term that's called 'bro-gramming' instead of programming" because there are so many men in computer science (UD, 2016). Dr Zargham knew that the environment for teaching and learning in computer science needed a major overhaul. He was prepared to model servant leadership by embracing pedagogical and curricular changes in his own courses, as well as by creating the favorable conditions for department-wide changes (Powell, 2008).[6]

As to the third major initiative, prior to the release of the TIDES call for proposals, Dr Zargham had begun a conversation about the landscape for computer science education with colleagues in the Office of the Dean of the College of Arts & Sciences. Together, they began to explore literature about barriers to student success in STEM. The SSPT had identified high rates of D/F/W rates in introductory computer science courses. As is well demonstrated in the literature, poor performance in introductory STEM courses effectively drives students out of STEM degrees and the STEM pipeline, even when they are otherwise capable of succeeding (Haak, HilleRisLambers, Pitre, & Freeman, 2011). Dr Zargham

---

[5]At UD, academic units that offer undergraduate courses of study are: the College of Arts and Sciences; the School of Engineering; the School of Business Administration; and the School of Education and Health Sciences.

[6]In her chapter on major changes to the computer science learning environment at the University of Pennsylvania. Rita Manco Powell underscores the impact of having the department chair teach a foundational course. Namely, "the department chair's teaching CSE 120 [the foundational course] has sent a strong message of the importance of students' early experiences in the major."

took this as a personal challenge. He was confident that he and his computer science colleagues could create learning environments that would genuinely teach students from all backgrounds and cultivate STEM talent not just among students who arrived in the classroom already knowing how to code.

Dr Zargham and Dean's Office colleagues saw that the barriers faced by underrepresented students at UD were not unique to our institution. At the same time, they also were certain that UD's unique culture would make it possible to develop and implement interventions that could change the learning environment for the better. The challenge was to develop a manageable, scalable intervention that drew upon UD's strengths. Based upon their assessment of UD's culture, which is highly decentralized and relational, they chose to focus on the classroom environment and faculty development, both of which involved pedagogical and curricular changes.

Guiding Literature

UD's approach for the TIDES project is rooted in literature on STEM student success, as well as within literature on computer science education. Prior to his arrival at UD in 2013, Dr Zargham had begun to look more closely at the research on the lack of equity in computer science, especially between male and female students (Goode, Chapman, & Margolis, 2012). Two institutions, Carnegie Mellon and Harvey Mudd College, had addressed this disparity with considerable success (Alvarado, Dodds, & Libeskind-Hadas, 2012; Klawe, 2013). Literature produced by key stakeholders at those institutions and by scholars elsewhere offered some critical guidance (Alvarado & Dodds, 2010; Margolis & Fisher, 2001). Based upon his review of the literature, Dr Zargham was optimistic that some of the interventions that were successful for boosting participation among women would also be appropriate for engaging all underrepresented populations in computer science. In particular, research pointed to the value of incorporating more inquiry-based pedagogy and collaborative learning into the classroom as a way of boosting student engagement.

Another evidence-based strategy was to develop an institutional solution for giving students a common "landing" or entry point in computer science by providing an accessible and inviting course for students from many different backgrounds. Although very tempting for faculty and administrators, the focus of the landing point was never on student deficiencies, also known as the deficit model (sometimes referred to as "fixing the student") (Brownell & Tanner, 2012). Instead, the focus was on building a common curricular foundation for success. UD's decision to focus on students at the beginning of their postsecondary education was informed by the 2012 report from the President's Council of Advisors on Science and Technology (PCAST, 2012), which stressed the importance of the first two years of college and/or university studies as critical for retaining students in STEM.

The project was also shaped by a growing body of literature on the importance of cultural competency, which came to undergraduate education from medicine and nursing education and is still going strong in those fields (Stanley,

Hall, & Berger, 2009; Waite & Calamaro, 2010). There is often a mismatch between some students' cultural experiences and expectations and that of the dominant culture of an institution. Faculty often fail to recognize this mismatch, and may even attribute it to deficiencies on the part of students, because they may simply argue that students are not sufficiently prepared or that the students are not ready for (or right for) university-level studies. Factors ranging from classroom climate to evaluation have dramatically different effects on various student populations (Barthelemy, Hedberg, Greenberg, & McKay, 2015). The results can be disastrous for student success and persistence (Gay, 2000). When faculty learn to develop pedagogy that is increasingly culturally responsive, they can begin to create learning environments that are authentically responsive to the experiences of all students (Murphy & Treisman, 2008). However, changing faculty pedagogy is a significant challenge because it asks faculty members to rethink – and change – expectations about learning that may have been formed during their own undergraduate experiences or sometimes ever earlier. During a faculty focus group conducted by our evaluator in December 2014, a faculty member was explicit about this mindset and the need to change it, saying:

> I think we tend, in computer science, to think about, "Oh, how did we learn in our undergraduate and graduate [programs], let me do that here," but the world is changing […] it's okay to explore. (UD, 2015)

Remarks such as this underscore how cultural change in the classroom cannot simply be directed at students; it needs to be directed at faculty, as well.

Implementation and Methodology

The project was designed for development and implementation over a three-year period. The project formally began with an intensive team workshop in the summer of 2014 and concluded in the summer of 2017 with another workshop. We note here that UD elected to extend the project evaluation by a year, at the University's expense, in order to assess impact over a four-year period. Doing so allowed the project team to gather and evaluate longitudinal data that can validate UD's approach. Specifically, it allowed us to assess graduation data, as well as multi-year retention, on the majority of students who engaged with the project starting in Year 1.[7] Included in the evaluation are rich qualitative data that offer insights into both faculty and student experiences related to the project.

---

[7]Although not all students graduate within four years of matriculation, we expect to have data on outcomes and impact for a sizable cohort of students who matriculated in Fall 2014. That data and subsequent analysis will not be available until after the publication of this volume.

We would be remiss here if we did not call out the role and contribution of our external evaluator, Dr Suzanne Franco. Dr Franco, Professor of Leadership Studies in Education and Organizations at Wright State University, was instrumental in the planning process, especially with regard to aligning our objectives and measurable outcomes. In focus groups conducted with faculty and with students, Dr Franco easily established rapport. Faculty, in particular, who engaged in some very sensitive conversations related to issues of bias and culturally competent teaching during their focus groups, were very open in their conversations with Dr Franco. Over the grant period, Dr Franco has proven to be a valuable partner in UD's efforts to promote student success given the high quality of her research and level of engagement with the project.

Following is an overview of the project's objectives and planned activities.

Objective 1: Overcome barriers to student interest and persistence in computer science, especially among underrepresented students.

Related Activities:

1.1. Utilize evidence-based research in order to understand and remedy barriers to entry and persistence.
1.2. Develop faculty capacity in culturally competent and innovative pedagogies.
1.3. Create a new, introductory-level, required course intended to boost interests and competency in computer science among underrepresented students.
1.4. Redesign additional courses intended to maintain interest and enhance student competencies through the critical second year of studies.

Objective 2: Monitor, assess, and disseminate outcomes from project implementation.

Related Activities:

2.1. Establish baseline data for underrepresented student outcomes and persistence.
2.2. Monitor Program implementation via data gathering (timeline, student feedback, video documentation).
2.3. Develop evaluation plan and metrics, conduct interim and summative evaluation intended to measure program impact.
2.4. Report on Program outcomes to campus audience and national community of STEM high education using traditional and novel vehicles.

Objective 3: Institutionalize and scale project initiatives to other disciplines.

Related Activities:

3.1. Create task force with administrators and faculty in other units to assess feasibility of expanding program elements.

3.2. Cultivate leadership support for expansion or continuation of successful program elements.

3.3. Solicit institutional support for sustaining program and develop plans for doing so.

Curricular Changes

As noted above, planning work for the project grew out of curricular and departmental reforms that were underway and intended to reframe the entire undergraduate educational experience. Curricular changes were implemented through the creation of a new foundational course, the substantial renovation of two additional courses, and smaller-scale changes in a number of other courses, namely, the introduction of active- and inquiry-based learning. Although the most significant changes were planned for introductory courses, we anticipated that faculty development would, in turn, have an impact on students at all levels.

During the planning period and the first few months of Year 1, Dr Zargham completed the development of an entirely new, foundational computer science course called "Creative Media Applications" (CPS 149). It was offered for the first time in Fall 2014. The course was designed to target barriers to entry and persistence in computer science among underrepresented students. Its starting point was an acknowledgment of a major barrier to success in computer science, namely, that students who matriculate in computer science courses have a wide variety of precollege computer experience and expectations. As a result, when some students see that others in a class have more programming experience than they do – with white male students typically having the most programming experience – they immediately perceive that they are behind in their mastery of course content. The resulting loss of confidence by students in STEM courses, especially women and underrepresented minority students, has significant, negative implications for retention and persistence (Hill, Corbett, & St. Rose, 2010; MacPhee, Farro, & Canetto, 2013).

CPS 149 was conceived to promote inclusive excellence from different academic backgrounds by stimulating student interest and emphasizing a multidisciplinary, project-driven learning process. Dr Zargham was the first faculty member to teach the course; eventually two other professors, Dr Norman Bashias and Dr Ju Shen, also taught the course. Each faculty member utilized a different programming language, such as Maya or Blender, but all chose an accessible language that would serve as a foundational tool. Classroom pedagogy supported collaboration, with instructors grouping students with varying abilities. Sustained interactions among students were structured to promote in-class social cohesion; students moved from simply being classmates to being collaborators. Close monitoring ensured that the workload was balanced among students.

A significant curricular change to CPS 149 came in Year 2, but it had almost nothing to do with teaching computer science content or programming. A feature of CPS 149, from the beginning, was a major project in which students learned how to program animation. Animations are effective visual teaching tools because they are highly engaging and students can see immediate results.

Additionally, students learned to make iterative improvements as their skills develop. Moreover, the work of refining animation programming is highly collaborative, and students develop strong problem-solving skills (Kennedy & Odell, 2014). Student focus groups conducted as part of our program evaluation revealed that students turned to their classmates for advice – including those within and outside of their own working groups – they sought out instructional videos and shared recommendations with their classmates, made use of the course's graduate assistant, and went to the professor for guidance. As evidenced by semester-end focus groups, students sought the type of just-in-time support that was suited to their own situation and learning style.

For Year 2, Dr Zargham changed the learning landscape somewhat by assigning students a media project on a topic of their choosing, but the subject material had to be anchored in the themes of social justice or human rights. Thus, instead of creating an animation that was only intended to be entertaining, students had to create an animation of some kind that communicated a message and told a story. The response from students was overwhelmingly positive. Students created projects around topics such as food access, human rights, incarceration, and other significant subjects.

For Year 1, CPS 149 was offered primarily to computer science majors. As an indication of the broad interest in the course, in Fall 2017, three years after CPS 149 was first offered, 47% of all enrolled students had declared majors outside of computer science. Students were able to perceive what this variety meant for the instructor and for the class. In a focus group conducted in December of 2015 (Year 2), a student observed that the instructor "seems[s] to be understanding that we're all from different majors. I think [he has] a good idea of how to integrate us all together." Further, the student observed, the instructor seems to "have the idea of what pace everyone can work at and how we can help each other" (UD, 2016).

The project involved a major renovation of two additional courses: "Algorithms and Programming I" and "Algorithms and Programming II" (CPS 150 and 151, respectively). They were taught by five different faculty members during the grant period. These two courses are required for students in seven different majors in the College of Arts and Sciences and the School of Engineering. Students in other majors can also choose to enroll in these courses as electives. Typically, students take CPS 150 and 151 within their first two years of study, thus we expected any improvements to the learning environment to support students for the remainder of their degree programs.

A major content change to CPS 150 was a switch from C++ to Java. Whereas both are object-oriented programming languages, C++ can tend to overwhelm students with too many choices. The disadvantage of switching is that more students were likely to be already familiar with C++, but even that had an advantage: the lack of familiarity put more students on an even footing by requiring nearly everyone to learn a new programming language. Ultimately, faculty switched to Java because it is designed to be simple with consistent rules, which is better suited for an introductory-level course. In addition, faculty made CPS 150 more engaging by teaching algorithm development using the "Design

Recipe" and adding graphics-based lab projects and programming assignments. For all three of the foundational courses (CPS 149, 150, and 151), adding graphics-based content proved to be very successful in promoting content mastery and engagement. Finally, faculty teaching CPS 151 underscored the importance of collaborative work and social cohesion by pairing students for object-oriented programming. Faculty also emphasized project-based learning throughout with graphics-based lab projects and programming assignments (Smith, Sheppard, Johnson, & Johnson, 2005; Tseng, Chang, Lou, & Chen, 2013).

Faculty Development

Proceeding in parallel with curricular changes were a number of faculty development initiatives related to pedagogy. They might best be described as guided and intentional, but mostly unstructured. Although only three faculty members attended the first TIDES Institute in the summer of 2014, their experiences, with regard to culturally responsive pedagogy, had an impact on the entire department. Dr Zargham, in particular, utilized what he learned about perspectives of underrepresented students to engage each faculty member in the department in an individual conversation about culturally responsive teaching during the course of the fall 2014 semester. We wish to emphasize that from the beginning, faculty were sensitive to the distinction between "cultural competence" and "culturally responsive teaching." The former implies a one-time or permanent fix, whereas the latter more accurately suggests an ongoing response to the cultural backgrounds and experience of one's students. As such, faculty prefer the latter term.

In an effort to demonstrate leadership support for a renewed focus on teaching and learning, the Office of the Dean and the Department of Computer Science jointly sponsored the attendance of all computer science faculty at the AAC&U STEM conference in Atlanta in the fall of 2014. The endeavor was a success. For the first time, computer science faculty had the opportunity to attend a professional conference that was entirely concerned with teaching and learning, as opposed to a conference that was primarily related to their research. It was an eye-opening experience in the very best way, for the faculty took away ideas related to pedagogy and curricular changes that they could apply to their own classrooms and their own teaching to promote student success. In attending a wide variety of sessions, faculty found some reassurance in knowing that educators at other schools faced some of the same challenges that they do with regard to student engagement. Faculty left the conference with the impression that UD, as an institution, really valued pedagogy.

In addition, the experience served as a very significant exercise in social-professional cohesion around the idea of teaching, as opposed to the kind of experience that faculty typically have at conferences focused on their research. During breaks, meals, and even after the conference, faculty had the opportunity to engage in informal conversations with their own departmental colleagues about their shared endeavors in the classroom. It was at this AAC&U conference meeting that UD's computer science faculty seriously began to embrace the idea of curriculum as community property. Thanks to the positive experience enjoyed by computer science faculty at the conference, they returned to campus prepared to seek out additional campus-based professional development related to student success, student learning, and culturally responsive teaching. By the third year of the project, faculty were more willing to engage in difficult conversations about bias and cultural difference than they were at the beginning of the project (Mack, 2017; UD, 2015, 2017).

Overall, the faculty focus groups conducted throughout the project period revealed that the TIDES institutes and workshops and AAC&U STEM conferences had a powerful impact on pedagogy and curricula for the entire department, not only the three new or revised courses (CPS 149, 150, and 151) that were the project's primary focus. Importantly, it was the unstructured nature of the faculty development (i.e., they attended workshops, sessions, and poster discussions of their own choosing) that was so significant. Faculty took inspiration about unique ways to deliver course material that would help students overcome barriers. Seeing the ways in which faculty at other institutions were successful or met with challenges gave them the confidence to experiment on their own.

Results

We are pleased to report that UD met all of the objectives as set out in the project proposal. Following is a summary of those findings. With regard to Objective 1 ("overcome barriers to student interest and persistence in computer science, especially among underrepresented students"), UD began with faculty development and curricular changes. We provided faculty with the tools needed to better understand evidence-based research related to student success, and to apply that research to their own classroom environments. Some of these tools were shared individually and through faculty meetings, but faculty also pursued some on their own at conferences focused on undergraduate STEM education. By the end of the grant period, faculty felt much more comfortable engaging with the idea of cultural responsiveness and they reported having made changes in their teaching practices in order to engage students from all backgrounds. Based upon feedback from students, we found that the three courses that were either created or revised in connection with our TIDES project (CPS 149, 150, and 151) indeed were successful in promoting interest and retention among students from all backgrounds. Although our overall numbers are small when compared to those of other schools, we had major gains in the total number of majors, the total number of underrepresented students, and retention from the first to second year.

With regard to objective 2 ("monitor, assess, and disseminate outcomes from Program implementation), we owe a great debt to our evaluator, Dr Franco, for helping us to achieve it. At the conclusion of each project year, Dr Franco utilized project data to make recommendations for iterative improvements. She subsequently evaluated the implementation of those recommendations. Feedback received from faculty and students via focus groups and surveys indicated that the project team addressed and incorporated that feedback into efforts to improve the project.

With regard to objective 3 ("institutionalize and scale Program objectives to other disciplines"), we have achieved this objective, though not in the ways originally anticipated. We proposed the idea of creating a task force with administrators and faculty in other units to assess feasibility of expanding program elements but found it more effective to work through existing committees and offices, especially the University's Learning Teaching Center (LTC). The success of that collaboration is evidenced by a project that grew out of the TIDES work and subsequently obtained funding from the National Science Foundation (NSF). A computer science professor, who had been deeply engaged in the TIDES work, took what he had learned about improving student learning in introductory courses and applied it to his upper division course. He used preliminary findings to develop a successful proposal to NSF in collaboration with a biology faculty member associated with UD's LTC and a computer science faculty member at another university.[8] Student learning and retention are at the center of that project.

The project team was very successful in cultivating leadership support for expansion or continuation of successful program elements and in soliciting support for sustaining the program. In particular, the College of Arts and Sciences contributed additional staff time and resources to continue the project evaluation and to support faculty from other departments as they undertook their own faculty development work. The project team also incorporated major elements of the project into subsequent grant proposals to improve student success in other STEM departments – including those housed in the School of Engineering and School of Education and Health Sciences.

Discussion

The thing that we are most proud of is the impact of the project on students studying computer science. The quantitative data show gains in student retention and engagement, but the qualitative data shows us what that really means for students and faculty: a major shift in departmental culture. Introducing the idea of cultural responsiveness was a challenge, as was emphasizing student success in a STEM culture that can sometimes emphasize a "sink or swim" starting assumption. Both of these can make faculty defensive because of what they perceive to be – accusations of bias or incorrect teaching. Most faculty consider themselves to be student-centered; that is why they teach. Faculty sometimes think, erroneously, that being asked to engage in culturally responsive teaching means making their courses easier so that underqualified students can more easily complete the course. STEM faculty tend to think that revising their pedagogy so as to promote student engagement and active learning in the classroom comes

---

[8]NSF Award #1712406, "Collaborative Research: Engaged Student Learning: Reconceptualizing and Evaluating a Core Computer Science Course for Active Learning and STEM Student Success," 15 August 2017–31 July 2020. Saverio Perugini (computer science) and David Wright (LTC and biology) are the project co-PIs.

at the cost of content delivery and student mastery. In a focus group from Year 2, a faculty member said as much: "The level of rigor that I used to give was quite high and now I realized that if I'm going to bring everybody along, I'm going to have to bring it down a bit" (UD, 2016). Research, however, does not bear out the idea that faculty have to give up rigor. By changing the delivery, or pedagogy, faculty can improve learning without sacrificing content mastery (Freeman et al., 2014; McConnell, 1996; Simurda, 2012).

Even with these concerns, faculty voices reveal that they have come a long way in thinking about their approach to learning, diversity, and student success. Our faculty have a much greater sensitivity to the ranges of experiences that students bring to the classroom, a cultural variation that manifests itself in everything from the ways that some students interpret test questions to the personal interests that really get them engaged in projects. One faculty remarked, "[…] for me, cultural responsiveness is the ability to recognize and respond [to the fact] that every student in my classroom has arrived at that classroom at a very different path from each other, and [from] the path that I took when I was sitting in that seat" (UD, 2016). Simply being able to see the classroom experience through the eyes of their students has genuinely changed how faculty approach the classroom. We expect this new awareness to have an impact on subsequent student populations as computer science faculty continue to develop both their awareness of student needs and their capacity to respond to difference in the classroom.

Conclusion

We had a number of challenges ahead of us when we began the TIDES project in 2014. Like many other universities, including those with a religious mission, the UD community found that its institutional culture, policies, and commitments to diversity and inclusion did not always reflect the fullest expression of our mission to serve students from all backgrounds. In particular, our student profile reflected limited diversity, although that profile is changing. UD is recruiting and retaining a more diverse population. Having a faith-based mission, especially one that calls for action based on self-reflection, provided us with a touchstone for reorienting our work and ensuring that UD, at all levels and in all ways, truly reflects a diverse, inclusive, and equitable learning community. As great a challenge as we had ahead of us when we started the TIDES work, we have nevertheless been able to demonstrate that a small group of committed faculty and staff really can bring about institutional change and hopefully provide the impetus for even greater change across a wider range of curricula and faculty development efforts.

The Last Word

The team from UD wishes to convey to faculty and staff at other institutions that are seeking to promote student success, that such an endeavor need not be an "all or nothing" proposition. Institutions and individuals should not be afraid to make small changes for the fear that they will not "move the needle." Cultural change starts with one person who is inspired to take on one small challenge. Positive changes with regard to inclusive excellence happen one student at a time. Choose to make the difference for that one student and invite a colleague to join you in doing the same. You, too, can turn the tide.

References

Alvarado, C., & Dodds, Z. (2010). Women in CS: An evaluation of three promising practices. *Proceedings of the 41st ACM Technical Symposium on Computer Science Education* (pp. 57–61). doi:10.1145/1734263.1734281

Alvarado, C., Dodds, Z., & Libeskind-Hadas, R. (2012). Increasing women's participation in computing at Harvey Mudd College. *ACM Inroads, 3*(4), 55–64.

Barthelemy, R., Hedberg, G., Greenberg, A., & McKay, T. (2015). The climate experiences of students in introductory biology. *Journal of Microbiology and Biology Education, 16*(2), 138–147.

Brownell, S., & Tanner, K. (2012). Barriers to faculty pedagogical change: Lack of training, time, incentives, and … tensions with professional identity? *CBE-Life Sciences Education, 11*(4), 339–346.

Chaminade University of Honolulu, St. Mary's University, & University of Dayton. (2006). *Characteristics of Marianist universities. A resource paper.* Retrieved from http://wasc.chaminade.edu/documents/appendix2/Appendix_I.5_Characteristics_of_Marianist_Universities.pdf

Chen, X. (2013). *STEM attrition: College students' paths into and out of STEM fields.* Statistical Analysis Report. NCES 2014-001. National Center for Education Statistics.

Freeman, S., Eddy, S., McDonaugh, M., Smith, M., Okoroafer, N., Jordt, H., & Wenderoth, M. (2014). Active learning increases student performance in science, engineering, and mathematics. *Proceedings of the National Academy of Sciences, 111*(23), 8410–8415.

Gay, G. (2000). *Culturally responsive teaching: Theory, research, and practice.* New York, NY: Teachers College Press.

Goode, J., Chapman, G., & Margolis, J. (2012). Beyond curriculum: The exploring computer science program. *ACM Inroads, 3*(2), 47–53.

Haak, D. C., HilleRisLambers, J., Pitre, E., & Freeman, S. (2011). Increased structure and active learning reduce the achievement gap in introductory biology. *Science, 332*(6034), 1213–1216.

Habjan, J. (2007). Society of Mary: Marianists. *Journal of Catholic Education, 11*(2), 198–217.

Hill, C., Corbett, C., & St. Rose, A. (2010). American Association of University Women (2010). *Why so few? Women in science, technology, engineering and mathematics.* Washington, DC: American Association of University Women website. Retrieved from https://www.aauw.org/resource/why-so-few-women-in-science-technology-engineering-mathematics/

Kennedy, T., & Odell, M. (2014). Engaging students in STEM education. *Science Education International*, *25*(3), 246–258.

Klawe, M. (2013). Increasing female participation in computing: The Harvey Mudd College story. *Computer*, *46*(3), 56–58.

Louvel, S. (2013). Understanding change in higher education as bricolage: How academics engage in curriculum change. *Higher Education*, *66*(6), 669–691.

Mack, K. (2017). Reconsidering STEM faculty professional development: Daring approaches to broadening participation in STEM. *Diversity and Democracy*, *20*(4). Retrieved from Association of American Colleges & Universities website https://www.aacu.org/diversitydemocracy/2017/fall/mack

MacPhee, D., Farro, S., & Canetto, S. (2013). Academic self-efficacy and performance of underrepresented STEM majors: Gender, ethnic, and social class patterns. *Analyses of Social Issues and Public Policy*, *13*(1), 347–369.

Margolis, J., & Fisher, A. (2001). *Unlocking the clubhouse. Women in computing.* Cambridge, MA: MIT Press.

McConnell, J. (1996). Active learning and its use in computer science. *ACM SIGCSE Bulletin*, *28*(SI), 52–54.

Murphy, T., & Treisman, U. (2008). Supporting high achievement in introductory mathematics courses: What we have learned from 30 years of the Emerging Scholars Program. *Making the Connection: Research and Teaching in Undergraduate Mathematics Education*, *18*(73), 205–305.

Pérez-Peña, R. (2012, June 21). Muslims from abroad are thriving in Catholic colleges. *The New York Times*. Retrieved from http://www.nytimes.com

Powell, R. (2008). Improving the persistence of first-year undergraduate women in computer science. *ACM SIGCSE Bulletin*, *40*(1), 518–522.

President's Council of Advisors on Science and Technology. (2012). *Engage to excel: producing one million additional college graduates with degrees in science, technology, engineering, and mathematics.* Retrieved from US Department of Energy website https://www.energy.gov/sites/prod/files/Engage%20to%20Excel%20Producing%20One%20Million%20Additional%20College%20Graduates%20With%20Degrees%20in%20STEM%20Feburary%202012.pdf

Simurda, M. (2012). Does the transition to an active-learning environment for the introductory course reduce students' overall knowledge of the various disciplines in biology? *Journal of Microbiology and Biology Education*, *13*(1), 17–20.

Smith, K., Sheppard, S., Johnson, D., & Johnson, R. (2005). Pedagogies of engagement: Classroom-based practices. *Journal of Engineering Education*, *94*(1), 87–101.

Stanley, N., Hall, G., & Berger, L. (2009). The case for cultural competency in psychotherapeutic interventions. *Annual Review of Psychology*, *60*, 525–548.

Tseng, K., Chang, C., Lou, S., & Chen, W. (2013). Attitudes towards science, technology, engineering and mathematics (STEM) in a project-based learning (PjBL) environment. *International Journal of Technology and Design Education*, *23*(1), 87–102.

University of Dayton. (2015). TIDES Year One Evaluation Report (2014–2015).

University of Dayton. (2016). TIDES Year Two Evaluation Report (2015–2016).

University of Dayton. (2017). TIDES Final Evaluation Report (2016–2017).

Waite, R., & Calamaro, C. (2010). Cultural competence: A systemic challenge to nursing education, knowledge exchange, and the knowledge development process. *Perspectives in Psychiatric Care, 46*(1), 74–80.

Witherspoon, A., Poe, D., & Sexton, S. (2017, November). *Increasing retention for undeclared students at a private mid-sized research university.* Proceedings of the 13th Annual National Symposium on Student Retention, Destin, Florida, November 6–9, 2017. [Forthcoming].

Chapter 5

In Search of Hidden but Accessible Truths: Coding for All at Queens College

Eva M. Fernández and Christopher Vickery

Reflection

On a train ride from New York City to Washington, DC, one early summer day in 2015, during an animated and likely over-caffeinated conversation about our project, our institutional context, our aspirations for our students, our aspirations for the good of the nation, or a combination of any of those topics, one of us made a comment memorable enough that it was promptly recorded for future reference: we are here in search of *hidden but accessible truths*. The comment captures one small but central dimension of the TIDES experience—the ways to increase diversity and equity in STEM are accessible truths. We have the empirical evidence, the pedagogical know-how, and the model theories of change. Yet, these truths continue to remain hidden, resulting in progress that is unacceptably slow and bumpy. Stimulating change must then begin with shining light on those accessible truths—truths that we were learning from our TIDES family and bringing back to our campus and our university system.

In this chapter, we tell the story of a transformation – institutional as well as personal–prompted by Queens College's participation in TIDES as an Honorable Mention institution. Without funding for a large-scale intervention, we have little to report in the way of data: we contributed infinitesimally small numbers to the structured evaluation of the project. Nonetheless, participating in the TIDES summer institutes and developing a strong affiliation with our TIDES family has stimulated, we think, profound changes in the way we and our institution are enacting the TIDES' call to action: the call to enhance underrepresented student interest, competencies, and retention in STEM, and to empower STEM faculty to practice inclusive and culturally sensitive teaching. *Sapere aude!*[1]

Institutional Context

Queens College (QC), a four-year institution in the City University of New York (CUNY) system, is a large, urban, public liberal arts college offering bachelor's, master's, and doctoral[2] degrees to one of the most ethnically diverse student populations in the nation: residents of the New York City (NYC) county of Queens. The county (the locals call it a "borough") is a microcosm of new immigration trends for the United States, given its location in one of the nation's major entry ports. The county of Queens, along with the rest of NYC, has seen recent significant growth in residents with Asian and Hispanic backgrounds (Furman Center, 2012), and has an almost even mix of Asian (27%), Black (18%), Hispanic (28%), and White (25%) residents (see the top panel of Figure 1). The QC student population (see the left side of the second panel in Figure 1) is primarily local, and demographic shifts in our surrounding community are the underlying source for the changes in the diversity of our student body, which has in the past ten or so years seen a sharp increase in proportions of Asian and Hispanic students. These shifts have led to our designation by the United States Department of Education as an Asian American and Native American Pacific Islander Serving Institution (AANAPISI) and, more recently, as a Hispanic Serving Institution (HSI).

Queens College could be an ideal setting for increasing the diversity of people entering the tech workforce in NYC. And yet the undergraduate Computer Science programs at QC mirror national trends in serving a very specific subset of our magnificently diverse population: some 27% of our undergraduate students majoring in CS identify as belonging to an underrepresented minority group, compared to 38% for the entire undergraduate population (see the right side of the second panel in Figure 1). When we add gender to the analysis, our CS students perfectly replicate the national trends:[3] only 17% of our CS undergraduate students are women.

The lack of diversity within the CS major is dissonant with CUNY's mission, which calls for a "commitment [...] to the provision of equal access and

---

[1] *Sapere aude* is Latin for "dare to know." Immanuel Kant chose this expression as the motto for the enlightenment in his 1784 essay "Beantwortung der Frage: Was ist Aufklärung?" ('An answer to the question: What is enlightenment?'). We come back to the topic of enlightenment thinking below.
[2] We offer doctoral degrees through our consortial relationship with the CUNY Graduate Center. Three doctoral subprograms in Psychology are based at QC; all other doctoral work (in areas ranging from English to Economics to Environmental Science) is based at the CUNY Graduate Center.
[3] In 2014, 18% of women pursuing Bachelor's degrees were enrolled in computer science (National Science Foundation, 2017).

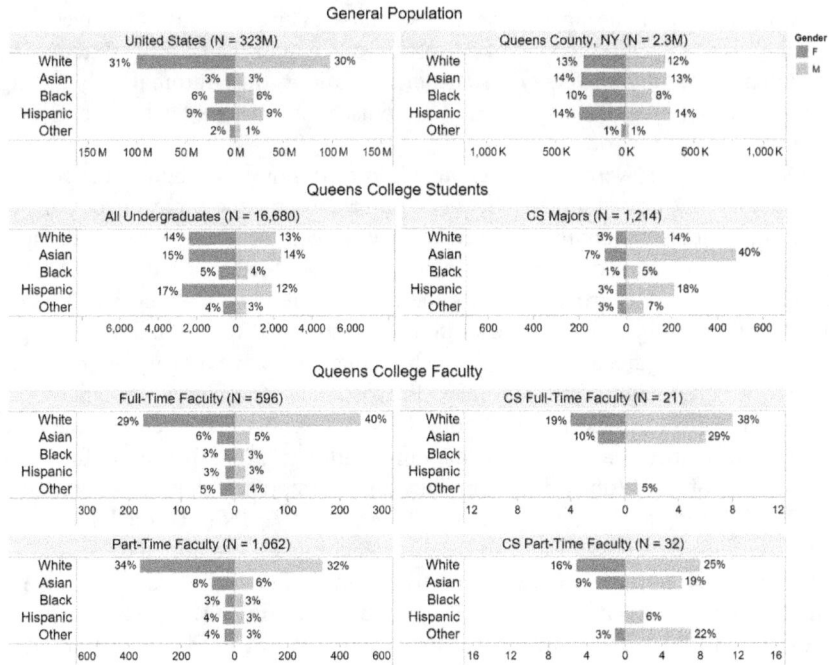

Figure 1: Ethnicity Estimates for the Populations of: the United States and the NYC County of Queens (top); All QC Undergraduates and Only Computer Science (CS) Majors (second panel); and all QC Faculty and Only CS Faculty Full-time (FT) and Part-time (PT) (bottom). *Note*: Data for the nation and the county are from the 2016 US Census population estimates (United States Census Bureau, 2018); QC student and faculty data are from the fall 2017 institutional census (Queens College Institutional Effectiveness). The category "Other" in QC student and faculty data includes international students and faculty.

opportunity for students, faculty and staff from all ethnic and racial groups and both sexes" (City University of New York, 2017). As we embarked on our TIDES journey, we started to learn how QC—despite the exceptional diversity in our surrounding community—is far from exceptional in countering national trends in CS demographics among students. We are also not exceptional in the demographics of our faculty (bottom panel of Figure 1), which resemble those for the nation much more than they resemble those of our community or our student body.

When we developed the idea for this project, we were acutely interested in taking advantage of several contextual factors. First, we imagined that the characteristics of our general education curriculum could be leveraged to attract female students to computer science courses. Second, we understood that our proximity to NYC's vibrant technology community could serve as a relevant backdrop and provide an experiential sandbox. Third, we saw ourselves in a possibly useful position as one of 24 institutions within the CUNY system (one of the largest public university systems in the nation), thus automatically having access to a population of faculty and administrators that might be receptive to learning from our work.

Our initial ideas were not well enough informed, however, about some contextual factors that turned out to play a central role in how the project evolved. For one, enrollments in computer science have surged with unprecedented vigor (National Academies of Sciences, Engineering, and Medicine, 2017), and QC's computer science department reflects the national trend in that regard. In addition, we found ourselves in an institution unaccustomed to examining data, specifically data disaggregated to display achievement gaps by ethnicity or gender. A change in QC's administration (new Provost, new President) brought about important shifts in thinking about both the surge of interest in tech and the need for a strategic focus on diversity within our institution. More fuel to our fire came in the form of the Women in Technology and Entrepreneurship in NY initiative (WiTNY, http://cuny.edu/witny), jointly launched by CUNY, Cornell Tech, and Verizon, with broad support from industry partners, with the specific aim of increasing the number of women working in technology. Lastly, the NYC broader context turned out to serve as an interesting stimulus, especially as word got out that QC had the largest enrollment in CS of any academic institution in NYC. External entities soon became very interested in accelerating our internal change, most importantly through initiatives coming from the NYC Office of the Mayor, including CS4All (http://cs4all.nyc) and the NYC Tech Talent Pipeline (http://www.techtalentpipeline.nyc). Other groups, like the Coalition for Queens (C4Q, http://www.c4q.nyc), eagerly sought out our partnership. We discuss these partnerships and collaborations in more detail in the *Evangelizing* section, below.

Background and Significance

With our submission to TIDES (titled *Coding for All: Increasing the Participation of Women in Computer Science through General Education*), we set out to increase the number of women entering computer science, using general education as the platform. An important tenet of our approach was our appreciation of a distinction drawn by Charette (2013) in the flagship publication of the leading engineering society in the country, *IEEE Spectrum*. In his provocatively titled article, "The STEM Crisis Is a Myth," Charette (2013) argued convincingly that the workforce actually has an overabundance of students who graduate with majors in STEM disciplines; what is needed is to increase the number of graduates who are able to leverage STEM-related skills effectively across a wide range of disciplines. This observation applies to computer science skills perhaps more pervasively than to other STEM-related skills, given that interacting with software and hardware, and developing (or at least having a foundational understanding of) code and algorithms is part of the everyday experience of people in many sectors, including those that are non-STEM.

Although many disciplines position the entry-level course for the major as a general education course in order to attract a large population of potential majors, this strategy is flawed in two relevant ways. The first flaw is that there can be a conflict when a course is used both to select students who should continue in the major and to satisfy a degree requirement for students who have no intention of continuing with the major. Although a well-structured course can certainly serve both audiences effectively, we see many instances where faculty are satisfied, or even pleased, to have high failure rates as evidence of strong selectivity. In sum, getting faculty to take responsibility for making such courses successful rather than placing the blame on unprepared or lazy students would be a valuable endeavor, but that was not the focus of this project.[4]

The second flaw, the one this project was set up to address, is for the introductory computer science course to be simply a programming course, using mastery of Java, C++, Python, Scheme, or some other programming language as the perceived goal of the course. The consensus is that it is important to introduce students to good coding practices early to avoid development of bad habits that will be difficult to unlearn later. This attitude, which dates as far back as Edsger Dijkstra's famous declaration that the Go To statement is "harmful" (Dijkstra, 1968), is perfectly correct as far as it goes. The problem is that this approach generates the misguided sense that in computer science you have to follow rules you might not understand because just following those rules makes things work. Since blindly following obscure rules is difficult, this approach to introductory CS courses leads to a second misconception our work was set up to address: the idea that only "geniuses" can do computer science.

While it is a mistake to use stereotypes to differentiate between populations, it is clear that a gender-related issue (driven by biological or societal factors, or a combination of the two; Ceci, Williams, & Barnett, 2009; Susan Pinker, 2008) leads more men than women, by a large margin, to thrive (or simply survive) in this type of introductory CS course. But rather than hypothesize what this issue might be, with no empirical evidence to bolster our position, our project adopted the approach of broadening the appeal of computer science to a wide range of students, including female students, without trying to make a course designed specifically for women or including patronizing features to make it appear more appealing to women, or something other than what it actually is.

Because the data indicate that there is a cultural bias that leads women to avoid CS courses, our project also addressed recruitment and aimed to incorporate culturally sensitive pedagogies. That is, we set out to devise a curriculum that is equally accessible to men and women, formulated on well-understood principles of how people learn (Ambrose, Bridges, DiPietro, Lovett, & Norman, 2010; Bransford, Brown, & Cocking, 2000) and supported by pedagogical

---

[4]Improving success rates in entry-level courses in STEM is the focus of a project currently underway at QC, *STEM Bridges Across Eastern Queens* (http://hsistem.qc.cuny.edu), designed and led by one of us (Fernández), and drawing deeply from expertise developed through TIDES.

approaches that are sensitive to diversity (Cole & Griffin, 2013). We designed and offered (and are still offering) a college-level introduction to fundamental concepts of the discipline that emphasizes the creativity, applicability, and accessibility of computing, as well as its interdisciplinary applications, rather than relying on the traditional rule-based, learn-to-program approach.

The working title of our computer science course is *Information and Intelligence*, and it seems appropriate to indicate here how it is designed with the intention to achieve the curricular aspect of the project. We decided that making our course "for all" was a more promising approach than overtly targeting a particular audience (women; see, e.g., Leach, 2010). We made a conscious decision to avoid terminology that carries "societal baggage" or that identifies computer science with conventional male-oriented stereotypes. We talk about "coding" instead of "programming" and we talk about "computing" or "technology" instead of "computer science." The semantic differences are minimal, yet extraordinary. We also avoided pejorative images like the 400-pound hacker sitting on his bed.

Although there are only two nouns in the course title, there are actually three threads running through the design of the course: (1) Information Theory, (2) Artificial Intelligence, and (3) Coding.

(1) The Information Theory thread deals with how digitally encoded data can and does represent virtually all types of information that we deal with in our everyday lives, in commerce, in science, and in our culture. Shannon's insight (Shannon, 1948) that the capacity of a telephone line for conveying information could be measured numerically has emerged as the basis for one of the most profound shifts in human thinking and behavior to date: the emergence of the digital information age and the shift from thinking of computation as "number crunching" to "information manipulation."
(2) As a discipline, Artificial Intelligence (AI) has been slow to measure up to the expectations raised by early researchers in the field. But advances in the discipline have indeed developed to the point that they are pervasive in our daily lives (e.g., ask Google; ask Siri; ask Alexa). Progress in AI requires mastery of fundamental principles of computer science, and the course is designed to introduce students to that relationship.
(3) The course ties Information Theory and Artificial Intelligence together through the model of encoding the behavior of intelligent agents. But rather than focus on algorithms in abstract situations, the course uses small-scale hardware devices (Arduino micro controllers) to give students the experience of writing code that causes physical responses to the device's environment (inputs) in order to have effects on its environment (outputs). There is not enough time in the course to generate full-blown problem-solving intelligent agents, but AI provides the context for the algorithmic aspects of the coding projects, and information theory provides the basis for understanding the characteristics of the controller's memory and the sensors and actuators attached to it.

> *Example of an Assignment Prompt That Relates AI,*
> *Information Theory, and Coding*
>
> When a mouse enters a cell in a maze, it senses three bits of information: whether or not there are walls to the left, to the right, or straight ahead. Your project is to simulate this information using three pushbuttons, and to light up NeoPixels to show which of four directions the mouse should go (left, right, forward, or turn around) based on that information and according to the "follow left wall" rule for traversing a maze.

The Arduino devices currently used in the course can be programmed in several languages, including Python and MakeCode (https://makecode.adafruit.com/). But the course is based on the traditional Arduino language, which is C++ with a built-in runtime library to support digital and analog I/O.

Implementation

Our project proceeded in two intertwined ways: the Course and the Evangelizing. The former advanced modestly, because our Honorable Mention status meant we had no budget to support project activities. The latter evolved in unpremeditated fashion: it was not part of the design, and in some respects we did not see it coming. We first turn to the course, then discuss the evangelizing, and wrap up this section with a discussion specifying how both activities were intricately supported by our participation in the TIDES community of practice.

Course Recruitment, Pedagogy, and Outcomes

Information and Intelligence was designed to instill in students something about the wonders of algorithmic thinking and computer science: the loftiest of ideals, at the most elementary levels. The course would plant seeds in freshmen which would, we hoped, grow them into successful (and gender- and ethnically-diverse) CS majors. The most fertile ground for this kind of seeding, we thought, would be the learning communities offered to freshmen at Queens College through its Freshman Year Initiative (FYI) program. FYI assigns almost all incoming students[5] to a course in some general education discipline paired with the first

---

[5] All freshmen entering in fall semesters are eligible for FYI, except for students who do not have the required proficiency in English to take *College Writing*. The learning communities thus only exclude international students with scores lower than 500 in the Test of English as a Foreign Language (TOEFL) and the handful of entering freshmen who enter in the spring semester.

required English Composition course (ENGL 110, *College Writing*). In these learning communities, the same 20 students take those paired courses, where the two instructors know each other, plan their syllabi and assignments in collaboration, sometimes include joint assignments or activities, and sometimes also engage students in out-of-class outings.

We very quickly learned that using "computing" in the name of our learning community was a naïve mistake: the first time we did this the course filled up with men before we could figure out what to do about it (15 men, two women)[6].

This accidental discovery had a highly positive outcome, as it propelled us to develop, in collaboration with the QC Office of General Counsel (with then-General Counsel Meryl Kaynard) and with the QC FYI directors, a method for controlling registration. Title IX regulations prohibit institutions from discriminating on the basis of sex in recruiting students (34 CFR § 106.23(a)), but Title IX also specifies that institutions can work to overcome the effects of conditions resulting in limited participation by one sex by undertaking additional recruitment efforts (34 CFR § 106.3(a)). The demonstrated disparity in the number of women (15–2) served to grant us the go-ahead to engage in specialized recruitment.[7]

In subsequent semesters, both in the fall when the course is part of a learning community and in the spring when it is not, the course has been open to both men and women, but as soon as the proportion of men reaches 50% of the total number of seats available, any new male registrants are placed on a waiting list, and invited to enroll in the course in the following semester, thereby meeting our legal obligation to serve all students.[8]

In addition to controlling registration, we have the active cooperation of FYI advisors, who draw attention to the special nature of the course during freshman orientation sessions. We have also been experimenting with specialized emails to recruit women enrollees. An example, used for the Spring 2018 term, is provided in Figure 2.

Controlling registration had a significant impact on our ability to recruit women into the course. Since the learning communities involve almost all freshmen (anywhere from 1,200 to 1,500 in a given fall), a scarcity of enrollments was never an issue. For the following seven semesters our enrollment has been

---

[6]This invites speculation about applications of this anecdotal discovery to tilting the balance in women-majority disciplines: imagine an introduction to psychology course called *Computers and the Human Mind*, or a course on language called *Computational Studies of Speech Production and Perception*.

[7]At the time of writing this chapter, we are unsure whether other CUNY colleges have adopted processes like this for controlling registration, but we have offered this insight at several university forums, to very interested audiences.

[8]Few (if any) of the waitlisted men have ever bothered to take the course in the spring. Most likely they meet the requirement some other way, or simply forget they were ever interested.

In Search of Hidden but Accessible Truths 81

> Dear Natalie,
>
> This is to alert you to CS 100, a Pathways "Scientific World" course being offered by the Computer Science Department next semester. The course is a "real computer science" course (you will learn to write code), but it is not part of the CS major. It is specifically designed for students who have little or no formal computing experience, but who recognize the importance of learning to work with technology as part of a liberal arts education.
>
> The course is open to both men and women, but in an effort to increase the number of women who study computer science, registration preference is being given to women. The flyer below describes the course and registration process in more detail.
>
> Sincerely,
> Dr. Christopher Vickery
> Professor of Computer Science
>
> CS 100 Flyer.pdf (https://bit.ly/2ko5MMx)

Figure 2: Sample email sent in December 2017 to undergraduate women not majoring in CS.

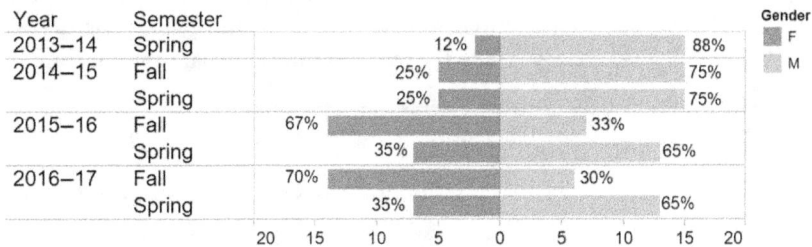

Figure 3: Enrollments (*N* and %) in CS 100 by gender, for five semesters including the entire TIDES implementation period (2014 fall through 2017 spring).

steady at over 40% women, and over 60% for the fall semesters when the FYI controls are in place (see Figure 3).

The course had been offered several times before we became involved in the TIDES project, and reflected Vickery's interests in computer architecture, including programmable logic devices, and real-time systems. Although not formally articulated, the prior goal could be summarized as "knowing how computers really work is a good thing."

When we submitted our TIDES proposal, Fernández was the director of the Center for Teaching and Learning, and brought insight into educational best practices to our work. In addition to being a member of the Computer Science faculty, Vickery was (and is) the Director of General Education at the college, and brought experience with curriculum development in those contexts to the project. Our TIDES experience, described in more detail in the *TIDES Community of Practice* section below, has served as a critical catalyst for the evolution of the course. The process continues to this day, but some notable steps along the way are described below.

Learning Focus

The TIDES experience has led to a shift in the perceived role of the instructor. Instead of being the organizer of subject matter so that it can be delivered in a coherent manner, the instructor now serves more as the facilitator of student learning. The criterion for a successful semester has shifted from how many students "got" the material to how engaged the students were with the material.

Student Feedback: Takeaways

At the beginning of each class, each student is given a piece of paper with a list of questions intended to encourage reflection on what happened during the class and to comment on what was problematic. The exact questions change from term to term and within each term as well. Completing these "Takeaways" counts a small amount toward the course grade, encouraging regular attendance in the course, and by making "good" comments, students can offset missed classes. More importantly, the takeaways become the basis for the first part of the following class meeting. The instructor still has to determine how much energy to put into a concept, but the students are engaged in the process of making that determination.

> A Question From a Recent Takeaway
>
> What question do you have as a result of today's class, and how will you try to answer it before next time?

Student Feedback: Quizzes

Quizzes are typically seen as a formative assessment tool that lets students know how well they are doing in a course as opposed to a summative assessment tool that determines a student's grade and the successfulness of the course. In our course, quizzes have evolved into a complement to the takeaways: they provide feedback to the instructor about how the class is doing in addition to motivating students and providing preparation for the summative midterm and final exams. Currently, there is a quiz at the beginning of each class, encouraging students to prepare ahead of time, yet being so numerous as to be truly a low-stakes activity. Students soon learn that questions that can cause difficulty are likely to be repeated across quizzes, encouraging deeper engagement with the material than "I didn't get that, but now it's over."

Group Work

Although teamwork is the norm in industry, the attitude in many academic computer science programs (including ours) is that individuals must master the skills and techniques of the subject matter before they can meaningfully contribute to a team. How to allocate academic credit to the members of a student team is a perennial problem: one or two people do the work, but everyone gets credit for it.

The "think-pair-share" approach (Lyman, 1987) helps us engage students, but the pairs that do not report out often seem to be the ones that do not "get it." Our thinking on the issue continues to evolve, but our use of low-stakes daily quizzes led to the following instructions for a recent one.

The Instructions for Today's Quiz are Different!

Do not hand this quiz in until you have discussed it with others and are sure that all your answers are correct. Everyone in the class has to submit the same answers.

- If anyone hands in a different answer from everyone else, everyone will get a "not ok" for the quiz.
- If everyone gets all the answers right, everyone will get a "good" for the quiz.
- Let [the TA] or me know if anything is unclear.
- You can use the whiteboards as you work on the answers.

The quiz created a lot of buzz, and in their Takeaways that day most students commented on how much they liked the experience. But, the most telling comments came from students who were *not* the leaders in the class. They observed the leaders being actively engaged in solving the quiz problems rather than "just knowing the answers," and more than one of the strugglers reported that they no longer felt like the outsiders to the process that they had thought they were.

Projects for All

In our goal of not catering to male stereotypes, we attempted to assign projects that might appeal more to the creative interests of women. Wearable electronics seemed like a good idea, but led to mixed results. In one case, male students tried sewing NeoPixels onto a necktie, but failed (conductive thread is hard to work with) and were frustrated. An attempt to collaborate with the Dance Department to produce costumes for one of their performances generated a lot of interest, but was not a success: the *Information and Intelligence* students could not come up to speed within the time constraints of the *Dance* students' semester deadline. Since then, the college has introduced a makerspace environment where projects like this will have a better chance of serving everyone's interest. We are currently exploring ways to incorporate culturally responsive pedagogy into curriculum changes tied to the makerspace.

At the same time, we thought that we should avoid robots and "techy" things because they would feed into negative male-oriented stereotypes. We do not have data to support this, but it looks like we were wrong. The women in the class seem just as interested in writing code to control motors, learning to solder, etc., as the men.

The TIDES Continue to Ebb and Flow

The analyses of course outcomes data must be interpreted with caution, as the dataset is extremely small. As discussed earlier (see Figure 3), the course was administered six times: controlling registration in three fall semesters (2014, 2015, 2016, controlling registration for the latter two and three spring semesters (2015, 2016, 2017).

Figure 4 offers a glimpse of course outcomes as measured by final grades, disaggregating by the dimension of most interest to this project: gender. The figure includes, for comparison, outcomes for the course as it was offered the semester before TIDES (spring 2013). For the TIDES semesters (2014 fall and forward), there is no appreciable gender gap, in either direction: 73% of the women pass, compared to 74% of the men. We do observe a gender gap in the semesters with controlled registration (fall 2015 and fall 2016), with women outperforming men: 81% of the women pass the class, compared to 77% of the

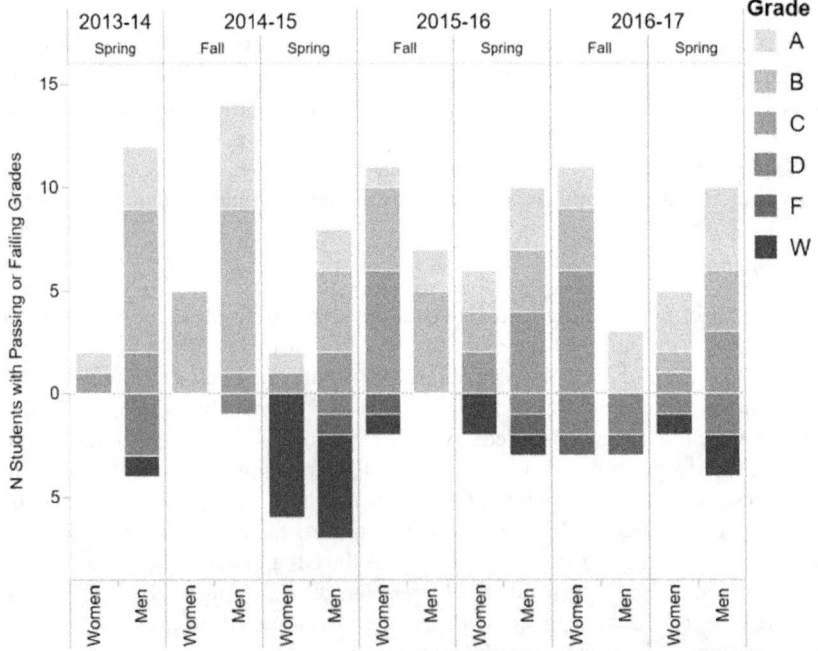

Figure 4: Grade distributions for CSCI 100, by semester and gender. Passing is defined as a grade of C or better (displayed above the horizontal axis).

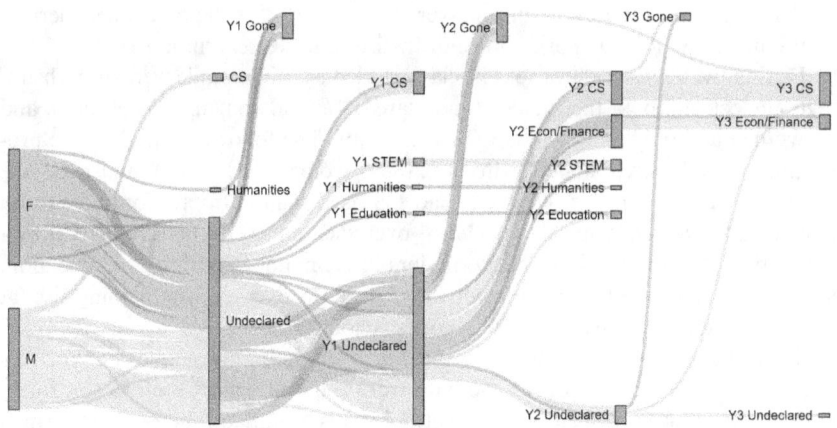

Figure 5: For the Three Cohorts Starting as Freshmen (fall 2014, 2015, and 2016), Academic Plan (major) Flows for Women (F, dark gray flows) and Men (M, light gray flows), From the First Semester, to Year 1 (Y1, all cohorts), Year 2 (Y2, Cohorts 2014 and 2015 only), and Year 3 (Y3, Cohort 2014 only). *Notes*: Majors: CS (Computer Science), Econ/Finance (economics, accounting, finance, and related), Humanities (majors in the Division of Arts & Humanities), Education (majors leading to preliminary certification as teacher in New York State). Other labels: Gone (absent from student records for relevant semester), Undeclared (no major).

men.[9] A larger sample size (and a proper comparison group) would allow us to examine the extent to which this finding is stable and replicable.

Figure 5 is a Sankey diagram[10] to help us explore whether the course had an impact on selection of major. The diagram shows the declared majors for students enrolled in the three fall semesters the course was offered persisted for up to three years after they took the course. We chose these three semesters because for all three (60 students total) the cohort included only first-time freshmen. The data for the display include declared majors during the fall the students took the course and for the following three fall semesters (Y1, Y2, and Y3 in the display). The sample is 53% women, very much in line with the college average.

Figure 5 provides a window into retention patterns (but not graduation, since none of the students in this sample have graduated within the analysis period): the year 1 retention rate is approximately 92% for the sample, which is

---

[9]In the US, women outperform men at all educational levels (see, e.g., Diprete & Buchmann, 2013).
[10]Sankey diagrams are visualizations of the transitions of multiple components in a complex system. The diagrams are typically read left-to-right (inputs-to-outputs), with nodes sized proportional to their inputs.

moderately higher than the college average (84–85% for the equivalent period; City University of New York, Office of Institutional Research, n.d.).

During the semester they took the class, students in the sample were overwhelmingly undecided about their major (undeclared: 97% of women, 93% of men), and no women and only two men had CS as a major. The following fall (Y1) the proportion of undeclared students dropped (88% women, 74% men), and only one woman,–but as many as five men–had CS as a major. Impressionistically, we observe that women who take this class, overwhelmingly, do not choose CS as a major path, converging instead into majors in economics and finance, education, and the humanities. The men, in contrast, choose CS over almost anything else (at a college where they have over 100 majors to choose from).

The inputs into the rightmost nodes are overwhelmingly male, but for this phase of the diagram we only have data from the first cohort (before controlled registration processes went into effect). At this point, all but 1 of the men remaining are majoring in CS; the only woman remaining is in a major related to economics or finance.

We will continue to watch the ebbs and flows of the enrollment patterns in this course. The course's strategic recruitment strategy has increased the participation of women in it. The pedagogical practices developed for the course instantiate many inclusive teaching practices. It is therefore not accidental that students (and instructor) are engaged, which leads to balanced outcomes for both men and women. However, the recruitment strategy along with the pedagogical practices do not seem to have an impact on the trend for women to stay away from CS. We say this with caution, given the paucity of data.

Evangelizing

As an Honorable Mention institution within the swell of TIDES, we were unchained from implementation or the more extensive reporting duties of the full awardees. This afforded us ample opportunity to network and expand. The time was ripe at QC, with a new President, Félix V. Matos Rodríguez, leading our college with its largest CS department in the NYC metropolitan region. One of President Matos' earliest public acts was participating in a televised panel on the topic of the value of a liberal education, where he showcased this fact (NY1, 2014). This and a constellation of other networking efforts on the part of our administration got us noticed by some of the major players in CS education within the university and within NYC.

The fact is that being the largest CS department in the NYC area is easy to brag about, and we got good mileage out of it. Our participation in TIDES gave us an automatically authoritative voice within this (sometimes politicized) discourse: our connection to a national organization working with a nationwide set of institutions made our perspective be one that people took notice of. Within months after returning from our first TIDES summer institute, we were engaged in conversations with organizations like Girls Who Code and Black Girls Code. We also connected with an organization in Queens County called C4Q

(Coalition for Queens, http://www.c4q.nyc), a nonprofit organization that provides training, with the specific objective of diversifying the tech community.

CUNY enrolls a quarter-million students at any given time, and the vast majority of them continue to live and work in the New York metropolitan region after graduation. These facts have not escaped the notice of the NYC Mayor's office and CUNY's central administration. Three NYC/CUNY initiatives with which we have been involved based on our "We are TIDES" mantle include CS4ALL, the Tech Talent Pipeline (TTP), and Women in Technology New York (WiTNY).

CS4ALL is an ambitious initiative by the Mayor's Office to incorporate computer science into the K-12 curricula for all NYC students. Vickery was asked to serve as a member of the CS4ALL Advisory Board, which consults with the research group tasked with evaluating the CS4ALL project.

An additional opportunity to share our growing expertise in inclusive excellence in STEM was through WiTNY (Women in Technology and Entrepreneurship in NY, http://cuny.edu/witny), which, as mentioned earlier, is a joint CUNY-Cornell Tech-Verizon initiative, supported by industry partners, aiming to increase the number of women working in technology. WiTNY has developed initiatives that include opportunities for rising freshman women at CUNY to develop incipient skills in programming; scholarships, internships, and specialized mentoring for CUNY undergraduate women pursuing tech-related majors; and opportunities for faculty to learn about inclusive teaching pedagogies and to develop courses that will narrow existing achievement gaps. We were invited to contribute to a workshop in summer 2016, attended by over 25 faculty from Computer Science departments around the CUNY system. Our contribution (Fernández & Vickery, 2016) offered an overview of the CSCI 100 course intervention, described some preliminary findings, and concluded with a brief tutorial on topics learned at TIDES, focused on how to recognize and reduce implicit bias and stereotype threat and encourage growth mind-set.

WiTNY consults with us on occasion, particularly on ways of exploring data trends for the entire university based on the smaller datasets we reported for QC for TIDES. WiTNY has also become a resource in ongoing expansion of the CSCI 100 course, which continues to be offered (now in two sections per semester) with partial support from WiTNY.

We think of TIDES as part of the social justice movement, with economic advantages to the students as just one of the positive outcomes of successful projects. Politicians have a complementary goal called workforce development, which attempts to enhance the regional economy by fostering development of a well-educated pool of workers to draw employers to the area. The NYC Government's Department of Small Business Services has partnered with local tech employers in a workforce development initiative called the Tech Talent Pipeline (TTP). QC was invited to be an initial partner in the effort, in part, because of the size of our CS Department, and in part because of TIDES reputation. The *TTP Residency at QC* funded paid internships to four cohorts of QC students over the course of approximately two years, with added programming for the student interns consisting of pre-internship training, networking opportunities, professional development, and support in job placement. In addition, the project was designed to provide feedback from industry to the Computer Science Department at QC, that would help identify and implement recommendations to improve job readiness for QC CS graduates. Industry's recommendations overwhelmingly focus on pedagogical approaches (e.g., project-based learning) that would in theory also have the effect of improving learning for all students. The CS Department administration has been reluctant to change its formal curriculum to meet industry's recommendations, but they recognize the value of providing a bridge for students to efficiently enter the workforce.

The TIDES Community of Practice

The TIDES program was designed to involve participation from a wide variety of institutions serving radically different student populations. The summer weeklong TIDES Institutes in DC and the AAC&U STEM Conferences each autumn have been described in this volume. Here we offer examples of how being part of TIDES impacted us.

Each institution's TIDES team was assigned a coach for the Institutes. Ours was Dr Beverly Bickel of the University of Maryland Baltimore County. Her mentorship and friendship through the years have been invaluable. In particular, she provided us with some suggested reading material at the first Institute. Looking back, it is hard to believe that we had not yet read Claude Steele's *Whistling Vivaldi*. During that first Institute, another coach, Dr Sumun Pendakur of the University of Southern California, exhorted everyone to become familiar with Carol Dweck's work on reinforcing a growth mind-set in learners. And at that same Institute, Nathan Klingbeil of Wright State University was a guest speaker who opened our eyes to the demonstrable effects that curriculum revision could have on the success of so-called underprepared students. We learned about implicit bias from Brian Nosek, about student mentoring from Erica Camacho, and about developing strong logic models from Kate Winter in the first summer institute.

We had a TIDES Workshop in conjunction with the AAC&U STEM Conference in Atlanta the first year, and a group exercise there was particularly enlightening for one of us. In the exercise, we were asked to categorize several traits, including race, gender, sexuality, religion, able-bodiedness, etc., according to which traits were more advantageous to the individual, and then where we aligned with those traits personally. Being an able-bodied, white, heterosexual male, who is Protestant, had never seemed particularly noteworthy (except for a few "WASP" jokes). But when the meeting leader asked, almost as an afterthought, whether anyone in the room had identified with all the advantageous traits, one of us was the only person in the room whose hand went up. The notion of being a person of privilege, and what that implies, was brought home more clearly than reading essays or listening to lectures on the topic could ever have accomplished. In hindsight, Vickery is not the only person of privilege in the TIDES community, but the perspective that experience provided has had a lasting impact on his outlook on the work we have been doing.

Discussion

In reflecting over how the past four years of TIDES have transformed us and our institution, we identified the following five areas where we have been able to uncover hidden, but accessible truths:

(1) *CSCI 100: Information and Intelligence.* We have developed a highly viable course to introduce students to CS in a way that is not only designed to present content accessibly to all students, regardless of gender (as originally intended), but that also incorporates some best practices in inclusive teaching and learning, as we learned to do through TIDES. Our miniature dataset from six semesters of CSCI 100 suggests that the course's design (including its controlled enrollment procedures) produces outcomes with no gender-based gaps in student achievement. The course is still running, and could run in many more sections.

(2) *Pedagogical expertise to inform other STEM education initiatives.* What we have learned about inclusive teaching through CSCI 100 is highly portable, and continues to impact other initiatives focused on STEM education at QC. One beneficiary is the US Department of Education funded project, *STEM Bridges Across Eastern Queens* (http://hsistem.qc.cuny.edu) mentioned earlier (footnote 4). In this project, faculty are redesigning entry-level STEM courses in seven disciplines at QC and our largest feeder, Queensborough Community College. CSCI 100 has also infused our thinking in a new initiative, still very much under development: we are considering adopting components of an approach called Design-Make-Play, developed by colleagues at the New York Hall of Science (Honey & Kanter, 2013), as a framework to develop a set of general education courses that will feature opportunities for hands-on improvisational learning-through-making. These courses will take advantage of resources from QC's new makerspace.

(3) *One course is not enough.* We have also learned that changing students' disciplinary objectives is difficult, and in this respect our findings suggest that a general education-focused intervention is not sufficiently strong to recruit and retain women into CS. This is in line with insight that has been reported elsewhere (e.g., Ganley, George, Cimpian, & Makowski, 2017) that students enter majors with steadfast preconceptions about who belongs in what discipline. It takes sustained social encouragement to lead students from populations traditionally underrepresented in CS to choose a technical career (Google, 2014). Authenticity in the learning environment to encourage personal creativity, sharing, and validating identity and belonging is what ultimately leads to shifting attitudinal constructs about studying CS (McKlin et al. 2018), but general education courses are perhaps too tangential to students' career pursuits. Building larger curricular pathways (and changing the culture, Frieze & Quesenberry, 2015) is the logical next step.

(4) *The power of disaggregating data.* TIDES has helped hone our institutional data analytic skills (despite the small number of data points, making statistical significance impossible to even explore). We have learned how

disaggregated data can be used to tell a story that can lead to evidence-based decision making (as cliché-ish as that sounds). This has had an impact within QC as well as throughout CUNY. TIDES has further provided us with a window into best practices at other institutions, and with sharp information about national trends in the impact of STEM and CS education on underrepresented groups. We use both of these sources of external data as comparison points to measure our institutional successes (and failures).

(5) *No funding does not necessarily mean no action (and context matters more than you think)*. We cannot underestimate the impact the project had in terms of making noise: TIDES allowed us to engage with and amplify the effects of preexisting but loosely related initiatives. Somewhat ironically, despite the limited scope of our TIDES funding, we have achieved a university-wide authoritative voice. Our original proposal was to change the CS department by using CSCI 100 as a model for curriculum change. As it turns out, we have been able to contribute to much larger efforts of the university and the city, in their ambitions to diversify the tech workforce. To do so, we had to be responsive to the many outside entities wanting to engage with the largest CS department in the NY Metropolitan area, something we had never anticipated doing. In addition, we have moved beyond encouraging the department to review its role in educating CS students to being part of a movement that connects our work to other STEM disciplines through the development of a makerspace and to preliminary discussions around the creation of a data science school. These new initiatives allow the department to focus its available resources on its perceived mission of providing a rigorous computer science curriculum while allowing the college to serve its students' needs for broader experience with technology and data analytics, which in turn relate very closely to our project's initial goal: coding for all.

Conclusion

We have provided an overview of the institutional and personal transformation that TIDES incited at QC and for the authors of this chapter. TIDES set out to enhance underrepresented student interest, competencies, and retention in STEM, empowering us to articulate why change is desirable and providing us with a lens through which we can see how change is possible. We have described how our contribution as an Honorable Mention institution was small in scale and yet wound up having (is still having) a broad impact. Our TIDES course, CSCI 100, used registration controls to increase exposure to CS for women undergraduates, and incorporated pedagogical practices designed to make all students in the class be able to master the course content and skills. Our participation in the TIDES community of practice, which was a significant stimulant in our personal transformation, also had the consequence of positioning us to become deeply involved (more than we would have been otherwise) in how STEM education plays out at our institution (QC and CUNY). Because of TIDES and our newfound expertise, we have also been able to secure external funding and recruit partners from our local community, all with the ultimate goal of advancing this mission-critical work.

The Last Word

We started this chapter invoking Immanuel Kant's (1784) motto for the enlightenment: *sapere aude!* ('dare to know!'). TIDES dared us to learn about increasing diversity and equity in STEM, by spreading expertise about best practices in inclusive teaching. In the four years that have passed, we have tried to enact this call to action, with a focus on CS. Kamau Bobb, in his TIDES keynote address at the 2016 summer institute, declared that "CS education is at the lead of the ship of equity," and we have come to see our role as helping to steer that ship in the right direction.

CS education is very much in the public eye, perceived as an easy way into a lucrative job by students and their parents, or as an essential way to maintain a strong national economy by politicians and media commentators. In a college context, CS education means a guaranteed flood of enrollments for departments, and suggests access to funds for institutional improvements to administrators. If we change the narrative so that the focus is on access, inclusion, and equity, we stand to make a positive difference.

We end this chapter invoking a recent rallying call for enlightenment thinking (Steven Pinker, 2018), which, put simply, is all about uncovering truths. Modern science, Pinker reminds us, informs on how we are to understand the human condition, through an evidence-based rational approach, which draws from the intrinsically human powers of abstraction and recursion. It is not lost on us that abstraction and recursion are central topics in any course on *Information and Intelligence*; one would only find those topics better covered in an introduction to linguistics. In the context of CS education, let data on how people learn and learn to persist in STEM drive pedagogical practices and institutional designs; let these designs be studied and the emerging patterns they generate serve to drive new pedagogical practices and institutional interventions, so that ultimately every student succeeds.

TIDES Resources

In our 2016 workshop for WiTNY (Fernández & Vickery, 2016), we offered participants a list of materials for further information. We replicate that list in its entirety below, with some updates and some comments about the relevance of each.

Stereotype threat and implicit bias are two barriers to enacting the TIDES call to action. Understanding the way each works is the first step to lowering or eliminating those barriers.

- Claude Steele (2010), *Whistling Vivaldi: How Stereotypes Affect Us and What We Can Do;*

- Reducing Stereotype threat (http://www.reducingstereotypethreat.org), online resources to disseminate research about stereotype threat to a broad audience, including an extensive bibliography (http://www.reducingstereotypethreat.org/articles/); and
- Project Implicit (http://www.projectimplicit.net/index.html), co-founded by Tony Greenwald (University of Washington), Mahzarin Banaji (Harvard University), and Brian Nosek (University of Virginia), to educate the public and to offer virtual tools to collect data on hidden biases.

Improving student success in any discipline involves adopting a growth mind-set, that is, an understanding that expertise can be honed through dedication and hard work. Psychologist Carol Dweck contrasts growth mind-set (which leads to learning, motivation, and productivity) to fixed mind-set (which stifles productivity and learning), adopted by people who focus on their intrinsic intelligence or talent and take these to be fixed traits.

- Carol Dweck (2008), *Mindset: The New Psychology of Success*; and
- Carol Dweck, The Power of Believing You Can Improve, TED Talks (https://www.youtube.com/watch?v=_X0mgOOSpLU).

We pointed many of our colleagues to the work by Nathan Klingbeil and colleagues on re-engineering Engineering Math, for a number of reasons: their design (to improve outcomes for all) is very similar to our original design; they provide extensive materials and documentation; and we find their results highly compelling.

- "Wright State Engineering Math", (https://engineering-computer-science.wright.edu/research/engineering-mathematics/the-wright-state-model-for-engineering-mathematics-education); and
- Nathan Klingbeil, Questioning the Equation, TEDxDayton (https://youtu.be/CWCWq155hyc).

On the interrelated topics of diversity, diversity in computing, and the gender gap:

- Beryl Nelson (2014), The data on diversity; Nelson also presented her work at a Google Tech Talk, available online https://youtu.be/Am3tHJzqnMk;
- Carol Frieze and Jeria Quesenberry (2015), *Kicking Butt in CS: Women in Computing at Carnegie Mellon*; and
- Susan Pinker (2008), *The Sexual Paradox: Men, Women, and the Real Gender Gap*.

A manual for teaching programming to students in non-STEM disciplines:

- Nick Montfort (2016), *Exploratory Programming for the Arts and Humanities*.

Acknowledgment

Both authors are at Queens College of the City University of New York. We thank our TIDES "coach" Beverly Bickel (University of Maryland, Baltimore County) for her wisdom, encouragement, and moral support. We also thank administrators at Queens who have been particularly supportive: President Félix Matos Rodríguez, Provost Elizabeth Hendrey, and General Counsel Meryl Kaynard.

References

34 CFR § 106.23. Code of Federal Regulations – Recruitment. US Government Publishing Office, https://www.gpo.gov/fdsys/pkg/CFR-2017-title34-vol1/pdf/CFR-2017-title34-vol1-sec106-23.pdf

34 CFR § 106.3. Code of Federal Regulations – Remedial & affirmative action & self-evaluation, https://www.gpo.gov/fdsys/pkg/CFR-2017-title34-vol1/pdf/CFR-2017-title34-vol1-sec106-3.pdf

Ambrose, S., Bridges, M. W., DiPietro, M., Lovett, M. C., & Norman, M. K. (2010). *How learning works: seven research-based principles for smart teaching.* San Francisco, CA: Jossey-Bass.

Bransford, J. D., Brown, A. L., & Cocking, R. R. (Eds.). (2000). *How people learn: Brain, mind, experience, and school: Expanded edition.* Washington, DC: The National Academies Press.

Ceci, S. J., Williams, W. M., & Barnett, S. M. (2009). Women's underrepresentation in science: Sociocultural and biological considerations. *Psychological Bulletin, 135*(2), 218–261. doi:10.1037/a0014412

City University of New York, Office of Institutional Research. (n.d.). *Institution retention and graduation rates of full-time first-time freshmen in baccalaureate programs by year of entry: Queens.* Retrieved from http://www.cuny.edu/irdatabook/rpts2_AY_current/RTGI_0007_FT_FTFR_BACC_SR-QC.pdf

City University of New York. (2017). *Mission and history.* Retrieved from http://www2.cuny.edu/about/history/

Charette, R. N. (2013). The STEM crisis is a myth. Retrieved from http://spectrum.ieee.org/at-work/education/the-stem-crisis-is-a-myth

Cole, D., & Griffin, K. A. (2013). Advancing the study of student-faculty interaction: A focus on diverse students and faculty. In M. B. Paulsen (Ed.), *Higher education handbook of theory and research* (Vol. 28, pp. 561–611). Dordrecht: Springer. doi:10.1007/978-94-007-5836-0_12

Dijkstra, E. W. (1968, March). Go To statement considered harmful. *Communications of the ACM, 11*(3), 147–148.

Diprete, T. A., & Buchmann, C. (2013). *The rise of women: The growing gender gap in education and what it means for American schools.* New York, NY: The Russell Sage Foundation.

Dweck, C. (2008). *Mindset: The new psychology of success.* New York, NY: Ballantine Books.

Fernández, E. M., & Vickery, C. (2016). Workshop presented at Women in Technology and Entrepreneurship in New York (WiTNY) event, New York, July 12. Retrieved from https://goo.gl/tm0HCW

Frieze, C., & Quesenberry, J. (2015). *Kicking butt in computer science: Women in computing at Carnegie Mellon University*. Indianapolis, IN: Dog Ear Publishing.

Furman Center for Real Estate & Urban Policy, School of Law and Wagner School of Public Service, New York University. (2012). *The changing racial and ethnic makeup of New York City neighborhoods*, Retrieved from http://furmancenter.org/files/sotc/The_Changing_Racial_and_Ethnic_Makeup_of_New_York_City_Neighborhoods_11.pdf

Ganley, C. M., George, C. E., Cimpian, J. R., & Makowski, M. B. (2017). Gender equity in college majors: Looking beyond the STEM/Non-STEM dichotomy for answers regarding female participation. *American Educational Research Journal*, *55*(3), 453–487. doi:10.3102/0002831217740221

Google. (2014). *Women who choose computer science—What really matters: The critical role of encouragement and exposure*. Retrieved from https://edu.google.com/pdfs/women-who-choose-what-really.pdf

Honey, M., & Kanter, D. E. (Eds.). (2013). *Design, make, play: Growing the next generation of STEM innovators*. New York, NY: Routledge.

Kant, I. (1784). Beantwortung der Frage: Was ist Aufklärung? *Berlinische Monatsschrift*, *12*, 481–494. Archival copy available at *Deutsches Textarchiv (DTA)* http://www.deutschestextarchiv.de/book/view/kant_aufklaerung_1784?p=17

Leach, A. (2010, September 29). The ten worst tech ads for women. *Jezebel*. Retrieved from https://jezebel.com/5650960/the-ten-most-patronizing-tech-ads/

Lyman, F. (1987). Think-Pair-Share: An expanding teaching technique. *MAA-CIE Cooperative News*, *1*, 1–2.

McKlin, T., Magerko, B., Lee, T., Wanzer, D., Edwards, D., & Freeman, J. (2018). Authenticity and personal creativity: How EarSketch affects student persistence. In *SIGCSE '18: 49th ACM Technical Symposium on Computer Science Education*, February 21–24, 2018, Baltimore, MD: ACM, 6 pp. https://doi.org/10.1145/3159450.3159523

Montfort, N. (2016). *Exploratory programming for the arts and humanities*. Cambridge, MA: The MIT Press.

National Science Foundation, National Center for Science and Engineering Statistics, Directorate for Social, Behavioral and Economic Sciences. (2017). Computer sciences – field of degree: Women. *Women, minorities, and persons with disabilities in science and engineering*. Retrieved from http://www.nsf.gov/statistics/2017/nsf17310/digest/fod-women/computer-sciences.cfm

National Academies of Sciences, Engineering, and Medicine. (2017). *Assessing and responding to the growth of computer science undergraduate enrollments*. Washington, DC: The National Academies Press. doi:10.17226/24926

Nelson, B. (2014). The data on diversity. *Communications of the ACM*, *57*(11), 86–95.

NY1. (2014). *Inside city hall*. Aired 7 pm and 10 pm September 23, 2014. http://www.ny1.com/content/politics/inside_city_hall/216040/ny1-online-cuny-presidents-discuss-high-demand/ (content no longer available)

Pinker, Susan. (2008). *The sexual paradox: Men, women, and the real gender gap*. New York, NY: Scribner.

Pinker, Steven. (2018). *Enlightenment now: The case for reason, science, humanism, and progress*. New York, NY: Penguin Random House LLC.

Shannon, C. E. (July 1948). A mathematical theory of communication. *Bell System Technical Journal, 27*(3), 379−423. doi:10.1002/j.1538-7305.1948.tb01338.x

Steele, C. (2010). *Whistling Vivaldi: How stereotypes affect us and what we can do.* New York, NY: W. W. Norton & Company, Inc.

United States Census Bureau. (2018). Race/ethnicity and gender for US population and Queens County population. *American fact finder.* Retrieved from https://factfinder.census.gov. Accessed on May 2018.

Chapter 6

Fostering an Environment for All Students to Succeed in Computer Science: Integrating Culturally Responsive Pedagogies with Curricula Redesign

Kiron Sharma, Laila Khreisat, Diana Cvitan and Gurjot Singh

Reflection

The settings of Fairleigh Dickinson University's (FDU) two New Jersey campuses each offer unique symbolism for the experience of the TIDES project. The Metropolitan Campus is divided by the Hackensack River, a tidal river with varying levels throughout the days, while the Florham Campus is represented by the emblem of a blooming rose.

Our work on the project over the past three years has very much felt like the ebb and flow of the river's tide. During low tide, the hidden content of the mud flats is uncovered, and the birds join to celebrate in the newly exposed treasure. However, our perspective of the river is always changing and adapting to our new understanding, as the water rises and presents new opportunities for waterflow or the occasional kayaker to appreciate the river's beauty.

Similar to the struggle of the river's flow, the blooming petals of the rose reveal many complex layers of great beauty. Nurturing the flower and understanding what it needs to develop takes focus, change, and dedication, but the end result makes the work worthwhile.

The change and growth associated with our work on the TIDES project, while symbolically described above, was very much as real an experience for the faculty as it was for the students. Opportunities for professional development and self-reflection enabled faculty to understand and view their pedagogy through a different lens. Facing the endeavor required openness on the part of the faculty member and a true willingness to see the learning experience from the perspective of their students. It took time to understand how even small actions, statements, and class elements could have a great impact, but seeing those small changes make a difference was reaffirming and provided the feedback needed to sustain the work. Each faculty member experienced that transformation in their own unique way.

From Sharma

I remember my first semester as a graduate student in computer science where I was the only female student in a department of 140 students, as well as part of a cohort of 30 students and an all male faculty. That journey, as being the odd one out, continued for 20 months through my course work, group projects, and exams. Memories and experiences from that same journey many years later made me wonder why more women did not enter or persist in the field of computer science. At that time, I was more intrigued by computer science topics and complex mathematical calculations that led to publications and research in probabilistic algorithm design, rather than the social implications of culturally inept systems of education that failed the dreams of many students.

I had very little awareness and even less time to dwell on that aspect back in graduate school and as I later worked to succeed in my field of computer science. Then came a faculty position, tenure track years, and administrative responsibilities and then some more. In between, there were large chunks of time with students while doing some of my most favorite activities: teaching classes or mentoring students for one-on-one research and senior projects. This is when I began exploring underlying reasons that led to lower retention, hurdles in recruitment and persistence of women and minority students in many of the STEM fields, but particularly in computer science. At my current institution, the demographics nowhere near mirrored the STEM enrollment, especially in computer science programs that had disproportionately low numbers of female students and lacked diversity, along with high attrition rates in the identified demographics. The same disconnect was being played out at other institutions. And the most surprising thing for me was that the needle had not moved much since I was a graduate student, even though there had been heightened awareness, and plenty of documentation and discussions around the topic of equity, recruitment, retention, and persistence of women and minorities in STEM.

I was determined to explore the issue at a deeper level and to make a difference at my own level. After exploring some published research in the area and attending mentoring conferences, I embarked upon the journey of developing mentoring programs for students in middle and high schools that involved strong role models who were women and minority students at our university. This program was well received in the local school districts and provided leadership opportunities for our students.

Soon after I had established a mentoring program, the TIDES project came to my attention. We got together a team of faculty, and prepared a proposal to be a part of the TIDES group that would explore culturally responsive pedagogies and bring attention to the problem that was haunting our nation's institutions. We were thrilled when our proposal was accepted.

The plenary session of the first TIDES Institute in the summer of 2014 introduced Project Implicit (https://implicit.harvard.edu/implicit/aboutus.html) and challenged all the participants to dig in, recognize, and acknowledge implicit biases. We discussed the benefits of self-affirmation and timely interventions that have been shown to improve education and other outcomes, with benefits that can be long lasting (Cohen & Sherman, 2014). The entire group discussed how self-affirmation and self-efficacy can have lasting benefits when they could trace an adaptive, positive feedback loop between the social network and the individual.

This plenary session, followed by three additional years of intriguing and self-exploring professional development, resulted in fresh approaches that I implemented in my classes and that I discussed with numerous colleagues over the past few years. The outcome was a realization that each student has a story and that story needs to become a part of their educational journey. The biases that we all carry, and do not even notice, prove to be impediments towards the very goal we seek to achieve: to help our students succeed to their fullest potential! During the past four years, I have been able to bring my personal experiences of being a minority woman in STEM, to study high quality research, and to seek guidance from experienced coaches who have done extensive work and explored the issue of culturally relevant pedagogies. I now view my relationships with my students as personalized and my role as a mentor first and professor second. This book chapter provides an insight into our ride with the TIDES program and our resolve to sustain and grow the progress we have made as TIDES family.

From Singh

At the beginning of my teaching career at FDU in the fall of 2015, my vision of teaching was limited to delivering lectures, preparing quizzes, and grading papers. For me, students were individuals who always act rationally and would not let their problems affect their studies in the classroom. I had absolutely no idea how their cultural background, home environment, and other social factors affected their behavior in the classroom. Since they were paying good money to attend college, they would know the value of education and would pay undivided attention to what I am teaching in class.

"If they don't understand something, they will ask." So I thought. The realization dawned on me after grading their first quiz; surprisingly, students who asked questions got higher marks than the ones who did not. I did not understand how this could be possible. If students did not ask questions, does that not mean they understood everything I covered in class? Aren't academically weak students the ones who are supposed to ask questions? "Maybe I should start paying more attention to how and if the students are learning."

For the next few lectures, after covering a topic I started asking:

"Did everyone get what I just explained?" Silence.
"Are you sure you got it?" Few nods.

There was something else going on here. Either they were not comprehending or they were not comfortable acknowledging in front of the class that they did not understand the material. Was it something like the Bystander effect – a question is asked to a group of people, everyone thinks someone else will answer it? Maybe, I wondered, I should start asking individually. So, after every class, I started asking individual students if they understood the material or not. Responses were always personalized, either yes or no, with a subtle hint of uneasiness. It felt like students were somewhat distant when asked if they understood the material. This behavior did not make any sense as I had only good intentions in my heart for them.

This behavior of the students started making sense after attending my first TIDES conference in November 2015. I became aware that I subconsciously divided students into certain groups based on my preconceived notions and their interactions with me in the first week of the semester. If someone was outspoken and raised their hand in response to the question I asked in class, I subconsciously perceived him/her as intelligent and others as average or below. As a result, when asking if they understood the material, I focused on only those students that I perceived to be weak. While students appreciated individual attention, they also felt uncomfortable being singled out as weak students.

As I attended more TIDES workshops and conferences, I became more cognizant of how my interactions with students in the classroom affect the learning of different students, such as non-traditional students, minority students, first-generation students, etc. Even though different students learn differently, all students need mentoring and nurturing to reach their full potential.

As a result of my exposure to TIDES, I made several changes in the way I teach my classes. The first and most important change was to realize individual differences between different students and respect their individual learning styles. While a few students are confident enough to speak up on their own, others need encouragement and care to make them comfortable to interact with their teacher and their fellow students. It is my responsibility as a teacher to encourage and guide students without singling out weak students or alienating strong students. Now in my classroom, I tend to question all students, to make sure that they have gotten the concept, and to encourage individual students to speak up.

I also saw a pattern in a few students who do not score decent grades on tests in the first few weeks of the semester, and then tend to give up and not put any effort into the next tests. Often it is the fear of failure turned into a self-fulfilling prophecy, where students start believing that since they did not do well on previous quizzes and their grade is low, they won't do well on the next test. To encourage students, I allowed retaking of all tests and assignments to dissociate learning from the fear of failure. I handed the control over to them; if they study the same topic and retake a test, they can improve their grades. I also made sure to teach the same topic again if students requested it. An important factor for success of this strategy is timely feedback; the sooner they see their grade, the more motivated they are to grab on to the opportunity to improve their grade by retaking tests and homework.

From Khreisat

I started teaching introductory programming courses at FDU back in 2005. My classes were not very diverse, but as the years went by, I started to see more minority students in my classes.

Programming can be hard for students to grasp due to the abstract nature of the process. Most women and most minority students have no background in the area of computer science prior to their first computer programming course as freshmen. They have never been exposed to these topics in high school and many computer science majors have no knowledge of what skills are required of computer science professionals. For these students, the programming courses seemed abstract and unrelatable. I started to observe this in my classes as they became more diverse. I wanted every student to succeed and that resulted in a research phase where I came across articles on culturally relevant pedagogy and how it is being used to reach and teach every student.

The TIDES institutes that I have attended over the past three years have really helped me gain a better understanding of cultural competence, which in turn, has allowed me to be a more effective teacher in the classroom. The first TIDES workshop, "Theories Related to Cultural Competence," held in Atlanta, Georgia, was an eye-opener for me. It helped me relate many issues that I was seeing in the classroom but was unable to understand. For example, in my classes, I create a very interactive setting where all students participate, as well as ask and answer questions I pose to them. However, there are always a few students who simply do not participate, even after I encourage them to do so.

The TIDES workshop pushed me to try to understand my students better in an effort to help them learn. Being part of this project was a great educational experience for me. This educational journey has continued for me throughout the three years of attending the TIDES workshops and it has helped me reach and teach my students more effectively.

Institutional Context

A comprehensive university, and the largest private institution in New Jersey with an enrollment of close to 12,000, Fairleigh Dickinson University has historically drawn distinct student populations on its two New Jersey campuses. FDU's Metropolitan Campus, set ten miles outside New York City, draws a very diverse mix of students, including international students, and maintains a designation as a Hispanic-Serving Institution (HSI). The Florham Campus offers a traditional residential campus setting in a small campus environment set in the outer suburbs. The student population at the Florham Campus has traditionally been less diverse, and the University some years ago recognized the need and importance of recruiting a base of students who more accurately reflect the diversity of our region.

Reflecting on these efforts, the Math, Computer Science, and Physics department recognized the challenges faced in STEM fields with significantly lesser participation by Hispanic, African American, and female students.

Introduction/Background and Significance

Our institution has a history of supporting and helping students from all demographics and we have focused our attention on recruiting minority students and female students to computer science programs, in particular. Our data showed that although our recruiting efforts were paying off, the retention and graduation numbers told a different story. The success of minority students is important so they could graduate from college in time, not incur unnecessary debt, and join the workforce. One snapshot of data from our computer science program revealed that the numbers of minority students and female students dwindled from freshman year (33%) to the senior year (9%) and only a small number of students completed their final year as a computer science student. Some of these students changed their major, and others left the institution.

Retention of minority students and women became a major area of concern for our department. We found freshman students struggling to grasp introductory programming concepts due to the abstract nature of the subject and because of students' minimal exposure to the real-life applications and long-term implications of technological advances. Students who were unaware of how the discipline of computer science has evolved and how it is embedded in every aspect of our lives, felt disenfranchised when they needed to engage in complex problem solving and develop algorithms to solve problems. Additionally, we identified several factors that could hinder students from majoring in computer science in general, and at FDU in particular. These factors include, but are not limited to stereotyping, initial low grades, and low confidence (Cohoon & Aspray, 2006), particularly for female students. Additionally, minority students often lack knowledge about the field of computer science and possible career paths (Scarlatos et al., 2008). Female students are usually attracted to programs that are relevant to the "real world" (Seepersad, 2016).

We were keen to improve retention rates and attract new students to the CS program by adding innovative components to our program, but particularly to all of the introductory computer science courses. We were seeking a student-centric approach with interventions in the program with a view to making the challenging introductory courses interesting and relevant, especially to women and minority students. We wanted students to see their learning in action with simulated robotics and novel human—computer interaction. Not only were we planning to design new courses, we also wanted all of our faculty members in the cognate departments to be professionally trained to address the issue of equity in STEM and the challenge of improving retention of minority students, while instilling grit and self-efficacy for students to persist and work hard. We planned to offer courses that encouraged discovery and hands-on analysis, augmented with activities to help integrate knowledge to application – recommended for female students in science disciplines (Freeman et al., 2014; Lou, Shih, Diez, & Tseng, 2010). Activities included simulated robotics and novel human—computer interaction, where students were able to see the programs they code in action. Additionally, we began to focus our energies on program design and evaluation to strengthen departmental understanding of the relevance of culture. Our intention was to build a program that would support early identity formation with connections to the field of computer science and a focus on success with rigor and self-efficacy by making connections with students' and their backgrounds.

Implementation/Methodology

The process that followed over the course of the project was quite straightforward and well-grounded in theory. All faculty members in our STEM disciplines are individuals who have high expectations of our students and who genuinely care about the success of each one of the students. Nonetheless, we all needed to get a deeper understanding of culturally responsive approaches to pedagogy that validate, facilitate, liberate, and empower ethnically diverse students while simultaneously cultivating their cultural integrity, individual abilities, and academic abilities (Gay, 2010). It was imperative that culturally responsive education be facilitated at all levels, from office staff and advising to the classroom.

The goals of our project were to:

- advance student interest in computer science topics in introductory courses;
- recruit women and minority students to minor and major in computer science; and
- improve retention rates of women and minority students in computer science.

Our approach was student-centered, where each intervention in the program was proposed with the view of making the challenging introductory courses in computer science interesting and relevant, especially to women and minorities. Course redesign enabled students to learn by discovery and hands-on analysis. Additionally, the first introductory programming course engaged students in Problem-Based Learning by unveiling pre-written, real-world programs, and by discovering shortcomings and errors intentionally injected by the instructor. Such activities help integrate knowledge to application.

In addition, part of our approach was to develop a model of teaching introductory courses that maintains a persistent focus on student success. This model modified pedagogical practices and techniques in the classroom, instituted frequent and low-stakes assessment of student learning, with attention on correct placements. Additionally faculty document each culturally sensitive pedagogical approach that they implemented. The redesigned courses included: Introduction to Computer Science with C++ (CSCI 2215) and Introduction to Computer Programming with C# (CSCI 1205).

Integrated into the courses were real-world examples, which helped students with abstract concepts and provided a context for their work. Some examples included:

- a history of the cell phone and an African American telecommunication pioneer who held seventy-five patents and helped make the cell phone possible;

- introduction to Bitpim cell phone forensics and the use of python in bitpim (http://www.bitpim.org/);
- Cyberlink Brain Body Interface for the handicapped (Doherty, Bloor, & Cockton, 2009);
- human–computer interaction and some of the great African American men and women who made significant contributions to computing; and
- robotics with EZ-robots for decision structures and repetition (https://www.ez-robot.com).

CSCI 2215 Introduction to Computer Science is our second-semester, first-year programming course. The original format of the course employed the traditional approach to teaching where students learn the fundamental concepts of the programming language coupled with programming assignments. The class meets twice a week for 200 minutes, with the first 50 minutes of the class dedicated to introducing the topic of the day, followed by student engagement in several in-class programming assignments. As part of the redesign of the course, we introduced several interdisciplinary and hands-on components, including:

(1) Human–computer interaction: Input and output devices for human interaction including speech recognition software, modified keyboards and mice engineered for the disabled, and mouth sticks for the physically disabled. Advances in computer technology to assist the physically disabled were analyzed and there was a demonstration of a robotic arm to feed the disabled. Dr Eamon Doherty developed the robotic arm as part of a previous project. Cyberlink as a mind and brain–body interface, is a software tool that was introduced to the students, where they learned how brain waves can be used as input signals for people who suffer from acute disabilities and paralysis.
(2) Virtual Reality and Mental Health: They were introduced in the classroom, including issues such as phobias, anxiety, substance abuse, and posttraumatic stress disorder (PTSD) among veterans. We picked this subject matter for the reason that there is heightened awareness of mental health problems in our society. Moreover, historically, our university has taken pride in supporting veterans from the time of its founding. The university continues to participate in the Yellow Ribbon Program, which ensures that GI Bill-eligible veterans can attend FDU at no charge.
(3) Nanotechnology and its applications: Concepts of very large and very small measurements, storage devices, and molecular robots. This topic puts cutting edge research front and center for students and encourages them to explore the newest inventions in a timely manner.
(4) Binary Number System and computational methods: The topic of number systems helps students relate to historical advances in computations, development of electronic circuity, and advances in hardware.
(5) Limitations of computing with respect to software and hardware: Our students learn problems that are hard to crack even with the most sophisticated computers and how hardware advances have affected development of computer systems.

The introduction of these topics has provided undergraduate students with insights into the applications of computer science in ways in which they are not often exposed. We emphasized hands-on activities and collaborative teamwork in the classroom, in the form of pair and group programming assignments, to foster active learning and collaboration. Frequent low-stakes assessments were introduced in the form of:

- several (25–30 in number) programming projects throughout the semester covering each new programming construct introduced;
- frequent quizzes; and
- three major tests

Students received prompt feedback on their performance with the aim of identifying areas of weakness and difficulty. Students were provided with opportunities, both inside and outside the classroom, to seek additional help on programming projects, as well as at group review sessions before tests.

The second course that was redesigned was CSCI 1205, Introduction to Programming. This is the first-semester, freshman-year course for the computer science major and a cognate course for the mathematics major. The course is an introduction to Computer Programming using the C# programming language. The majority of women, and most minority students, who enter the computer science major have no background in computer science prior to their first programming course. They have never been exposed to these topics in high school and many are unaware of the skills needed to become a computer science graduate. The programming course seems abstract and unrelatable to this group of students. To help students realize the importance of computer science and to spark their interest in the field we introduced three interdisciplinary topics:

(1) Introduction of cybersecurity and cyber-crime topics using BitPim, an open-source forensics program used to analyze cell phone data, and Guidance Software's Encase (https://www.guidancesoftware.com/) program, that enables recovery of criminal data on PDAs.
(2) Robotics – EZ-Robots. Students learn to program EZ-Robots, implementing simple C# constructs that perform simple tasks.
(3) Game-programming assignments to develop games of strategy. Students learn introductory programming constructs using C++ and are introduced to UNITY (https://unity3d.com/), a game development platform.

The newly introduced topics teach students about the skillsets they will develop as they move through advanced courses in the major. Early introduction to complex applications have motivated students to seek internships and research projects in interdisciplinary fields.

As part of the project we also instituted professional development for our faculty. The project included structured professional development seminars and discussion sessions for all STEM faculty at FDU. During these sessions, faculty documented and shared best practices and techniques that work in classrooms with diverse student backgrounds and that provide motivation to minorities and women to advance their studies in STEM fields. These activities helped to bring about institutional change at a broader level that encouraged all STEM faculty and advising staff to be aware of culturally sensitive pedagogical techniques.

We held a seminar in each of the three years of the grant period. During the first year, we hosted an external speaker who was knowledgeable about culturally responsive teaching and ideas about appropriate instructional adjustments. Dr Orlando Taylor, Vice President of Strategic Initiatives and Research at Fielding Graduate University presented a talk titled "The Cultural Competence Imperative in Higher Education: Who Benefits?"

This seminar brought focus to knowledge about cultural values, beliefs, learning styles, perceptions, and historical legacies of ethnic groups. Subsequently, each year, faculty members shared the practices and steps that they have implemented and shared the effects on student retention and achievement in STEM classrooms. These efforts dovetailed the professional development programs organized as part of the AAC&U TIDES Institutes attended by our team members. The seminars at FDU also offered a platform for sharing the practices learned at the AAC&U TIDES Institutes. With a deeper understanding of Culturally Responsive Teaching methodologies, our faculty was able to develop authentic approaches to their teaching practices, revised approaches to assessment and grading, and connections to students in and out of the classroom. However, over the course of the three-year project, several changes and adaptations needed to be made to its implementation.

Peer mentoring was an initiative that we had proposed as part of the TIDES project, however, it was not funded. We recently received funding from NCWIT (National Center for Women and Information Technology) to establish a mentoring program for our introductory computer programming courses to provide support and help to students with a special focus on women and minority students. We are also looking to expand the peer mentoring approach to developmental math courses offered by the department. We included all STEM faculty at FDU in our professional development seminars and workshops to help expand their perspectives and experiences with underrepresented students. Our experiences with low-stakes assessments in the project have led to the expansion of the practice to other courses as well.

Results

During the first year, the project was estimated to have an impact on 60 computer science students and five faculty members at Fairleigh Dickinson University's Florham Campus alone. Over the second year of reporting, the impact was expanded through the professional development workshops for faculty, and by the interventions in specific computer science courses, to reach over 2,341 students and 20 faculty members across multiple campuses and institutions through professional development and course redesign and interventions. In the third year, the project is estimated to have cumulatively impacted over 3,095 students and 36 faculty members across University and neighboring institutions, including Drew University, The County College of Morris, Essex Community College, and The College of Saint Elizabeth. In this final extension year, the project continued its work to impact an additional 1,240 students and 36 faculty. All told, the cumulative impact over the span of the grant period has been measured to reach 97 faculty members and 6,736 students!

In the fall of 2016, class enrollment in the primary course, CSCI 1205, was 94 students. Of these 26 (32%) were underrepresented minorities, and 17 (21%) were unknown, which may indicate that the total number of URM is higher. While the enrollment in fall 2016 is just slightly more than 2015 (93), it still represents a significant increase over fall 2014 (65) and continues to be a positive indicator of increasing impact. In the spring of 2017, enrollment in CSCI 1205 is lower (17 students total) due to the fact that this primary course is more often taken with fall entry. In sum, a total of 110 students were enrolled in our CSCI 2215 and CSCI 1205 courses in fall 2016, representing a 57% increase in enrollment in those two courses over fall enrollment of 2015.

Class enrollment in CSCI 2215 for the spring of 2017 consisted of 83 students in total (a significant jump in enrollment over the 44 students enrolled in the spring of 2016 and the 41 students enrolled in spring of 2015). There were a total of 100 students registered in CSCI 1205 and CSCI 2215 in spring 2017. A total of 210 students have attended or are attending the modified courses since the last report, representing a 19% increase over last year.

The calculated number of students taught by the faculty members attending the workshops ($N = 36$) is 1,240. This number is based on the reported class enrollment for classes taught by the faculty participants in the fall 2016 and spring 2017 semesters.

While the total number of students taught is lower than that of the previous year, it may not fully reflect the long-term impact and reach the participating faculty may have on students. A number of the workshop participants were faculty presently assigned to administrative and supervisory positions at the University. As such, the number of courses taught in the 2016–17 year is low or nil. However, in future years, the typical teaching load of these administrators would bring the number of courses taught and students impacted to a total comparable to the previous year. In addition, by including the administrators in faculty supervisory and training roles, the workshop material has the chance for greater dissemination and a multiplier effect in future years.

A review of enrollment of computer science majors on the Florham Campus continues to show a promising trend. Total enrollment continues to increase year over year (showing a jump of 19% to 114 students in 2016 which increased to 149 students in 2017) and enrollment of underrepresented minorities is also steadily increasing, maintaining a representation of 38% of the population. In addition, female enrollment demonstrates a positive upward trend from 2013. At 17% of the population, we can see signs of a return to the higher levels of 2011 and 2012.

Table 1: Percentage of female and minority students at enrolled in Computer Science on Florham Campus.

Students	2011	2012	2013	2014	2015	2016
Hispanic, Black, American Native, and Multi-ethnic	25%	33%	33%	38%	38%	38%
Females	19%	18%	11%	14%	14%	17%
Total No. of Students	36	63	64	84	92	114

The following table provides demographic information from the last six years for the Computer Science major in Becton College (Florham campus) (Table 1).

Overall, FDU computer science major enrollment continues to grow with female and URM student enrollment steadily increasing in numbers, while maintaining or raising their proportionate representation in the population. Most notable is the significant upward trend in female representation. Female student confidence rates highly in all of the data gathered (pre- and post-survey and focus groups). This confidence, buttressed by faculty support and nurtured through course delivery modifications, may play an important role in the positive student outcomes.

TIDES Course Enrollment

Enrollment and increased interest in computer science are the other indicators we have monitored. In the previous years of the TIDES grant, there were documented increases in the female and underrepresented minority enrollment. For fall 2016 and spring 2017, the female and underrepresented male enrollment did not demonstrate as large of a representation. Females represented 41% of CSCI 1205 class and 26% of the CSCI 2215 class. Underrepresented minorities represented 28% of the CSCI 1205 class and 33% of the CSCI 2215 class. The lower number of underrepresented minorities may be due to a higher percentage of students falling into the unknown category. About 20% of the students in CSCI 1205 and 19% of students in CSCI 2215 were identified as unknown, but we are unsure if that identification was the result of data collection error or the student's selection to identify outside of the single option, or to not identify altogether. Given the continued success of previous years in increasing enrollment of females and underrepresented minorities, this issue requires some further evaluation to determine if they reflect general enrollment trends or something more specific to the computer science courses.

The following table presents retention data in percentages for all disciplines at the Becton College of Arts and Sciences (Table 2).

Table 2: Year to year Retention Data for all majors at Becton College, Fairleigh Dickinson University.

2009	2010	2011	2012	2013	2014	2015
53%	64%	64%	71%	76%	74%	81%

Table 3: Computer Science retention at FDU's two New Jersey Campuses in 2016.

Florham Campus			Metro Campus		
% Retained in Computer Science			% Retained in Computer Science		
	Female	Male		Female	Male
Black	0.00	71.40	Black	100.00	100.00
Hispanic	66.70	80.00	Hispanic	0.00	100.00
Asian	0.00	75.00	Asian	100.00	100.00
White	100.00	88.20	White	0.00	100.00
Unknown	0.00	100.00	Unknown	0.00	100.00
Total	60.00	82.10	Total	100.00	100.00

Retention data for underrepresented students in computer science programs is presented below for both Florham and Metro Campuses. Promising changes over 2016 are seen in retention levels of Black and Hispanic males as well as the overall retention on both campuses (including the 100% retention on the Metro campus!) Less promising is the lower retention rate on Florham of Hispanic females and females overall. It is important to note that where small populations are involved, respective retention rates may be misleading (Table 3).

Graduation rates

Our six-year graduation rates for first-year students enrolled in computer science on the Florham Campus as of fall 2014, fall 2015, and fall 2016, are noted below for comparison. Enrollment in the fall 2008 semester was low, as was the graduation rate for that cohort (fall 2014 graduation). We do, however, see a slight increase in the overall graduation rate for the following years. We anticipate that the increased enrollment in subsequent years will yield more substantial data on graduation rates (Table 4).

Table 4: Computer Science at Florham Campus 6-year Graduation Rate.

Fall 2014 Graduation Rate with CSCI Degrees			Fall 2015 Graduation Rate		Fall 2016 Graduation Rate	
	F	M	F	M	F	M
Hispanic	0.0%	0.0%	0.0%	0.0%	0.0%	66.70%
White, non-Hispanic	0.0%	50.0%	0.0%	75.0%	100.0%	66.70%
Total	0.0%	40.0%	0.0%	50.0%	100.0%	66.70%

Grades

As a student outcome, grades provide one measure to assess the modifications made to the entry-level computer science course. Females enrolled in the primary course CSCI 1205 during both fall 2016 and spring 2017 performed at the same level as the general population of students. However, 77% of females enrolled in the secondary course CSCI 2215 during both semesters earned an A or B in the course (as compared to 60% for males). The higher performance by females in the course is even more defined when we look at the assignment of A grades – 58% of females earned an A in the course, while 33% of males earned an A. Female respondents in the pre- and post-survey and focus groups continue to express high confidence in their ability and persistence, as well as strong comfort and perceived support from faculty. In the administered post-survey, 100% of females believed faculty were happy when they did well. In addition, with a predominately female faculty, female students may identify with their instructors in a more direct way.

In underrepresented minority males, we saw significant improvement in grade performance. In the CSCI 1205 course in fall 2016 and fall 2017, 65% earned a grade of A or B, which is significant improvement over fall 2015 where only 20% of underrepresented males achieved an A or B final grade. Among the African American students, we have also seen improvement, with approximately 58% earning A and B in the primary course, compared to 50% in the previous year. Further, feedback was solicited from student participants during our project. Focus group sessions were conducted with students majoring in mathematics and computer science along with an online survey of respondents from the same population. The goal of the focus group and survey was to ascertain the self-perceptions of the students. Students were recruited from the campus TIDES course and participants represented a range of racial identities. Results of the sessions and survey revealed some positive perspectives on gender and racial stereotypes and their impact on the way women and minorities view themselves and perform in math and computer science. Positive peer interaction and support came across in both survey and focus group results with 13% indicating some or little judgement from peers (and none indicating significant judgement).

Some focus group respondents stated that peers/others in the major were "all really supportive and friendly." For example, most female participants in our focus group expressed increased confidence in their abilities and a greater sense of persistence in their academic work.

The students, likewise, perceived little to no difference in treatment from faculty, based on gender or race. Only 7% responded that they had a minor perception of different treatment based on gender, and only 3% held that same minor perception of different treatment from professors, based on race. This view was also borne out in the focus group results where students pointed to faculty (particularly the full-time faculty) as kind and caring. However, students in the focus group were less satisfied with the support of adjunct faculty, whom they regarded as well meaning, but less prepared with pedagogical skills and classroom approaches. One area for continued improvement may be additional training in culturally relevant pedagogy with a tie to general didactic approaches, especially designed for and delivered to adjunct faculty.

Discussion

Computers are becoming increasingly prevalent in our everyday lives and with it, the need for computer professionals is increasing rapidly. Academic institutions are not producing enough graduates to catch up with this need; furthermore, there is a huge under-representation of minority and women students in this area. Our efforts in this project were directed towards the overarching goal of advancing student interest in computer science. As the main goal, we focused on recruitment and retention of women and minority students in computer science.

At the center of computer science lies the essential skill of computer programming, which is a cognitively intense activity that requires analyzing computational problems, critical thinking, and designing solutions by mentally visualizing effects of algorithms on data. For a computer science student, successful acquisition of these skills requires high levels of attention and engagement in introductory programming classes. Any factors that negatively affect student motivation and engagement lead to substandard learning that results in attrition in computer science.

In our effort to retain students in our department, our first action was to identify any general problems in the learning process faced by all CS students, as well as any specific problems faced by underrepresented minority (URM) students. We uncovered many general factors that affect all student populations, such as the abstract nature of the subject, minimal exposure to real-life applications, and the disconnect between individual CS concepts and real-world systems. With the help of TIDES resources and through the resulting self-reflection and introspection, we also found many factors that specifically affect URM students, such as stereotyping, implicit bias, lack of role models to relate and aspire to, lack of knowledge of possible career paths, and low confidence due to a sense of not belonging. All these factors result in lack of motivation and disengagement that subsequently results in dropping out of the computer science major or college altogether.

Our second action was to tackle these problems through changes in our CS curricula. To deal with the inherent learning difficulties in computer science, we incorporated novel learning tools (e.g., robot programming, cybersecurity and forensics software, and game-programming tools), as well as new pedagogical techniques (e.g., problem-based learning, inquiry learning, and frequent low-stakes assessments with immediate feedback). In addition, several seminars and talks were organized for freshmen students that covered diverse real-world applications where computer science systems are helping the general population (e.g., human computer interfaces for physically disabled, brain−body interface for paralysis, virtual reality for mental health therapy, and nanotechnology). To address factors specific to the URM students, programming courses were augmented with several topics that are culturally relevant to URM students (e.g., talks and discussion about notable African American and women scientists, who made significant contributions to computing). We empirically measured effects of these efforts on student retention and morale and found significant improvement. FDU computer science major enrollment continues to grow with female and URM students, with increases in graduation rates. In addition, there was an increase in the grades earned in programming classes with URM and female student grades shifting towards more A and B grades, resulting in increased confidence to pursue a career in computer science.

Encouraged by these results, our third action was to disseminate the knowledge gained from these findings to other faculty at our campus, as well as the surrounding campus community. We instituted professional development for our faculty through seminars and discussions on culturally sensitive pedagogy. In these sessions, faculty documented and shared best practices and techniques for classrooms with diverse student backgrounds to motivate their careers in STEM fields. All these efforts over the span of the grant period significantly influenced the lives of both students and faculty. While faculty became more cognizant of how to adjust their teaching style to teach classes with diverse student backgrounds more effectively, students also appreciated the efforts of faculty by actively participating in the learning process with increased attention and engagement.

Conclusion

We stayed focused on the goals we had set before embarking on the TIDES journey. Our strategy of enhancing our courses with interdisciplinary topics relatable to students was extremely successful in advancing students' interests in computer science. Our students embarked on projects in interdisciplinary fields, we experienced better retention in introductory courses, and we have seen a marked surge in the number of students pursuing a graduate program in computer science.

Our activities that focused on women and minority students resulted in greater numbers of women and minority students in our program, and retention rates of the demographics improved. Our department faculty remain energized with causes that directly relate to student success and, as a result, we have created a new club for women in computer science with funding from the National Council for Women & Information Technology (NCWIT). With support and funding from Google, we also developed an outreach program targeting middle school students by providing them with experiences in computer programming and mobile app development. As part of a university-funded initiative, we created a learning community of computer science students and have initiated regular field trips and invited speakers to keep the students engaged by participating in interdisciplinary and computer science-related events.

At the university level, we have held workshops for faculty to introduce techniques of culturally responsive pedagogies and our provost is initiating a Women in Science Group. Our TIDES project supported our ideas of curricula revision, encouraged us to focus on students as individuals rather than a group or "student body," and brought into perspective the various kinds of scaffoldings that help diverse students prosper and persevere in an arena that has been historically unreceptive to women and minority students. The changes we have made are sustainable and our institutional leadership is supportive of promoting underrepresented students in STEM.

The Last Word

Moving forward, it is helpful to consider some of the main takeaways identified through our experience in the project. We began the work on our "Computer Science Talent Advancement Project" with the recognition that there is much student talent and potential for the computer science field in underrepresented populations. Through careful attention to course delivery and nurturing of these student populations, their talent and abilities can shine through and lead them to academic success. By removing unseen structural barriers and building new frameworks, it becomes easier for the students to see themselves as successful in the field of computer science and then, as a result, make that success a reality.

However, as we learned along the way, enabling the talent to shine and propelling the student forward are only parts of the equation. While a focus on changing the underrepresented student's perception on his or her abilities and future success is critical, it is just as important to work towards changing the perspective and perceptions of those around the student. Through the curricular and pedagogical adaptations, we saw the positive impact on all students in the program (not only for those in the underrepresented population) and believe the experience has led to deeper understanding and enhanced perspective for all, including the faculty.

Perhaps the most important (and least expected) contributing factor to the success of the project was the transformation experienced by the engaged faculty. As their reflections reveal, the impact of the activities led to their significant personal and professional growth. By investing in the development and preparation of those faculty and staff most closely responsible for guiding and supporting student learning, and by supporting culturally relevant pedagogy in the curriculum, institutions can reap rewards for students and faculty for years to come.

References

Cohen, G. L., & Sherman, D. K. (2014). The psychology of change: Self-affirmation and social psychological intervention. *Annual Review of Psychology, 65*, 333–371.

Cohoon, J., & Aspray, W. (Eds.). (2006). *Women and information technology: Research in underrepresentation.* Cambridge, MA: MIT Press.

Doherty, E., Bloor, C., & Cockton, G. (2009). *The "Cyberlink" Brain-Body Interface as an Assistive Technology for Persons with Traumatic Brain Injury: Longitudinal Results from a Group of Case Studies.* Published Online doi:10.1089/cpb.1999.2.249

Freeman, S., Eddy, S. L., McDonough, M., Smith, M. K., Okoroafor, N., Jordt, H., & Wenderoth, M. P. (2014). Active learning increases student performance in science, engineering, and mathematics. *Proceedings of the National Academy of Science if the United Stated of America, 111*(23) 8410–8415.

Gay, G. (2010). *Culturally responsive teaching: Theory, research, and practice* (2nd ed.). New York, NY: Teachers College Press.

Lou, S.-J., Shih, R.-C., Diez, C. R., & Tseng, K.-H. (2010). The impact of problem-based learning strategies on STEM knowledge integration and attitudes. *International Journal of Technology and Design Education, 21*(2), 195–215.

Scarlatos, L., Lowes, S., Sklar, E., Chopra, S., Parsons, S., Rudowsky, I., & Holder, H. (2008). Building bridges: The 2006 summer institute. *Journal of Computing Sciences in Colleges, 23*(3), 23–30.

Seepersad, C. C. (2016, October). How to involve more women and girls in engineering. U.S.News & World Report. Retrieved from https://www.usnews.com/news/stem-solutions/articles/2016-10-17/how-to-involve-more-women-and-girls-in-engineering

Chapter 7

Culturally Responsive Strategies for Addressing Recruitment and Retention of Women in STEM: Online Modules for Building STEM Majors' Computational Skills

Mark Matlin, Elizabeth McCormack, Douglas Blank and Jennifer Spohrer

Reflection

From McCormack

Reflecting on what we learned through the TIDES' initiative through readings, presentations, conversations, and our own experimentation within our project, two insights have stayed with me. One is the power of shifting from a student-deficit model to a student-difference model. Culturally responsive teaching does this by striving to level the playing field for all students. The potential negative impact of students' lack of cultural capital is minimized and the possible enrichment of cultural resources is enhanced. In our project, we built in discussions, peer-to-peer activities, journal prompts, and assignments to make explicit our pedagogical approach and the rationale for the structure of the course, to set clear expectations for demonstrating learning, and to provide various means for us to get to know one and other. Journal prompts and assignments were also used to tap into student's intrinsic values and aspirations in addition to the many extrinsic factors that can dominate student motivation, dedication, and commitment. A variety of assignments provided different kinds of learning opportunities and inclusive examples of what academic success can look like. Having adopted the student-difference model, we embraced an iteration through a variety of specific course elements to determine what worked best in our project to enhance belonging and enrich learning. Learning specific techniques to make teaching more inclusive and equitable was a game changer for me. I felt empowered to make a difference.

My other takeaway was of an entirely different nature. It was a true gestalt shift in how I understood my work in this area in relation to others. It concerns notions of ally-ship and advocacy. At our second annual TIDES Institute, we had a facilitator working with us on the strong tension between expectations to assimilate to majority structures and a desire to disrupt the status quo and transform those majority structures. Is our purpose to help students and faculty to learn to navigate a system not built for them, or to aid them in dismantling and transforming the system to find a better way? This tension snapped when a white man spoke up to describe what he imagined were the experiences of URMs and what he thought should be done. His comments generated a reaction of anger from another member of our group whose response became further complicated as she then felt compelled to defend her loud and angry response and the stereotype she subsequently felt entrapped by. In the subsequent "fishbowl" exercise, designed to debrief and gain insight into the encounter, I faced the uncomfortable position of being told my help was not asked for, needed, nor fundamentally necessary. Why were the white majority here I asked? To serve as an ally from within the majority system to gain resources. I learned that day that many members of underrepresented minority groups within our TIDES cohort felt strongly that they need to be in the lead with this work and prefer that members of the majority group learn to function as allies, not leaders. Majority members can also help by being advocates for students and faculty when they encounter difficulty within the majority system. The tension shows itself once again in my expected ally-ship and advocate roles. I had been cast as a member of a group, not seen as an individual, but with group characteristics. This reminded me that it is indeed a privilege to be seen as a unique person first, and as a representative of a group, second. Déjà vu ensued, as I recalled my years as a female physicist.

This new context deepened my understanding of the discursive landscape in which we operate everyday around the work of equity and inclusion. I've learned to apply what I originally learned for my teaching in the classroom to every encounter I have − listening, explaining, sharing, exploring, creating new possibilities for learning.

From Matlin

The "fishbowl" event referenced above also was seminal for me. It, together with some of the presentations we heard at the TIDES Institutes (e.g., one on the fallibility of perception), made me grasp, at a deeper level than before, how differently individuals might interpret a given event, comment, or action as a result of their personal backgrounds and experiences. It also made clearer to me how much of a struggle it can be for members of non-dominant groups to navigate daily life; that realization resonates with the events that have prompted the births of the Black Lives Matter and Me Too movements. As a result of these TIDES experiences and the wider cultural environment, when interacting with students now, I find myself to be more thoughtful in several ways. I'm more conscious that they might not be interpreting what I'm saying the way I would interpret it (i.e., the way I mean it). I'm also more aware that the privileges and good fortune I have mostly taken for granted as a white male might not have been available to my students. Additionally, I'm more sensitive to how the lack of those privileges might play into a student's performance in a course or interactions with me. It could be very valuable to come up with a way to reproduce the fishbowl experience at other institutions, but the sensitive nature of the issues involved would necessitate the services of a highly experienced leader to ensure that the interaction was a thoughtful and productive one.

From Blank

Although all of us have been teaching at an all-women's college for many years, the TIDES project provided me with a new, deeper, and more personal understanding of diversity and equity than I have ever had. I believe that this was possible because the TIDES Institutes worked very hard to make these topics explicit and connect them directly to our specific educational goals and materials.

The conversations at the Institutes were sometimes uncomfortable and messy. We often discussed topics (such as race and gender) that went beyond the reach of any type of meeting possible back on campus. Our TIDES colleagues from other institutions were honest, sensitive, and raw. Our TIDES mentors were compassionate, knowledgeable, and thoughtful. Through this ordeal, I learned much about weaving together ideas from education, technology, social science, and psychology to create a better classroom experience for all. For me to effectively carry out these lessons, it is required that I consciously bake them into every aspect of teaching. Some ideas are subtle, and others are more straightforward. These techniques did not necessarily come naturally for me at first. By making them explicit on the syllabus and in the readings, activities, and assignments, it is my hope that they will eventually come more naturally for me.

From Spohrer

Although I did not participate in the TIDES Institutes with my colleagues, we drew on their experience and on TIDES programming to develop our own faculty development workshop on Teaching to Increase Diversity and Equity in STEM. We prepared that workshop in consultation with faculty across disciplines and career stages, and their concerns and needs align with the reflections here: information-sharing was not sufficient, they needed a safe space in which to critically examine their own assumptions and practices, and work through potential alternatives with their peers.

Institutional Context

Bryn Mawr College is a small (1,350 undergraduate students), all-women's, liberal arts college about 10 miles outside of Philadelphia, Pennsylvania. The College itself has a very diverse student body, with approximately 33% of the student body being US students of color. However, while the physics department attracts many international students, generally we enroll few students from domestic underrepresented groups. The TIDES program offered us an opportunity to develop instructional materials at the interface between physics and computing, which we hoped would attract and retain more underrepresented students in physics. This is crucially important on the national scale, since only about 20% of bachelor and PhD degrees in physics are earned by women, and less than 3% are held by African Americans (APS/Source: IPEDS Completion Survey).

Over the last decade or so, Bryn Mawr College has graduated 5–8 physics majors per year, representing approximately 2–3% of each graduating class. This is roughly 20 times the national average for women graduating with undergraduate physics degrees in the United States. (In recent years, our numbers of majors have increased significantly: 11 graduated last year, 16 are expected to graduate this year, and 12 are on track to graduate next year.) More broadly, on average 27% of Bryn Mawr College students graduate with a STEM major, as compared to the national average of 8% for women (Bryn Mawr College, Office of Institutional Research, 2012). Given these statistics, Bryn Mawr has the potential to impact the national scene in a significant way.

Computation is now a significant part of the work done by many practicing scientists, yet it is not universally taught in undergraduate science departments. Our initial interest in the TIDES program stemmed from two facts: (1) alumnae surveys of our physics majors indicated that many of them would have liked more exposure to scientific computation during their academic careers at Bryn Mawr, and (2) while the physics department attracts many international students to the major, few students from US underrepresented groups have majored in physics. It was our hope that, through the TIDES program, we could address both of those issues. However, we wished to do so in a way that would not increase faculty workload or major requirements for our students.

Participation in early TIDES activities, and the "fishbowl" incident in particular, led us to realize that solving the second problem would require more than just creating a course or curricular materials – we would need to engage physics faculty members in thinking about how our teaching might be changed in order to attract students from underrepresented groups. A key element of this process would be familiarizing ourselves and our colleagues with the academic literature on topics such as stereotype threat, microaggressions, and inclusive teaching.[1]

---

[1] Stereotype threat refers to an individual's concern that they might confirm a negative stereotype about a group (usually a non-dominant one) to which they belong. A microaggression is "a subtle but offensive comment or action directed at a minority or other non-dominant group that is often unintentional or unconsciously reinforces a stereotype" [dictionary.com]. Inclusive teaching aims to provide a learning environment that treats all students equitably and makes all students feel welcome and supported in their learning.

Introduction/Background

Bryn Mawr College has at the core of its mission the rigorous education of undergraduate women in the liberal arts. Our TIDES project contributes to this goal with the development of two components: (1) one intended to introduce scientific computation to women (especially women of color), and (2) the other to engage faculty members in expanding their understanding of the issues involved in teaching a diverse student population.

For the first component, we are using a "blended" (combined online and classroom) teaching and learning approach to embed computational skills development throughout the sequence of courses required for the Physics major. Blended learning (also known as hybrid learning) is a combination of online, self-paced learning and face-to-face classroom instruction. Research conducted prior to 2011 showed blended learning could increase student engagement, satisfaction, and learning outcomes in large classes at universities and community colleges (Aspen & Helm, 2004; Association for the Advancement of Computing in Education, 2007; Dziuban, Hartman, & Moskal, 2004; Lovett, Meyer, & Thille, 2008; Means, Toyama, Murphy, Bakia, & Jones, 2010).

Our strategy in the first year of the grant was to design a Computational Methods course, primarily for physics majors but also for other students in the physical sciences, that would serve as a temporary vehicle to develop, pilot, and assess modular learning units in a blended learning format, and to gain experience with teaching practices that support diverse classrooms. In the second and third years of the grant, this course then would be broken apart and the vetted learning modules embedded in required physics courses at the introductory, intermediate, and advanced levels (thereby avoiding the need for additional staffing). These modules explicitly contain many of our best practices, described below, for increasing diversity and equity. Additionally, we would train faculty to use the modules and support their work to develop blended teaching approaches to meet the needs of students from diverse backgrounds. The idea behind this approach of embedding the modules throughout the curriculum was to provide repetition and reinforcement of the students' programming skills and ongoing practice in the development of their metacognitive faculties.

The second component of our program was to educate faculty members about the potential barriers to learning experienced by STEM students from underrepresented groups, and to provide guidance on adopting teaching approaches to address those barriers and better serve all students. To that end, two of us (McCormack and Spohrer) worked with recent Bryn Mawr College graduates, Jancy Munguia and Esther Chiang, to develop a faculty workshop titled "Teaching for Diversity and Equity: Scholarship and Practice." This workshop, which incorporates case studies and small-group breakout sessions, presented multiple techniques for inclusive teaching (Tanner, 2013). During the grant period, the workshop was offered four times: twice on Bryn Mawr College's campus to the tri-college community (i.e., affiliates of Swarthmore, Haverford, and Bryn Mawr Colleges), once at a national meeting, the March 2016 AAC&U Conference on Diversity, Learning and Student Success: "Shifting Paradigms and

Challenging Mindsets," and once by colleagues at Allegheny College, who offered it using our materials on their own campus. A complete packet of facilitator materials is available at the GitHub site listed in the TIDES Resources section below.

Implementation/Methodology

Implementation/Methodology: Computational Modules

At the core of our methodology for developing the computational materials was an open-source technology called a "computational notebook." A computational notebook integrates text, formatted equations in LaTeX (LaTeX Project, 2018), computation, visualizations, and other media such as sound and video, and renders it in a web browser window. Computational notebooks easily allow students to author code, reproduce (and adapt) code, and insert text and hyperlinks. We believed the notebook format of computation would allow us to implement our blended approach to create "modules" that could be used by and distributed to other institutions. Most importantly, the notebook platform allowed us to integrate culturally responsive material and assignments directly into the computational instructional modules. In addition, computational notebooks could be used by the students to express their own narratives and personal connections in the form of "reflections" directly alongside their coding work. An example reflection on one of the modules is:

> I think we should have been made to make the original code for 1-D kinematic motion. It was good that we had to modify it for the other questions, but I think I would have learnt more if I had had to create the code by myself. I still get confused about how to append and input while statements, so this would have been great practice. Question 1 was too simple of a task. Exercise 2 was a much better exercise. It was difficult and took a long time to figure out, but it really helped me understand how to use the original code and modify it.

Specifically, for our project we used the Jupyter open-source notebook framework, which supports over 40 computing languages (Kluyver et al., 2016). A significant advantage to utilizing an open-source platform is that students will have access to it free of charge, even after they have left Bryn Mawr College.

To more widely advertise the benefits of notebooks for teaching, we organized a conference around notebook-based pedagogy, as embodied in the modules, called "JupyterDayPhilly: Transformative Teaching with the Jupyter Notebook" and hosted it at Bryn Mawr College in May 2017 (JupyterDayPhilly, 2017). We had 10 invited speakers and over 30 participants. The conference website (see the TIDES Materials section below) is a useful resource for anyone wishing to explore the technology for computing with diversity and equity goals, including our own modules.

We developed our fourteen modules (one with multiple parts) as Jupyter notebooks, and chose the Python programming language for all modules.

Python is especially well-suited for computing education, but also is used by researchers in a variety of fields, including biology, physics, chemistry, linguistics, and computer science. Using authentic tools on authentic problems has been shown to be effective in education (Forte & Guzdial, 2005). Module 0 provides an introduction to computing in general and, over three parts, Module 1 introduces the basics of programming and Python, as well as some software library packages that extend the power of Python for scientific computing. The other modules present mathematical techniques and applications to physics. An instructor's guide to the modules, including a flowchart of module dependencies, is provided with the modules (see the TIDES Resources section).

The Computational Methods course was designed with several features intended to help meet the goals of the TIDES project to enhance diverse and inclusive learning. Some of these features were formulated with the principles of Universal Design for Learning ([UDL], CAST, 2018) in mind. Consistent with the UDL philosophy, it was our intention to facilitate learning through features that would assist *all* students, including those from underrepresented groups in STEM. The features are:

- *Context information*: The start of each module lists the prior modules with which students must be familiar in order to undertake the current module, a time estimate for reading and working through the module, the learning goals for the module, and a brief list of some interesting applications of the mathematical tools presented in the module. (Module 0 omits the last element, as well as features 2–5 below.)
- *Scientist profile*: Each module contains a personal profile of a scientist connected with computing that describes their work and some interesting facts about their life; most of these profiles were generated by students. In constructing the profiles, the students were asked to focus on contemporary individuals whose lives or work they found inspiring in some way. We plan to continue to ask students working with the modules to generate such profiles. (A sample profile is shown below, as is some sample feedback from students on the profiles.)
- *Breakpoints*: These are quick questions meant to prompt students to stop and think about what they have just read – along with answers to those questions – so students can confirm their understanding immediately. (Student feedback from the pilot course motivated inclusion of the breakpoint answers in the modules themselves rather than in separate solution sets.) A couple of example breakpoint questions, from the module on numerical differentiation, are "Prove this claim that b is the derivative of the quadratic curve $y = ax^2 + bx + c$ at $x = 0$" and "Write out the expression for the quartic (degree 4) approximation to the derivative."
- *Exercises*: These ask students to put into practice the concepts they learn in the modules. Those in early modules are relatively straightforward to complete; the exercises increase in difficulty as students progress through the sequence of modules and build their skills and confidence. Many of the

exercises involve standard applications or computations that students will encounter in their physics courses. (We intend to add application problems from other scientific disciplines as the project progresses and where appropriate.)

- *Reflection prompts*: During the Computational Methods pilot course – which was run as an interactive session, sometimes including a short lecture but with the bulk of the time used for students working independently and in groups – we periodically posed questions to the students designed to improve their metacognitive skills. Those questions and others have been incorporated into the module notebooks themselves so that students will encounter them no matter which context they engage with the modules in. Examples of reflection questions posed in the modules are "Which components of this module did you find more difficult to work through, and why do you think they were challenging?" and "When you got stuck, what did you do to get unstuck? Could this or similar actions be helpful if you get stuck in future work?"
- *Recaps*: Bullet-point lists near the end of each module summarize the key takeaway ideas.
- *Term project*: As part of the pilot course, students completed a term project applying computation to some problem of personal interest to themselves. Most students chose project topics related to other courses they had taken or were taking, but one student chose a topic connected to her personal interest in music. As we learned during various TIDES Institutes throughout the grant period, assignments that invite connections with a student's personal goals and interests can enhance motivation and persistence, two elements of learning found to be key in the retention of students from underrepresented groups in STEM (Harackiewicz & Hulleman, 2010; Harackiewicz, Tibbetts, Canning, & Hyde, 2014).
- *E-portfolio*: To encourage students to see the connections between the modules and to recognize the full scope of their work, we asked each student to compile all of their module-related activities into an electronic portfolio ("e-portfolio") which they will be able to use as evidence of their computational skills when applying to jobs or graduate schools.

Example Scientist Profile

Mark Dean is an inventor and computer engineer, born on March 2, 1957 in Jefferson City, Tennessee. Dr Dean earned a bachelor's degree in Electrical Engineering from the University of Tennessee, a master's in Electrical Engineering from Florida Atlantic University, and a PhD in Electrical Engineering from Stanford University. Upon graduating from college, Dean soon started working at a young IBM, where he rose to become the first African American IBM Fellow, the highest recognition of technical excellence at the company. In his time at IBM, where he spent the majority of his career, Dean became famous for three main contributions to the worlds of computer science and computer engineering: he helped develop the Industry Standard Architecture (ISA) systems bus, which allowed outside devices like the mouse and disk drives to be plugged directly into the computer; some of his work also helped lead to the development of the first color PC monitor; and, finally, he is known for leading the IBM team that created the first gigahertz processing chip. As evidence of his influence on the field, Dean holds three of IBM's original nine patents, and he has more than 20 patents in total to his name. His inspirational story as a pioneering African American in the sciences has been and continues to be a source of inspiration for aspiring computer scientists of all races.

Sample Student Comments on the Scientist Profiles

"To me, the most inspiring thing about this story was that Dean grew up in a very difficult time for black Americans, yet still succeeded academically and professionally to a huge degree. It reminds me that no matter where you come from or what disadvantages you might start out with, if you are dedicated, work hard, and love what you do, nothing can stop you from achieving your goals. I think I can apply this to my academics and career choice to help me decide what I spend my life doing based on my true interests."

"His [Dean's] story was very inspirational considering he was an African American growing up in the 60's and 70's and was able to achieve so much despite any adversity he faced. He was able to work on many large projects, not just one, which is something I aspire to do."

Implementation/Methodology: Faculty Workshops

The Teaching for Diversity and Equity: Scholarship and Practice workshops were designed to introduce faculty to relevant research findings and give them an opportunity to discuss how they might be applied to particular teaching challenges. We developed this approach through a series of planning conversations with small groups of interested Bryn Mawr College faculty across a range of fields and career stages. Participants in these conversations generally felt they would benefit from learning more about the particular challenges faced by different groups of students and from gaining concrete pedagogical strategies to address those challenges. They also articulated concerns about practice, ranging from personal anxieties about saying or doing the "wrong" things when working with students whose background differed from their own, to broader institutional questions about reconciling perceived tradeoffs between student-centered teaching and academic rigor. An effective workshop would clearly need to not only give faculty information, but also provide a chance to discuss possibilities for, experiences with, and potential ramifications of applying that information in their own teaching.

The final version of the workshop consisted of four parts: (1) a large-group discussion of motivations and goals; (2) a presentation of the scholarship that informs practices of inclusive teaching; (3) a small-group activity in which participants discussed case studies and practiced applying inclusive teaching techniques; and (4) an invitation to make commitments to turn workshop takeaways into concrete action. The first and last parts were designed to help participants develop individual and collective goals and takeaways for the workshop. We began each workshop by asking participants to take a few minutes to individually reflect on their reasons for attending and their overall goals for students. We then asked volunteers to share some of their reflections with the larger group and, through a discussion of their responses, developed a shared sense of what participants hoped to achieve. At the conclusion of the workshop, we asked participants to reflect back on their reasons for coming and their overall goals, and to write down one or two concrete ideas from the workshop that they would put into practice to achieve those goals when they returned to the classroom.

The second part introduced faculty to the research surrounding diversity and equity in higher education, starting with the core finding that students are less likely to succeed in college if they are a member of an underrepresented group, a first-generation college student, and/or an economically disadvantaged group, although not because of under-preparedness. In other words, differences in college readiness do not fully explain the success gap. We then introduced other variables that have been found to negatively impact student success, including cognitive barriers such as stereotype threat (Steele, 2010), microaggressions (Sue et al., 2007; Sue, Lin, Torino, Capodilupo, & Rivera, 2009), imposter syndrome (Clance & Imes, 1978), a "fixed" mindset (Dweck, 2006), and structural barriers such as observer perspective (Steele, 2010), and "dysfunctional illusions of rigor" (Nelson, 2010).[2] In all cases, we referenced widely available and accessible sources (also cited here) that faculty could read for more information, and brought in examples from our own teaching experiences and work with Bryn Mawr College students (Cook-Sather & Agu, 2013). We closed the presentation

---

[2]Imposter syndrome refers to a tendency of some to doubt their worthiness and to fear being exposed as a "fraud." Carol Dweck distinguishes "fixed" and "growth" mind-sets: the fixed mind-set takes abilities to be innate and essentially unchangeable, while a growth mind-set holds that practice and effort can enhance one's abilities. Observer perspective denotes the limited knowledge that an "observer" possesses when viewing an "actor," who may be responding to stimuli outside the observer's field of view. In the educational arena, the observer would be a teacher or other authority figure and the actor would be a student (whose behavior or performance might reflect individual circumstances unknown to the observer). Craig Nelson's "dysfunctional illusions of rigor" are a set of seven notions about teaching, now seen as outdated and false, such as that students fail in courses primarily because of their own shortcomings; that old-fashioned, uniform, rigid teaching methods are unbiased and superior to those that "pamper" students; etc.

with the image below, taken from the pamphlet *Step Up and Lead for Equity*, by the Association of American Colleges and Universities ([AAC&U], 2015). We used it to frame a whole-group conversation about the distinct concepts of equality and equity, and how a shift toward seeking equity would impact pedagogy.

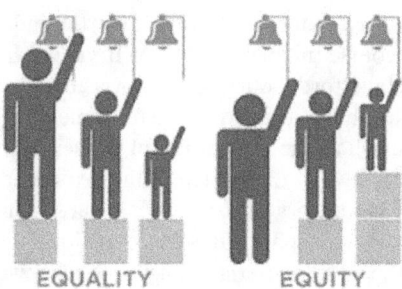

For the third and longest part of the workshop, we asked participants to break into small groups for a facilitated discussion of case studies. Experienced faculty and staff facilitators served as discussion leaders, and started the activity by reading aloud a faculty perspective and a student perspective on a scenario that raised issues of equity. These scenarios were based on the research and/or real-world experiences of faculty and former students who assisted with workshop development and were designed to illustrate some of the barriers to equity and inclusion raised in the presentation, such as imposter syndrome and racial stereotyping. The group discussed issues raised by the scenario, and then each participant received a card with an inclusive teaching strategy, derived from articles containing practical guidance on culturally responsible, engaging, and equitable teaching for college instructors (Cook-Sather, Cohen, & Shumate, 2011; Tanner, 2013). Participants took turns reading their cards and discussing how and why they might use the strategies they contained if they were the faculty member in the scenario. Facilitators raised questions about how the scenarios and recommended practices might intersect or vary across contexts (e.g., different campus cultures, different class sizes), if participants did not do so themselves.

After a short break, the breakout groups returned for a final intention-setting exercise and wrap-up discussion. We gave participants time to strategize how they might apply one or two recommended practices in their own teaching and asked them to write down a formal commitment to do so on a sticky note to share with the group. We also asked participants to write down a question they still had about inclusive teaching on a sticky note. Participants posted both notes on the walls and walked around the room reading each other's commitments and outstanding questions in preparation for a final discussion in which they were invited to share observations, questions, and commitments. At the end of the workshop, each participant received a packet to take home containing the case studies, copies of the two pedagogical articles from which the recommended practices were taken, a bibliography of further reading, and a copy of *Step Up and Lead for Equity* (AAC&U, 2015).

Results

Results: Computational Modules

The pilot course produced extensive feedback on the individual modules from the 17 students in the course (nine women from Bryn Mawr College, one woman and seven men from Haverford College), which was used to improve their clarity and sequencing. The feedback resulted in the refinement of breakpoints and self-reflection prompts, as well as the integration of the scientist profiles directly into the modules. The first few of the updated and expanded modules were next taught as part of the laboratory accompanying our second-semester, calculus-based, mechanics course for physical science majors. There, we found that attempting to teach the basic material in a few weeks' worth of two-hour lab meetings to primarily first-year students was an overreach. Most of them had no programming experience, and the challenge of learning that skill on top of the physics they were learning in the course, not to mention the other demands of being a freshman in college, was a bit too much to handle for many of them.

After an extensive departmental discussion, we decided to rearrange our sophomore-level labs so that one of them could be converted to an exclusively computational lab. By placing the basic modules in a second-semester, sophomore lab, we intended to leverage the students' greater mathematical maturity while still introducing them to computing early enough in their college careers that they would have ample opportunities to reinforce and further extend those abilities in their junior and senior years. The first offering of this computational lab occurred in Spring 2017, and was taught successfully by a new faculty member who had had no involvement in the development of the modules. The results were promising: the students were able to get through the first five modules, apparently without significant difficulty, and the faculty member was able to learn and adapt the modules into the course pedagogy. We will continue to introduce the computational learning project in this way each year. The additional modules will be assigned in upper-level physics courses, culminating in the capstone senior seminar when students will complete and present their e-portfolios with a final reflection on their computational learning.

Results: Faculty Workshops

Variants of the workshops were delivered four times: (1) at the Blended Learning in the Liberal Arts Conference (Bryn Mawr College, May 2015); (2) as a Tri-College workshop (August 2015) for Bryn Mawr, Haverford, and Swarthmore faculty members; (3) as an Allegheny College faculty workshop (August 2015), and (4) at AAC&U's Diversity, Learning, and Student Success Conference (Philadelphia, 2016). Combined, they involved 118 participants from at least 37 institutions. The iterations at the Blended Learning in the Liberal

Arts and AAC&U conferences involved faculty and staff from many geographically distributed institutions, whereas the Tri-College and Allegheny College workshops involved participants from a single college or closely-knit consortium. Participants were asked to provide feedback via a paper questionnaire distributed at the end of the workshop.

Table 1 shows aspects of the workshop that participants were asked to rate via a Likert scale. Averages in almost every case were positive (above 4, which was neutral). The statement that participants were most likely to disagree with, "the workshop covered content that was new to me," reflected participants' prior knowledge of workshop content, rather than attitudes toward the workshop itself. Participants most strongly agreed with statements that "the workshop addressed important topics" and "concepts were clear." Most agreed that they planned to act on knowledge or use strategies as a result of the workshop, but they were less sanguine in response to statements that they were more prepared or had learned something new as a result of the workshop.

Responses to the open-ended questions included on the survey provide a more nuanced reading of the results. For example, although Likert scores for the statement "the workshop covered content that was new to me" suggest that many participants were familiar with the content before attending, when asked "what, if anything did you learn that was new to you?" the most common responses referenced the scholarship behind barriers to learning and approaches for dealing with classroom scenarios; that is, what one might consider the "content" of the workshop. This suggests that while many college faculty and staff are already somewhat familiar with research on diversity and equity in higher education and/or strategies for creating more inclusive and equitable classrooms, there are still a significant number of individuals who benefit from learning more about specific strategies and having an opportunity to explore their use.

Feedback on the workshops also resonated with the hypothesis we formed when soliciting input from faculty in the workshop planning stage, namely, that providing participants with opportunities to discuss experiences and strategies was as important as raising awareness about research and best practices related to diversity and equity in higher education (see, for example, National Center for Women and Information Technology, 2017). Participants overwhelmingly mentioned that small-group discussions in which they reviewed case studies and strategies or shared experiences with colleagues were the most successful aspects of the workshop. When asked about possible improvements, they recommended more time for such discussions and more time to develop a concrete plan to incorporate what they had learned into their teaching practice.

Discussion

The effectiveness of the modules at engaging and retaining students from traditionally underrepresented groups is difficult to assess due to the small numbers of students who have used the modules at Bryn Mawr so far. While roughly a half dozen faculty members at other institutions requested our modules, we do

Table 1: Participant Feedback — Scale of 1 (Strongly Disagree) to 7 (Strongly Agree).

	Blended Learning Conf. (May 2015)	Allegheny (Aug 2016)	Tri-College (Aug 2016)	AAC&U (March 2016)
The workshop addressed important topics	6.7	6.6	6.0	6.7
I plan to share information from today's workshop with others	6.1	6.0	5.6	6.7
The concepts presented by the instructors were clear to me	6.6	6.3	6.1	6.6
I felt comfortable asking questions	6.2	6.3	6.0	6.4
I plan to use what I learned today in my courses	6.2	6.4	5.9	6.3
Having participated in this workshop, I can more effectively help students learn	5.4	6.0	5.1	6.3
I am satisfied with what I gained from this workshop	6.1	6.1	5.2	6.3
Sufficient time was provided for me to ask questions	6.1	5.8	5.5	6.0
As a result of this workshop, I am better prepared to teach diverse learners	5.2	5.7	4.8	5.8
I discussed with others how I can apply the concepts covered in today's workshop to my courses	5.8	6.1	5.3	5.8
I learned strategies for teaching diverse learners	5.0	5.5	4.5	5.7
The workshop was about the right length in time	5.4	6.0	5.5	5.4
I learned about the research on diverse learners	5.2	5.2	4.3	5.4
I learned strategies for advising diverse learners	4.1	5.2	4.2	4.7
The workshop covered content that was new to me	4.3	4.8	3.5	4.3

not yet have any feedback from them on their use of our materials. However, recent classes of physics majors at Bryn Mawr have been significantly larger than in previous years, so we anticipate improved numbers and therefore better data on the impacts of the modules going forward.

The attempt to introduce the early modules in the freshman year was not effective for our students. However, introducing students to the modules in the second semester of their sophomore year does appear to be a successful strategy. This observation essentially was confirmed during a second offering of the computational laboratory in the Spring 2018 semester, but further tweaking of the module exercises and the pacing of the lab was indicated.

The prompt given to the students in the computational methods pilot course to generate the module scientist profiles focused on relatively contemporary individuals who inspired the students. We hoped that this would lead to the students finding individuals with backgrounds similar to their own who had overcome significant obstacles to achieve their accomplishments. While that turned out to be the case for most of the profiles, especially those done by the women students, there were some that featured well-known white males. During the pilot course, we probed a little bit into why the students chose those individuals, but upon reflection it would have been valuable to have had a longer discussion about bias against women and people of color in the computing community and high-tech industry and how it results in the failure of those communities to adequately recognize the contributions of people from diverse backgrounds. We will encourage faculty members who teach the modules in the future to engage in this sort of discussion explicitly.

Finally, we plan to assist students in forming a computational study group to provide peer support for those students who work through modules independently of a class or as part of an advanced class in which they are asked to complete modules on their own. Most likely, that learning community will be a blended one, having both face-to-face and online elements, to enable students to interact with each other both in person and virtually.

Overall, our TIDES project has had two significant effects at Bryn Mawr College. First, computational notebooks modeled on our modules, including the "Reflection" and "Breakpoint" techniques, have been adopted in Physics, Biology, and Computer Science. This research resulted in a number of publications, including O'Hara, Blank, and Marshall (2015), Blank (2017), Hu, Blank, Chan, and Doom (2017), and Lewis, Blank, Bruce, and Osera (2016). Second, faculty who participated in the Workshop to Increase Diversity and Equity have increased their capacity to teach in culturally sensitive and relevant ways and have made modifications to their course assignments and pedagogical practices.

Conclusion

With the twin goals of providing training in scientific computation to our majors and recruiting more students from US underrepresented groups to STEM fields by familiarizing faculty members with the key ideas around inclusive teaching, we developed, piloted, and made publicly available both curricular materials on scientific computing and workshop materials for faculty training.

We intentionally embedded and integrated learning-promoting features such as personal profiles and various reflection prompts into the instructional modules in order to send a strong signal to both students and other faculty members that we value diversity in our classrooms, and to make it less likely that these features will be overlooked or dropped due to time constraints. The modules designed in this way may also serve as a model for other faculty members who might adapt these materials or design their own. Building the modules and considering which of their features might best contribute to inclusive student learning also will carry over to other courses and future curricular material development.

Our curricular materials can be incorporated into curricula at other institutions. Outcomes will be highly dependent not only on the details of those curricula, but also on the prior knowledge and experiences of students, as well as their expectations.

The Last Word

Those of us who started teaching having had little or no actual training in pedagogy often simply do what we have seen our own teachers do. Teaching in a way that successfully benefits the diverse range of contemporary students means that we must continue to educate ourselves about how people learn, to use that knowledge to inform how and what we teach, and to be self-aware when we interact with students. Only in this way can we optimize the opportunities for *all* of our students to participate, learn, and grow.

TIDES Resources

The authors found the following readings particularly helpful in developing the modules and workshops for this project:

- Henderson, C., Beach, A., & Finkelstein, N. (2011). Facilitating change in undergraduate STEM instructional practices: An analytic review of the literature. *Journal of Research in Science Teaching, 48*(8), 952–984. A meta-review of articles on promoting change in STEM education practices. Key findings are that developing and disseminating curricular materials and top-down policies were *ineffective* methods of creating change, compared to interventions – aligned with or designed to change instructor beliefs – that last at least a semester and are designed to work within the institution in which they're implemented.
- Cook-Sather, A., Cohen, J., & Shumate, T. (2011). Embracing productive disruptions. *Teaching and Learning Together in Higher Education, 4*. This article, freely available online, offers concrete strategies for culturally inclusive teaching based on field research in college classroom.

- Tanner, Kimberly D. (2013). Structure matters: Twenty-one teaching strategies to promote student engagement and cultivate classroom equity. *CBE Life Sciences Education, 12*(3), 322–331. A similar compilation of strategies, but with a focus on the sciences.

The authors have published both the computational modules and the workshop materials as open educational resources and welcome others to use and adapt them:

- The complete set of computational modules together with supporting documentation are available at https://github.com/BrynMawrCollege/TIDES.
- The workshop materials and a recording of the presentation from the original iteration of the workshop are available on the Bryn Mawr digital commons repository: http://repository.brynmawr.edu/blended_learning/2015/2015/37/.
- The JupyterDayPhilly talks and resources are available at https://jupyterday.blogs.brynmawr.edu/schedule/

References

Aspden, L., & Helm, P. (2004). Making the connection in a blended learning environment. *Educational Media International, 41*(3), 245–252.

Association for the Advancement of Computing in Education. (2007). Perspectives on blended learning in higher education. *International Journal on E-Learning, 6*(1), 81–94.

Association of American Colleges and Universities. (2015). *Step up and lead for equity: What higher education can do to reverse our deepening divides.* Retrieved from http://www.aacu.org/publications/step-up-and-lead

Blank, D. S. (2017, May). *Computational storytelling in the liberal arts.* Presentation at JupyterDayPhilly, Bryn Mawr College, Bryn Mawr, PA. Retrieved from http://nbviewer.jupyter.org/format/slides/urls/jupyter.brynmawr.edu/services/public/dblank/jupyterday/Computational%20Storytelling.raw.ipynb#/

Bryn Mawr College, Office of Institutional Research. (2012). *Science graduates: Bryn Mawr and national.* Retrieved from http://www.brynmawr.edu/institutionalresearch/sciencegrads_national.html

CAST. (2018). *University design for learning guidelines version 2.2.* Retrieved from http://udlguidelines.cast.org

Clance, P. R., & Imes, S. A. (1978). The imposter phenomenon in high achieving women: dynamics and therapeutic intervention. *Psychotherapy: Theory, Research & Practice, 15*(3), 241–247.

Cook-Sather, A., & Agu, P. (2013). Students of color and faculty members working together toward culturally sustaining pedagogy. In J. E. Groccia & L. Cruz (Eds.) *To improve the academy: Resources for faculty, instructional, and organizational development* (pp. 271–285). San Francisco, CA: Jossey-Bass.

Cook-Sather, A., Cohen, J., & Shumate, T. (2011). Embracing productive disruptions: Excerpts from an ongoing story of developing more culturally responsive classrooms. *Teaching and Learning Together in Higher Education, 4.* https://repository.brynmawr.edu/tlthe/vol1/iss4/5

Dweck, C. (2006). *Mindset: The new psychology of success.* New York, NY: Random House.

Dziuban, C. Hartman, J., & Moskal, P. (2004). Blending learning. *ECAR Research Bulletin, 7.* Retrieved from https://library.educause.edu/resources/2004/3/blended-learning

Forte, A., & Guzdial, M. (2005). Motivation and nonmajors in computer science: Identifying discrete audiences for introductory courses. *IEEE Transactions on Education, 48*(2), 248–253.

Harackiewicz, J. M., & Hulleman, C. S. (2010). The importance of interest: The role of achievement goals and task values in promoting the development of interest. *Social and Personality Psychology Compass, 4*(1), 42–52.

Harackiewicz, J. M., Tibbetts, Y., Canning, E. A., & Hyde, J. S. (2014). Harnessing values to promote motivation in education. In S. Karabenick & T. Urden (Eds.) *Motivational Interventions, Advances in Motivation and Achievement* (Vol. 18, pp. 71–105). Bingley, UK: Emerald Publishing.

Hu, H. H., Blank, D., Chan, A., & Doom, T. (2017). Panel: Teaching to increase diversity and equity in STEM. *Proceedings of the 48th ACM Technical Symposium on Computer Science Education* (pp. 665–666). https://doi.org/10.1145/3017680.3017695

JupyterDayPhilly. (2017). Transformative teaching with the Jupyter notebook. May 17 – Thursday, May 18, 2017. Retrieved from https://jupyterday.blogs.brynmawr.edu/

Kluyver, T., Ragan-Kelley, B., Pérez, F., Granger, B., Bussonnier, M., Frederic, J., … the Jupyter Development Team. (2016). Jupyter notebooks – a publishing format for reproducible computational workflows. In F. Loizides & B. Schmidt (Eds.) *Positioning and Power in Academic Publishing: Players, Agents and Agendas* (pp. 87–90). Gottingen, Germany: IOS Press Ebooks. https://doi.org/10.3233/978-1-61499-649-1-87

LaTeX Project. (2018). Retrieved from https://www.latex-project.org

Lewis, M. C., Blank, D., Bruce, K., & Osera, P-M. (2016). Uncommon teaching languages. In *Proceedings of the 47th ACM Technical Symposium on Computing Science Education* (pp. 492–493). https://doi.org/10.1145/2839509.2844666

Lovett, M., Meyer, O., & Thille, C. (2008). The Open Learning Initiative: Measuring the effectiveness of the OLI statistics course in accelerating student learning. *Journal of Interactive Media in Education.* http://eric.ed.gov/ERICWebPortal/detail?accno=EJ840810

Means, B., Toyama, Y., Murphy, R., Bakia, M., & Jones, K. (2010). *Evaluation of evidence-based practices in online learning: A meta-analysis and review of online learning studies.* Washington, DC: U.S. Department of Education, Center for Technology in Learning.

National Center for Women and Information Technology. (2017). Engagement practices. Retrieved from https://www.engage-csedu.org/engagement/make-it-matter

Nelson, C. E. (2010). Dysfunctional Illusions of Rigor: Lessons from the Scholarship of Teaching and Learning. In L. B. Nilson & J. Miller (Eds.), *To Improve the Academy: Resources for Faculty, Instructional, and Organizational Development* (Vol. 28). San Francisco, CA: Jossey-Bass.

O'Hara, K., Blank, D., & Marshall, J. (2015, May). *Computational notebooks for AI education.* Paper presented at International Florida Artificial Intelligence

Research Society Conference (FLAIRS), Hollywood, FL. https://doi.org/10.13140/2.1.2434.5928

Steele, C. M. (2010). *Whistling Vivaldi: How stereotypes affect us and what we can do.* New York, NY: W. W. Norton.

Sue, D. W., Capodilupo, C. M., Torino, G. C., Bucceri, J. M., Holder, A. M., Nadal, K. L., & Esquilin, M. (2007). Racial microaggressions in everyday life: Implications for clinical practice. *American Psychologist, 62*(4), 271–286.

Sue, D. W., Lin, A. I., Torino, G. C., Capodilupo, C. M., & Rivera, D. P. (2009). Racial microaggressions and difficult dialogues on race in the classroom. *Cultural Diversity and Ethnic Minority Psychology, 15*(2), 183–190.

Tanner, K. D. (2013). Structure matters: Twenty-one teaching strategies to promote student engagement and cultivate classroom equity. *CBE Life Sciences Education, 12*(3), 322–331.

Chapter 8

Culturally Responsive Computational Science through Research Experience in Core-curriculum Courses

Lior Shamir, Franco Delogu, Melinda Weinstein and Hsiao-Ping Moore

Reflection

As a computer science undergraduate student, I remember sitting in diverse classrooms. But when I became a computer science professor, I noticed that things had changed, and my classes were far less diverse than the classrooms I used to sit in as a student. That anecdotal observation was well aligned with national enrollment numbers (Krause, Polycarpou, & Hellman, 2012). While in the mid-1980s 37% of computer science graduates were women, the enrollment of women dropped to 30% in the early 90s. Graduation rates continued to decline to ~27% in the late 90s (Camp, 2001), and as low as ~12% in 2012 (Zweben, 2012). That is, while in most STEM disciplines the participation of women has increased, it has decreased sharply in computer science. The percentage of underrepresented minorities in computer science has also been extremely low, with no signs of change over the years. Although it seemed odd, at that time I did not have the tools to understand the low participation of minorities and women in computer science. I simply had to accept it as the reality of my discipline.

My acceptance of the lack of diversity in computer science changed with TIDES, which provided me with the tools to observe the reality of computer science through a completely different lens. In particular, I began to understand how the "geek" culture developed in computer science plays a major role in attracting a certain group of students, while excluding the others. That led to the development of this project, an attempt to initiate a process of creating a new kind of computer science education. The computer science education created in this project aims to be less "geeky," and can make a friendly learning environment for many students who would otherwise not feel that computer science is a natural environment for them.

During that process, I began to understand that the primary enemy of diversity in computer science is not necessarily the professor who advises the struggling female student that she would do better if she changed her major to English. It is also not the teaching assistant who becomes noticeably impatient when answering questions from students of color. These people may have a negative impact, and they clearly do exist, but they cannot be held responsible for the massive systemic diversity crisis that we experience in computer science.

Through TIDES, I began to understand that the real enemy of diversity in computer science is the department chair who announces that increasing the number of underrepresented minority students by 50% is a primary goal for the next five years, but will not change the curriculum for that purpose. The real enemy of diversity in computer science is the professor who argues that sensor network optimization is a gender-neutral topic. The real enemy of diversity in computer science is the dean who announces that underrepresented minorities are encouraged to apply for an open faculty position, but who will not approve the hiring of faculty who do not have a research program in an established sub-field that has computer science journals, conferences, and NSF programs. The real enemy of diversity in computer science can also be the CEO of the tech company desperately looking for qualified women to hire, but will not change the fraternity-like environment in their company. So, as is often the case, the real enemy of diversity in computer science is not those who oppose diversity, but those who agree with the cause, but will not make the necessary changes.

TIDES helped me understand that the enemy of diversity in computer science is us – the entire discipline of computer science. Addressing the problem effectively will not be through "patches" like summer stipends for women or sending underrepresented minority students to conferences. Addressing the problem at the national level will require a comprehensive change in the discipline. That includes changing the academic contents as well as moving the discipline away from the "geek culture" that hijacked and currently controls computer science as an academic discipline. The project described in this chapter is an attempt to take the first steps to create an environment in which students can express their identity, culture, and ethnicity through computing, in a new computer science learning environment.

Institutional Context

Despite being located in an ethnically diverse area in Southeast Michigan, Lawrence Technological University has attracted a relatively low population of underrepresented minority students. As a STEM institution, nearly 75% of the students at Lawrence Technological University are men. Less than 10% of the student population are underrepresented minority students. Another important aspect of our campus is that about 75% of students do not live on campus, and many of them are part-time students. The need to increase the number of students from underrepresented minorities has been a topic of major concern since 2012, when Dr Virinder Moudgil became the President of Lawrence Technological University. The back wind from campus leadership was a substantial catalyzer for the growth of the TIDES project, which later expanded far beyond its original plans.

An important benefit of Lawrence Technological University is its relatively small class sizes, normally of 20 students. The small classes enable student research as part of the course, such that each student owns their project and can choose different content and hypotheses for their research.

Introduction

Many institutions of higher education define a core curriculum as a set of courses that all students are required to take as a requirement for graduation. In many cases, these courses are introductory humanities courses that cover world culture, including literature and the arts. Some core-curriculum courses provide students with basic information about the social or natural sciences such as introductory physics or biology.

Since computer science courses rarely serve as core-curriculum courses, non-computer science students are normally not exposed to computer science. Consequently, most students graduate without obtaining knowledge about computing beyond the immediate computer applications that they use for basic common tasks in their daily lives (e.g., using a word processor or basic online services such as Facebook).

The limited access of many students to computer science reinforces an intervention that can expose a broader population of students to computing. Undergraduate research is a proven effective intervention that has demonstrated its efficacy and impact on engagement, recruitment, retention, and GPA increases of STEM students (American Association for the Advancement of Science, 2011; Freeman et al., 2014; Hippel, Lerner, Gregerman, Nagda, & Jonides, 1998; Kinkel & Henke, 2006; Seymour, Hunter, Laursen, & DeAntoni, 2004). It was found superior to "cookbook" experiments with known results (Braxton, Hirschy, & McClendon, 2004; President's Council on Advisors on Science & Technology [PCAST], 2012). The studying of open-ended questions in a project-oriented environment or problem-based learning has demonstrated efficacy in the field of computer science (Dolog, Thomsen, & Thomsen, 2016; Gestwicki & McNely, 2016).

However, while incorporating independent research is ideal, undergraduate student research is limited by the availability of funding for student stipends (Ramirez, McNicholas, Gilbert, Saez, & Siniawski, 2015), as well as the time commitment required of faculty to mentor an undergraduate student (Schmolitzky & Schummer, 2008). The limited research assistantship positions often lead to a selection process in which the students with the highest GPA are more likely to win research assistantship positions. That practice might exclude many students who might need the intervention. That is, those students who struggle to graduate and are at the highest risk of dropping out have limited access to research experience, a proven high-impact practice that is accessible only to the most privileged students.

Classroom-based research experience (CRE) is an inclusive intervention that provides research experience inside the classroom as part of courses that are part of the curriculum, so that all students are provided with the opportunity to participate in research. In CRE, students investigate a scientific question that cannot be answered by the existing literature. While CRE courses have been implemented successfully in the biological and chemical sciences (Clark et al., 2009; Colabroy, 2011; Hoskins, Lopatto, & Stevens, 2011; Willbur, Vail, Mitchell, Jakeman, & Timmons, 2016), computer science programs rarely involve authentic research in the form of CRE as part of first-year level courses.

Here, we describe a novel approach that allows students to experience computing in its broader sense while applying computational tools to research questions in art history, psychology, and biology as part of first-year, core-curriculum courses. This allows the students to experience authentic research using computing in diverse fields that are different from the "traditional" fields of research in computer science. This also allows the students to own their research and select their research questions, as well as provides them with the opportunity to express their culture and identity through computing.

Implementation

The proposed modules are taught by two instructors: the discipline instructor, who teaches the entire course; and a computer science faculty, who joins the class only during sessions related to the research modules. The modules are designed for four one-hour sessions. The computer science faculty are available to the students of the course during office hours. Although most of the technical work is done in the classroom, assistance during office hours is normally given to those who did not attend the class.

As mentioned earlier, the modules are designed for introductory freshman-level courses that are not computer science courses. The courses in which the modules were implemented are Introduction to Psychology, Introduction to Biology, and World Masterpieces 1, which is an introductory humanities course. Students who did not necessarily choose computer science as their major are thereby exposed to computer science education in the context of its application, rather than the current introductory computer science courses that focus more on abstract terms such as loops and variables.

Before starting the experiments, the students are provided with the protocol of the experiment. Although each experiment is different, the differences between the experiments are limited to the hypotheses and the data being analyzed. The methodology is similar for the experiments of all students. The protocols provide a step-by-step set of instructions for completing all stages of the experiments, including the software tools and commands needed to execute. The detailed protocols for the modules described in this paper are free and available to the public, and all software used is also available for free download.

The students work in pairs, helping them to develop teamwork skills (Auchincloss et al., 2014; Vivian, Falkner, Falkner, & Tarmazdi, 2016). Working in teams makes it easier to complete the tasks, as some of the tasks can be labor-intensive. In some cases, students might want to study a certain question that is of no interest to other students. In these cases, students are allowed to work alone. The opportunity to study questions of personal interest is a key element that allows the student to express their personality, identity, and interests through computing and research. In addition to collaboration, the modules are also designed to cover the other four CRE elements (Auchincloss et al., 2014), which are (1) scientific practices, (2) iteration (3) producing new knowledge, and (4) relevance to the field.

Interdisciplinary Computer Science and Art History Module: Quantitative Analysis of Art History

The computer science research component is added to a humanities core-curriculum course, "World Masterpieces 1," which covers art, literature, and their cultural and historical perspective from the ancient world through the Renaissance. Among these topics, the course also has an art history section that normally consumes two weeks of the course, in which the students discuss art and artistic movements. That section is typically taught in the traditional lecture-based fashion with classroom discussions.

In the new art history module, the students first propose a hypothesis regarding art history. The hypotheses need to be approved by the instructor before the work begins. For example, students may choose to study whether the artistic style of two painters is more similar compared to other artists, or whether the artistic styles developed in different countries or geographic locations are more similar compared to artistic styles developed in other regions. This allows the student to not just own the research, but to also express their identity by selecting painters related to their culture, ethnicity, etc. The students then test their hypothesis, by collecting the relevant image data (digital paintings) and analyzing them quantitatively using computational tools.

The students work in groups, normally of two students, to encourage teamwork. The computer analysis module is co-taught by one humanities faculty and one computer science faculty. The humanities faculty supervises the selection of project ideas and art history hypotheses, works with the student to develop preliminary ideas into mature plans leading to art history experiments, and then put the analytical findings into their art history context. The computer science faculty assists the students with the computational analysis and explains the different computational methods used in the process.

Enabling Tools for Computational Analysis of Visual Art

Automatic analysis of visual art is a complex task for computing machines, and since the course is a first-year course the students clearly do not have the training and knowledge required for developing such methodology from scratch. Therefore, the students use several existing open-source tools such as secure copy (SCP) and secure shell (SSH), as well as image analysis and data visualization tools. An important element of the course is the image analysis and pattern recognition technology that enables the computer analysis of visual art. The primary computer programs used in the course are WNDCHRM (Shamir et al., 2008) and Version 3.5c of PHYLIP (1993), both open-source programs that can run on Linux and Windows.

WNDCHRM is an image analysis software that can analyze paintings automatically (Shamir, 2012; Shamir, Macura, Orlov, Eckley, & Goldberg, 2010). The program first converts each image to a set of numerical values that reflect its content such as fractals, textures, shapes, colors, and more (Shamir, 2012; Shamir et al., 2010; Shamir & Tarakhovsky, 2012). It then applies pattern recognition algorithms to perform automatic classification of the paintings. The software also analyzes the similarities between the different artistic styles and visualizes them using a phylogeny powered by the PHYLIP software package. A phylogeny visualizes the similarities between elements in the form of a graph. It was originally developed to visualize genetic similarities between organisms, but in this work, it is used to visualize differences between artistic styles. Previously, it demonstrated its efficacy in analyzing visual art in the context of art history (Shamir, 2012; Shamir et al., 2010; Shamir & Tarakhovsky, 2012), as well as experiments related to art perception (Shamir, 2015; Shamir, Nissel, & Winner, 2016).

WNDCHRM is a program that works through a terminal window and receives its parameters by typing a command line. Its input is a path to a folder that contains subfolders such that each sub-folder contains images of paintings. Its output is a set of numerical values representing similarities between the folders, deduced by comparing the visual content of the images in the different folders. These similarity values can be transformed using PHYLIP into a phylogeny that visualizes the similarities. In other words, the process of applying WNDCHRM followed by PHYLIP can be conceptualized as an image analysis process that receives a set of folders of digital paintings as input, and provides a map of similarities between them as output. This simple design leads to an easy implementation, allowing students to carry out the experiments.

Computational Art History Module Implementation

After the research questions are defined, the students use the Internet to collect images of digital paintings representing the studied artistic styles. Normally, the students have around five different artistic styles and collect 30 images for each style so that the data set for each experiment contains about 150 images. The data collection is done by the students outside of the classroom.

The images are then copied to a Linux server using SCP, and processed by WNDCHRM to compute the numerical image content descriptors, a set of values that reflect the visual content of the image. The use of a Linux server with multiple cores is required due to WNDCHRM's computational complexity. It also exposes the students to work with remote servers and Linux, as the students need to use the command line over secured SSH to run several instances of WNDCHRM as daemons.

The processing can take as long as one day, and when completed the students copy the files containing the values of the numerical image content descriptors of each image back to their computers. The students then download and use the Windows version of WNDCHRM, and use basic machine learning practices to classify the artistic styles and create a confusion matrix and a similarity matrix. Using PHYLIP, the similarity matrix created by WNDCHRM is visualized as a phylogeny, the students analyze their results and prepare their final paper according to the computer analysis, which they critique in light of the historical and artistic perspectives of the art.

Figure 1 shows the results of a simple experiment performed by students. The students collected different paintings from different geographical regions such as China, India, the Middle East, Spain, Germany, France, and Italy. Each geographical region was represented by 30 paintings. Another set of paintings only included works by the painter Titian. After the paintings were collected, the students tested the similarities between the artistic styles developed in different parts of the Old World. Two different students collected Chinese paintings, and the computer correctly identified the similarity between the two artistic styles, which are essentially the same. Because Titian is an Italian painter the computer correctly placed him close to the Italian art.

After the students choose their research project, the art history module requires four 60- to 90-minute meetings with the students. In the first meeting, the students are introduced to the data collection and are given instructions and tips to collect their data. In the second meeting, the students copy their data to the remote Linux server and launch the image analysis daemons using

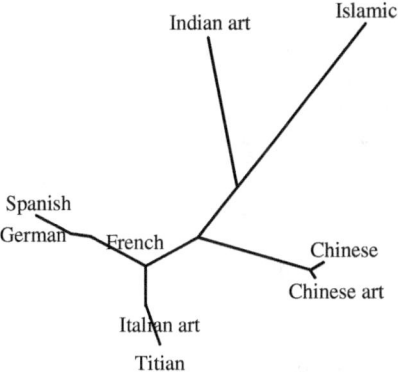

Figure 1: Computer-generated Phylogeny of Similarities between Artistic Styles in Different Geographical Locations and Several Individual Artists.

WNDCHRM. In the third meeting, the students copy the data back from the server and perform basic analysis such as classification using the Windows version of WNDCHRM. In the fourth meeting, the students analyze their results using PHYLIP and produce the final results of the project. Once the results are produced, the students write their final paper in which they analyze the computer analysis in light of the art history perspective. During the semester, the students also receive help from the computer science faculty when needed outside of the classroom.

The project exposes the students to both computer science and art history, and allows the students to study research questions related to the artists of their choice.

Psychology and Computer Science Module: Studying Patterns in the Use of Social Media

The goal of the course-based research experience in the CS-interdisciplinary psychology module is to investigate feelings, motivations, and fields of interest that are shared using Facebook status updates (FSUs). For instance, people of different age groups might choose to express different topics through Facebook. Clearly, data from other social networks (e.g., Twitter) could also be used. With Facebook, FSUs are used to broadcast personal states and experiences or to share opinions about things considered interesting or relevant. Social media is designed specifically to allow people to express themselves, therefore, using Facebook data allows students to select topics of their choice related to their own identity and interests.

During an entire semester, students collect and analyze FSUs and cross the data with demographic information of the posters. The annotators determine for each FSU the activation, length, use of quotes, and originality, as well as rank the relevance of the FSU to music, sports, religion, food and drink, art and esthetics, comedy, opinion and society, and daily life (Delogu, Franetovic, & Shamir, 2015).

After the FSUs are collected, the students propose hypotheses and test them using automatic analysis of the text. Students use the Unstructured Data Analysis Tool (UDAT) text classifier (Shamir, Diamond, & Wallin, 2016). For instance, the students can propose a hypothesis that people younger than 25 tend to write longer posts than those who are older than 25. To organize the data, the students can separate the data by the age of the poster, and apply the text analysis tool to compare the mean and standard error of the length of the posts of each group. That allows the students to perform research on social media by using computer tools and analysis.

Social Media Analysis Module Implementation

The social media analysis is done as a group project such that the entire class participates in the collection and annotation of the data. Each group of students defines their own research questions to study. For data collection, the students copy and paste the Facebook posts of their Facebook friends after asking their permission to do so. Each post is saved as a plain text file and assigned a unique file name. The students then annotate each post with characteristics of the person who wrote it, such as age, gender, level of education, and so on. The students also annotate each post by its content. The annotation can be the classification of the topic discussed in the post, such as music, sport, and daily life, as well as the emotion expressed in the post (e.g., anger, happiness). Clearly, different annotations can be made based on the research questions, but in order to allow the studying of as many research questions as possible, it is required to make numerous annotations so that students can then have sufficient variety from which to select the research questions of their interest.

The data are organized in one single Excel file so that each Facebook post is a row in the spreadsheet. The first column is the file name, and the other columns contain the annotations of the students. With a spreadsheet file, the students can use UDAT (Shamir et al., 2016) to perform text analysis. UDAT can classify and identify differences between classes of text files. For instance, the students can classify between posts about sports and posts about politics, and then use UDAT to identify differences between the two classes such as the length of words, length of sentences, different usages of punctuation, higher variety, and repetition of words. The differences between these values reflect the differences between the classes. The statistical significance of the difference in the form of a t-test score is also provided by UDAT, and the students can use simple online statistical calculators, such as GraphPad QuickCalcs[1], to deduce the statistical significance of the difference they identified.

The combination of the characteristics of the posts and the annotations provide a virtually limitless number of hypotheses that can be easily identified and tested, by students. That allows students to perform the research of their choice by combining psychology data and computer analysis.

Biology and Computer Science Module: Quantitative Analysis of *C. elegans* Microscopy Images

In the computational science and biology module, the students perform research using computer-based microscopy image analysis. In this course, the students test the effects of an environmental toxin of their choice on a model organism using image analysis. The model organism used in the module is *C. elegans*, an important and commonly used model organism that is relatively easy and inexpensive to grow and maintain, and is suitable for introductory courses (Girard et al., 2007). Working with *C. elegans* does not require expensive facilities or equipment; therefore, the proposed course module can be taught at almost any institution of higher education (Stiernagle, 1999).

---

[1] http://www.graphpad.com/quickcalcs

In addition to the possibility of analyzing the effect of a yet-untested substance, the novelty in the experiment is the image analysis, which allows quantifying subtle differences that are the result of a certain treatment. That is, while the effect of toxins or other treatments is normally measured by survival determined by counting the number of live worms, here the effect of the treatment can be measured by analyzing the microscopic images of the worm while the worm is still alive, which provides a potentially more sensitive analysis that detects the effect of the treatment before it becomes fatal. The purpose of the module is to allow students perform biology research as part of a biology lab, while using computer methods.

Computational Microscopy Image Analysis Module Implementation

In the first part of the experiment, the students expose the *C. elegans* to a substance chosen by each group of students. To provide a sufficient amount of data, the students need to collect 30 images periodically from the control and treatment groups. Each worm can only be imaged once. Since *C. elegans* adulthood occurs in 2.5 days and the life span is two to three weeks, the data acquisition part can fit in a single semester. After the images are acquired, the students separate the images of different body parts of the worms such as the corpus, the terminal bulb, the intestine, and the tail. Each image of a segmented body part must be of the same dimensionality, and different body parts cannot be mixed in the same experiment. If a group of students decides to study the terminal bulb, only images of the terminal bulb can be used in that experiment.

The separation of the regions of interest from the image is done by the students manually. The task requires a simple image editor, and numerous publicly available image editors can be used for that task. The image editor used by the students in this project was the free IrfanView (Skiljan, 2012). The advantage of IrfanView is that it also has batch-processing capabilities, so that the students can separate a larger region of interest than they need, while ensuring that it is centered on the body part of interest. Then, they can normalize the size by applying a batch process. The process can be done with any other body part to test further hypotheses.

The images of each set of worms need to be placed in a separate folder. For instance, if the experiment tests the effect of a certain dose of substance, the images of worms exposed to each dose need to be in a different folder, so that the analysis software can make the connection between the image and the dose. Then, the WNDCHRM tool is applied followed by PHYLIP, in a process similar to the automatic analysis of art history. The separation to different folders is done so that WNDCHRM can separate between the classes based on the folders they are in.

The first outcome of the analysis is the classification accuracy, or how well the image classifier can identify the dose by analyzing the image of the worm. If the classification accuracy is above mere chance accuracy, it can be considered as preliminary evidence that the machine learning system can provide useful information about the data. For instance, if there are five doses (five classes), classification accuracy of 20% would indicate that the system has no signal or that the toxin at that dose had no measurable effect, as classification accuracy of 20% can be achieved by random assignment of the samples to classes, and does not require any analysis of the data. But if the classification accuracy is higher than 20%, it provides evidence that the machine learning is capable of associating the microscopic image with the corresponding dose in accuracy higher than mere chance. Therefore, the analysis of the microscopic image is sensitive to the dose to which the worms were exposed.

A more informative part of the results is the similarity matrix, which shows the morphological similarities between worms exposed to different doses. The similarity matrix is visualized by a phylogeny using the PHYLIP package to show the similarities between the classes. These outcomes of the analysis can show the does–response effect by combining the biology experiment with computer science methodology.

Results

Participants

The questionnaire was administered to 138 students of Lawrence Technological University (43 female and 70 male).

Evaluation Method

To assess the attitudes of students attending TIDES courses, we designed a 31-item survey including questions about the following six thematic focuses: (1) Interest and Proficiency in STEM, (2) Interest and Proficiency in Computer Science, (3) General Academic Self-Efficacy (Self-Efficacy), (4) Interest and Proficiency in conducting Research (Research), (5) Concerns about Ethnicity Issues (Ethnicity), and (6) Concerns about Gender Issues (Gender). The survey also included questions about the demographic and academic background of the participants. The scaling method of the survey was a 5-point Likert scale ranging from "1" (very strong disagreement) to "5" (very strong agreement). The survey was administered twice (before and after the course) to an experimental sample of students who took TIDES courses, and to a control sample of students who took the analogous sections of these courses that did not have a TIDES component. The TIDES courses involved in the assessment were Introductory Psychology, Biology 1 Lab, World Masterpiece 1, and Biology 1.

Analysis

To analyze the survey results, a multifactorial analysis of variance was conducted. The answers to the single questions were grouped and averaged according to their thematic focus. The variables are *Gender* (M vs F), *Topic* (STEM, CS, Academic Self-efficacy, Research, Ethnicity Issues, Gender Issues), *Group Condition* (control group vs Experimental group) and *Ethnicity* (Caucasian vs

Other) as between-subjects factors, and *Treatment* (pre-course survey vs post-course survey) as a within-subject factor. Only students who completed the survey both before and after the course were included in the analysis for a total of 88 students (28 female and 60 male).

Evaluation Results

The results show a significant effect of the main factor *Topic*, $F(5, 420) = 342.74$, $p < 0.0001$. Post-hoc analysis showed that participants answered with higher scores to questions about the importance of STEM with mean of ($M = 4.17$) and academic self-efficacy ($M = 4.18$) than computer science ($M = 3.38$) and research ($M = 3.5$). Also, responses had low scores for questions concerning the presence of issues of ethnicity ($M = 1.4$) or gender ($M = 1.44$). All other main factors were not significant: *Treatment*, $F(1, 84) = 0.00865$, $p = 0.92612$; *Gender*, $F(1, 84) = 0.12875$, $p = 0.72063$; *Ethnicity*, $F(1, 84) = 0.66479$, $p = 0.41718$ and *Condition*, $F(1, 84) = 1.5070$, $p = 0.22303$. Interestingly, a significant interaction was observed between Gender and Topic, $F(5, 420) = 6.9803$, $p = 0.00000$. Post-hoc analysis shows that men ($M = 4.18$) were generally more interested in computer science than women ($M = 3.07$), ($p = 0.00012$), and that women ($M = 1.66$) were more concerned about gender issues than man ($M = 1.20$), ($p = 0.0011$). The interaction between *Topic* and *Ethnicity* was also significant, $F(5, 420) = 2.3293$, $p = 0.04185$. Post-hoc analysis showed that non-Caucasian participants ($M = 1.60$) were more concerned about ethnicity issues than Caucasians ($M = 1.18$). The post-hoc analysis showed that the interest in STEM in the control group was significantly higher than in the experimental group before treatment ($p = 0.0003$), but not after treatment ($p = 0.08$). Finally, participants after treatment were more concerned about *Gender issues* than before treatment ($p = 0.007$), but not in the control group ($p = 0.19$).

Evaluation Conclusions

The analysis indicates that STEM and academic self-efficacy were more attractive and less intimidating than computer science and research. Also, participants were not concerned about issues of gender and ethnicity. When separated by gender, the results show some gender differences; in particular, male students demonstrated a greater interest in computer science, and women were more concerned about gender issues than men. When separated by ethnicity, non-Caucasian students were more concerned about racial discrimination than Caucasians.

Concerning the influence of the TIDES courses, we found that students who attended a TIDES course increased their interest in STEM, while the control group tended to show less interest in STEM. We also found decreased academic self-efficacy in the TIDES courses. This counterintuitive result may be interpreted as a consequence of the particular set of TIDES courses and the timing of administration of surveys. TIDES classes involved a non-selected population of students who did not choose to include computer science in a non-computer science course. Computer science, even when applied to daily life contexts and taught with nonintimidating, inclusive methods, can be perceived as challenging by students that have low computer science literacy. Moreover, the post-test survey was administered in the final week of classes, which is likely to be the more stressful time of the semester. In such conditions, it is not surprising that the self-reported evaluations show a seemingly paradoxical negative influence of TIDES courses.

Discussion

Undergraduate research experience is one of the most effective proven interventions that increase student's engagement and academic performance (American Association for the Advancement of Science, 2011; PCAST, 2012). However, in the traditional form of an undergraduate research assistantship, the research experience is difficult to perform at large scales due to the limited resources that are required in order to engage and train each student.

Here, we describe research modules that can be used in freshman-level courses to expose students to research, and introduce them to basic computational science and data analysis. The modules are designed to provide students with ownership of their research by allowing them to define their own hypotheses. By design, the research modules allow for different scientific questions by different students, yet with a similar methodology so that the research activity can support the participation of multiple students and can be performed in the classroom. The ability to scale the research projects was a key component in the success of the implementation, allowing each student to choose their own hypothesis.

The research allows the student to work on topics of their interest, and express their identity and culture through computing. For instance, the art history module allows students to select the artists or artistic styles of their interest, and since there is a strong link between art and culture, students can select those artists and artistic styles that represent their cultural background.

The culturally responsive approach also makes it easier for the instructor to include culturally sensitive content in the courses. With this approach, the instructor is not required to actively lead the students to work on a topic related to their culture, a task that might intimidate some instructors. Our approach provides the student with the option to express themselves through their projects, without the explicit direction of the instructor.

One of the important lessons from the TIDES' experience is that to reach a true change in inclusion requires more than implementing best practices. The change needs to come with a sense of a mission – a movement that can draw members and lead to a true change in the institutional culture.

Conclusion

Introductory humanities, social science, or natural science courses are part of the core curriculum in many academic institutions. We transformed introductory core-curriculum courses into courses that involve discovery-driven computational science activities, with the purpose of exposing non-CS students to computing. The modules were designed for students with no prior knowledge of computer science, and involve the analysis of data using advanced computational tools to study different hypotheses, potentially leading to scientific discoveries.

This new form of computer science is designed to start a change in computer science education. That change aims to reduce the technical or "geeky" materials, and add more content that appeals to those students who would not normally choose computer science as their major.

We used research experience as a proven high-impact practice, but primarily as an intervention through which the students can express their identity, culture, or ethnicity. The modules were also designed in a culturally responsive manner, to allow students to express their identity, culture, and ethnicity through computing. By taking a responsive approach, we created an environment where it is easier for the teacher to use culturally sensitive content in the course.

The Last Word

Driven by the government's top policy-makers and the corporate sector, current trends in higher education largely focus on attracting more students to STEM education (PCAST, 2012). The attempts to increase the number of STEM majors often comes at the expense of disciplines such as the social sciences and the humanities. The project described in this chapter is one of many such attempts to shift students from social science and the humanities into computer science. However, the STEM-rush that we are practicing and its impact on the future of our society should be reviewed carefully. While a STEM-led society will have clear advantages in terms of economy and technological development, weakening the social sciences and humanities can have its own implications on our culture and structure of our future society.

That STEM-oriented mindset also impacts the motivation for adopting inclusive practices. The stated motivation for inclusion in computer science or STEM is often associated with economic implications, efficient use of the pool of talent, or strengthening the scientific community. In other words, the arguments made by inclusion advocates are often about how inclusion can help the "establishment." Arguments related to social justice, opportunities for all, and shaping a healthy society and culture are often neglected or considered peripheral. It is our hope that the association of technology with the social sciences or the humanities will gradually lead to a new generation of professionals and scientists, who can address and understand all angles of inclusion in STEM.

TIDES Resources

A detailed description and step-by-step protocols of the modules described in this chapter are available at http://vfacstaff.ltu.edu/lshamir/downloads/CRE.

The WNDCHRM software and source codes are available at: http://vfacstaff.ltu.edu/lshamir/downloads/ImageClassifier.

The UDAT software and source codes are available at: http://vfacstaff.ltu.edu/lshamir/downloads/udat.

Several videos have been prepared by George Terrell, a student who took two of the CRE courses in his freshman year, and then prepared videos about the students taking these courses in the following semesters. These videos summarize the modules, and can be viewed at: https://www.ltu.edu/blogs/cre/2017/06/21/cre-student-makes-videos-of-cre-courses.

References

American Association for the Advancement of Science. (2011). *Vision and change in undergraduate biology education: A call to action*. Retrieved from http://visionandchange.org/files/2011/03/Revised-Vision-and-Change-Final-Report.pdf

Auchincloss, L. C., Laursen, S. L., Branchaw, J. L., Eagan, K., Graham, M., Hanauer, D. I. ... Dolan, E. L. (2014). Assessment of course-based undergraduate research experiences: A meeting report. *CBE-Life Sciences Education*, *13*(1), 29–40.

Braxton, J. M., Hirschy, A. S., & McClendon, S. A. (2004). *Understanding and reducing college student departure: ASHE-ERIC Higher Education Report* (Vol. 30, No. 3). Hobokan, NJ: Wiley Periodicals, Inc.

Camp, T. (2001). Women in computer sciences: Reversing the trend. *Syllabus Magazine*, 24–26.

Clark, I. E., Romero-Calderon, R., Olson, J. M., Jaworski, L., Lopatto, D., & Banerjee, U. (2009). "Decon-structing" scientific research: A practical and scalable pedagogical tool to provide evidence-based science instruction. *PLoS Biology*, *7*(12).

Colabroy, K. L. (2011). A writing-intensive, methods-based laboratory course for undergraduates. *Biochemistry and Molecular Biology Education*, *39*(3), 196–203.

Delogu, F., Franetovic, M., & Shamir, L. (2015). Keep me posted! Human and machine learning analysis of Facebook updates. *Proceedings of the 8th international conference on mobile multimedia communications* (pp. 141–144). May 25–27, 2015, Chengdu, China.

Dolog, P., Thomsen, L. L., & Thomsen, B. (2016). Assessing problem-based learning in a software engineering curriculum using blooms taxonomy and the IEEE software engineering body of knowledge. *ACM Transactions on Computing Education*, *16*(3), Article No. 9.

Freeman, S., Eddy, S. L., McDonough, M., Smith, M. K., Okoroafor, N., Jordt, H., & Wenderoth, M. P. (2014). Active learning increases student performance in science, engineering, and mathematics. *Proceedings of the National Academy of Sciences*, *111*(23), 8410–8415.

Gestwicki, P., & McNely, B. (2016). Interdisciplinary projects in the academic studio. *ACM Transactions on Computing Education*, *16*(2), 8.

Girard, L. R., Fiedler, T. J., Harris, T. W., Carvalho, F., Antoshechkin, I., Han, M. ... Chalfie, M. (2007). Wormbook: The online review of Caenorhabditis elegans biology. *Nucleic Acids Research*, *35*(Suppl. 1), D472–D475.

Hippel, W. V., Lerner, J. S., Gregerman, S. R., Nagda, B. A., & Jonides, J. (1998). Undergraduate studentfaculty research partnerships affect student retention. *The Review of Higher Education, 22*(1), 55–72.

Hoskins, S. G., Lopatto, D., & Stevens, L. M. (2011). The create approach to primary literature shifts undergraduates self-assessed ability to read and analyze journal articles, attitudes about science, and epistemological beliefs. *CBE-Life Sciences Education, 10*(4), 368–378.

Kinkel, D. H., & Henke, S. E. (2006). Impact of undergraduate research on academic performance, educational planning, and career development. *Journal of Natural Resources & Life Sciences Education, 35*(1), 194–201.

Krause, J., Polycarpou, I., & Hellman, K. (2012). Exploring formal learning groups and their impact on recruitment of women in undergraduate CS. In *Proceedings of the 43rd ACM Technical Symposium on Computer Science Education* (pp. 179–184). New York, NY: ACM.

PHYLIP [Phylogenetic inference computer software package]. (1993). Retrieved from http://evolution.genetics.washington.edu/phylip.html

President's Council on Advisors on Science and Technology. (2012). *Report to the president - engage to excel: Producing one million additional college graduates with degrees in science, technology, engineering, and mathematics.* Retrieved from US Department of Education website: http://files.eric.ed.gov/fulltext/ED541511.pdf

Ramirez, M., McNicholas, J., Gilbert, B., Saez, J., & Siniawski, M. (2015). Creative funding strategies for undergraduate research at a primarily undergraduate liberal arts institution. *CUR QUARTERLY, 36*(2), 5–8.

Schmolitzky, A., & Schummer, T. (2008). Patterns for supervising thesis projects. In T. Schümmer & A. Kelly (Eds.), *Proceedings of the 13th European Conference on Pattern Languages of Programs (EuroPLoP 2008)*. New York, NY: ACM.

Seymour, E., Hunter, A.-B., Laursen, S. L., & DeAntoni, T. (2004). Establishing the benefits of research experiences for undergraduates in the sciences: First findings from a three-year study. *Science Education, 88*(4), 493–534.

Shamir, L. (2012). Computer analysis reveals similarities between the artistic styles of van Gogh and Pollock. *Leonardo, 45*(2), 149–154.

Shamir, L. (2015). What makes a Pollock Pollock: A machine vision approach. *International Journal of Arts and Technology, 8*(1), 1–10.

Shamir, L., Diamond, D., & Wallin, J. (2016). Leveraging pattern recognition consistency estimation for crowdsourcing data analysis. *IEEE Transactions on Human-Machine Systems, 46*(3), 474–480.

Shamir, L., Macura, T., Orlov, N., Eckley, D. M., & Goldberg, I. G. (2010). Impressionism, expressionism, surrealism: Automated recognition of painters and schools of art. *ACM Transactions on Applied Perception, 7*(2), 8.

Shamir, L., Nissel, J., & Winner, E. (2016). Distinguishing between abstract art by artists vs. children and animals: Comparison between human and machine perception. *ACM Transactions on Applied Perception, 13*(3), 17.

Shamir, L., Orlov, N., Eckley, D. M., Macura, T., Johnston, J., & Goldberg, I. G. (2008). Wndchrm – An open source utility for biological image analysis. *Source Code for Biology and Medicine, 3*(1), 13.

Shamir, L., & Tarakhovsky, J. A. (2012). Computer analysis of art. *ACM Journal on Computing and Cultural Heritage, 5*(2), 7.

Skiljan, I. (2012). Irfanview [Graphic computer software]. Retrieved from https://www.irfanview.com/

Stiernagle, T. (1999). Maintenance of c. elegans. *C. elegans*, *2*, 51–67.

Vivian, R., Falkner, K., Falkner, N., & Tarmazdi, H. (2016). A method to analyze computer science students teamwork in online collaborative learning environments. *ACM Transactions on Computing Education*, *16*(2), 7.

Willbur, J. F., Vail, J. D., Mitchell, L. N., Jakeman, D. L., & Timmons, S. C. (2016). Expression, purification, and characterization of a carbohydrate-active enzyme: A research-inspired methods optimization experiment for the biochemistry laboratory. *Biochemistry and Molecular Biology Education*, *44*(1), 75–85.

Zweben, S. (2012). *Computing degree and enrollment trends*. Retrieved from Computing Research Association website: http://archive2.cra.org/uploads/documents/resources/taulbee/CRATaulbeeReport-StudentEnrollment-07-08.pdf

Chapter 9

A Journey of Discovery

Alla Webb, Raymond Gonzales and Monica Parrish Trent

Reflection

Before we began our TIDES journey, our understanding of culturally responsive teaching (CRT) was very limited. More specifically, we were not sure how CRT could contribute to improving the success and retention of underrepresented student populations in Computer Science and other STEM and non-STEM disciplines. At the same time, we harbored several assumptions about this approach. Like many, we thought CRT mainly involved connecting course content to our students' ethnic backgrounds. We also assumed that implementing CRT would simply be a matter of adding or revising specific exercises, activities, and modules to our existing courses to reflect cultural content. Coming from a highly diverse community college, we were also under the naïve presumption that we probably did not have as much to learn about cultural responsiveness as our TIDES colleagues from less diverse institutions. In other words, despite our limited understanding of CRT, we did not think it would be a difficult concept to grasp and put into practice. However, we have learned that CRT is a multilayered concept that requires time, effort, and experience to understand and appreciate.

Breakthroughs

Some of our breakthroughs have been those moments and developments that have helped us to understand CRT's various layers. One such breakthrough came during early discussions with an in-house "CRT Team" of faculty we formed to explore what CRT might mean at our highly diverse two-year institution. They were well versed in the field and pointed out that a student's culture involves much more than her or his ethnicity or race. It is, in fact, comprised of all those factors that may impact one's learning – such as age, interests, work and family situations, and previous learning experiences. It was exciting in the sense that it helped us to better understand the potential obstacles and opportunities impacting our students' success. Even more, it implied new possibilities in regard to interventions that could utilize information about these "cultural factors" to better support our students. Our next challenge was to somehow clearly convey this idea of culture and our understanding of CRT to faculty. Not surprisingly, feedback from faculty who attended our early workshops revealed confusion. For example, some participants asked how CRT was different from "good teaching practices." Conveying CRT in a conceptually clear way to faculty has been and continues to be both an ongoing imperative and a challenge for us.

The next breakthrough was our conceptualization of CRT as a three-step process: (1) discovering our students' "cultural factors," such as their work schedules and previous learning experiences; (2) adjusting one's teaching based on what we learn in the discovery stage; and (3) ongoing assessment of these adjustments and students' learning, which leads to potential additional adjustments in a recursive process. Presenting CRT as a process has helped us to convey this approach as much more than just a matter of going through a checklist of prescribed activities or adopting a particular "best practice."

It seems, however, that each breakthrough in our understanding of CRT has been followed by even more new realizations about CRT's many layers. At our annual TIDES Institutes, for example, we learned through various shared experiences that cultural sensitivity and responsiveness necessarily requires educators to struggle with the obstacles to inclusiveness within themselves. These obstacles often stem from different types of ignorance. For example, one TIDES Summer Institute speaker increased our awareness of different types of privilege one may enjoy by virtue of accidental factors such as race, gender, or zip code. Ignorance of such privilege prevents us from recognizing the full spectrum of inequity experienced by underrepresented populations in society, and in education, specifically. This, and other TIDES experiences, confirmed that we cannot truly practice CRT unless we are aware of our own unconscious biases, positions of privilege, and roles in perpetuating inequity in higher education. We also learned that the process of becoming self-aware of these obstacles to inclusiveness is uncomfortable, by nature. If it had not been for these TIDES experiences, we would have continued to see CRT as mostly a process or set of activities to follow, divorced from any significant personal introspection.

Institutional Context

Montgomery College (MC), situated in the suburbs of Washington, DC, has one of the largest and most diverse student populations among all community colleges in the country. Founded in 1946, its three campuses are located in Montgomery County, Maryland, a majority—minority county with significant international populations. Montgomery County is ranked fourth out of the 10 most diverse US counties, with 40% of its population speaking 138 languages in their households. At MC, over 150 nationalities are represented among its 23,000 credit students. Most MC students lead complex lives. As community college students, they balance demanding work schedules, family obligations, personal and cultural identities, and responsibilities associated with their educational aspirations.

While our student population reflects the county's demographics, and diversity has long been a point of pride for the institution, in 2013, the Closing the Achievement Gap Task Force (CAGTF) submitted its final report and recommendations to the college community. Recommendations from the CAGTF to "develop special college-wide programs to specifically address the academic success, retention, and completion of African American and Latino students" and to "enhance the cultural competence of faculty to welcome students of diverse ethnic backgrounds," were foundational to our TIDES efforts. Grounded in evidence that the college's Black and Latinx students were not achieving at the same rates as their White and Asian counterparts, these recommendations challenged the institution to do more to achieve equitable outcomes for all students.

In addition to the college's CAGTF efforts, Theme I: Educational Excellence of the MC 2020 Strategic Plan, states, "Students of all races and ethnicities [will] succeed at the same high rate." Moreover, "students [will be] guided and mentored with personal attention appropriate to their academic needs." Thus, the TIDES project was an opportunity for Montgomery College to not only increase the representation of women and minorities in the college's computer science courses, but also to be intentional in its efforts to support and professionally develop faculty who must engage a very diverse student population. Doing so required advocacy from the administration in the form of financial assistance, increased communication about the importance of this work, and collaboration with internal and external institutional partners.

Introduction/Background and Significance

We made a conscious decision to leverage MC's in-house experts to guide the development of our project's CRT conceptual framework, including our definitions of culture, CRT, and our Discover–Adjust–Assess process. Our "CRT team" consisted of faculty from MC's English Language for Academic Purposes Program (MC's academic English as a Second Language program). We elected to work with faculty from this program because: (1) they are trained in multicultural education, intercultural communication, and other fields relevant to CRT; and (2) they are familiar with the college context in which our CRT interventions would occur. The CRT Team provided significant assistance to the TIDES project team because they drew from the works of major scholars in CRT and related fields, such as Dr. Geneva Gay, Dr. Zaretta Hammond, and Dr. Edward Hall. The collaboration with the CRT Team was powerful because it facilitated discussions about how to best apply CRT to MC's context. This collaboration also helped to produce our project's theoretical framework consisting of our definitions of culture, CRT, and our Discover–Adjust–Assess process.

In the early stages of the project, the team formulated an operational definition of CRT: "Utilize information about our students' backgrounds and learning to tailor instruction in ways that increase their opportunities for success." We felt this definition was appropriate for our project in several ways. First, we hoped its simplicity would make it more accessible. Second, its explicit goal of student success was highly relevant to both the faculty and the college administration.

Scholarly Influence

We relied on the work of Gay (2010), including her concept of culture. According to Gay (2010),

> Culture, like any other social or biological organism, is multidimensional and continually changing. As manifested in expressive behaviors, culture is influenced by a wide variety of factors, including time, setting, age, economics and social circumstances (p. 10).

Gay's (2010) point that culture is multidimensional confirmed our view that our students' cultures extend well beyond their ethnicity, with which culture is often equated. Her idea that culture is constantly changing reflected our belief that our students' cultures, including their self-identities and "cultural factors," such as work-family situations and interests, are always changing. This viewpoint prompted us to emphasize in our professional development events that CRT must be a continual process throughout the entire semester. Seeing CRT in this way makes it more likely that our teaching takes into account possible changes in students' situations.

Hall's (1976) "cultural iceberg" model has helped us to communicate to faculty the "deeper" or "hidden" aspects of culture. These include communication styles and attitudes towards authority, as opposed to traditional "surface" aspects such as celebrations, religion, and food. We emphasize that being aware of these deep cultural influences can help faculty avoid misinterpreting certain behaviors, which can have potentially damaging effects on the teacher−student relationship, a critical part of student learning and success.

Hammond's (2015) "Components of Academic Mindset" model in her book, *Culturally Responsive Teaching and the Brain*, helped us to show faculty that CRT, again, is more than just a set of activities to bring to the classroom. For example, one component involves helping students feel that: (1) they belong to the academic community; (2) they can succeed; (3) their efforts lead to growth and competence; and (4) the work they are doing is valuable (Hammond, 2015, p. 109).

Implementation/Methodology

At an early point in our project, we had come to realize that infusing CRT across the institution through a broad faculty professional development effort, rather than one solely focused on computer science faculty, was the most effective way to increase the impact and sustainability of our project. In our early presentations and workshops, our goals were to help faculty see the connection between CRT and their daily teaching, and to make CRT as accessible as possible to faculty. To further facilitate the implementation of CRT, we wanted to provide faculty with a variety of resources. These included tools to help them discover their students and make adjustments to their teaching. Our actual implementation revealed both the promise and challenges of applying a Discover–Assess–Adjust process to one's teaching.

Making CRT Relevant

To connect CRT to everyday teaching, we asked our workshop participants to list both their main teaching challenges and the major obstacles to their students' learning. Typical responses included "lack of participation in class and group discussions" and "not finishing projects on time." We then asked our participants for culturally "unresponsive" ways to interpret and react to these challenges. For example, one "traditional interpretation" of students not participating in class and group discussions is that it demonstrates a lack of interest in the subject or a lack of preparation on the students' part. Next, we asked the participants to offer possible underlying reasons for these challenges. In the scenario mentioned earlier, for example, faculty offered alternative reasons such as not having the prerequisite knowledge needed to participate or students coming from a culture in which asking questions of the professor is considered disrespectful. We then connected this activity of identifying the possible underlying causes of these challenges to CRT, which involves leaving one's preconceptions at the door and taking the time to discover the actual obstacles to our students' learning.

In subsequent workshops, we added an activity that asked participants to think of ways in which they had already dealt with these challenges or possible new adjustments they could make to address them. Our goal was to help faculty see how CRT could help them in their courses. In addition, we wanted them to see that many were already employing cultural responsiveness without necessarily identifying it as such. However, we realized in conducting this activity that participants were not exploring the full range of possible culturally responsive adjustments they could make to navigate these challenges. As a result, we began providing participants with a list of "unofficial CRT principles" that we had inferred from the literature and discussions with our CRT team (a complete list of these principles can be found on the MC TIDES website: http://cms.montgomerycollege.edu/mctides/). These included "create a comfortable learning environment" and "empower students." This step helped participants to reflect more on their own teaching and to generate more ideas. The ideas that they provided expanded our own appreciation of the potential of CRT to help students succeed.

As we made progress in helping faculty see the relevance of CRT, early post-workshop feedback revealed that questions persisted about the nature of CRT itself. This helped us to realize that we needed to make CRT even more accessible to faculty.

Making CRT Accessible

As we were thinking about how to make CRT more accessible, we realized that our definition of CRT, as well as our expanded notion of culture, pointed to a process. This realization resulted in the creation of a diagram depicting a three-part process, "Discover–Adjust–Assess," depicted in Figure 1.

As Figure 1 indicates, faculty first discover their students. More specifically, professors identify students' "cultural factors," such as work schedules, interests, and previous learning experiences, which may have a significant impact on their ability to persist and succeed in their studies. These factors represent challenges to and/or potential assets to facilitate learning. For example, students' interests can be connected to course content to increase motivation. On the other hand, their work schedules can be considered a challenge, if, like many MC students, they work 20–40 or more hours per week. Sometimes, one factor can be both a challenge and an asset. For instance, the challenge of managing busy work schedules, family responsibilities, and school could be turned into an asset by using student information regarding these variables as content for a coding assignment in a computer science course.

Then, based on this information, faculty make changes to their teaching in the "Adjust" stage to guide their students to success in achieving the course outcomes. These adjustments can take many forms from minor "tweaking," such as slowing down the pace of one's lessons about challenging material, to more significant interventions like employing a partial or fully flipped classroom approach. Most importantly, the "Discover" stage of the process is what determines the adjustment. In other words, there is no "one size fits all" approach as each class of students has its own "cultural makeup" that determines which adjustments to make.

Finally, faculty constantly evaluate their students' learning and the effectiveness of their adjustments throughout the semester in the "Assess" stage. This

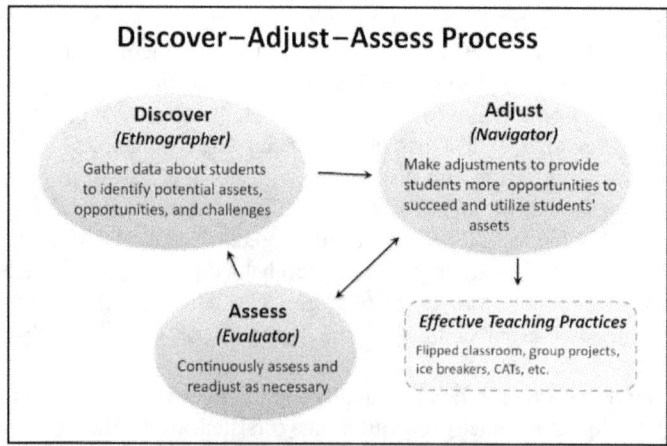

Figure 1: MC TIDES CRT "Discover–Adjust–Assess" Process.

process is meant to be cyclical and iterative, reflecting the reality that our students' "cultures" (i.e., "cultural factors") and their understanding of various concepts are constantly changing.

To further increase the accessibility of CRT to faculty, we have used analogies in the process and in our presentations. As shown in the diagram, professors play the role of "ethnographer" in the "Discovery" stage, objectively observing and gathering information about their students. Then, in the "Adjust" stage, they put on the "navigator's" hat as they make adjustments to their teaching based on what they have discovered about their students in the previous stage. In the final stage, they act as "evaluators" who constantly measure their students' learning and the impact of their adjustments in the "Assess" stage.

CRT Application: Providing Resources

Understanding and implementing CRT are two very different things. In addition, our faculty have very busy schedules. Therefore, we wanted to provide as much assistance as possible to help them put the Discover–Assess–Adjust process into practice. This involved gathering tangible resources as well as creating multiple mechanisms for accessing and delivering them. These resources and mechanisms also allowed faculty outside of the MC TIDES project to implement CRT.

Culturally Responsive Tools for the "Discovery" Stage. To help the Computer Science faculty discover their students, we revised an AAC&U/Project Kaleidoscope survey designed to explore students' perceptions of STEM fields, including their interest levels and sense of self-efficacy. The revised survey (see Appendix A, "Start of Semester Survey") was more appropriate for our community college context. It was also used as a "pre/post" measure of the impact of applying the Discovery–Adjust–Assess process.

We also added several items to the demographic information part of the survey instrument to create a "Getting to Know You" survey with questions more targeted to our student population (the complete survey can be found on the MC TIDES website: http://cms.montgomerycollege.edu/mctides/). For instance, we asked students how many hours they work per week. Additionally, we added several open-ended questions. For example, "What can I [the professor] do to make this class an enjoyable learning experience for you?" Questions like these could give faculty ideas at the very start of the semester about what types of adjustments they could make to their teaching.

Further, we provided faculty with a "Midterm" survey for students consisting of open-ended questions. For example, "What is preventing you from performing better in this course?" We hoped that results from this survey would provide "critical intelligence" about student learning that could inform timely adjustments to one's teaching.

Gathering Ideas for "Adjust" Stage. As with the professional development component of the project, we have relied heavily on our faculty in the implementation stage. For example, one of our first steps was to ask Computer Science and other

STEM faculty to provide us with the various activities and strategies they were already using to achieve their course objectives. Our thinking behind this approach included many levels. First, these resources would serve as a "toolkit" of teaching ideas for all faculty to use. In addition, we believed that our diverse and experienced faculty were the best source of these resources. They were already highly experienced in teaching our diverse student population. Though they may not have labeled it as such, they were already engaging in CRT in various ways.

Disseminating Resources to Facilitate CRT Implementation. To make the surveys, activities, and classroom assessment techniques (CATs) accessible to both faculty involved in the implementation and college-wide, we created several resources for faculty.

- **The "Teaching Toolkit"**: It is an electronic database containing activities, strategies, and other resources created by faculty and instructional designers in our college's professional development division, E-learning, Innovation, and Teaching (ELITE).
- **The Hub: A Virtual Space for Teaching Resources by MC Faculty**: The Teaching Toolkit is housed on "The Hub" (http://mcblogs.montgomerycollege.edu/thehub/). "The Hub" itself arose out of a joint MC TIDES and ELITE collaborative effort. ELITE's support for MC's TIDES project has been critical to its success and sustainability.
- **Teaching Tips of the Month from the MC Community**: It, also supported by ELITE, is a monthly e-newsletter sent to the entire college community showcasing faculty teaching tips, strategies, and resources. The full collection of these "Tips" is also housed on "The Hub."

Implementation Pluses

Post-implementation faculty interviews revealed both the challenges and promise of the Discover–Adjust–Assess approach to CRT. Many professors were able to make meaningful adjustments to their teaching based on their students' survey data. For example, two professors tailored their content based on information about their students' majors. Other professors noticed that significant numbers of their students were working 20 or more hours per week, leading them to change office hour times and to incorporate advising focused on time management. It is also important to note that even when faculty did not seem to grasp our conceptualization of CRT, they were experimenting with strategies that could still be described as culturally responsive. One example was a professor who held weekly meetings with students to discover what they were finding challenging in their course. There are, after all, multiple ways to apply CRT. Our goal is to promote its intentional and systematic use.

Implementation Deltas

At the same time, a significant number of professors did not have enough time to sift through the survey data or had trouble identifying adjustments based on these data. Our future goals include finding ways to make these surveys more practical tools to discover one's students, perhaps through further streamlining, and to help faculty connect students' cultural factors to teaching adjustments. We also noticed in our post-implementation surveys that a few professors still either did not fully understand the concept of CRT or did not see its value. Though somewhat disappointed by this, we also realized that there are many factors that determine whether a particular approach or methodology will be understood and adopted by faculty.

Summary

We believe that the Discover–Adjust–Assess process implementation support structure that we have created with the help of ELITE is a solid foundation for the sustainable practice of CRT at MC. For any approach to take hold, however, it requires persistent efforts over the long term. Therefore, we will continue to reflect on how to refine and best promote CRT so that it will be used and adopted by as many faculty as possible.

Results

Our main implementation goals were to increase faculty capacity and confidence to employ CRT in their teaching and, through this, to increase the enrollment and performance of women and minorities in computer science courses. The broadening of the project's initial limited scope in regards to professional development allowed us to reach many more faculty than originally planned. Through our professional development activities at the department, area, and college-wide levels, we have "touched" over 300 MC faculty and staff over the last 4 years. In addition, we have presented and conducted workshops on CRT to over 260 attendees at various conferences outside MC. These numbers do not include the additional faculty and staff we are reaching through the "Teaching Tips of the Month" publications, the "Teaching Toolkit," "The Hub," and the CRT Video Series that was also created with the help of ELITE. These resources will also help to ensure the sustainability of our professional development efforts over the long term.

Impact on Faculty

We are seeing an impact with "spinoff" professional development events. For example, a recent ELITE Faculty Showcase (December 2017) was organized around the theme of CRT. At this event, several of the faculty presenters referred to aspects of the MC TIDES project including the "Teaching Toolkit" and definition of CRT.

In addition, we were pleased to see the positive survey and interview feedback from faculty in regards to their use of CRT in their classes. In answering the question, "Has the Discover–Adjust–Assess process changed (1) the way you teach? (2) the way you view your students?", sample responses included, "It has helped me to step back more and see where we are going" and "It made me a better teacher [...] more empathetic [...] [able to] relate more to students [...]" One professor indicated that she now has a greater sensitivity to students' situations and is willing to be more flexible in her teaching. These are precisely the types of responses we would hope to see if professors utilized the Discover–Adjust–Assess process in their classes. They also reflect a shift in teaching mindset that we had hoped to see, a mindset characterized by a greater awareness of and sensitivity to students' "cultural factors." This also includes adaptiveness in regard to adjusting one's teaching based on knowledge of these factors.

Impact on Students

We were also happy to see improvements in several measurements directly related to our project's impact on students. One of these was an increase in the number of female and underrepresented minority students (African Americans and Hispanics) majoring in Computer Science. Figure 2 shows an increase from 2014 to 2017 for each group. In addition, we hoped that our project's CRT application would have a positive effect on student success in Computer Science I (CMSC 203). Figure 3 shows notable increases in success, as measured in the number of students receiving grades of A, B, or C, for the same groups from 2014 to 2017 in this course, especially for African American and Hispanic students.

We also saw statistically significant increases in several pre- and post-Likert survey responses focused on general student perceptions of Computer Science and other STEM courses (see a complete survey with scale in Appendix A). The following results (Figure 4) are for matched students and not for overall results.

We were particularly pleased with these last two results as they can be seen as measures of a professor's caring for her or his students. Caring is a central aspect of CRT and something that we would expect to see if our CRT process was

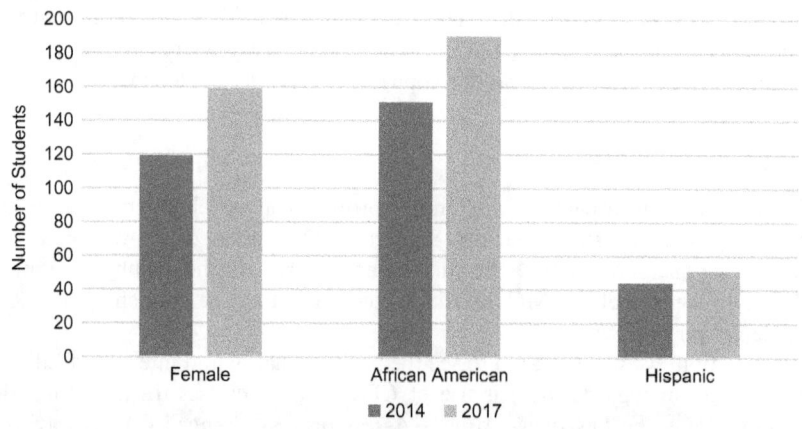

Figure 2: Students Majoring in Computer Science.

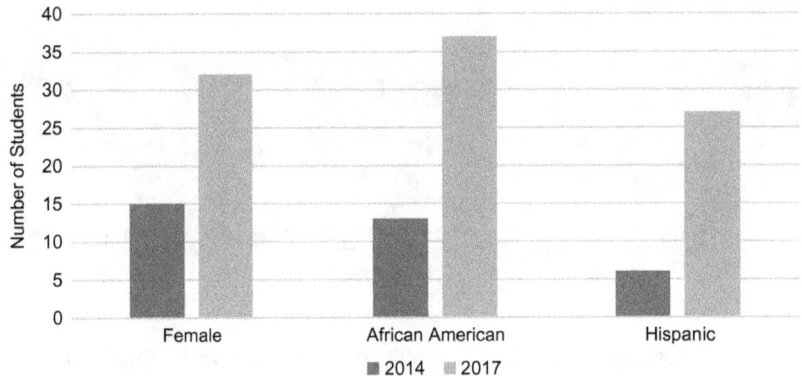

Figure 3: Student Success in CMSC 203 "Computer Science I" (Completion with Grades A, B, or C).

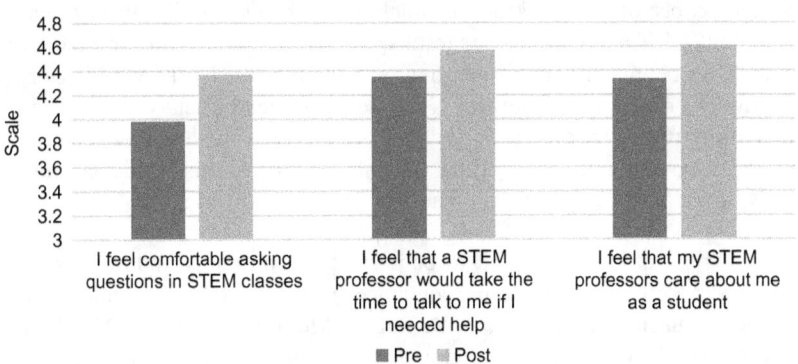

Figure 4: Student Perceptions of Computer Science and STEM Courses (Spring 2017 Semester).

being implemented by faculty. Furthermore, these results may also partly explain the increases in computer science majors.

Finally, we saw statistically significant increases in measures related to student's self-efficacy (Figure 5). If, through the use of CRT, professors are more caring, attuned to their students' learning, and adaptive in their teaching, the following results would actually be expected.

All results shown in the graphs above are from data gathered by our project's internal evaluator, Dr Brian Ault, from the Office of Institutional Research and Effectiveness (OIRE) at Montgomery College. He wrote in the 2017 Annual Report, "In sum, across time, students are reflecting greater confidence and increased capabilities by the end of each term. These redesigned classes are having the intended effects."

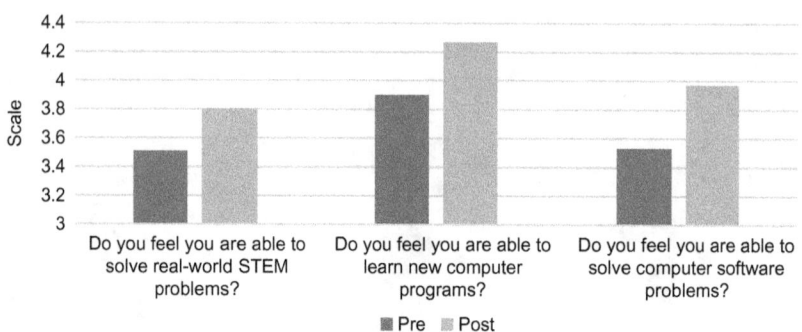

Figure 5: Measures of Student Self-efficacy in Computer Science and STEM Courses (Spring 2017 Semester).

Discussion

The significance of our work lies as much in what our TIDES journey revealed to us about CRT as in any of our results. We learned that trying to operationalize CRT to be effective in a "real-life" setting involves hard work. Because of its complex, multilayered nature, CRT does not lend itself well to a simple explanation and cannot be packaged as a step-by-step methodology. Because it requires discovering and navigating the cultures of not only students, but also faculty, great patience is needed. The journey was frustrating and humbling at times.

In this regard, it is important to be part of a community and/or have a network of support. The support and guidance from the TIDES community, especially from our institutional coach, Dr Patrice McDermott, and TIDES director, Dr Kelly Mack, was critical to helping us get through challenging periods. In addition, there must be significant institutional support. From the beginning, the TIDES effort at MC was blessed with wide-ranging support from various quarters. In many of our workshops, for example, we teamed up with faculty involved in other STEM student success initiatives. We were also able to bring our CRT workshops and presentations at MC directly to large groups of faculty and administrators because of deans, provosts, and senior vice presidents who granted us significant portions of their division and leadership meetings throughout the duration of the project. We understand that this level of administrative support is not always a given. We attributed this support mainly to the college's focus on student success, particularly for underrepresented students, as expressed in its MC 2020 Strategic Plan and Closing the Achievement Gap Task Force documents. Finally, as previously noted, ELITE has and will continue to play a critical role in the success and sustainability of the TIDES effort, in facilitating not only professional development events but also direct support for the "Toolkit," "The Hub," and the "Teaching Tips of the Month" publication.

Finally, we believe our project demonstrated that CRT can become a part of the student success culture at a diverse community college. A clear conceptual framework, faculty involvement, and mechanisms to gather and store CRT resources can help faculty see CRT as a "real" tool to improve student outcomes. Most importantly, when CRT is applied, students feel better about their learning experience and most faculty feel better about their teaching.

Conclusion

Our TIDES project began with both a limited focus and understanding of CRT. As we learned more about CRT during our TIDES journey, we saw a greater potential to expand the scope of the project by broadening the professional development component to include faculty college-wide and beyond. This expanded scope fittingly addressed new professional development-related recommendations identified by the college's Closing the Achievement Gap Task Force, namely to "enhance the cultural competence of faculty to welcome students of diverse ethnic backgrounds" (Montgomery College, 2013, p. 5).

From the beginning, we felt strongly that it was important to draw on our own faculty's existing knowledge and expertise as a starting point. We gathered data from our professors, including existing teaching activities and perceived teaching challenges. Also, the early discussions of the in-house CRT team resulted in the formulation of an operational definition of CRT and the Discover–Adjust–Assess process. These early "foundations" have been and continue to be refined and expanded. For example, we continue to gather teaching activities from faculty to add to the Teaching Toolkit and feature in our Teaching Tips of the Month Newsletter. We also continue to refine the Discovery–Adjust–Assess process depicted in Figure 1 to reflect new insights about CRT.

During our TIDES journey, we also discovered that trying to achieve cultural responsiveness can be quite humbling. As mentioned earlier, we learned at our TIDES summer institutes that CRT involves a realization of our own shortcomings, including our implicit biases. We realized during our project that this critical component of CRT was missing from our process. As a result, we have started and will continue to incorporate aspects of this vital dimension of CRT into our professional development events. Another realization through surveys and interviews is that despite our best efforts, CRT remains a vague or unimportant concept to at least some faculty who have participated in our workshops or even been directly involved in the implementation. Given our understanding of cultural responsiveness as a continuous process, we are now more likely to persist in tackling such challenges.

The Last Word

If it had not been for our TIDES journey, we would never have realized the great potential of cultural responsiveness. This journey has helped us to see its capacity to positively impact students' outcomes and faculty's view of teaching. More importantly, through its process of discovery and adjustment, it points the way to greater justice and equity, not just in higher education but also in society as a whole. Indeed, our realization of its applicability to multiple disciplines and contexts is why we did not focus exclusively on computer science courses in this chapter.

TIDES Resources

The following are resources mentioned in this chapter that was created to help faculty apply CRT in their courses.

- Montgomery College TIDES project: http://cms.montgomerycollege.edu/mctides/
- The HUB: http://mcblogs.montgomerycollege.edu/thehub/
- The following MC TIDES resources are located on The HUB and mctides website:
  - The Teaching Tip of the Month Newsletter.
  - The Teaching Toolkit.

The following are suggested resources we have found helpful throughout the work of the project.

- Angelo, T., Thomas, A., & Cross, K. P. (1993). *Classroom assessment techniques: A handbook for college teachers* (2nd ed.). San Francisco, CA: Jossey Bass.
- Booth, S. (2001). Learning computer science and engineering in context. *Computer Science Engineering, 11*(3), 169–188.
- Brown-Jeffy, S., & Cooper, J. E. Cooper. (2011). Toward a conceptual framework of culturally relevant pedagogy: An overview of the conceptual and theoretical literature. *Teacher Education Quarterly, 38*(1), 65–84.
- Frank, J. (2013). Raising cultural awareness in the English language classroom. *English Teaching Forum, 51*(4), 2–11.
- Gay, G. (1994). *A synthesis of scholarship in multicultural education.* Oak Brook, IL: North Central Regional Educational Lab.
- Ladson-Billings, G. (1995). Toward a theory of culturally relevant pedagogy. *American Educational Research Journal, 32*(3), 465–491.
- Leonard, J. (2008). *Culturally specific pedagogy in the mathematics classroom: Strategies for teachers and students.* New York, NY: Routledge.
- Milner, H. R. (2011). Culturally relevant pedagogy in a diverse urban classroom. *Urban Review, 43*(1), 66–89.
- CAST (2018). *Universal design for learning guidelines.* Retrieved from http://udlguidelines.cast.org
- Nieto, S. (2009). *The light in their eyes: Creating multicultural learning communities* (10th Anniversary Ed.). New York, NY: Teachers College Press.
- Shaw, P. A., & Bailey, K.M. (1990). Cultural differences in academic settings. In R. C. Scarcella, E. S. Andersen, & S. D. Karshen (Eds.), *Developing*

communicative competence in a second language (pp. 317–328). Boston, MA: Heinle & Heinle Publishers.
- Weinstein, C., Curran, M., & Tomlinson-Clarke, S. (2003). Culturally responsive classroom management: Awareness into action. *Theory Into Practice, 42* (4), 269–276.

References

Gay, G. (2010). *Culturally responsive teaching: Theory, research and practice.* New York, NY: Teachers College Press.

Hall, E. T. (1976). *Beyond culture.* Garden City, NY: Anchor Press.

Hammond, Z. (2015). *Culturally responsive teaching and the brain: Promoting authentic engagement and rigor among culturally and linguistically diverse students.* Thousand Oaks, CA: Corwin.

Montgomery College. (2013). *Closing the achievement gap task force: Final report and recommendations.* Retrieved from http://cms.montgomerycollege.edu/WorkArea/DownloadAsset.aspx?id=62317

Appendix A: Montgomery College Start of Semester Survey

(1) Your Experiences in College-level Computer Science/Math/Engineering/ Science (CS/MA/EN/SC) Classes Before This Semester

If you have not taken a college-level Computer Science, Math, Engineering, or Science (CS/MA/EN/SC) class you may skip to the next table of questions.

To What Extent is Each Statement in next page True for You? How True is Each Statement for You?

0 = Never; 1 = Rarely; 2 = Sometimes; 3 = Often; 4 = Always; NA = Not Applicable to Me	0	1	2	3	4	NA
1. I can call, ask, or text another student from my CS/MA/EN/SC classes if I have a question about an assignment or the class.						
2. I feel comfortable asking questions in CS/MA/EN/SC classes.						
3. I feel that a CS/MA/EN/SC professor would take the time to talk to me if I needed help.						
4. I feel comfortable participating in class activities such as pair work and small group and whole class discussions in my CS/MA/EN/SC classes.						
5. I feel my CS/MA/EN/SC professors respond to my work quickly and helpfully.						
6. I feel my CS/MA/EN/SC professors care about me as a student.						
7. My CS/MA/EN/SC professors sometimes do not answer my questions.						
8. I feel my CS/MA/EN/SC professors encourage me to contribute ideas in class.						
9. My CS/MA/EN/SC professors ask for their students' comments about the course and make changes to the course based on those comments.						

(2) Your Interest in Computer Science

How Likely are You to Do the Following?

0 = Never; 1 = Not Very Likely; 2 = Somewhat Likely; 3 = Very Likely; 4 = Definitely; NA = Not Applicable To Me	0	1	2	3	4	NA
10. Major in computer science?						
11. Minor in computer science?						
12. Pursue a four-year degree in computer science?						
13. Pursue a career in computer science?						

(3) Self-perceptions of Computer Science/Math/Engineering/Science (CS/MA/EN/SC) Abilities

Do You Feel You Are Able to the Following?

0 = Never; 1 = Rarely; 2 = Sometimes; 3 = Often; 4 = Always; NA = Not Applicable to Me	0	1	2	3	4	NA
14. Solve real-world CS/MA/EN/SC problems?						
15. Understand articles, textbooks, and information about CS/MA/EN/SC?						
16. Learn new computer programs?						
17. Solve computer software problems?						
18. Work on a project using CS/MA/EN/SC concepts?						
19. Have a career in CS/MA/EN/SC?						
20. Remain in *Computer Science* after next semester?						
21. Do very well in *Computer Science* after this semester?						
22. Complete the math requirements for a *Computer Science* major?						
23. Complete a degree in *Computer Science*?						

(4) Handling Challenges in Computer Science/Math/Engineering/Science

How Likely Are You to Do the Following?

0 = Never Likely; 1 = Not Very Likely; 2 = Somewhat Likely; 3 = Very Likely; 4 = Definitely Likely; NA = Not Applicable to Me

	0	1	2	3	4	NA
24. Continue in CS/MA/EN/SC classes even if you did not see people like you in the class?						
25. Continue in CS/MA/EN/SC classes if you feel you are not doing as well as other students in the class?						
26. Find tutoring help in CS/MA/EN/SC?						
27. Find ways to overcome communication problems with CS/MA/EN/SC professors.						
28. Continue on in CS/MA/EN/SC even if you felt that, the environment in these classes was not very welcoming for you?						
29. Deal with unfair treatment in CS/MA/EN/SC classes?						

Chapter 10

Equity through Access to Computer Science Learning at a Small Liberal Arts College

Kathleen Purvis-Roberts and Thomas Poon

Reflection

"An edited volume which calls for self-reflection?" That is exactly the question we, the coauthors, asked each other. From that point on, we knew that working on this book chapter would be different from anything we had ever published in our careers. Realizing that we come to our current moments in time from entirely different trajectories, we present our separate but convergent reflective narratives below.

From Purvis-Roberts

One of the aspects I like most about being a professor is working with students, whether in the classroom, teaching laboratory, or doing independent research. I have always strived to be supportive of all students, no matter their gender identity, racial and ethnic background, religion, etc. In the last couple of years, though, I have learned that we all have implicit biases. I have been working on recognizing these biases and making sure that they do not affect the way that I interact with my students. As a female chemistry professor, I went through all of my own educational experiences without female mentors. All of my male mentors were very supportive and encouraging of my academic endeavors, even though their experiences obviously differed from mine as a woman in science. As a professor, I decided to use the model of mentorship they used with me for my students: building their confidence in their abilities and then trusting them to accomplish their goals, although always being present to support them when they needed extra help. I would encourage and support any student who wanted to major in science, no matter their background.

In my teaching, I have always been careful to call on all students in my classes to encourage them to answer questions, and I provide equal opportunities when recruiting students to work in my research laboratory. During one of our first TIDES Institutes, we had a session about implicit biases, which are preconceived opinions about someone that you do not realize that you have. I had taken an online test (Greenwald, Nosek, & Banaji, 2003) for implicit biases (Greenwald, McGhee, & Schwartz, 1998) against women scientists and did not show a bias, so I figured I was clear and had no biases at all. As someone who thinks about inclusion in the sciences when teaching and doing research, I thought I could not be biased against students of different races and ethnicities. Thus, I was surprised when we took the test about race, and I did show a bias. To be honest, I was shocked and a little embarrassed too. I care so much about all of my students, and I did not think that deep down, I might be thinking about them differently. This experience made me more determined than ever to intentionally face the implicit biases I might have and to avoid complacency in addressing them. After taking the test in the TIDES Institute, we talked about how to be more aware of our biases, as well as how to confront them in the classroom. This session helped me to guard against complacency during my work as an educator and administrator. For example, now when I walk into my classroom or teaching laboratory, I check myself and think about any implicit biases that might affect the way that I teach and interact with my students that day. Similarly, as an administrator, when I was developing programming or applying for funds to support programs, I thought about how we could best serve students of all backgrounds and spread scarce resources more effectively and equitably.

From Poon:

As a first-generation student, I did not have the advantages of learning from relatives in-the-know when it came to navigating my education. It was always "work hard, get good grades." This came easily to me in high school, but college presented a new reality where I was no longer the smartest person in the room. In fact, I wasn't even close. Learning how to succeed in college was a slow journey that did not reach a positive conclusion until my junior year, when I finally made the Dean's list. Back then, the terms implicit bias (Greenwald & Banaji, 1995), microaggression (Lilienfeld, 2017; Pierce, 1970), and model minority (Petersen, 1966) had yet to become part of the public vernacular. As an Asian American student, I experienced ample amounts of implicit bias and microaggressions, and felt I was held to the standards of the model minority.

Fast forward to summer 2013, the year these two coauthors applied for a grant from the National Science Foundation's (NSF) Scholarships in Science, Technology, Engineering, and Mathematics (S-STEM) program. I had long since dedicated my career to helping students navigate the challenges that come with majoring in a STEM field. However, it was not until I started working on our grant proposal that I came across the aforementioned terms and acquired a framework for mentoring students through their first-generational challenges. This framework came from the work of our colleague, Professor Roberta Espinoza, in her book, "Pivotal Moments: How Educators Can Put All Students on the Path to College" (Espinoza, 2011). The book had such a powerful influence on our grant proposal that we asked Professor Espinoza to join us as a co-Principal Investigator.

Eight months later, we learned that our NSF proposal had been funded, while our AAC&U TIDES proposal was awarded an Honorable Mention. Being an honorable mention institution did not allow us to receive the full funding, but it did allow us to participate in the TIDES Institutes. It was through TIDES that I learned about my implicit biases, the importance of students seeing people who look like them in charge of the classroom or in higher level positions (Milem, Chang, & Antonio, 2005), the power of teaching mathematics in applied ways that are relevant to one's major (Klingbeil & Bourne, 2014), and so much more. All of these lessons would prove vital to me in my role as interim president as we navigated the campus climate issues that came to the fore both locally and nationally during the tumultuous 2015–16 academic year (Hartocollis & Bidgood, 2015, A16).

Overall, the TIDES institutes have continued to shape administrative policy as we work with our communities and constituencies. In addition to the thought-provoking sessions, such as the ones on implicit biases mentioned above, we were able to learn from the other colleges and universities represented at the institutes. We faced similar struggles to many of these institutions. How do we make sure we are developing an inclusive campus? How do we improve certain programs and majors where students are struggling? How do we think about mechanisms to encourage a diverse range of students? TIDES helped us keep focused on the important issues on our campuses.

Institutional Context

Pitzer College is a highly selective, four-year liberal arts institution in Claremont, California, 35 miles east of Los Angeles. Pitzer currently has 1,062 students enrolled on campus, and is also part of the Claremont Colleges Consortium, which has over 6,000 undergraduate students across five campuses. Approximately 46% of Pitzer students receive financial aid. One of the priorities for Pitzer College, as an institution, is to increase the diversity of students and faculty. One of our community goals is diversity, as we learn from the rich and complex histories, viewpoints, and life experiences of those in our community. We value and celebrate the synergy created by our differences and similarities. Our Office of Admissions recruits excellent students from diverse backgrounds from all around the country and the world (Figure 1).

At Pitzer College, a core value that distinguishes our approach to education is intercultural understanding. We believe that an

> individual perspective and approach to the world is informed by the culture in which one resides. Intercultural understanding enables Pitzer students to comprehend issues and events through cultural lenses beyond their own. From Los Angeles to Botswana to Nepal, Pitzer students are educated to thrive and succeed in an ever-changing global community (Pitzer College, 2018a).

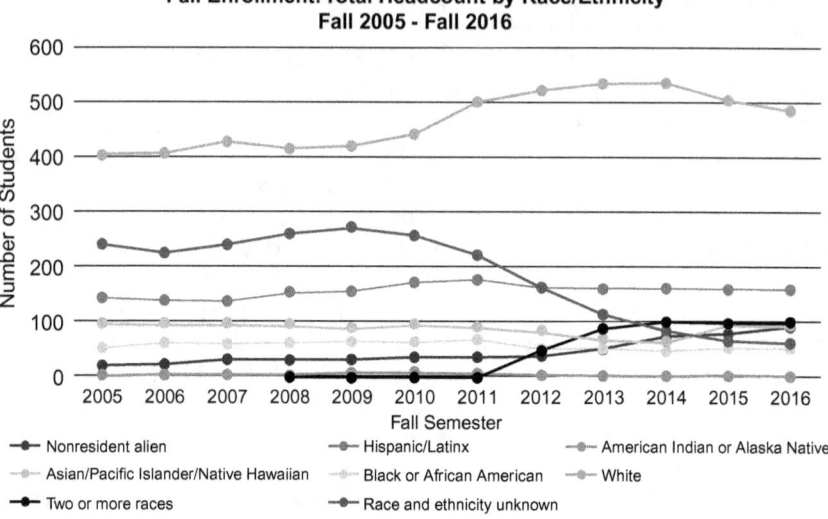

Figure 1: Summary of Ethnic and Racial Backgrounds of Pitzer Students Over the Past Decade.

Faculty believe that
> by learning about their own culture and placing it in a comparative perspective, students appreciate their own and other cultures, and recognize how their own thoughts and actions are influenced by their culture and history. This understanding supports a set of cognitive, affective, and behavioral skills and characteristics that facilitate effective and appropriate interaction in a variety of cultural contexts (Pitzer College, 2018b).

Just a couple of years ago, Pitzer College faculty developed new educational objectives around social justice theory and praxis to provide students with a more comprehensive way to learn and practice intercultural understanding. In order to meet the student learning outcomes for this objective, students take three types of courses. First, students must demonstrate intercultural understanding from an international or global perspective, either by finishing an approved study abroad program or taking a course that addresses a culture outside of the United States. Students also take a course that demonstrates intercultural understanding from a domestic or local perspective. Further, students take a course that addresses historically marginalized cultures in the United States, which could include offerings in Ethnic Studies, Gender and Feminist Studies, American Studies, and LGBTQ theory. One of these courses must focus on the theory of social justice while one of the others must get students out into the community or the world to practice intercultural understanding outside of the classroom.

Introduction/Background and Significance

The United States experienced noticeable gains in science and engineering (S&E) degree attainment between 2004 and 2014. Table 1 shows that all but one demographic group experienced significant increases in S&E degrees awarded. Most notable is a 116.8% increase in S&E degree attainment by Hispanic students (National Science Foundation [NSF], 2018).

Despite these upward trends, Table 1 starkly reveals that the total number of S&E degrees conferred for each ethnic minority group is well below the number awarded to White students. In fact, other studies show that persistence in S&E majors is much lower for women and underrepresented minorities than it is for White males. In a 2012 executive report to the President, the President's Council of Advisors on Science and Technology (2012) reported that fewer than 40% of entering STEM students complete a STEM degree. Women and underrepresented minorities (nonWhite, nonAsian) earned 50.0% and 20.3%, respectively, of the total S&E degrees awarded in 2014. These proportions do not match the proportions of women (28.4%) and underrepresented minorities (11.2%) employed as scientists and engineers (data for 2015; NSF, 2018), suggesting that these affinity groups do not persist in S&E fields after college.

Table 1: Increase in Science and Engineering Degrees Awarded between 2004 and 2014 (NSF, 2018).

	S&E degrees		% Increase, 2004 to 2014	% of total S&E degrees in 2014
	2004	2014		
All	458,658	635,915	38.6	NA
Male	227,861	318,015	39.6	50.0
Female	230,797	317,900	37.7	50.0
American Indian or Alaskan Native	3,264	3,192	−2.21	0.502
Asian, Native Hawaiian, or Pacific Islander	41,403	58,942	42.4	9.27
Black	38,737	52,647	35.9	8.28
Hispanic	33,748	73,179	116	11.5
White	297,708	372,882	25.3	58.6

Our inability to retain students who express interest in S&E fields is often referred to as the "pipeline leak" (Allen-Ramdial & Campbell, 2014). Our original goal in applying for the NSF S-STEM and TIDES funding was to implement best practices (Griffith, 2010) in addressing this pipeline leak.

Pitzer College, with 33.0% faculty of color and 38.0% students of color, is well positioned to support and produce graduates in S&E majors. Pitzer is part of the Claremont Colleges Consortium, which includes five undergraduate colleges (Claremont McKenna, Harvey Mudd, Pitzer, Pomona, and Scripps Colleges) along with two graduate institutions (Claremont Graduate University and Keck Graduate Institute). Students can take courses at colleges across the consortium, and even major in fields not offered by their home institution. For the past five years, Pitzer College has been struggling with the need to provide computer science (CS) courses to a student body that is yearning for CS courses. The College does not offer CS courses, and we have no CS professors on the faculty. Pitzer College students can take CS courses at Claremont McKenna, Harvey Mudd, and Pomona Colleges. However, since seats in CS courses are at a premium, it can be difficult to enroll in the introductory courses. Once students declare a major in CS though, they are treated like majors from the host institution and have the same access to courses as any major at Harvey Mudd or Pomona.

Pitzer students are not choosing to major in CS in great numbers since CS is not a major at our home campus. Instead, they are taking introductory CS courses to complement and strengthen their majors. The number of CS majors from Pitzer has increased from one student in 2006 to five students in 2017. In some years, there are no CS major graduates at all from Pitzer. As expected, many science students are taking computer science courses to learn how to program and analyze data for laboratory courses and/or senior thesis research. However, students taking introductory CS courses vary widely in terms of major, from Media Studies and Studio Art to Economics and Intercultural Studies. Students want to learn the basics of programming to complement their major curriculum and/or extra-curricular activities, but it is often difficult to provide enough seats in these courses to satisfy demand.

Pitzer's President, Dr. Melvin Oliver, is very supportive of STEM as a means to achieving equity. He has said many times that "STEM is now a means to diversity and equity for college campuses." This begs the question, "Can we use CS course offerings as a way to attract and retain students from underrepresented groups?"

Implementation/Methodology

While we were Pitzer College administrators, we observed an increase in Pitzer student interest in Computer Science courses, especially the Introduction to Computer Science course, CS5, at Harvey Mudd College. As Pitzer College does not have its own Computer Science Department, the Deans of Faculty at the five undergraduate Claremont Colleges worked closely together to facilitate Pitzer student access to computer science courses at not only Harvey Mudd

College, but also at Pomona College and Claremont McKenna College, where other introductory CS courses are also offered. The average class size at Pitzer College is 16.5 students, and this is similar across the Claremont Colleges. CS5 at Harvey Mudd has grown to 350 students, which is likely the largest class size offered in Claremont Colleges history. This allowed most of the students who wanted to take Introductory Computer Science to take an important exploratory step.

The CS Department at Harvey Mudd College also realized that the vast majority of students were taking the introductory course and deciding not to major in CS. They developed a course for these students that will help them apply the knowledge they gained in CS5 to projects that students would like to pursue. The course, CS for Insight (CS35), is being offered for the third time during the Spring 2018 semester. CS35 cannot be used as a major course in Computer Science; it is designed as a terminal course for students who want to learn the basics of programming but do not intend to be computer engineers. The motivation behind development of CS35 is to encourage students to develop and practice "investigative computing" skills. The faculty who developed the course wanted students to create small prototype programs that use data, simulations, and/or other computing to gain insight into fields other than CS. They also wanted students to develop capabilities/confidence with existing libraries that support these investigations.

The CS Department at Harvey Mudd was wonderful to work with, but it took time to work out the details to allow Pitzer students to take courses there, and even with such a large introductory course, sometimes students have a hard time securing a seat in the class. Therefore, we found alternative options for students to learn how to code. For example, Pitzer has a subscription to Lynda.com, where students can start learning the basics of computer programming. Other online sources, such as Codecademy (www.codecademy.com), can help students learn how to code interactively. The key is to find resources to help students accomplish the goals that they have set for themselves. Perhaps they do not need a full semester course in computer science, but rather can benefit from online sources that can provide them with the skills and knowledge that they seek.

The administrative team at Pitzer appreciated working with the Harvey Mudd CS faculty, especially their willingness to think outside the box about ways to serve students who are not currently majors and do not intend to be majors. We also appreciated their commitment to opening up their introductory courses so that many, many more students could be introduced to CS. This has benefitted them too. Pitzer College is one of the most diverse undergraduate Claremont College in terms of its student body. Harvey Mudd's classes became richer in diversity, which provided differences in thought and helped the institution's faculty and students to see how CS can be applied in a variety of different ways. As the number of majors from Pitzer increases, the diversity of majors in Harvey Mudd's department will increase too. Some of these majors will eventually become employees at tech companies, a business sector which historically has lacked diversity.

Results

Between 2006 and the present, a larger and more diverse cohort of students from Pitzer College has begun to take computer science courses at Harvey Mudd, Claremont McKenna, and Pomona Colleges. Over the last decade, the enrollments in computer science courses by Pitzer students have grown exponentially (Figure 2). In the past few years, the number of upper division courses taken by students has started to decline, but the number of introductory courses is continuing to increase. We think that this is a direct result of initiatives aimed at improving access and equity in STEM education at our institution.

The diversity of students taking computer science courses has also been increasing. While the majority of the Pitzer students enrolled in both lower and upper division CS courses are White, the percentage of Asian students taking CS courses has increased (Figures 3 and 4). The percentage of Native American/ Alaskan, Hispanic/Puerto Rican, and multi-racial students from Pitzer College has fluctuated over the years, but regardless, these students add increased diversity of thought to CS courses across the Claremont Colleges.

Discussion

Pitzer College's emphasis on culturally responsive teaching and learning has allowed the institution to identify unmet students' needs and find ways to meet those needs. Pitzer has responded to its students' desire to become more proficient in CS by identifying pathways that facilitate CS learning. Sometimes administrators have obvious solutions, as we did in working with nearby institutions that offer courses that our students want to take and facilitating their enrollment. At other times, we needed to think outside the box, such as offering

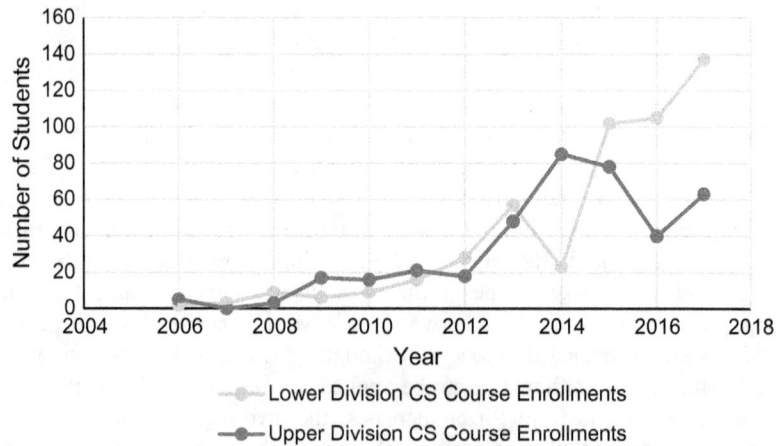

Figure 2: Total Number of Students Taking Computer Science Courses Over the Past Decade, Separated by Lower Division Courses and Upper Division Courses.

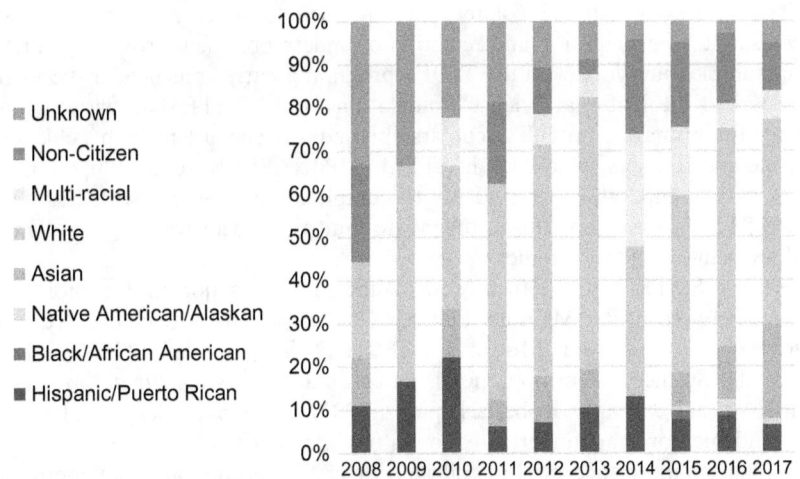

Figure 3: Summary of Percentage of Pitzer College Students Enrollments for Lower Division Computer Science Courses.

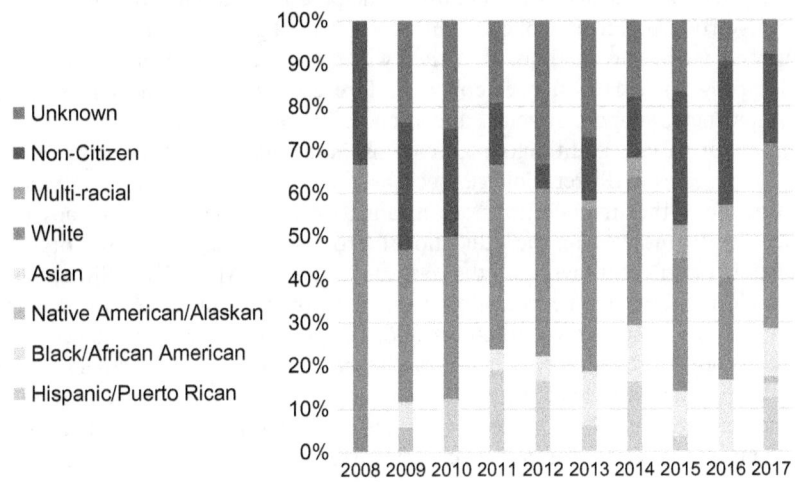

Figure 4: Percentage of Pitzer College Students by Race And Ethnicity Enrolled in Upper Division Computer Science Courses.

access to online resources, so that students can learn the skills that they want. Even without access to a higher education consortium like Pitzer's, institutions could partner with the business community, other institutions of high learning in their area, or offer access to online resources so that their students can learn the skills in CS that they need to succeed in today's world.

The success of our CS collaboration has led to other programs that are increasing the participation and retention of underrepresented groups in STEM. For example, our work with the TIDES program greatly influenced a successful proposal to the National Science Foundation for an S-STEM initiative grant. The grant primarily provides scholarship funds to encourage high achieving, low-income students to succeed in STEM at Pitzer. These scholarships replace loans with grants, allowing students to complete their degrees with less debt. The S-STEM grant also allows students to limit time spent working on campus and focus more on their studies.

Pitzer's S-STEM grant focuses on students who major in the molecular sciences. We call it "Mentors Enable, Connect, Help, Advocate, Nurture, Intervene, Sustain, and Motivate (MECHANISM) for SUCCESS in the Molecular Sciences." Our approach is based on a book called *Pivotal Moments*, written by our colleague Roberta Espinoza (2011). The main idea is that educators and mentors can undertake thoughtful interventions in students' lives to help them be more successful in college. For first-generation and/or underrepresented students, such interventions may provide them with the cultural capital necessary to succeed in college.

The interventions offered by the MECHANISM program are varied. First, the majority of students in the cohort participate in a summer bridge program before starting at Pitzer College. This introduces them to some of the science faculty as well as to methods that they will use in lab. More importantly, the bridge program creates a peer cohort, before classes begin, who can serve as study partners, support systems, and friends. During the school year, we meet monthly for various additional interventions. Some introduce students to various support services at Pitzer College, such as career services, the library, Student Affairs, etc. Other interventions are meant to teach students how to advocate better for themselves in the educational process. For example, we organize lunches with different faculty in the sciences so that the MECHANISM students can build relationships with faculty in the fields they are interested in pursuing. Then, when students have questions about classes or the major, they are not afraid to talk to the faculty. Finally, we introduce the scholars to Pitzer alumni who have gone on to successful careers in research and medicine. The scholars can see someone who was once in their shoes on campus, having similar struggles, and is now successful in their chosen career path. These alumni often act as mentors to students, too.

Finally, as PIs, our most important role is to mentor the students. We meet with students often, both individually and in groups. We help them to think about majors and which classes they need to take to succeed in the major. We identify potential research opportunities, both on and off campus, and we encourage students to talk with faculty about opportunities to work in their research laboratories. We help them find resources when they are struggling with a class, and we let them know that we believe in them and that they can make it through a difficult exam, problem set, or course. Mostly, we are advocates who believe that these students are going to be successful and remind them of that when they lose their confidence.

The MECHANISM program has contributed to a pattern of increasing enrollment in science from traditionally underrepresented populations at Pitzer College, which is very exciting. One of the sessions at a TIDES Institute helped us to think about access and equity in STEM education, which we can apply directly to what we are attempting to achieve at Pitzer. Faculty from the Wright State University Engineering Department explained that they did research to figure out what their roadblock courses were and then revised their curriculum to increase the success of underrepresented students in their engineering major (Klingbeil & Bourne, 2014). For the Engineering Program at Wright State University, the roadblock course was calculus.

Originally, general chemistry and calculus were roadblocks at Pitzer, because the math tended to cause problems for students who did not have a strong science and math background. About ten years ago, we developed a new section of general chemistry for students who had weak math and science backgrounds from high school. The class followed the same curriculum as all of the other sections, except it was limited in size and had a mandatory problem-solving session associated with it. More than anything, this course built student confidence in their own abilities. The faculty teaching the course know that the students can be successful in the course; we just have to convince the students taking the course that this is true. Historically, students who complete the designated section performed as well as all of the other students when they entered the second semester of chemistry (Hatcher-Skeers, Yong, & Packard, 2016). At Pitzer, the math faculty actually added a similar course for the introductory sequence, where students have mandatory problem-solving sessions along with the course itself. We are now in conversation with the physics faculty to see if they could offer a similar section of physics to provide additional support and mentoring for students with weaker math backgrounds.

Overall, as we increase the number of traditionally underrepresented students in science here at Pitzer, we need to encourage and support these students. As faculty, we need to think about the way we teach and increase our cultural competency. We need to show students the broad diversity of successful scientists today, and mentor students to be equally successful in their own pursuits.

Conclusion

Pitzer College benefitted greatly from being a part of the TIDES program. TIDES helped us to think deliberately about how to help our students achieve the goals they set for themselves, whether taking an introductory computer science course to learn enough programming to supplement their major or as a pathway towards majoring in CS. By facilitating the enrollment of Pitzer students historically underrepresented in science in CS courses, we have been able to diversify the viewpoints and classroom environments in the CS curriculum as well. Eventually, we will start to increase diversity and equity in the CS field.

The coauthors benefitted personally from the TIDES Institutes, too, as the material learned positively impacted their teaching and work as administrators.

We learned to be more inclusive in our classes and work with students. The learning augmented our work on a National Science Foundation S-STEM grant and allowed us to apply further those principles of equity and inclusion we focused on during the TIDES Institutes to a new cohort of science students at Pitzer College. Diversity and equity initiatives like TIDES expand their impact beyond the intended targets, as we have observed at Pitzer College.

The Last Word

Institutional change can be scary, especially when it seems like you have so far to go. If you take small steps but keep moving, you can make big changes over time that you never imagined possible.

What we learned through this process is that first, you need to listen to your students and utilize institutional data to determine their needs. Then, you can look for solutions to serve your students best and help them achieve the goals that they set out for themselves. When we first observed the demand for computer science courses from Pitzer students, we were not sure what to do. It did not make sense for us to start a Computer Science Department, especially since we already had three programs in town at our consortial colleges. When we started conversations about opening more seats in classes, we never dreamed that the CS departments would be so collaborative and willing to educate our students.

The point is that once you identify a problem, you need to jump in and find creative solutions to benefit your students.

TIDES Resources

Throughout our time as a TIDES Honorable Mention Institution, we have utilized many of the resources provided or presented to us at TIDES meetings. As we have detailed throughout this chapter, we have utilized implicit bias theory to check our implicit bias and to create awareness among our faculty undergoing tenure-line faculty searches. Presentations on the importance of students seeing STEM professionals who look like them have changed the content of what we teach. Our colleagues have also created a document that highlights the accomplishments of women scientists and scientists of color. This document has been made available to faculty in our science department so that they may incorporate examples within our courses and teaching. Further, the sessions and emphases on culturally responsive pedagogies (Sleeter, 2012) were strategically woven throughout the entire period of the TIDES Initiative.

All of the preconference meetings connected to AAC&U Conferences were helpful in introducing our team to new concepts (e.g. Systems Thinking), fostering camaraderie among institutions seeking structural change in their curricula, and reinforcing concepts learned in the summer TIDES Institutes.

Perhaps the most salient requirement was that an institutional administrator be part of each TIDES team. Our TIDES team included various administrators at various times over the three years. We had two Associate Deans, an Interim Dean, and an Interim President. These administrators recently transitioned from faculty positions and, therefore, were able to bring both perspectives to bear on the team's work. Administrative buy-in also made implementation of new initiatives more nimble.

References

Allen-Ramdial, S A., & Campbell, A. G. (2014). Reimagining the pipeline: Advancing STEM diversity, persistence, and success. *BioScience, 64*(7), 612–618.

Espinoza, R. (2011). *Pivotal moments: How educators can put all students on the path to college.* Cambridge, MA: Harvard Education Press.

Greenwald, A. G., & Banaji, M. R. (1995). Implicit social cognition: Attitudes, self-esteem, and stereotypes. *Psychological Review, 102*(1), 4.

Greenwald, A. G., McGhee, D. E., & Schwartz, J. L. K. (1998). Measuring individual differences in implicit cognition: The implicit association test. *Journal of Personality and Social Psychology, 74*(6), 1464–1480.

Greenwald, A. G., Nosek, B. A., & Banaji, M. R. (2003). Understanding and using the implicit association test: I. An improved scoring algorithm. *Journal of Personality and Social Psychology, 85*(2), 197–216.

Griffith, A. L. (2010). Persistence of women and minorities in STEM field majors: Is it the school that matters? *Economics of Education Review, 29*(6), 911–922.

Hartocollis, A., & Bidgood, J. (2015, November 11). Racial discrimination demonstrations spread at universities across the U.S. *The New York Times, 165*(57,047), p. A16. Retrieved from http://www.nytimes.com

Hatcher-Skeers, M., Yong, D., & Packard, P. (2016, November). *CS 3: Deliberate investment: Strategies for sustaining inclusive STEM classrooms for first-generation students.* Paper presented at the Association of American Colleges & Universities' STEM Conference, Boston, MA.

Klingbeil, N. W., & Bourne, A. (2014). *The Wright State model for engineering mathematics education: A longitudinal study of student perception data.* Paper presented at the 121st ASEE Annual Conference & Exposition, Indianapolis, IN.

Lilienfeld, S. O. (2017). Microaggressions: Strong claims, inadequate evidence. *Perspectives on Psychological Science, 12*(1), 138–169.

Milem, J. F., Chang, M. J., & Antonio, A. L. (2005). *Making diversity work on campus: A research-based perspective.* Washington, DC: Association of American Colleges and Universities.

National Science Foundation (NSF). (2018, March 26). Women, minorities, and persons with disabilities in science and engineering 2017. [Online] Retrieved from https://www.nsf.gov/statistics/2017/nsf17310/data.cfm

Petersen, W. (1966, January). Success story, Japanese-American style. *New York Times Magazine, 9*(6), 20–43.

Pierce, C. M. (1970). Black psychiatry one year after Miami. *Journal of the National Medical Association, 62*(6), 471.

Pitzer College. (2018a). Mission and values. Retrieved from https://www.pitzer.edu/about/mission-and-values

Pitzer College. (2018b). Educational objectives of Pitzer College. Retrieved from http://catalog.pitzer.edu/content.php?catoid=6&navoid=429

President's Council of Advisors on Science and Technology. (2012). *Engage to Excel: Producing One Million Additional College Graduates with Degrees in Science, Technology, Engineering, and Mathematics. Report to the President.* Retrieved from https://obamawhitehouse.archives.gov/sites/default/files/microsites/ostp/pcast-engage-to-excel-final_2-25-12.pdf

Sleeter, C. E. (2012). Confronting the marginalization of culturally responsive pedagogy. *Urban Education, 47*(3), 562–584.

Chapter 11

Challenging Us to Change

Helen H. Hu, Patricia B. Campbell, Jessica C. Johnston, Brian Avery, Greg Gagne and Julie Stewart

Reflection

"If I'd taken this class earlier, I'd have been a computer science major!" Quotes like this one from a female senior math major inspired the Westminster computer science (CS) department to develop a new CS course for first-year students as our Westminster TIDES project. To qualify as a first-year requirement, this new CS course was paired with Biology, Chemistry, and Sociology courses, involving five Westminster faculty over three years. Throughout the project, we were repeatedly confronted by the disparities in privilege and were challenged to meet our students where they were, rather than where they "should" be. We learned to question the way things worked in the system, and we became braver in trying new ideas to help our students. TIDES Institute presentations helped us to better understand the challenges faced by our first-generation students, which led us to recognize in ourselves a tendency to perceive students' deficiencies. We learned to be more empathetic with our students and to help our students to the best of our abilities. After hearing about the Wright State Model for Engineering Mathematics Education at the first TIDES Institute, we started to question the systems in place in our departments and our college. Prerequisites for courses were reduced, major requirements were modified, and even the registration process was adjusted to improve gender balance in our TIDES learning communities.

The most impactful moments for us were the unscripted interactions among our overall TIDES community, when we learned first-hand about white fragility and about the importance of the perception of our actions (rather than the intention of our actions). While these moments did not lead to specific changes, they transformed our mind-sets. Over four years, we had journeyed together and learned much about culturally responsive teaching, supporting our students, and transformative innovations. We still have room to grow and improve.

Culturally Responsive Strategies for Reforming STEM Higher Education:
Turning the TIDES on Inequity, 187−200
Copyright © 2019 by Emerald Publishing Limited
All rights of reproduction in any form reserved
doi:10.1108/978-1-78743-405-920191011

Institutional Context

Westminster College is a private, comprehensive, liberal arts college with an undergraduate enrollment of approximately 2300 students. Although 60% of Westminster College undergraduate students are female, Computer Science (CS) classes at Westminster have historically had very low female enrollments. From 2002 to 2012, only 18.7% of all Westminster CS majors were female (21 out of 113). Only four of these 113 students came from traditionally underrepresented backgrounds (African American, Hispanic, and/or Latino). To increase diversity in the CS program, the CS faculty had already adopted instructional practices that have been demonstrated to be effective at engaging more students, including adopting pair programming in labs, teaching programming via media computation, and showing and discussing video clips on the diverse range of CS opportunities and applications in introductory CS classes. These efforts attempt to improve retention once students are enrolled in their first CS course, but do little to encourage students to consider CS courses prior to and during enrollment.

The Westminster TIDES project sought to increase the interest in the CS course by developing a new CS course for nonmajors (Computer Science Principles) and offering this course as part of Westminster's Learning Community Program. Because all first-year Westminster students are required to take part in a learning community, 81 first-year students took the CS course as part of a learning community over three years, 20 of whom went on to take additional CS classes. In the two years following the introduction of CS learning communities, 34.5% of graduating CS majors were female (10 out of 29 from 2015–2017) and 3 of these 29 students were from traditionally underrepresented backgrounds.

Introduction/Background and Significance

Learning Community Background

Learning communities are high-impact courses that produce self-reported gains in deep learning by students (Kuh, 2008). Since 2006, all of Westminster's first-year students are required to take a learning community course as part of their liberal education degree requirements. Taught by two professors, learning communities pair two traditionally different subject areas with a common theme. Students learn about each discipline and are actively involved in the process of integration of ideas from those disciplines. As a result, students use an integrated lens as they develop critical thinking skills. Students grow and understand that problems can be successfully solved using this approach. From a catalog of approximately 20 learning communities, students each choose one learning community that matches their interests or a promising new area they wish to explore. The Westminster TIDES project offered three learning community pairings, each targeting a different type of student:

- a Human Genetics/Computer Science learning community (offered Spring 2015, Fall 2015, Fall 2016) directed at undeclared majors who were curious about science;

- a General Chemistry/Computer Science learning community (offered Fall 2015 and Fall 2016) directed at Biology, Chemistry, Physics, and Pre-med majors; and
- a Sociology/Computer Science learning community (offered Fall 2016) directed at students who were not interested in science.

In the first years of implementing learning communities, prior to it becoming a requirement in 2006, retention rates for all Westminster students in learning communities was 81%, compared to 67% for those students not participating. Over the years, the structure of the learning communities has grown to include specific mentoring responsibilities for those who teach the courses. The learning community structure provides each first-year student with a direct, sustained interaction with a full-time faculty member. Students in learning communities build strong ties with fellow students and faculty. This structure is helpful to all students; it may be particularly valuable to students who experience difficulty as they transition to college.

Process Oriented Guided Inquiry Learning

Process Oriented Guided Inquiry Learning (POGIL) is a student-centered learning approach where teams of 3–4 students collaborate to learn the course content together (http://pogil.org). POGIL activities encourage student growth in process skills like critical thinking, teamwork, and communication, by assigning students roles in their teams. Each activity includes sequences of questions that guide students to explore the new material, invent key concepts, and apply their new understanding (Hanson, 2013). Students are more likely to participate in a POGIL classroom because they are accountable to the other members on their learning team as they work together in-class to complete the activities. A recent survey of CS POGIL instructors found that 92% of them agreed that students were more engaged in classrooms when using POGIL activities, and 88% agreed that students were more active in their own learning process (Hu, Kussmaul, Knaeble, Mayfield, & Yadav, 2016).

While POGIL classrooms will vary, a typical POGIL classroom will involve:

- Students working collaboratively in self-managed *learning teams*, where each student is assigned a unique role and set of responsibilities for the class period. The instructor acts as a facilitator to help these learning teams work, rather than as the presenter of information.
- The assignment of *guided inquiry* materials, which use a learning cycle approach (explore – invent – apply) to help students construct their own understanding of the course content.
- A focus on *process skills* development, in the POGIL activities and by the instructor who is acting as a facilitator in the classroom.

The *learning teams* usually consist of three to four students, working together for multiple weeks, which allows students to rotate at least once through each of the four roles. Different POGIL instructors prefer different role names and responsibilities, but a typical set of roles would include a manager, a spokesperson, a recorder, and a reflector. Distributing role cards can help remind students of their responsibilities; a variety of role cards can be found online.

The most defining element of the POGIL methodology is the *guided inquiry materials*, which guide students through a series of "models" and questions to construct their own understanding, rather than providing an explanation of the material in lecture or written format. Superficially, these POGIL activities resemble worksheets, but they are written to follow a learning cycle approach of exploration, concept invention, and application. Each POGIL activity will usually consist of three or four models, where new information is provided to serve as a basis of the new understanding that will be constructed. Each model is followed by a series of five to ten questions. The first few questions are typically exploration questions, where the student is guided to consider various aspects of the model. Concept invention questions follow prompting students to discover patterns and develop concepts typically before the standard terms for these ideas are introduced. Finally, the concept is reinforced and extended in the application phase with exercises and problems. Ideally, at least some of these questions are too difficult to be answered individually, and will require the learning team to collaborate to reach satisfactory answers.

All four, Computer Science, Human Genetics, and General Chemistry, professors involved in the TIDES learning communities adopted POGIL pedagogy in their classrooms, while the Sociology professor modified her course to include more collaborative learning and POGIL-like class activities. In particular, the CS POGIL activities were the first POGIL activities deliberately developed to be culturally sensitive POGIL activities, intended to broaden participation in CS. These CS POGIL activities were piloted for the Westminster CS course for non-majors and later adopted by three partner institutions (Cornell College, James Madison University, and Saint Xavier University).

Implementation

Westminster

Each year, three Westminster faculty from the CS, Biology, and Chemistry departments attended the weeklong TIDES Institutes and learned about teaching strategies for broadening participation. The Westminster TIDES Project also invited multiple experts to present two three-hour workshops on unconscious bias (July 2014 and May 2015) to Westminster faculty. Based on feedback from the 2014 workshop, the 2015 workshop included more concrete steps that faculty could take to make their teaching more inclusive, with less time spent on the importance of inclusive teaching.

At the start of the project, one CS faculty member and one Chemistry faculty member were already experienced POGIL authors and classroom facilitators; the other three faculty from CS, Biology, and Sociology faculty all attended a three-day POGIL workshop to become more familiar with POGIL pedagogy.

The workshop include sessions on the following: (1) Classroom Facilitation, (2) Improving Facilitation, (3) Effective Responses, (4) Polling, (5) Activity Structure, and (6) Learning Objectives. As noted, the CS, Biology, and Chemistry faculty adopted POGIL pedagogy in their learning community. While the Biology and Chemistry faculty adapted existing POGIL activities for their classes, at the start of the project, no POGIL activities existed for a nonmajors CS course or for Sociology; therefore CS and Sociology faculty designed new classroom strategies. The Sociology professor modified her classroom to be more collaborative by creating some POGIL-like classroom activities, whereas the CS professor developed a set of POGIL activities with cultural relevance in mind. (The CS POGIL activities were later adopted by other CS faculty at Westminster and the partner schools.) To assist Westminster faculty in developing culturally responsive activities, Dr. Jean Aguilar-Valdez created a rubric with seven criteria: (1) voice, (2) differentiation, (3) access, (4) connection, (5) higher-order thinking, (6) social justice, and (7) equity (Hu & Avery, 2015). The CS POGIL activities often included questions asking students to identify if the day's CS course content was relevant to their interests. For example, when learning about pseudorandom number generators, students were asked how their favorite games relied on unpredictable, random events. When studying about the internet, students looked up their IP addresses, and when studying about file compression, they checked how many more music files or movie files they could store on their laptops. These activities are available at http://tinyurl.com/CSPpogil.

Recruitment of students into the learning communities was challenging because the students registered for the learning communities before their arrival on campus. In the first year, a flyer was sent to all first-year students, but only ten students registered for the Spring 2015 learning community. To recruit students better for the Fall 2015 and Fall 2016 learning communities, faculty met with counselors and student workers in the Westminster START Center to discuss how to describe the learning communities to appeal to a wider range of students. Faculty and staff who advised incoming first-year students were given a flyer to help them differentiate between the three learning communities that involved CS classes. These following descriptions were included in a 2016 learning communities brochure sent to all first-year students:

Understanding You: Unlocking the Mysteries Behind Your Aptitude, Interests, and Attitudes (Spring 2015, Fall 2016, Fall 2017)

> Why are people good at certain things, but not at others? Why do some people enjoy eating, while others live to exercise? Why some people hold rigid attitudes, while others float between extremes? The answer to these questions about you – and many more – can be partially answered by genetics. In this learning community, students learn fundamental principles of genetics and get answers to some of life's most interesting questions, questions that look at how much of our life is shaped by our family

inheritance and how much by our environments. Students in this learning community will develop apps for their Android devices while discovering how computing answers questions and drives innovation in genetics and other fields.

Atoms and Apps: The Role of Computers in Science and Medicine
(Fall 2016, Fall 2017)

Computers are helping advance discoveries in science and medicine; the 2013 Nobel Prize in Chemistry was awarded for computational chemistry research. Students in this learning community will develop mobile apps for Android phones and tablets while also discovering how computing is driving innovation in science and medicine. Some of the apps students develop in CMPT 140 will be used directly in CHEM 111 to assist in data collection and analysis.

Wired or Fired: Understanding the Digital Divide in Society (Fall 2017)

Your generation is the most connected in history. And your phone is the key. You watch TV, monitor your exercise, check your bank account, and send texts all on your phone. But who is creating this technology? First, the good news: Creating phone apps is something everyone can do, including you. Now, the bad news: Have you heard about the digital divide? This refers to the "haves" and the "have nots" in terms of technology. It also applies to those who create technology. Unfortunately, many people think they can create technology. But this can all change. In this learning community, we will explore the social factors that contribute to low numbers of women, people of color and non-wealthy studying and working in Science, Technology, Engineering, and Math. Learning about these social factors of exclusion will help us to change this, beginning with you. You will learn the principles of computer science and will develop apps for Android devices.

All learning communities at Westminster were expected to build community between students, by including an off-campus activity. One of the more successful off-campus activities was the Chemistry–CS learning community attending a screening of "The Martian", a movie that included both chemistry and CS concepts in the story. The Sociology–CS learning community visited the Leonardo Museum, with its exhibits to "explore the ways that science, technology, art, and creativity connect". Finally, some of the learning communities incentivized peer-led study groups, where students received extra credit for organizing or attending study groups before quizzes and exams.

Partner Institutions

In the second and third year of the project, three partner institutions used the POGIL CS curriculum developed at Westminster in their CS for nonmajors classes. The CS faculty at these institutions also attended the three-day POGIL Regional Meetings (described above) and a three-hour "Teaching to Diversity in CS" workshop to concepts such as combating micro-aggressions and discussed promising engagement practices to address students' narrow ideas about computing. The students at the three institutions took the same pre/post surveys as the Westminster students, and the three CS instructors were interviewed by the evaluator.

At the end of the first year of the project, a high number of the Westminster students enrolled in the Spring 2015 learning community expressed interest in taking future CS courses. However, these promising results were not replicated at the partner institutions in the second year of the project. Interviews with the instructors at the partner institutions helped us recognize that while they were willing to change their pedagogy, they were not yet convinced about the importance of connecting the curriculum to students' interests. Some instructors skipped the questions that tried to prompt students to draw connections between the material and their interests, while one instructor even questioned whether these questions were appropriate to the course.

To improve on engaging students at the partner institutions, we developed the following two-dimensional framework to assess levels of POGIL implementation tied to participation and context (Hu & Campbell, 2017). The first dimension, levels of student participation, helps teachers consider changes to how they teach, whereas the second dimension, stages of relevant curriculum, helps them consider changes to what they teach. All CS teachers were introduced to this framework before the third year of the project and encouraged to reflect on the degrees of student participation and relevant curriculum in their CS courses.

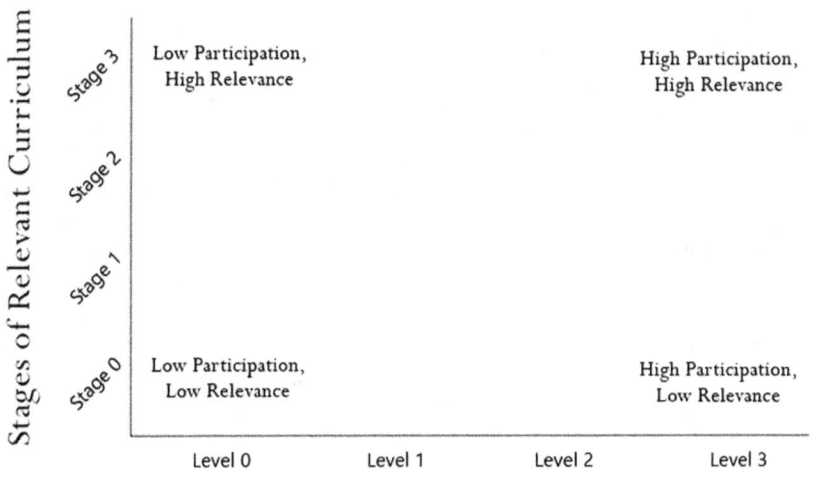

Results

Westminster CS results

Over the three years of the project, 81 Westminster students completed one of the six TIDES learning communities. Even though 60% of all Westminster students are female, only 42% of the learning community students were female. Female participation improved each year of the project (30%, then 36%, and finally 50%), as we reworked the marketing of the learning communities to attract more female students. The Biology–CS learning community rebranding was especially successful (female enrollment was 30% and 33% before the rebranding, and 71% with the "Understanding You" theme), however the last offering of the Biology–CS learning community also had the fewest students continue on to additional CS courses. The Sociology–CS learning community also did reasonably well, with 45% female students in its first and only offering. The Chemistry-Computer Science learning community averaged only 35% female students over the two years (actually decreasing slightly in the second year), making the learning community General Chemistry class the least gender-balanced section of General Chemistry at the college.

Twenty-five percent of the 81 learning community students enrolled in additional CS courses after their learning community. Disappointingly, fewer female students (5 out of 34) went on to take additional CS courses than the male students (15 out of 47). Anecdotally, we know that some students were interested in CS before enrolling in the learning community, even though we had tried to direct most incoming CS majors into our first CS course for majors and not our learning communities. We also know of multiple students who had no interest in CS until the learning community and now plan to major in it. Finally, since our learning community students have not yet graduated, we continue to see more of them enroll in CS courses, so we expect the 25% to increase, but we do not expect any more students to major in computing degrees.

Westminster Chemistry results

More than half the TIDES learning community students also took the General Chemistry (CHEM 111) in their first semester at Westminster. Thirty-four students participated in a CS–Chemistry learning community, while an additional 9 General Chemistry students participated in a CS–Biology learning community and 1 General Chemistry student participated in a CS–Sociology learning community. A total of 29 of these 44 students (66%) continued on to take CHEM 112, the second semester of General Chemistry, with a higher retention rate in the non-Chemistry learning communities (8 of the 10 continued on to CHEM 112). These retention rates are approximately equivalent to the retention rates across all General Chemistry classes (66% in 2015 and 2016).

Following a poor average performance on the second midterm exam in the 2015 General Chemistry class, students were incentivized with a trivial amount of extra credit to form and attend peer-led study sessions. Fourteen of nineteen students attended at least one study session during the remainder of the semester, while eleven students attended three or more study sessions. The student leading each session was responsible for announcing the planned study session in class, submitting a list of students who attended, and detailing topics discussed during the session. The improvement between the second and third midterm exam for students who attended study sessions was astounding. In particular, the improvement was most extreme for students who had failed midterm exam 2: an average increase of 18% on midterm exam 3! This improved performance persisted for those students who continued to attend peer-led study sessions.

The Chemistry professor added a question to anonymous end-of-semester course evaluations to assess student attitudes toward the peer-led study sessions. All feedback was positive, but one comment from a student really stood out:

> I attended a majority of the student-led study sessions and definitely believe that they were beneficial. We not only are able to work on assignments and discuss current Chemistry topics with each [other], but we have a great time doing it. The study session helps for both educational purposes, as well as built stronger bonds... making [our] learning community a tight knit group. Just seeing the progression of our class from Day 1 [...] to now meeting 4-6 times a week, in class and out, is unbelievable. The study group is a great idea and I strongly encourage it for next semester [...] and for future generations that choose to attend Westminster and take Chemistry.

In response to these encouraging results and overwhelmingly positive student feedback, the Chemistry Department adopted a standard departmental extra credit policy to encourage all students to join study groups. Students can earn a 0.5% increase in their final grade simply by attending at least three peer-led study sessions with at least three students throughout the semester and an additional 0.5% extra credit for attending campus events and volunteering at outreach events. Affecting this type of departmental change was actually quite easy, as the department already embraces student-centered, team-based learning at its core.

CS results across institutions

The POGIL activities for the CS course were adopted at three additional institutions in Fall 2015 and Fall 2016 (Cornell College, James Madison University and Saint Xavier University). In Fall 2016, 120 students (31% female) took a non-majors CS course at the four institutions (including Westminster). These students were invited to complete a pre/post survey that included the Computer Attitude Questionnaire for Computer Science Freshmen (CASF) as well as questions about their interest in taking more CS courses, their major, classroom climate in the learning community, and student demographic information.

Matching pre/post responses were received from 65 students, 18 (28%) of whom were women. Student interest in taking more CS courses significantly increased during the semester, from 3.5 to 3.8 (f = 3.4, p = 0.04) with interest among women increasing from 3.2 to 3.6 and men from 3.6 to 3.9 on a scale from 1, absolutely not, to 5, absolutely yes.

Analysis of their CASF responses revealed three factors (Hu & Campbell, 2017):

- Factor 1: Ease and comfort with computers and technology;
- Factor 2: Positive feelings about the roles computers play; and
- Factor 3: Interest in computing careers and spending time on computers.

With regards to ease and comfort using computers (factor 1), all students had a significant increase over time (f = 9.1, p = 0.002) with gender differences decreasing over the semester from 0.3 to 0.1. All students also saw an improvement in their feelings about the value of computing (factor 2) over time (f = 8.3, p = 0.003). Encouragingly, female students became significantly more positive in their perceptions of the value of computers (factor 2) to the extent that gender differences seen at the start of the semester were almost eliminated by the end of the semester, from 0.4 to 0.1. There were no significant changes in interest in computing (factor 3) over time for the class taken as a whole, but there were significant gender differences. While men came into the non-majors CS courses significantly more interested in computing careers and spending time on computers than women (f = 7.7, p = 0.007), this gender gap decreased over the course period (from a 0.7 difference to a 0.2 difference on a five-point scale, as seen in Table 1).

The post-survey in the third year of the project also included questions on classroom climate, to measure the impact of the Levels and Stages framework. Students had very positive perceptions of the classroom climate, particularly in terms of the encouragement of mutual respect among students. Students felt they participated in the classroom and were comfortable asking questions, and there were no gender differences in their perceptions. The degree to which they felt they could express their interests and experiences in the course rated the lowest, however, the rating was still quite positive (see Table 2).

Discussion

The Westminster TIDES project successfully engaged 81 Westminster first-year students in a new CS course that met not only a first-year learning community requirement, but also met a general education Science and Math graduation requirement by the end of the project. In addition, many other students took a similar CS course based on the same CS POGIL activities at three other institutions. About 25% of the Westminster students went on to take additional CS courses, and gender differences were almost eliminated in students' perceptions of the value of computers. We were pleased that the learning communities appeared to increase most students' interest in CS, but we also realized that having three CS learning communities simultaneously in the last year of the

Table 1: Changes in Students' Computer Attitudes, Fall 2016 (1 = Very Negative to 5 = Very Positive).

		Factor 1		Factor 2		Factor 3	
		Comfort with computers		Value of comp.		Interest in comp. careers	
		Pre	Post	Pre	Post	Pre	Post
Women $N=18$	Mean (SD)	3.9 (0.6)	4.2 (0.5)	3.9 (0.9)	4.4 (0.6)	3.3 (0.3)	3.7 (0.9)
Men $N=46$	Mean (SD)	4.2 (0.6)	4.3 (0.6)	4.3 (0.8)	4.5 (0.6)	4.0 (0.7)	3.9 (0.8)
Total $N=65$	Mean (SD)	4.1 (0.6)	4.3 (0.5)	4.2 (0.8)	4.5 (0.6)	3.8 (0.8)	3.9 (0.9)

One student did not indicate gender.

Table 2: Student Assessment of Classroom Climate, Fall 2016 (1 = Very Negative to 5 = Very Positive).

	Female Mean (SD)	Male Mean (SD)
How would you rate the value of the hands-on activities, with the four team roles (POGIL) in this course?	4.2 (1.1)	4.1 (0.8)
To what degree do you feel the course provided opportunities for you to include your interests and experiences?	3.9 (0.9)	3.8 (0.8)
To what degree does the instructor encourage mutual respect among all students?	4.7 (0.6)	4.7 (0.6)
To what degree do you participate in the course?	4.3 (0.7)	4.3 (0.8)
How comfortable do you feel speaking up/asking questions in this course?	4.1 (1.1)	4.3 (0.9)

project also made it more difficult to attract female students in high numbers to all three learning communities. In the third year, many of the female science students eligible for the Chemistry–CS learning community instead registered for the other two learning communities and enrolled in a stand-alone General Chemistry course. Like many other CS departments, we are currently understaffed, but we remain committed to the idea of offering one CS learning community each year to attract CS students to computing.

A major takeaway from TIDES for us was the message of "Be Empathetic", which in turn helped us become better teachers. We worked to get into the mind-sets of helping every student to the best of our abilities, rather than being disappointed with what we had previously perceived to be students' deficiencies. Our Chemistry professor introduced a new extra credit policy to encourage students to form peer-led study groups and convinced many of us in other departments to introduce this same extra credit policy. For students who don't really know what it means to study, having peers to emulate is so beneficial. The discussion of difficult concepts with other students forces students to confront the fact that maybe they're not as comfortable with the material as they thought.

In addition, some of us have started including more metacognition and self-assessment exercises in our classes to encourage students to think about what they know, what they need more help with, and how they're studying for the class. The feedback provided by students allows us to tailor suggestions with specific ways to improve in the class. These assignments also remind students that their goal is not to complete POGIL activities in class as quickly as possible, but rather to learn the underlying concepts.

The energy from our Westminster TIDES Project led to our participation in many similar initiatives. In 2015, we received a $5000 Google CS Engagement Award to add more context to labs and homework assignments in our first-year CS courses. The Westminster CS Department was selected as a National Council for Women & Information Technology (NCWIT) Pacesetter School for two years (January 2016–December 2017), where we worked with a cohort of leaders from academia and industry to make measurable progress on broadening participation goals. Starting in 2018, we are taking part in one of NCWIT's Extension Services Learning Circles, where we work directly with a consultant to increase our female enrollments and graduation rates. The Westminster Math, Physics, and CS departments collaboratively applied for and received Westminster's first Scholarships for STEM program award, funded by the National Science Foundation, which provides financial and academic support for Westminster students majoring in our three disciplines. CS faculty from Westminster and a partner institution also applied for and received a five-year NSF IUSE Award to study faculty adoption of POGIL and the effect of POGIL activities in introductory CS courses for majors.

Finally, we have watched our campus institutionalize diversity efforts. At the start of our project, the Westminster TIDES faculty ran workshops over two years on understanding bias and teaching for diversity for Westminster faculty. By the end of the project, Westminster reorganized the Diversity Office, hiring a new Director of Student Diversity & Inclusion in March 2016, and a new Associate Vice President of Diversity, Equity, and Inclusion (AVP-DEI) in

September 2016. The college now sponsors several college-wide activities encouraging self-selected faculty and staff in their efforts to better support student success for all students. These include faculty and staff reading groups and courses on diversity and privilege, as well as a "Continuing the Conversation" Series on culture, bias, and other diversity issues.

The Last Word

Learning to teach for diversity is an ongoing process. All nine faculty involved in the Westminster TIDES project have remarked about wanting to do more, but not always knowing how to do it. Changing their course content took both faculty prep time, as well as class time away from other areas, but as one faculty noted:

> I'm working on infusing culture. I've moved from having to cover all the material to saying "What's the point of covering it, if the students don't get it and don't find it relevant?"

Another faculty member noted that in his discipline, it is no longer possible to cover every topic in an introductory first-year course by lecturing, which has helped him select a smaller set of topics to concentrate on using active learning instead.

While all nine faculty involved were committed to active learning techniques at the start of the project, several came to the realization that the classroom environments they developed are just as critical to their students' success. One faculty member noted:

> Having joined the faculty directly out of graduate school, I had a very "sink-or-swim" mentality. I had to work to get into a mindset of helping every student to the best of my ability, rather than being disappointed with what I perceived to be students' deficiencies […] . I now reach out to students proactively when their performance shows any sign of slipping, while I previously waited until a student was failing to let them know they should probably drop the class.

Thanks to the TIDES project, we now realize that being more explicit about what we expect our students to do, with a more descriptive explanation, and more obvious connection of class content to students' lives, can lead to higher, not lower, standards. We work harder to design classes to include more of our students, by learning who they are at the start of the semester and identifying what they need to learn, rather than mechanically covering all the chapters in a textbook. For example,

> I have started including more metacognition and self-assessment assignments in my class to encourage students to think about what they know, what they need more help with, and how they're studying for the class. The feedback provided by students allows me to tailor suggestions with specific ways to improve in the class.

Each of our successes goes beyond a single instructor's class, because we share our ideas with other faculty, both those involved in the TIDES project and those in our departments and divisions. Thanks to this sharing, the entire Chemistry department and much of the CS department now offer extra credit points for students who form and/or participate in peer-led study groups. In other cases, prerequisites have been evaluated and reduced, not just in our departments, but also most notably in the Westminster Math Department.

All of us are grateful to AAC&U and the TIDES Institute for teaching us that empathy and high expectations go hand in hand. We are better teachers because of the experience, and our students benefit from our evolution.

TIDES Resources

Experiencing POGIL in a workshop is critical to helping most instructors to really understand the key principles and practices. The National POGIL Project website (http://pogil.org) maintains a calendar of three-hour, one-day, and multiple-day workshops held across the United States. Ninety-minute and three-hour workshops are also held often at STEM education conferences like the ACM SIGCSE Technical Symposium.

For those unable to attend a workshop, the National POGIL Project website (http://pogil.org) provides a FAQ to POGIL, a downloadable implementation guide, and lists of POGIL curricular materials, primarily in STEM disciplines. Others find the *Instructor's Guide to Process-Oriented Guided-Inquiry Learning* (Hanson, 2013) to be a useful introduction to POGIL pedagogy.

References

Hanson, D. M. (2013). Instructor's Guide to Process-Oriented Guided-Inquiry Learning. Pacific Crest, 2013. http://pcrest.com/research/POGIL_Instructor_Guide2014.pdf

Hu, H. H., & Avery, B. (2015). CS Principles with POGIL Activities as a Learning Community. *Journal of Computing Sciences in Colleges, 31*(2), 79–86, December 2015.

Hu, H. H., & Campbell, P. B. (2017). A Framework for Levels of Student Participation and Stages of Relevant Curriculum. in *Computing in Science & Engineering, 19*(3), 20–29, May–June 2017. doi:10.1109/MCSE.2017.44

Hu, H. H., Kussmaul, C., Knaeble, B.., Mayfield, C., & Yadav, A.. (2016). "Results from a Survey of Faculty Adoption of Process Oriented Guided Inquiry Learning (POGIL) in Computer Science", in Proceedings of the 2016 ACM Conference on Innovation and Technology in Computer Science Education (ITiCSE '16). ACM, New York, NY, USA, 186–191. DOI: https://doi.org/10.1145/2899415.2899471

Kuh, G. D. (2008). *High Impact Educational Practices: What They Are, Who Has Access to Them, and Why They Matter.* Washington, DC: American Association of Colleges and Universities (AAC&U). http://www.neasc.org/downloads/aacu_high_impact_2008_final.pdf

Chapter 12

The Rising TIDE of Wright State University: Context, Connections, and Consequences

Travis Doom, John Gallagher, Michael Raymer and Kathleen Timmerman

Reflection

In Fall 2012, anticipated changes to State of Ohio policies on allocation of educational resources provided strong motivation for all state-affiliated, four-year universities to adopt semester-based academic calendars. As Wright State University was still on a quarter-based academic calendar prior to 2012, all academic units were charged to reformulate their curricula. While reimagining our computer science curriculum, we initiated a fairly typical content review to determine what discipline topics would be covered in each of the new semester-term courses. However, during the review, we realized that we had a rare opportunity to not only repackage our existing content, but to also consider how we could introduce additional modifications to encourage student success. Our existing quarter-based curriculum in Computer Science had a first-year progression rate into the second year course offerings of less than 50%. Four-year retention rates for declared majors in computer science were near the national norms of 40%. Given the national context, the fact that our first-year sequence includes both majors and non-majors, and the less selective nature of the institution's admissions policies and mission, this success rate was not considered unusual. However, with the curriculum transition, we saw an opportunity to redesign our curriculum specifically to address issues, which impeded the progression of students. We chose to think about *how* we should teach the material (and eventually to *whom* we would teach the material), rather than simply *what* would be taught in each course.

A small team of faculty in the department's curriculum body researched the impacts of in-classroom/active learning approaches on student success. The whole of the Department Faculty, convinced by that research, authorized a trial offering of our Computer Science I (CS I) course based on the North Carolina State University (NCSU) SCALE-UP approach (Beichner, 2008; Beichner et al., 2006). SCALE-UP refers to Student-Centered Active Learning Environment with Upside-down Pedagogies (previous definitions have also cited the UP to stand for "Undergraduate Physics" or "Undergraduate Programs" as the approach has evolved.)

SCALE-UP was initially introduced to increase success in large-enrollment general education physics courses. SCALE-UP methods require teaching spaces with collaboration resources (group tables, whiteboards for small groups, shared networked computers, etc.) not typically available in traditional classrooms. The Wright State Computer Science and Engineering Department (WSU-CSE) did not alone possess the resources to create such a facility. Therefore, Department Faculty worked with the Department Chair, the College Dean, and the University Provost to secure matching funds to the Department's partial investment to make this in-classroom experiment viable. Faculty initially expressed concern that the need for this investment would doom this project to failure. To the contrary, we found that, once the potential impact on retention and progression were communicated, our upper administration whole-heartedly moved to support this Faculty-led initiative to impact student success.

The Fall 2012 WSU-CSE Computer Science I (CS1) SCALE-UP offering realized progression rates (percentage of students receiving a grade of A, B, or C and then enrolling for the next course in the sequence) nearly doubled those of traditional offerings in previous terms. That initial improvement in progression rate has been sustained since that first offering. Most interestingly, however, the success rates for female students increased more dramatically than that of the male students. Similarly, the success rates for URMs increased dramatically. The sample sizes were too small for the impact to be statistically observable, but these initial increases piqued interest in broadening the effort. Although our goal was to increase the success rates for all students, it became clear that this change in pedagogy might provide a mechanism to more effectively support and empower those historically considered "more at risk." Due to this compelling early evidence, our departmental faculty became even more open to considering how change in teaching style provided advantage and how specific barriers to progression might be best addressed. It also inspired the originating group of faculty to align with TIDES to seek advice and experience from those already well-established in overcoming specific barriers to student success.

Institutional Context

Wright State University (WSU) is a metropolitan research university located in Dayton, Ohio. Named after Dayton natives Orville and Wilbur Wright, WSU's educational mission is focused on providing research capability in the region and paths to higher education for all students graduating in good standing from high schools in the Miami Valley region of Ohio. In 2016, WSU had approximately

13,600 students with 12,500 of those being degree seeking undergraduate students. Of those degree seeking undergraduates, approximately 30% are first generation, 25% are underrepresented minorities, and 60% are women. Approximately 40% of incoming freshman have high school GPAs between 2.00 and 2.99 and the University's overall six-year graduation rate is approximately 45% (on par with institutions with similar mission and selectivity). The six-year graduation rate for URMs is less than half of the overall rate, at approximately 20%.

Like many Universities with a regional mission, Wright State has focused on improving first-year progression and retention. For our students, we observe the first year to be most critical and WSU students that progress through their second year of study are very likely (more than 70% likely) to graduate. At the time of our project, Wright State had implemented many campus-wide first-year programs, including: (1) a common first-year text, (2) first-year seminars, and (3) mandatory advising programs. These university-wide programs seemed to have had very limited success on our computer science and engineering programs. While the number of students with declared interest in computer science or computer engineering as an intended major remained high, the number of students progressing through the first-year computer science core was only a small fraction of those interested. Most concerning, the majority of the students exiting the university generally meet the same standards of academic preparedness met by their successful and progressing peers. In other words, students were leaving the computer science program, even though they had the preparation required for success.

Methods and Motivation

Inverted lecture-style instruction, in which lecture content is viewed at home and classroom time is used for active-learning activities, provides a clear opportunity for a revolution in undergraduate-level STEM education (Bergmann & Sams, 2012; Freeman et al., 2014; Lage, Platt, & Treglia, 2000). SCALE-UP teaching (Beichner, 2008; Beichner et al., 2006) has become a particularly prolific and emblematic representative of inverted pedagogy. Given its focus on the use of classroom technology, we felt that the SCALE-UP approach would be exceptionally well-suited for the instruction of computer science and engineering. We also felt that its model of active engagement was well-suited for developing investigational and synthesis skills that are critical for success in computer science and engineering.

Operationally, in a SCALE-UP classroom, the instructor is completely immersed in the student experience and learning environment with significantly less traditional lecture. The students are instead engaged in real-time computer science activities and interaction with their peers. There is evidence that course material is better retained as just-in-time learning (Novak, Patterson, Gavrin, & Christian, 1999) and peer-/group-based approaches remediate, develop, and reinforce skill and knowledge-based course outcomes. At least anecdotally, even without additions to basic SCALE-UP methodology, there is more occurring in the classroom. The practice of regularly engaging in group activities and in speaking and using the terminology and techniques of the field affirms each student's understanding of themselves as being successful in their studies. The potential impacts of this approach are consistent with Cohen's self-affirmation theory (Cohen & Sherman, 2014). Further, inverted classroom approaches may directly ameliorate the negative effects of the Impostor Syndrome (Clance & Imes, 1978). The imposter phenomenon, in which a student doubts their capability in an area of effort, even when all evidence demonstrates their proficiency, is well known in the STEM community. Underrepresented groups (particularly female students) might feel that they "do not get" mathematics or engineering as well as their peers simply due to the fact that they have not observed evidence of success of people they identify as similar to themselves in their classmates, instructors, or popular culture. This effect can be overcome through mandatory, in-class, peer-based activity that allows students to develop maturity and observe similar levels of mastery in their peers. These activities provide a platform from which to observe the "mountain climbing" that takes place in first-year engineering education. Perhaps even more importantly, this frequent use of classroom time allows faculty to interact with students in small groups, which facilitates cognitive apprenticeship (Collins, Brown, & Newman, 1987).

A question we asked ourselves early in our curricular redesign process was, if one could anecdotally expect powerful reductions to barriers to success just from using inverted instruction at all, what would happen if we were explicitly *intentional* about designing content to even further enhance those effects? Could this impact be sustained over an entire core curriculum? Could we really impact every student? Would this effort simply delay failure, or would it allow sustained progression? Would incorporating this redesign into our entire core sequence increase or decrease the likelihood of sustainability?

Implementation/Methodology

From our earliest discussions of curriculum reform at Wright State, we realized that we would face the same challenges that innovators in curriculum and pedagogy face everywhere: (1) How can we find the time to individualize classroom instruction when there is little enough time to cover core material as it is? (2) How do we incentivize often overburdened faculty to accept pedagogical changes when the institutional promotion and tenure system provides little or no reward for such activities? (3) How do we assess our results, accounting for difference in individual instructor effectiveness, class composition, and the myriad of other factors that influence the learning environment from semester to semester?

Like-minded peers at other institutions provided some significant inspiration. Across the nation and the world, adoption of new technology for the delivery of instructional material was allowing faculty to "flip" their classrooms. In a traditional classroom, lecture time is spent giving students their initial exposure to the material. Students are exposed to course topics for the first time in the classroom, and then spend out-of-class time reinforcing that learning via homework, group study, and test preparation. In a flipped class, this pattern is reversed. Students see the material first at home (i.e., through a video lecture or online interactive tutorial) and classroom time is spent in a mixture of brief reviews, small- and large-group team exercises, and other activities designed to challenge their understanding, reinforce learning, and help them to develop deeper and more abstract insights into the topic. One particular type of flipped classroom, the SCALE-UP model first piloted at North Carolina State University ([NCSU]; Beichner, 2008; Beichner et al., 2006) had shown promising results in physics classes. By redesigning the classroom environment, leveraging technology in and out of the classroom, and engaging students in well-organized, short, small-group, in-class exercises, SCALE-UP teaching has had a positive impact on student engagement and academic achievement in a wide range of disciplines and institutions. For example, NCSU Physics Department reports that physics students are 2.8 times more likely to fail in a traditional course compared to their SCALE-UP offerings of the same course. Encouraged by these successes, and driven by the objectives of the TIDES project, we decided to undertake the task of increasing student retention and academic performance, especially for students from traditionally underrepresented groups in computer science and engineering, by using the SCALE-UP model to flip every required core course in our curriculum. It was well-understood that this would not be a small task, but would require curriculum redesign, classroom re-engineering, and technology adoption on a grand scale. Additionally, it would require the support and engagement of a significant portion of our faculty, and institutional support at the department and college levels.

The first step in preparing to SCALE-UP the computer science and engineering curriculum was to remake the classroom layout. Front-facing desks in tiered lecture halls do not create an environment conducive to small group exercises and discussions. Fortunately, the WSU administration and our department invested in a new classroom featuring round tables seating nine students each, laptops at every seat, whiteboards covering nearly every wall, dedicated short-throw projectors near each table, and an instructor workstation with extensive AV controls and classroom monitoring and interaction software. With a total of six tables, the room would accommodate 54 students with sufficient space for group activities and instructor interaction.

With nine students at each table, small-group activities can be assigned for three groups of three at each table with larger discussions involving all nine students. Hierarchical exercises can be designed such that the three small groups at each table solve a problem independently, and then combine, discuss, or compare or compete their solutions, with each table then reporting their results to the rest of the class. With this type of exercise, the results of 54 students engaging in a learning activity can lead to a manageable number of six collectively-generated solutions to discuss with the class. Projectors around the room can be used to share a single image from the instructor workstation, or to project a student-generated image from a designated workstation at each table. Ample whiteboard space facilitates group brainstorming and problem solving with ample space to make and correct mistakes. Classroom management software at the instructor station allows the instructor to monitor student activities, quickly distribute documents and software throughout the classroom, and collect student results and comments. Instructors can, for example, quickly send a multiple-choice question to every workstation in the room, with student responses summarized in a pie-chart that the instructor can then optionally share with the rest of the class. Taken together, these features created a classroom environment that was well optimized for group discussions, problem solving, and brainstorming. As soon as it was ready for use, it was clear that curriculum and pedagogy could now be modified to leverage the value of this new learning space.

A primary motivation of our curriculum redesign was to free classroom time to allow interventions and activities designed to engage a diversity of students. As it would be both impractical and unproductive to increase student workload, curriculum changes would need to increase the efficiency and effectiveness of student learning time in and out of the classroom. We believe that the most limited resource in the classroom is the instructor's attention and that the most effective learning often takes place when the instructor is interacting directly with students. Therefore, most often, some material introducing students to new concepts and walking through problem-solving procedures should be delivered outside of the classroom so that instructor time can be preserved for active coaching and problem solving. To realize this idea, we began by collecting audio/video recordings and screen capture of every lecture delivered in a course. In practice, this meant placing cameras in the classroom and use of lapel microphones to collect high quality audio. It also meant replacing whiteboards or overhead projectors with digital pens and touchscreens so that the instructor's writing could be captured and incorporated into lecture videos. Instructors also repeated student questions out loud so that they would be captured in the recordings. Finally, after the collection of hours of raw lecture footage and captured annotated digital screens, we curated, edited, and produced a collection of short 5–15 minutes "best-of" videos covering basic course topics.

Once the videos were complete, we had the means to begin flipping the classroom. In subsequent semesters, students were assigned video lectures and readings in place of in-class lectures, and class time was opened up for other activities. The new in-class activities were designed to require students to interact with one another, using the language of the discipline, and to build proficiency and identity as computer scientists and engineers. By spending class time practicing discipline-specific skills, students were immediately aware of their skill levels relative to their peers and able to appropriately focus efforts, questions, and peer-aid towards increasing self and team mastery. Many basic questions were handled within each group as students aided each other in understanding. When an entire group faced difficulty, the diffusion of the potential for personal embarrassment made it far easier for them to reach out to request direction or aid.

As an example of how we designed in-class activities, we will use the example of our activity to introduce the topic of academic honesty and the consequences of violating it. This example was chosen for two reasons: it illustrates how extensive new learning opportunities were introduced in the newly freed and available classroom time; and it does not require deep understanding of discipline-specific computer science material.

In recent years, academic honesty and intellectual property messages have become very important in computer science courses, as nearly every algorithm, data structure, and design-pattern an instructor can imagine to assign to students is available in multiple programming languages on the web. Historically, students confronted with allegations of code-sharing or re-use often claim to be uncertain of where the line is drawn between healthy collaborative discussion or web research and plagiarism. For instructors, this is often a particularly morose course topic, and not a particularly comfortable or auspicious subject to cover in the crucial first class. Many instructors would rather not establish a negative relationship on day one. Enabled by the SCALE-UP classroom, we replaced the usual warnings and exhortations with an active classroom exercise entitled "*Is it cheating?*"

In this exercise, the students are first given a brief anecdote describing a clearly innocent academic interaction:

> "Professor X assigns her data structures class the task of writing a binary search tree that maintains groups of items in pre-sorted order. One student, Michael, is confused about where and which duplicate values should be stored in the tree structure. During a study session, Michael asks a classmate to explain it to him. The classmate explains, and Michael uses this information to write his binary search tree code. He earns an A on the assignment."

The students are then polled, anonymously, using the class management software: "Did Michael cheat?". The scenario is then altered slightly, such that the situation becomes more ambiguous. Perhaps Michael looks at some code on the web to answer his question, or perhaps Michael's classmate, unasked, shows Michael her own code to help him understand. After each scenario, students are asked to vote, and then to discuss the case in groups and reach a verdict at each table. After these discussions, the instructor weighs in with a personal perspective, and finally sets the ground rules for the course.

Surprisingly, in most cases we have found that the students' views on what constitutes cheating are far more rigid and strict than most instructors' own policies. Regardless, the students emerge from an active exercise having engaged the rules via an attempt to understand the issues. They are required to engage with their classmates and instructor, to communicate their views, and to wrestle with ambiguous problems. The time is not used to lecture students about rote rules, but rather to guide them toward a discipline-specific understanding of norms on the issue at hand. Further, each student begins to establish a relationship of trust with the instructor, to build integrity, and to utilize critical thinking skills on a topic.

A second example of an active learning implementation strategy is the use of high-frequency low-impact testing in which exams are frequent and with only small individual contribution to the final grade. Regular, limited-scope assessments help keep both the instructor and each student aware of how well each student is prepared for active classroom activities. With the ease of auto-grading, online testing aids, instructors can view results in real time and modify their lecture plan for the day to meet their students where they are. Frequent assessment also helps some students come to classes early in the term more fully prepared to engage in in-class group activities. Over time, the desire to be prepared for the in-class activity becomes its own justification for coming to each class well prepared. The commonality across the above two examples and most, if not all, of the interventions we developed, is the recognition that course instructors are better employed in guiding students through active engagement and not in reading content to them. By moving some, but not necessarily all, passively consumed content outside the classroom, we more efficiently leverage instructor face time and actually free up in-class time for activities that are more valuable, both in terms of content mastery and delivery of culturally informed barrier removal interventions.

Results

The initial results of a 2012 flipped-classroom trial at Wright State anecdotally suggested an increase in potential progression rate and an increase in retained student mastery of course concepts in their subsequent course. Based on these anecdotal results, in Fall 2014, Wright State's Computer Science and Engineering Faculty began studying the impact of active learning pedagogy in the courses for the common two-year introductory sequence for both the computer engineering and the computer science programs. Although the amount of active learning varied from instructor-to-instructor, all four courses in the CS&E common core (Computer Science I, Computer Science II, Computer Organization, and Data structures) now have SCALE-UP style active learning included in each class.

The barriers addressed and assessed by this project encompass both cognitive and non-cognitive issues. Additionally, since less classroom time is spent lecturing, clear evidence of equal course rigor in student outcomes must be demonstrated. Due to the range of assessment goals, several different assessment tools are deployed to measure the impact of the barriers to the student's progression rates, retained knowledge, and attitudes. Our work included four primary metrics for evaluation: (1) institutional enrollment/progression data, (2) course-level grade/completion data, (3) quantitative analysis of retained prerequisite knowledge (Timmerman & Doom, 2017), and (4) a pre-/post-course qualitative analysis of student attitudes.

The overall project appears to have statistically significant observable impact on the progression students with low levels of academic preparedness. When regularized interventions are shared with faculty and the faculty are able to use in-class time to specifically deal with overcoming barriers, progression rates in CS I significantly improve (largely due to the increase in progression of students with lower levels of academic preparedness). The greatest results (more than a 50% increase in student progression) were seen in a course taught by a TIDES-trained project investigator and the highest percentage of classroom time (more than 50%) invested in active learning activities. Faculty who did not attend a

TIDES institute, but who were trained by those who attended a TIDES institute, also showed less dramatic, but sustained, increases. The use of activity-focused class time and high-frequency, low-impact assessments appear to have the highest measurable contribution toward overcoming barriers to progression. The availability of out-of-class lectures does not necessarily inherently increase success itself, but is a means to free in-class time to be used more productively.

This positive impact is most dramatically observed in our data for the Spring and Summer term offerings of CS I. Students who are best prepared for the study of computer science generally take CS I in the Fall. Our fall offerings have an even balance of academic preparedness levels as measured by ACT math scores and high school GPA (36% high level, 36% medium level, 27% low level of academic preparedness). Spring term offerings, by contrast, include a higher percentage (52%) of less well academically prepared students who are advised or required to take prerequisites to CS I in the fall. Spring students, and similarly delayed summer students, traditionally have progressed from CS I at a much lower rate. When Computer Science I is taught using the new pedagogy of flipped with barrier interventions, a significant increase of students able to progress to the next course is observed for Spring and Summer terms (53% to 75% and 78% to 100% respectively). The 75% progression rate seen in Spring offerings under the new pedagogy rises to the same progression rate previously only seen for the most well-prepared students in Computer Science I Fall term offerings. For students with a low level of academic preparedness, the progression rate increased from 47% to 81%.

To ensure that the students progressing in the new pedagogy maintain the same standard of mastery, we administer a prerequisite quiz in CS II to assess mastery of critical knowledge areas. There was no statistical difference in mastery observed between fall and spring/summer groups of students progressing in the new pedagogy, even though spring and summer cohorts contained a much higher proportion of students that would have been likely to fail under the previous pedagogy. Similarly, rates of progression and student mastery were sustained throughout the entire two-year core sequences for this very different body of initial students progressing successfully through CS I.

To assess how the barrier interventions impacted underrepresented groups in STEM, two specific subpopulations of students were reviewed: (1) female students and (2) students from underrepresented ethnic backgrounds. For these results, all students from the subgroups in all the different courses were evaluated as a single group. When the female students are grouped according to their Academic Preparedness Level, they followed the same trend as the general population; the students with a low academic preparedness level have a significant increase from 51% to 76%.

The results for underrepresented ethnicity students were different from what were observed for the general population. The high level of academic preparedness from this group of students showed a statistically observable increase from 70% (n = 74) to 91% (n = 11). This result suggests that the interventions focusing on non-cognitive and social barriers were particularly impactful in helping these academically well-prepared students' progress.

We utilized a qualitative retrospective student survey developed by our project's external evaluator to explore the relative impact of several barrier interventions on a set of underlying factors that had been posited as potential barriers to student success. Collected data indicates that activity-focused class time and problem-solving exercises are rated as the most impactful changes by the students. The data indicates that the vast majority of students did not view any particular course element as having a negative impact.

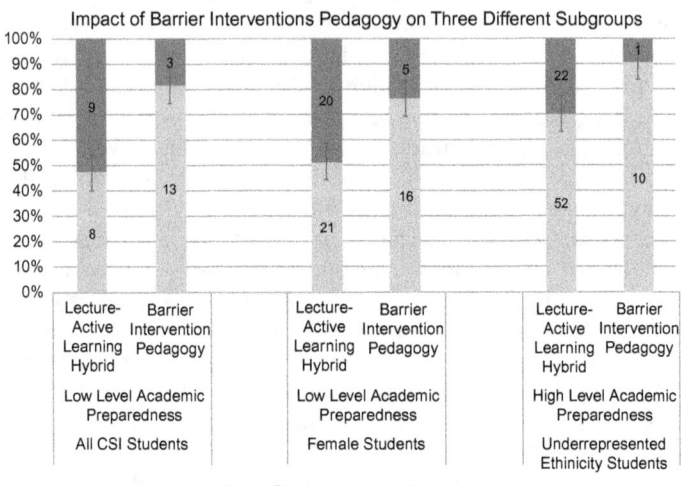

Student pre/post qualitative attitude surveys and end-of-course course evaluations showed no decrease in measured attitudes of students towards the class, instructor, or other commonly assessed metrics. Statistically observable increases were seen in responses to questions related to being more comfortable asking questions, knowing more people, confidence in ability to deal with STEM projects, and confidence in ability to deal with unfair treatment. The most significant increase was in whether or not "class time was well used" for which 92% of students provided a score of 5 out of 5 on student evaluations and the remaining 8% provided a score of 4 out of 5.

Discussion

Of interest to readers of this book are the following questions: (1) How do we find time in already crowded classes to actively address specific, individualized, student needs? (2) What style of intervention is both effective and practically sustainable? and 3) What interventions are particularly useful for overcoming barriers specific to underrepresented student demographics? We recognize that in many ways what we did to address those questions is not entirely novel in that it draws very heavily on existing inverted classroom models and specific training in cultural responsiveness provided by the TIDES institute. What is novel, perhaps, is that we were privileged with the opportunity to synthesize all that knowledge into a specific plan, run that plan in a coordinated manner over several classes in a coordinated sequence, and finally, provide some data-driven insight into each of the questions.

On the first question, there is little doubt that inverting a classroom shifts the focus of in-class time onto active learning engagement. We do not wish to suggest that this somehow lightens the load for the instructor. In fact, the amount of instructor effort usually increases at least moderately as instructors need to think on their feet and improvise more often. Carefully designed inverted activities, however, employ hierarchical structure to allow students to engage individually, but negotiate common solutions that are assessed in group and by the instructor. This blend does allow the use of more *impactful* activities and inherently helps build computer science and STEM identities. We were able to demonstrate that one could provide scaffolding to circumvent barriers for students, particularly those underrepresented, while maintaining content mastery and remaining within the time and resource boundaries of a typical course offering.

On the second question, our strategies seem both effective and sustainable. Assessments of retrained knowledge show no significant difference in preparedness for the next core course between the students in the control group and the students in the experimental group. The increase in progression rate for the fully flipped with barrier interventions pedagogy most greatly impacts less academically prepared students, lifting them to progression rates more in line with academically well-prepared peers. Even in course offerings which do not show an overall increase that is statistically observable, more detailed analysis shows a significant increase in progression among students with low levels of academic preparation, which is masked by the relative lack of change in the more highly prepared students.

Progression rates throughout the core sequence were sustained, when taught by faculty who were aware of and took action to address the barriers to progression. Specifically, the progression rates of such courses appear to be roughly equivalent to the progression rates of the courses as previously offered with more highly academically prepared students. Thus, the success of less academically well prepared students in the first course of the sequence does not "delay failure," but instead appears to allow sustained progression (at least when the subsequent core courses use similar pedagogy).

In our experience, the most difficult obstacle to overcome in conducting this work is not in convincing faculty that there is merit in this effort. The biggest obstacle is to balance that merit against the effort in change necessary to realize the advance. Changing course materials, preparing to use new teaching styles, and preparing entirely new in-classroom activities is a daunting and work-intensive task. Even more daunting is the task of mentoring others to conduct this work.

We have found that the key towards flipping an entire core curriculum and drawing in a wide number of faculty is to make this work easy for other faculty to adopt incrementally. There is no need to completely invert all aspects of a course simultaneously. Incremental advantage is possible. This allows the potentially daunting work to take place over multiple terms as each faculty member becomes more comfortable with the technique and develops fresh ideas for in-classroom activities appropriate to their students and take on the course material.

On the third question, the most salient observation is our finding that well-prepared students from underrepresented student groups succeed in greater numbers when engaged in active learning classrooms with tailored interventions. A tantalizing fact in the analysis is that the URM students that showed the most benefit from the project-deployed interventions are those that have a high level of academic preparedness. Non-URM students (including women) showed the most benefit in students who are least well academically prepared. We have yet to determine if this discrepancy is due to the nature of our classification mechanism for academic preparedness, chance, error, or a legitimate suggestion that URM students may have been failing to progress at disproportionate rates for reasons other than lack of aptitude or academic preparation. This suggests giving credence to the concept of using classroom time to ameliorate imposter syndrome and to help build a "computer scientist" identity.

In addition to the three core questions, one might also be curious about practical observations about making a curriculum-wide, culturally responsive, teaching strategy work. Perhaps the most critical practical observation is this: *Once a class is inverted and materials are developed, the teaching style itself does not add to ongoing regular workload, but simply changes it, allowing more focus on students in class.* Indeed, the inverted lecture framework lends itself to sharing activities and out-of-class materials (video lectures, etc.) that may actually simplify the process of teaching a class, particularly for the first time. Instructors will not necessarily know exactly what questions/problems a particular student group may have with in-class activities. This can be both exciting and terrifying. The most critical preparation for these interactions is simply mastery of the content. Appropriate elements of the discipline can then be shared, as needed to help lead students to overcome group-specific concerns. The faculty member may have a general idea of what is going to happen in a class period, but it will be the students who will specifically identify and communicate exactly how and where instructor support is most valuable. As those needs can change substantially from group to group and from term to term, flexibility in determining specific needs provides significant opportunity for increases in student success.

From the perspective of the student, a change of focus from what (or even how) we teach to a focus on whom we are teaching, better enables each faculty member to meet every student wherever they currently are in their progression. This applies equally to students new to the discipline as it does to an experienced practitioner in the field. This allowed the faculty in our project to take a much more active role in helping students to develop the ability to think like a STEMist. Mastery of that one fundamental skill might explain all other success of the project.

Conclusion

There seems to be little doubt that active learning in the classroom has potentially enormous impact on student success and both their identity and competence as a practitioner of their discipline. Students learn best when they are partners in learning. The most common objection from faculty is not doubt over the impact, but rather a belief that there is no time to conduct such activity. Although there may be some initial outlay of time required to flip a classroom, once this task is completed, it allows instructor time to be leveraged more efficiently. One may, therefore, have a reasonable expectation that one will achieve better results with the same amount of instructor time and effort.

Further, at least at our institution, there is little doubt there has been campus-wide effect. Faculty prepared to teach project courses report bringing these techniques into other courses under their instruction. During this project, faculty from across campus asked and were encouraged to use our experimental SCALE-UP classroom. These efforts encouraged, at least in part, the development of three additional large-scale active-collaborative learning (ACL) classrooms on campus designed to bring ACL to many large-enrollment general education courses. These efforts also contributed to the offering of the first campus-wide teaching symposium, "Teaching for Student Success Symposium: Reducing the Achievement Gap," at Wright State University (Aug 25, 2015). This event was scheduled as part of the new faculty orientation and included more than 100 new and returning WSU faculty members and instructional staff from throughout the university. The symposium provided an opportunity to expose WSU faculty to several project-related activities, including a panel on SCALE-UP/Active-Learning teaching, and poster sessions on engaging students, active-learning practices, and reducing the achievement gap for underprepared, underrepresented, or low-income students. The symposium has since been institutionalized as an annual event.

From our efforts, we conclude that both individual and institutional change to increase the success of all students is indeed possible. However, to be successful, the change has to come bottom-up and from the faculty. Administration cannot and should not attempt to force faculty to change how they teach. The decision of how to best teach students is, very rightly, a faculty freedom and responsibility. Making change, where appropriate, at the institutional levels requires a network of faculty to support change efforts, particularly when impact cannot be meaningfully assessed objectively for years. This network must work with administration to develop a culture of trust that enables experimentation and supports/facilitates incremental change.

The Last Word

The most important takeaway from our experience is the importance of continuous improvement and incremental change. Do not make this work into a project so large that it can never get started. Instead, the work should be considered and implemented as a series of small steps. These not only include your steps to change classroom experiences towards more "who-oriented" learning, but also your steps to aid your peers in their efforts. Try an activity or two. Get feedback from students. Share the experience with peers. Encourage peers to try the activity that you prepared; and in turn attempt yourself activities that they have prepared. Use those interactions to make that experience better next time, and to inform the transformation of another experience. Each reflection leads to another small step. Some steps will be in the right direction; some will be in the wrong direction. The incremental change allows room for error and improvement. This incremental and continued change and involvement of your community will be critical towards supporting incremental and sustained change that eventually impacts an entire program or institution and thus has long-term, meaningful impact on each student.

As a final reflection, we would be remiss if we ignored the difficulty of our initial faculty team being "some white guys from Ohio" beginning a project focused on the use of culturally responsive teaching strategies. We began this project as a general attempt to improve success for all of our computer science students through a specific reform. We would have been daunted by a project designed to develop a pedagogy to specifically deal with the matter of equity and inclusion. We were both surprised and overjoyed to see the particularly powerful impact of our general work on women and underrepresented minorities. At this time, there are relatively few women and underrepresented minorities on the faculty of most computer science departments. If we are to change this reality, then some of this work must be done and supported by people like us.

We cannot overstate the importance of the TIDES training in our development towards thinking not just about how we teach, but whom we teach. Some of the key areas where the structure and guidance of the TIDES community impacted this work include: (1) Framing the research in terms of its importance, potential impact, and necessity; (2) Facilitating the discussion of awkward questions, particularly regarding approaches that various groups might find constructive or off-putting; (3) Modeling interactions through participation in reflection, fishbowls, and other best practices; (4) Informing our efforts through pointers to specific best-in-class resources and providing the scaffolding to help use the material quickly; and (5) Encouraging self-assessment and reflection. The information contained in this book should be an invaluable resource to anyone looking to undertake similar efforts.

TIDES Resources

Before engaging in this work, we highly recommend that you read the works in the reference section of this chapter. In particular, the work of Abeysekera and Dawson (2015) on the flipped classroom, and the work of Beichner et al. (2006) and Beichner (2008) on the SCALE-UP Project provide critical context regarding the impact of carefully using both in-classroom and out-of-classroom time intentionally to best impact student learning. These readings will also help illustrate the potential importance of technology (for example, room design or the use of videos) towards success in this work. The SCALE-UP Project's web site (http://scaleup.nscu.edu) is an outstanding resource towards getting started in this work.

Lage et al. (2000), Bergmann and Sams (2012), and Freeman et al. (2014) are all excellent introductions to the potential impact of inverted-lecture practices. These readings may be helping in building faculty impetus towards attempting changes in pedagogy to facilitate increases in student learning. Clance and Imes (1978), Collins et al. (1987), and Cohen and Sherman (2014) provide critical insight into the psychology behind potential impact of this work. This insight may be vital to selecting appropriate activities to address specific barriers to a particular course, institution, or student group. Lastly, our published research results (Timmerman & Doom, 2017; Timmerman, Raymer, Gallagher, & Doom, 2016) may provide some context on specific techniques and barrier interventions we found most appropriate to our student body and some specific tools used to assess impact.

References

Abeysekera, L., & Dawson, P. (2015). Motivation and cognitive load in the flipped classroom: Definition, rationale and a call for research. *Higher Education Research & Development, 34*(1), 1−14.

Beichner, R. (2008). The SCALE-UP Project: A Student-Centered Active Learning Environment for Undergraduate Programs. National Academy of Sciences, September 2008. Retrieved from https://sites.nationalacademies.org/cs/groups/dbassesite/documents/webpage/dbasse_072628.pdf

Beichner, R., Saul, J., Abbott, D., Morse, J., Deardorff, D., Allain, R., ... Risley, J. (2006). Student-centered activities for large enrollment undergraduate programs (SCALE-UP) project. In E. F. Redish & P. J. Cooney (Eds.), *Research-based reform in university physics*. College Park, MD: American Association of Physics Teachers.

Bergmann, J., & Sams, A. (2012). *Flip your classroom: Reach every student in every class everyday*. Arlington, VA: International Society for Technology in Education World.

Clance, P. R., & Imes, S. A. (1978). The imposter phenomenon in high achieving women: Dynamics and therapeutic intervention. *Psychotherapy: Theory, Research and Practice, 15*(3), 241−247.

Cohen, G., & Sherman, D. (2014). The psychology of change: Self-affirmation and social psychological intervention. *Annual Review of Psychology, 65*, 333−371. Retrieved from https://doi.org/10.1146/annurev-psych-010213-115137

Collins, A., Brown, J. S., & Newman, S. E. (1987). Cognitive apprenticeship: Teaching the craft of reading, writing and mathematics (Technical Report No. 403). Retrieved from https://files.eric.ed.gov/fulltext/ED284181.pdf

Freeman, S., Eddy, S. L., McDonough, M., Smith, M. K., Okoroafor, N., Jordt, H., & Wenderoth, M. P. (2014). Active learning increases student performance in science, engineering, and mathematics. *Proceedings of the National Academy of Sciences of the USA, 111*(23), 8410−8415.

Lage, M. J., Platt, G. J., & Treglia, M. (2000). Inverting the classroom: A gateway to creating an inclusive learning environment. *The Journal of Economic Education, 31*(1), 30–43.

Novak, G. M., Patterson, E. T., Gavrin, A. D., & Christian, W. (1999). *Just-in-time teaching: Blending active learning with web technology.* Upper Saddle River, NJ: Prentice Hall.

Timmerman, K., & Doom, T. (2017, March). Infrastructure for continuous assessment of retained relevant knowledge. In *Proceedings of the 2017 ACM Special Interest Group Technical Symposium on Computer Science Education (SIGCSE 2017)*, Seattle, WA.

Timmerman, K., Raymer, M., Gallagher, J., & Doom, T. (2016, August). Educational methods for inverted-lecture Computer Science classrooms to overcome common barriers to STEM student success. In *Proceedings of the 2016 IEEE Research on Equity and Sustained Participation in Engineering, Computing, and Technology (RESPECT) Conference*, Atlanta, GA.

Chapter 13

Music as the Icebreaker for Learning to Code

Ani Nahapetian, Virginia Huynh, Omar Ruvalcaba, Ric Alviso and Gloria Melara

Reflection

The California State University, Northridge (CSUN), TIDES initiative (CSUN@TIDES) grew from a collaborative effort to infuse projects from music into computer science coursework. Early discussions revealed that the upper-division computer science courses lent themselves well to the incorporation of music applications. However, numerous instances of students switching majors due to early-class experiences made us resolve to address the first course in programming, instead.

The TIDES@CSUN team shared the vision of students learning to program with culturally familiar applications, and specifically using music to break the ice. The world music drum machine developed using an ASCII beep character and simple if-statements and loops became the clarifying example. The use of music in the programming work connected the two fields, and resulted in a close collaboration between faculty and student assistants from both the Computer Science and the Music Departments. Throughout our more than three-year collaboration, we held regular monthly team meetings with all of our faculty stakeholders and with student assistants involved in the development and implementation.

The distinctly different approaches to teaching challenged us. Music faculty pushed for more reflection by students and the Computer Science faculty struggled with its relevance and time requirements. Reciprocally, for those from the Music Department, fundamental parts of their experience were uncomfortable and questionable for their new collaborators, leading to bewilderment and frustration.

About a year into the project, when we set out to recruit faculty to use the new culturally relevant modules, we encountered hurdles. Using new programming modules in lectures and lab sections was clearly additional work, but faculty buy-in was a larger challenge than was originally anticipated. Faculty stipends, lab assistants, additional training, and custom tailoring of assignments were not sufficient to incentivize the majority of faculty members to participate.

Upon that realization, we took a step back and provided faculty members with easily accessible and field-specific information about the need for culturally responsive instruction. We also found avenues for intervention outside of the traditional faculty-student interactions – with peer mentors, the YouSpeak classroom interaction system, and the Festival of Computer Science.

Institutional Context

California State University, Northridge (CSUN), is a public university in the San Fernando Valley of Los Angeles. It has the largest student body of the 23 campuses of the California State University (CSU) system. It is the second-largest comprehensive university in the state of California, behind UCLA. CSUN's enrollment exceeds 41,000 students, making it one of the largest single-campus universities in the United States. It awards over 1% of the Computer Science degrees awarded from over 369 US universities and colleges (American Society for Engineering Education, 2016).

In addition to being a Hispanic-serving institution for nearly 20 years, CSUN achieved minority-serving institution (MSI) status in 2014. It currently has an undergraduate enrollment with more than 55% representing traditionally under-served minority (URM) populations (i.e., American Indian/Alaskan Native, Native Hawaiian/Pacific Islander, African American, and Latina/o). CSUN is the only four-year institution of higher education serving Los Angeles' multicultural San Fernando Valley, whose 1.8 million residents are 47% Latino.

With over 10,000 degrees awarded each year from more than 50 departments, CSUN graduates the potential to change the future workforce by creating a programming-capable workforce, if provided access to programming courses. Additionally, CSUN's culturally diverse student population has the potential to change the face of the next generation of computer scientists and programmers. Thus, it is a powerful venue for intervention.

There are also unique challenges. Namely, there is a significant discrepancy between the proportion of underrepresented minority women on the CSUN campus and those in the Computer Science Department. Totally 32.4% of the CSUN undergraduate population are URM women (29.6% Latina), while the Computer Science Department has only 6.3% URM women (4.9% Latina). The data for men are surprisingly inverted. URM men are only 23.3% of the CSUN undergraduate population (21.2% Latino men), but they represent 34% (31.6% Latino men) of the Computer Science Department.

Our intervention addressed the first programming course in a series of three, commonly referred to in the literature as CS 1. The course equivalent at CSUN is listed as COMP 110. This course is a required first course in computer programming for five majors at CSUN: (1) Computer Science, (2) Computer Information Technology, (3) Computer Engineering, (4) Mathematics, and (5) Information Systems. Enrollment in COMP 110 has a yearly average of approximately 300 students. Although it has a large enrollment, it also has a high fail rate. Thus, modification of COMP 110 coursework was a high-impact point in the curriculum to address retention in the Computer Science major.

We chose music – from salsa to hip-hop – to serve as our mechanism for intervention. With CSUN's more than 8,500 URM male students and more than 12,000 URM female students, we used culturally familiar music to cultivate a sense of belonging in COMP 110 throughout the inevitable struggles that students faced while working towards programming mastery.

Introduction/Background and Significance

Interest in computing majors, by "generation computing" (Roberts, 2016) students, has experienced dramatic growth (Roberts, 2011; Zweben & Bizot, 2018). During the personal computer (PC) and dotcom enrollment booms, resources – including faculty and course offerings – were not sufficient to match the dramatic and rapid growth of students. Therefore, Computer Science departments were forced to throttle student's enrollment. Women were much more likely to turn away from the major, in response to enrollment throttling (Roberts, 2016). We are again experiencing dramatic growth in Computer Science interest, and unfortunately the growth of resources is, again, outpaced by student enrollment. Therefore, it is imperative that solutions that address increased interest in computer science programs also address the retention of women and URMs.

Approaches applied broadly to other STEM fields cannot simply be ported to Computer Science. When Computer Science data are disaggregated from those of other STEM fields, Computer Science appears clearly distinct and unique (Lehman, Sax, & Zimmerman, 2017).

Studies have shown the significance of the introductory course in the retention of computing majors (Franklin, 2013). One such study found that women were more likely than men to leave an introductory programming class because of the teaching style (Blaney & Stout, 2017).

Implementation/Methodology

Through our TIDES@CSUN initiative, we invested in both culturally relevant content and culturally responsive instruction and engagement to ensure that students in STEM reflect the diversity of our community.

With the support of the AAC&U TIDES program, we created culturally relevant content through our project, "Learning to Code by Making Music: The Introduction of Computer Science Coursework with World Music Applications for the Retention of Underrepresented Students in STEM." Instead of using traditional examples based on board games (e.g., programming die rolls) and economics (e.g., programming the calculation of compound interest), we incorporated innovative references to music from various cultures into the instruction of a required core introductory programming course (e.g., programming a world music drum machine). Thus, by teaming up faculty in Computer

Science with faculty in Music, we created culturally relevant content in the context of computer science instruction and developed laboratory modules for introductory programming courses.

We elevated the voice of students in the classroom using a quiet and subtle platform, the YouSpeak classroom interaction system. YouSpeak enabled students, including those insecure in the classroom, to ask questions anonymously and have their comments posted alongside the instructor's presentation materials.

To support the culturally relevant content, we also developed modules for instructors to implement culturally responsive instruction, including reflection exercises and the promotion of mindful collaboration.

From the pool of students who recently completed the modified course, we hired mentors for our lab sections and started the near-peer mentor program. Coincidentally, all of the mentors were women of color. Following a focus group of the mentors, we found that the student mentor role clearly helped the mentors themselves redefine how they viewed their own abilities and career paths, and influenced their sense of belonging in the field.

We extended the culturally responsive engagement outside of the formal instruction to informal opportunities for interaction with faculty and fellow students. With our Festival of Computer Science event on the lawn outside our building, we had a DJ, live jazz music by our CSUN Music students, food, free t-shirts, and brain teasers. We had the participation of student clubs, including the Society of Women Engineering (SWE), the Society of Hispanic Professional Engineers (SHPE), and the National Society of Black Engineers (NSBE). We showed the diverse face of our student population at CSUN for students passing in and out of class and to the food court. Moreover, we provided fun and relaxed opportunities for interaction among our students and faculty.

Culturally Responsive Content Development

TIDES@CSUN incorporated topics from world music into its introductory programming course, COMP 110, in an effort to attract and retain underrepresented student interest in STEM fields. These topics were often culturally familiar to the traditionally underrepresented student groups we aimed to retain and support in the major.

As an applied field, computer programs are developed to address a need in an application area. However, typically, the application areas presented in lectures and assigned in homework carry little or no cultural relevance to underrepresented groups such as Hispanics, African Americans, or women. The previous practice at CSUN, and in most other institutions, was to use examples and projects inspired by topics such as mathematics, economics, board games, and science fiction, as evidenced by the introductory programming textbooks. For example, for-loops are presented by verifying the $3n+1$ conjecture. The Math library is practiced with the calculation of compound interest. Random number generation is presented with games such as craps. We, instead, used musical genres such as salsa, Mexican music, blues, and hip-hop to inspire lecture examples, programming projects, and lab modules that referenced musical topics such as rhythm, scales, and tones across cultures.

One of the programming projects, for example, asked students to create a drum machine with versatility to compose rhythmic beats from different cultures and musical traditions, including hip-hop beats and Latin rhythms. The students used standard software libraries and the basic building blocks of programming, including if-statements, loops, and arrays. Some example beats are shown below, and demonstrate how the topics of selection and iteration can be neatly combined to implement beats. In the representation, the types of beats are represented with lowercase and uppercase symbols, with 'x' representing the weak beat and 'X' representing the strong beat.

- duple/Polka (found in Mexican music): XxXxXxXx;
- triple/Waltz (also, found in Mexican music): XxxXxxXxxXxx;
- clave (found in Latin music including salsa): XxxXxxXxxxXxXxxx;
- blues: XxXXxXXxXXxX;
- hip-hop (a popular example): xxXxxxXx; and
- gospel: xXxXxXxX;

After identifying key computer science topics and matching them with topics from world music, we developed modules for use in any CS 1 course offering. The modules were developed with help from brainstorming sessions that included Computer Science and Music faculty members and students. We learned not only about our respective fields in these meetings, but also about the cultural differences between our fields and departments. Each module included a project description and specification, Java skeleton code, as well as peer-narrated YouTube video that guided students through the skeleton code, links, videos, and texts introducing the musical topics. We also included some web-based demonstration of the project to help students play around with and understand the musical concepts addressed in the project.

The development process intentionally engaged students as key members. The students helped inspire applications and topic areas that would be appealing to themselves; their voices were used for the videos developed. Both music and computer science students, mostly undergraduates, were involved in the project development. Coincidentally and fortunately, they shared their enthusiasm about the project with their friends, thus serving as an unexpected and powerful promotion and recruitment mechanism. The modules, detailed in Figure 1, were developed, tested, and implemented for the project.

Many of the modules allowed the students to choose their preferred musical styles. As a result, they were able to express their cultural diversity in a way that would have been limited, if the music had been prescribed by us. For example, in the lyrics processing problem, where the students found the text of their favorite songs to determine the most common words, a few students excitedly realized that they could use lyrics in Spanish or other languages, just as easily as those in English.

Modules Name	Programming Concept	Description
Scale of Words	Console I/O - print statements and reading values from the console. Basics of instantiating an object.	Sing a scale using a user entered word
Guess the Note	Selection - Branching with if, else if, and else statements; introduction to methods	Guess a played note and display whether the guess is correct, higher, or lower than the played note
World Music Drum Machine	Loops - for and while loops	Create different rhythmic beats from around the world
Random Music	Random Number Generation - Generating a random integer with the Random object or with Math.Random()	Randomly generate different combinations of music beats
Guess the Genre	Loops and Arrays - methods and double dimensional arrays	Make a game where the user needs to guess the genre of the played song
Strings To Beats	Strings – String class and string processing	Make a string processing drum machine
Lyrics Processing	File I/O – Reading and writing to a file; string processing	Count the occurrences of words in a song's lyrics
Text to Melody	File I/O – Reading from file; string processing	Read numbers from a text file to play a melody
Beat Creator	Object-Oriented Programming – Declaring classes, instantiating objects, working with multiple class file	Create a graphical user interface to play beats with appropriate timing
Sound Recorder	Object-Oriented Programming – Declaring classes, instantiating objects, working with multiple class file	Record and play sound

Figure 1: The Programming Modules, with the Programming Concepts They Explored and the Music-inspired Programming Prompts.

To grow faculty awareness of the need for culturally relevant course materials, at CSUN and in the broader LA area, we hosted workshops on the CSUN campus attracting STEM faculty from CSUN and neighboring Loyola Marymount University. One of our early training workshops was titled "Teaching Programming with World Music: Modules, Tools, and Ideas for Student Retention." The workshop provided an overview of the TIDES@CSUN modules developed for introductory programming courses. It discussed the experience of implementing CSUN's COMP110 course and laboratory. It also presented a hands-on introduction to YouSpeak, the classroom participation tool, designed to encourage the participation of students in the classroom through anonymous question and comment posting. Most powerfully, it included a panel of CSUN students representing diverse programming backgrounds, who discussed their experiences with the TIDES@CSUN modules and the redesigned COMP 110/L course in which they were enrolled or had just completed.

Adoption of the culturally relevant course materials was not as smooth as we had originally assumed. Interestingly, a similar challenge did not present itself with the culturally responsive instruction modules. Upon this realization, we began work to have the culturally relevant programming materials serve as the basis for the revised COMP 110/L courses, gave presentations at departmental meetings, and addressed recruitment efforts to new faculty who had not yet finalized their teaching outlines.

Culturally Responsive Instruction Modules

In addition to the implementation of culturally relevant programming modules, we also developed modules *for instructors* to integrate and increase culturally responsive instruction. The initial inspiration for this work was a well-received presentation entitled, "Microaggressions and Underrepresented Groups in Computer Science," by Virginia Huynh at one of our workshops. The talk addressed the common forms of microaggressions relevant to computer science, and the best practices for professors and mentors to create supportive and inclusive professional environments. The response and the demand for more materials awakened us to the need for accessible and field-specific culturally responsive instruction educational materials.

We developed culturally responsive instruction modules targeting faculty (not students) that addressed topics from the broader area of culturally relevant pedagogy. The modules break down the material into chunks so as not to appear burdensome to read or disconnected from classroom instruction. The instructor modules include links to videos found online, prepared YouTube videos, PowerPoint presentations, reports, websites, research articles, listicles, word clouds, newspaper articles, and data visualizations.

Modules cover topics relevant to culturally responsive instruction of programming and computer science, with a specific focus on instructors of introductory programming courses. The content is easily accessible (e.g., not requiring special subscriptions), diverse in its content presentation (e.g., text, videos, images), and targets both enthusiastic and reluctant instructors. Practical tips, hands-on classroom exercises, and links to a variety of resources are provided.

The culturally responsive instruction modules address topics including feedback culture, microaggressions, stereotype threat, and culturally responsive conflict resolution. Specific classroom activities are explored, including the BaFa BaFa multicultural activity, project-based learning, and reflection exercises. Community service learning, creating a caring community in the classroom, and confronting convention in the classroom community are also explored. Finally, motivating culturally responsive instruction and topics specific to women in programming are addressed.

Discussing the Gender Gap

Closing the gender gap was an exceptionally challenging problem for us. We invited Linda J. Sax, Professor with the UCLA Graduate School of Education and Information Science to give a talk entitled, "The Gender Gap in STEM: The Unique Case of Computer Science." The talk focused on a national sample of entering college students spanning 1971 to 2011 and revealed how women in Computer Science held a distinct set of characteristics compared to other STEM areas.

We did not stop with a keynote. With a room full of 22 faculty members from a range of departments and six members of the CSUN Administration, including the Dean of Engineering and Computer Science and the heads of CSUN's Offices for Faculty Development, Institutional Research, and Academic Resources and Planning, we invited the audience to form a working group to examine the challenges and strategies for recruiting and retaining CSUN women and traditionally underrepresented minorities in STEM.

The discussion questions were as follows:

- How do we change the public discussion about women and URMs going into STEM?
- What has worked at other institutions? How are we different at CSUN?
- Should we take a targeted approach?
- How do we attract women & URMs into STEM?
- What existing campus programs (or broadly) can we leverage?
- What pedagogy would best support achievement in the key coursework that constrains success?
- What resources are needed to retain women and URMs?
- From your discussions with students, what hurdles or turning points have STEM students experienced?

YouSpeak Classroom Interaction System

Throughout our TIDES@CSUN implementation, we provided students the opportunity to use the YouSpeak classroom interaction system to ask questions and comment anonymously. YouSpeak provided students (who were shy, intimidated, and/or working through a translator because they are hard of hearing or deaf) to have another avenue to participate in the classroom. All student comments, submitted through smart phones or computers in the classroom, were projected, thus elevating student voices to that of the course instructor.

YouSpeak is a web and mobile classroom interaction software system, developed at CSUN, which provides a framework for students to comment or to ask questions anonymously during class through its mobile or web-based app. Students can rate the comments of others in the class, up or down, allowing the most relevant questions to rise to the top of the list. Instructors project these comments alongside course materials, such as slides, documents, and videos, using the web interface.

YouSpeak enabled the collection of quantitative data about student participation in our TIDES@CSUN courses. The continuous and personalized data collected about students' understanding of course topics tailored the immediate course flow, and also informed the courses long term. The corpus of data produced was used to extract the contributing factors to student participation and the understanding of course topics.

While the well-known technology of clickers allowed students to give electronic feedback during lecture, YouSpeak went a step further. YouSpeak not only examined the understanding of concepts by the class as a whole, and with multiple-choice and freeform prompts, but also informed the instructor of the understanding of concepts by certain groups of students in the class.

Peer Mentors

After the first modified course offering concluded, we realized that we had access to a powerful resource, namely our own students. Accordingly, we hired mentors from the pool of students who had recently completed the modified course, and started a peer mentor program. The peer mentors assisted in the lab and organized study sessions. Through their interactions with other students, the peer mentors helped to change the image of who could be successful in Computer Science. Coincidentally, all of the peer mentors were women of color.

To prepare and support the peer mentors for their role, students would meet with faculty member Gloria Melara to: (1) reflect upon and discuss the culturally responsive environment of their previous COMP110 TIDES@CSUN course; (2) provide the necessary skills for the mentoring task; and (3) build self-confidence in the mentoring role. These meetings offered peer mentors the opportunity to talk about their mentoring experience, discuss what was or was not working in the lab, and provided them with a formal space to generate ideas, such as conducting workshops for students before the class's three lab examinations. Furthermore, the faculty/peer-mentor meetings provided us with the ability to collect information about the students' needs.

Similar to the students who assisted in developing the culturally relevant course content, the peer mentorship program became a growth opportunity for the mentors themselves. That is, it positively impacted their sense of belonging and confidence in their abilities.

Festival of Computer Science

For the first time, and hopefully not last, we held the Festival of Computer Science on the south lawn of our building, inviting CSUN students to interact with faculty, staff, and student clubs from the Computer Science Department. We had an excellent turnout of students from Computer Science, Engineering, and many other majors. We had food, a student DJ, and live Jazz music from CSUN Music Department students.

Several faculty presented posters at the event, showcasing topics from classes, research activities available for students, and topics related to careers in computing. Two additional breakout sessions were also hosted following the event, led by Computer Science Department faculty. Shan Barkataki gave a presentation on the path to graduation for transfer students; and Li Liu presented a Computer Science Department orientation for freshmen. Additionally, student clubs were invited to make presentations at the event, including those supporting underrepresented groups in STEM.

Throughout the event, all students were invited to participate in programming and computer science brain teasers. For completed attempts, students received T-shirts. This activity engaged students, sparked discussion with faculty, and encouraged students to work together. The event's first goal was to present computer science as a fun, thought-provoking field. The second goal was to encourage interaction and reduce the intimidation that students may feel about the field and its practitioners. This opportunity gave students a concrete topic of discussion with faculty and fellow students, thus decreasing the fear of sounding uninformed and removing the challenge of coming up with a technical topic or question.

Results

To quantitatively evaluate how effectively we have addressed the participation and the retention of URMs and female students with our modified COMP 110 course, we evaluated course enrollment, pass rates, and surveys of student confidence. We collected data, including grades and persistence in the major, to determine the effects of our intervention.

All groups in our last year of the TIDES-redesigned courses had a higher percentage of students who earned a C or higher, as compared with the control group. We are encouraged by the stronger overall student outcomes, particularly the performance of URM women and the increase in men's performance compared to previous years. Our data suggest that the development of culturally responsive instruction, paired with our redesigned course modules, contributed to the persistence of URM women and potentially improved grades for URM men. Overall, our intervention does not appear to benefit all women, but we are hopeful it has some value as women in the TIDES courses had an 11% higher pass rate than those in the control course.

In spring 2017, students completed a survey about their confidence in technical skills, confidence in accessing resources, and their satisfaction with the quality of relationships with faculty and students. In the TIDES-redesigned courses, men and women showed increased confidence in technical skills, but this increase was smaller among URM women and nonexistent for URM men. In the control courses, women did not gain confidence in their technical skills, and URM women in particular felt less confident. This suggests that enrollment in the TIDES-redesigned course may be beneficial for women in particular. However, enrollment in TIDES courses did not positively affect students' confidence in accessing resources or satisfaction in quality interactions.

A focus group of the peer mentors was conducted to understand the impact of the role of peer mentors. The focus group revealed that being a peer mentor helped students improve their own understanding of computer science concepts, realize the importance of professional opportunities in pursuing a computer science career and the impact of faculty mentors. It also helped them think about pedagogy and teaching computer science. They learned how to modify their approaches to address students' different learning needs and how to consider their students' perspective when teaching.

Discussion

Comparing the demographics of the computing majors with the rest of the campus, the absence of URM women, and especially Latinas, is stark. Therefore, it is imperative to disaggregate URM women from non-URM women and URM men in the data analysis. Moreover, it is important to understand that the only way the representation of URMs can reach its full potential is by recruiting and retaining URM women.

In our intervention, we found that a unique group of faculty were willing to participate in TIDES@CSUN, and use both culturally relevant course content and culturally responsive instruction. Surprisingly, not all faculty teaching the course were interested in having a student peer mentor. For the new programming assignments, we concluded that faculty buy-in was a critical barrier to change, and that buy-in had to take place in the first semester of the course. Otherwise, the course materials were already prepared and change usually was met with resistance. Faculty members teaching the introductory programming courses have a large impact on the retention of underserved students and on their sense of belonging.

Engaging students in peer mentorship and content development had an impact not only on the students enrolled in the course, but also on the students engaged in the project. Exploring further opportunities to engage students throughout their degree program is a powerful mechanism for improvement.

Conclusion

This project set out to prepare culturally relevant content to attract and retain underrepresented groups to and in the computing majors, respectively. Specifically, we chose to develop World Music applications in the programming work for an introductory CS 1 course at CSUN. In the process, we concluded that culturally relevant content is not sufficient if not paired with culturally responsive engagement. Therefore, we developed short, diverse modules for faculty to understand and incorporate culturally responsive instruction in their classroom. We also recruited peer mentors from the students who had recently completed the revised course. The impact of the peer mentors was not only demonstrated in the improvements of the enrolled students, but also on the peer mentors themselves.

The Last Word

Powerful, tangible changes were achieved when we fully and actively engaged students in the content development, through peer mentorship, in informal but substantive interactions, and with culturally relevant laboratory work in the classroom.

References

American Society for Engineering Education. (2016). *Engineering by the numbers: ASEE retention and time-to-graduation benchmarks for undergraduate engineering schools, departments and programs.* Retrieved from http://aeir.asee.org/wp-content/uploads/2017/07/2017-Engineering-by-the-Numbers-3.pdf

Blaney, J. M., & Stout, J. G. (2017). Examining the relationship between introductory computing course experiences, self-efficacy, and belonging among first-generation college women. In *Proceedings of the 2017 ACM SIGCSE Technical Symposium on Computer Science Education* (pp. 453–458). https://doi.org/10.1145/3159450.3159458

Franklin, D. (2013). A practical guide to gender diversity for computer science faculty. *Synthesis Lectures on Professionalism and Career Advancement for Scientists and Engineers, 1*(2), 1–81.

Lehman, K. J., Sax, L. J., & Zimmerman, H. B. (2017). Women planning to major in computer science: Who are they and what makes them unique? *Computer Science Education, 26*(4), 277–298.

Roberts, E. (2016). *A history of capacity challenges in computer science.* Retrieved from http://cs.stanford.edu/~eroberts/CSCapacity/

Roberts, E. S. (2011, September). Meeting the challenges of rising enrollments. *ACM Inroads, 2*(3), 4–6.

Zweben, S., & Bizot, B. (2018, May). 2017 CRA Taulbee survey: Another year of record undergrad enrollment; doctoral degree production steady while master's production rises again. *Computing Research News, 30*(5). Retrieved from https://cra.org/crn/2018/05/2017-cra-taulbee-survey-another-year-of-record-undergrad-enrollment-doctoral-degree-production-steady-while-masters-production-rises-again/

Chapter 14

Interventions Addressing Recruitment and Retention of Underrepresented Minority Groups in Undergraduate STEM Disciplines

Cleo Hughes Darden, Roni M. Ellington, Jigish Zaveri, Sanjay Bapna, Linda Akli, Stella Hargett, Prabir Bhattacharya, Ali Emdad and Asamoah Nkwanta

Reflection

We, at Morgan State University (MSU), feel fortunate to have been selected among 20 colleges and universities nationwide to participate in the Association of American Colleges and Universities (AAC&U) Teaching to Increase Diversity and Equity in STEM (TIDES) program. As a Historically Black College and University (HBCU), Morgan is passionate about finding novel and innovative ways to recruit and retain our largely African American student population in STEM fields. As such, the Morgan TIDES Program (MTIDES) centered its attention on addressing these issues by meeting the four goals identified by the TIDES program:

(1) To infuse computer and information science tools into basic science courses in chemistry, biology, physics, mathematics, and computer science for the purpose of graduating a workforce skilled in data science.
(2) To empower Morgan faculty, through carefully designed professional development workshops, to effectively integrate Computational Data Science (CDS) tools and implement culturally sensitive pedagogy into their practice.

Additionally, the MTIDES program identified two additional goals that are aligned with the goals of the TIDES program. They were:

(1) to develop a computational data science certificate program that targets both Morgan STEM and non-STEM majors; and
(2) to foster sustainable institutional change at Morgan State University through the systemic implementation of culturally sensitive instructional strategies and CDS techniques and instructional strategies.

Over the past three years, the MTIDES Program, with its interdisciplinary team of administrators and faculty members from several schools/colleges within the university (i.e., the School of Computer, Mathematical, and Natural Sciences; School of Education and Urban Studies; School of Engineering; School of Business and Management; and College of Liberal Arts), has worked strategically to produce and introduce novel courses, curricula, and workshops. The workshops included: (1) Cultural Competency, Computational and Data Science; (2) Uses of Big Data, R, Parallel R; and (3) Extreme Science and Engineering Discovery Environment (XSEDE). The main purpose of these workshops was to train and empower faculty with the tools and techniques to enhance culturally responsive teaching methods in STEM courses to primarily African American undergraduates. Before we attempted to make changes in our classroom pedagogy, and we worked assiduously to change our attitudes, our behaviors, and our expectations, as well as to increase mindfulness about our increasingly diverse student population. To do this, we attended yearly TIDES Institutes, which were designed to focus on culturally responsive teaching (CRT) and provide a safe and encouraging environment for us and the other TIDES teams to express thoughts about the successes and challenges of each of our projects. The TIDES Institutes introduced us to new pedagogical/social science concepts and information that would aid us in creating more inclusive STEM classroom environments, thereby helping us to retain our STEM students.

For the MTIDES Team members that participated in the TIDES Institutes, the on-campus workshops were designed to address culturally responsive pedagogies. The interdisciplinary MTIDES team founded the workshop, "Cultural Competence in STEM Undergraduate Teaching" where we received a clearer understanding on, through examples and hands-on activities, of how best to utilize selected culturally responsive pedagogies to create more inclusive STEM courses. The MTIDES team learned that a lack of cultural responsiveness, − defined as the ability to understand, communicate, appreciate, respect, and interact effectively with persons of various cultures (Coggins, Dupont, & Campbell, 2008; Cross, Bazron, Dennis, & Isaacs, 1989) can interfere with the learning environment in our classrooms, especially with a diverse, underrepresented student body. While we thought we had planned our courses well and thought we were "good teachers" in our respective disciplines, we certainly had not used a self-reflective process, as was advocated in these workshops, to design our courses for maximum delivery to and inclusion of our primarily STEM students.

At the workshops, we were challenged to ask three essential questions as we prepared our courses and entered our respective classroom: (1) Who am I? (2) Who are we? (3) Who are our students? This reflective process was transformative. The knowledge and insight gained through participation in the TIDES Institutes were immeasurable in how they empowered the MTIDES team to accomplish our own goals and objectives of being effective educators.

Not only did the strategies learned at the TIDES Institutes impact how we work with students, but they also affected how we worked with one another. We are not only an interdisciplinary group, but we also come from many different cultures (i.e., African, African American, Asian, and the Caribbean). By having an interdisciplinary multicultural team, we were able to ground our work in various disciplinary and cultural perspectives. This was particularly important for the development of the culturally responsive teaching principles that guided our work since these principles were not discipline-specific; therefore, they could be applied across many disciplines. Further, we applied some of the techniques learned in the TIDES institutes to develop a powerful and committed team that respected and valued the views and perspectives of various cultures. This made our team more sensitive to the needs of our diverse population of students and more willing to interrogate our personal biases when implementing these principles in our classrooms. This work was not always easy because the team members already had their own biases about improving student-centered learning and were not familiar with culturally responsive teaching pedagogies. However, working through these challenges and working together over the last three years with the common goal of success of the MTIDES project have certainly impacted the MSU community.

The MTIDES project has fostered interdisciplinary collaborations within the respective STEM departments and in the various schools and college within MSU. One of the team members, an administrator from the School of Business, noted that the computational resources provided by the MTIDES Project "has had a profound impact on the school." When asked to explain, he noted that by sharing the MTIDES project resources with his colleagues, the School of Business was considering a redesign of several of its courses to incorporate more computational thinking (a key focus of the MTIDES Project).

In many ways, faculty members were the true benefactors of the MTIDES project. They used the opportunities provided by the MTIDES project to enhance their research and teaching through the resources provided. Interdisciplinary collaborations were forged not only among the existing team members, but also among new interdisciplinary teams that have emerged across campus. Consequently, working together as one team (biologists, mathematicians, computer scientists, sociologists, engineers, educators, information technologists) provided us with the opportunity to learn from one another and to respect the strengths brought by each individual to solve "big data" (Manyika et al., 2011) problems. For example, faculty who participated in the Extreme Science and Engineering Development Environment (XSEDE) workshops worked in teams to create learning activities that were used in their classrooms. These activities drew on the skills and competencies from several disciplines and supported students in seeing how the concept of "big data" applied to complex situations. One Information Science and Systems faculty member expressed his gratitude for the interdisciplinary nature of MTIDES by simply saying, "Thank you so much for offering this important resource across campus, and I hope to promote more interdisciplinary research."

At the heart of the MTIDES project, was the desire to recruit and retain our largely African American undergraduate students in STEM fields, through introducing innovative ways to engage our students. One of the major impacts of the MTIDES initiative was that faculty participated in various summer institutes related to successfully implementing active-learning strategies in their STEM courses. For example, STEM faculty members from Biology, Chemistry, Physics, and Mathematics participated in week-long-intensive National Academies Summer Institute for Scientific Teaching (NASIST) training workshops (2013–2015). Of the twelve faculty members, two were MTIDES faculty and others were from either various programs on campus or other universities. The workshops focused on active-learning, student-centered pedagogical approaches, and assessment. The trained faculty members began implementing active-learning modules within their courses, largely impacting the School of Computer, Mathematics, and Natural Sciences. More recently (August 2017), NASIST came to MSU, during which earlier work participants, three MTIDES faculty, and two MTIDES administrators served as facilitators. Faculty who utilized the resources and workshops provided by the MTIDES project reported increased interest in STEM by their students, as well as positive learning outcomes. Faculty showed an increased willingness to integrate more computational tools and techniques into their diverse discipline courses. This integration was expected to have a positive impact on attracting more students to STEM disciplines, as well as on preparing more students for STEM careers.

Several faculty members noted that the MTIDES Project was responsible for

> promoting a broader computational thinking environment by expanding the number of courses being taught and faculty investing more time and effort into implementing computational science into every course that is given at the university, which is good for the university.

According to one faculty member,

> MTIDES provided a platform and created a mechanism for both students and faculty members to interact in ways that reflected mutual respect for various disciplinary and cultural perspectives. This made the integration of culturally responsive teaching and computational data sciences in the MTIDES courses more engaging for students in all disciplines. As a result, students exposed to MTIDES courses were more engaged and interested in learning about computational data sciences.

Institutional Context

Morgan State University was established in 1867 to train young Black men for the ministry, and has evolved into a public, co-educational, comprehensive, Carnegie-classified doctoral research university in Baltimore, Maryland. In 2016, MSU was named a National Treasure by the National Trust for Historic Preservation. In the state of Maryland, MSU is the largest Historically Black College and University (HBCU) and has been designated as "Maryland's Preeminent Public Urban Research University" in 2017 by the state's legislature. MSU has the responsibility of addressing the needs of urban populations in the city of Baltimore and the state of Maryland. MSU has an ethnically and culturally diverse student body and offers a range of programs, leading to degrees from the baccalaureate through the doctorate as well as offering programs in research and public services.

MSU enrolls a diverse undergraduate population, with over sixty percent supported by Pell grants and a large percentage of first-generation college students. This population of students faces challenges to degree completion. More than 65% of first-time freshmen test into developmental courses and have financial challenges to support their academic endeavors. In 2015, MSU launched the "50 by 25" campaign, which focuses on increasing MSU graduation rates to at least 50% by 2025. Currently, the graduation rate is 38%.

As noted earlier, MSU has challenges with improving retention and graduation rates. To address some of these challenges, the MTIDES Project was implemented in the School of Computer, Mathematics, and Natural Sciences in 2014. For the past three years, the MTIDES Team has infused computational tools into several science courses, as well as sociology, business, and engineering courses and Morgan faculty members actively participated and implemented computational science tools and culturally responsive/sensitive pedagogies into science, sociology, business, and engineering courses. The MTIDES team developed a computational data science certificate (CDS) program for Morgan STEM and non-STEM majors. The MTIDES team continues to systematically implement culturally responsive and computational instructional strategies into courses throughout the University.

Our analysis of various data reveals that many institutional changes are being realized because of the MTIDES project. For example, several key administrators, particularly those from the Computer Sciences and Information Science and Systems departments, hold positive attitudes and beliefs about the value of incorporating computational data science tools and strategies and culturally responsive teaching practices into courses taught in their departments. These positive attitudes and beliefs will be discussed in further detail in the sections that follow. To date, the MTIDES Project has produced fourteen MTIDES-influenced courses, six MTIDES Computational Data Science (CDS) courses, and three new courses, which are included in the CDS certificate program. The MTIDES team expects that the project's ultimate impact will be to increase the students' interest in computational data sciences and to provide STEM and non-STEM students with additional computational skills that will prepare them for the workforce and additional educational endeavors beyond the baccalaureate degree.

The Computational Data Science (CDS) certificate program is an interdisciplinary program developed by the MSU faculty and facilitated by the support of the TIDES program. The lead departments for the CDS certificate program include the Departments of Biology, Computer Science, Industrial Enginerring; Information Science and Systems, Mathematics, and Sociology. The upper-division certificate in CDS is designed as a fifteen-credit-hour certificate, where the core is nine credit hours (with an option of choosing three courses from an inventory of six courses). All of these courses require computational analytical techniques that can be applied to data sets.

Introduction/Background and Significance

In recent decades, considerable importance has been placed on increasing the number of Americans who pursue degrees and obtain employment in STEM (National Academies of Sciences, Engineering, and Medicine, 2017; Thomasian, 2011), which includes disciplines such as Computer and Information Systems, Computer Science, Computer Administration Management and Security, Computer Programming and Data Processing (Big Data), Information Sciences, Computer Networking and Telecommunications Sciences (Manyika et al., 2011; National Academies of Sciences, Engineering, and Medicine, 2017; Noonan, 2017). Increasing the number of STEM workers is important because the STEM workforce in the United States drives innovation, which fosters new ideas and commercializes patents, generates new businesses, and improves the economy (Thomasian, 2011). According to the 2017 STEM jobs report, in the United States, there were 9.0 million STEM workers in 2015, which is a 6.1% increase from 2010, for all workers in STEM jobs (Noonan, 2017).

STEM employment increased by 24% in the last ten years (2005–2015) and is projected to increase by 8.9% from 2014 to 2024 (Noonan, 2017). In order to maintain the pace of STEM employment, the US workforce will require 1 million more STEM professionals during the next decade to compete globally (President's Council of Advisors on Science and Technology [PCAST], 2012). However, attaining this goal will be a challenge due to the low rates of persistence to graduation for undergraduate STEM majors, which are even lower for women and underrepresented minorities (National Science Board, 2010; PCAST, 2012).

Several studies indicate that there are many factors that contribute to low persistence of STEM majors such as: (1) lack of interest in the general science courses, (2) ineffective teaching and advising, and (3) lack of preparedness for STEM majors (Bettinger, 2010; Brainard & Carlin, 1998; Chen, 2015a, 2015b; Cheryan, Master, & Meltzoff, 2015; Ost, 2010; Packard, Gagnon, LaBelle, Jeffers, & Lynn, 2011; PCAST, 2012; Rask, 2010; Seymour & Hewitt, 1997; Sithole et al., 2017; Strenta, Elliott, Adair, Matier, & Scott, 1994).

The STEM persistence gap results in fewer STEM students entering the STEM workforce or graduate programs. Therefore, the focus of the MTIDES project was to (1) develop, implement, and evaluate a project that would integrate computational data sciences and culturally responsive teaching in select

STEM and non-STEM courses, and (2) to create a computational sciences certificate. This project was created to help address the recruitment and retention of underrepresented students in undergraduate STEM disciplines, particularly computer and information sciences by redesigning courses in ways that would increase student engagement and provide students with skills and competencies that would make them more marketable.

A growing body of research suggests that infusing computational sciences and culturally responsive teaching practices into undergraduate STEM courses will support the skills and competencies needed by our students for future jobs requiring the use and analysis of big data (National Academies of Sciences, Engineering, and Medicine, 2017; Sengupta, Kinnebrew, Basu, Biswas, & Clark, 2013; Wilensky & Reisman, 2006); foster engagement in STEM disciplines (Guzdial, 2008); promote increased achievement (Guzdial, 2008; National Academies of Sciences, Engineering, and Medicine, 2017); solve unstructured problems and communicate information to others (Lee, Martin, & Apone, 2014); and enhance computational skills and competencies.

To improve MSU students' preparedness for graduate and professional schools and the STEM workforce, the two major goals of the MTIDES project focused on (1) infusing computer and information science tools into basic science courses; and (2) empowering Morgan faculty through carefully designed professional faculty development workshops to effectively integrate computational science tools and implement culturally responsive pedagogies into STEM courses.

For this project, faculty empowerment referred to the extent to which faculty had the interest, knowledge, and skills to effectively understand and implement Computational Data Science (CDS) and culturally responsive teaching (CRT) in their classrooms. In addition to these two major goals, there were two overarching MTIDES project goals. These goals were (1) to provide a Computational Data Sciences Certificate (CDSC) Program that attracts Morgan STEM majors and non-STEM majors and (2) to foster sustainable institutional change at MSU through the systemic implementation of CRT, CDS techniques, and instructional strategies. The CDSC program would be awarded to students who successfully completed the revised STEM curricula. To assist faculty and students, an external partnership with the XSEDE, an NSF-funded cyberinfrastructure project, provides advanced computing resources and training, and was leveraged to develop computational sciences curricula.

Faculty from the Schools of Computer, Mathematical, and Natural Sciences; Business; Liberal Arts; and Engineering participated in various activities designed to achieve the above goals. Project activities included (1) project meetings, (2) professional development activities focused on computational data sciences and culturally responsive teaching, (3) course redesign meetings and activities, (4) need assessment activities, (5) individual interviews and focus groups, and (6) classroom observations. The major outcomes for the project were to redesign STEM and non-STEM courses by infusing computational data science tools and culturally responsive teaching into these courses. Another major outcome was to offer an approved computational data science certificate program that appealed to STEM and non-STEM students.

Implementation/Methodology

The evaluation of MTIDES was guided by a SYSTEMS VIEW of Program Evaluation (Chen, 2015a, 2015b), which used logic models to determine the inputs, outputs, and key outcomes of the project and included both formative and summative evaluations (Chen, 2015a, 2015b). In addition, the project evaluation was guided by the Program Evaluation Standards developed by the Joint Committee on Standards for Educational Evaluation (Yarbrough, Shulha, Hopson, & Caruthers, 2011). Specifically, the standards related to program utility, feasibility, and accuracy were considered throughout the planning and implementation of the project-planning and evaluation processes.

Guided by the underlying conceptual lens discussed earlier, the evaluation of the MTIDES project included data collection and analysis from various sources throughout the duration of the project. These data were used to determine the extent to which the project was meeting its intended outcomes, to understand faculty perceptions of MTIDES activities, and to answer the evaluation questions. Since this chapter focuses only on the outcomes of the first two goals of the project, we have included the following relevant evaluation questions.

Evaluation Questions for Goal 1

(1) To what extent is computational and data science being infused in chemistry, biology, physics, mathematics, computer science, engineering, and information systems courses?
(2) How are faculty implementing computational and data science strategies, tools, and techniques into their chemistry, biology, physics, and mathematics courses?
(3) In what ways are the computational and data science tools, techniques, lessons, and modules developed in the workshops impacting student learning and engagement in chemistry, biology, physics, mathematics, computer science, information systems, and engineering courses?

Evaluation Questions for Goal 2

(1) How are the professional development workshops being designed and implemented to empower faculty to integrate both computational/data science and culturally sensitive teaching strategies and lessons into their courses?
(2) What are the experiences of STEM and non-STEM faculty in the professional development workshops?

Data collection methods included:

(1) evaluation surveys from professional development workshops;
(2) a faculty survey that measured faculty interest in and competency with computational data sciences and culturally responsive teaching;

(3) student survey data, which focused on students' interest in the computational data science certificate program, and their level of interest and engagement in MTIDES courses;
(4) administrative focus groups centered on administrators' interest in and support of the project;
(5) observation protocol developed and used to understand the extent to which computational data science tools and culturally responsive teaching were being integrated into the MTIDES courses;
(6) faculty syllabi; and
(7) student needs assessment data.

These data were collected and analyzed using thematic analysis of qualitative data (interview data, focus groups, classroom syllabi) and quantitative analyses of survey data, observation data, and needs assessment. The MIDES CRT workshops were grounded in the work of leading scholars in culturally responsive educational strategies including Ladson-Billings (1995), Gay (2010), and Moses and Cobb (2001). During these workshops, the MTIDES faculty developed a set of culturally responsive teaching principles (CRTP) that would shape their course redesign and classroom instruction to make their courses more culturally responsive and promote active learning. The principles were generated through an iterative process that began with a list of 15 core strategies of culturally responsive pedagogy drawn from the STEM literature. These strategies were distributed to individual faculty members, who were asked to rate each of the strategies on a scale from 1−5, based on (1) how critical that strategy would be to creating a culturally responsive STEM classroom, and (2) the extent of their willingness to integrate the strategy in their courses. Faculty were then grouped to discuss individual ratings and to develop a list of their top five strategies. Once groups developed their rankings, they were vetted by all faculty until an agreement was reached on the set of principles that would ultimately shape our CRP framework for the MTIDES project. CRP principles, as adopted by the MTIDES faculty, were to: (1) incorporate physical and hands-on activities in instructional practices; (2) incorporate more student-led discussions and teaching opportunities in class; (3) increase awareness of personal biases and judgments that shape perceptions of students and willingness to change these perceptions; (4) have student apprenticeships that foster empowered learning communities; and (5) use students' lived experiences as a context for course content and activities.

In addition to culturally responsive teaching practices, MTIDES faculty were charged with infusing computational data science (CDS) tools in their courses. Professional development workshops were given by the MTIDES partner, XSEDE, to assist faculty in understanding and implementing CORE/Basic Data-driven competencies and Simulation and Modeling in the context of their courses. XSEDE developed a set of basic and core competencies that students will need to understand in order to analyze large, complex data sets (see XSEDE, 2014 for a list of these principles). According to the competencies shaping CDS integration, students will: (1) understand how data originates from diverse sources; (2) be able to recognize factors affecting and techniques employed to cope with quality data; (3) be able to organize, describe, and manage data; (4) have a basic understanding of databases; (5) understand the diverse motivations and barriers associated with data sharing, production, and consumption; (6) be able to plan and practice the data lifecycle; and (7) be able to understand and explain the role of modeling in CDS. These competencies guided the ways in which faculty integrated CDS in their classes as well as how professional development evaluations and course observations were structured.

A workshop on "R and Parallel R" was also offered to faculty and graduate students to provide hands-on knowledge of computational skills thereby enable faculty to work with highly customizable analytics scripts and tools for their research. The R Foundation for Statistical Computing has developed the R programming language for statistical computing and graphics in a free software environment. Parallel R is a platform for on-demand, distributed, parallel computing using R and is used by statisticians and data miners for data analysis. Parallel R supports in-memory implementation, code parallelization, and high-performance computing for data analysis, data mining, machine learning, and AI. Mr David Walling of Texas Advanced Computing Center, Austin, Texas, was the instructor for the full-day R and Parallel R workshop. The workshop attracted over thirty participants from various MSU departments, as well as from other regional universities (Howard University, Johns Hopkins University, and the University of Maryland College Park). Participants included STEM and non-STEM faculty, graduate students, and postdocs. All participants were unanimously enthusiastic about the value of the workshop. One faculty member commented that this workshop had opened new avenues of research by providing new tools and techniques.

Results

Here, we provide insight into the extent to which faculty were empowered to integrate CDS and CRT into classroom practices, and the ways in which such infusion shaped students' engagement and achievement in STEM courses. This empowerment was fostered by carefully planned professional development experiences that were designed to assist faculty in understanding the goals and objectives of MTIDES. The professional development experiences provided faculty with the following: (1) an understanding of CDS and CRT, (2) shared ways that they can integrate these ideas into their work, (3) provided hands-on experiences with creating interdisciplinary activities and modules that reflect the tenets of CRT and CDS, and (4) provided support with effectively implementing these activities and modules into their courses.

Evaluation Question (1) for Goal 1: To what extent are computational data sciences being infused in STEM and Non-STEM Courses? Analysis of data collected for the three years of the project indicated that both STEM and non-STEM faculty became more aware of the importance of computational data sciences to their disciplines and developed strategies that exposed their students to CDS tools and techniques. For example, in our initial survey of faculty, many faculty members were not aware of CDS and many confused it with computer science or integrating various forms of computer technology. After participating in MTIDES professional development activities, faculty were able to not only articulate the meaning of computational data sciences, but also identify how CDS science tools could be used in their courses in ways that supported students in developing competencies in CDS, and how student-learning outcomes could be improved in their specific disciplines.

Student engagement and learning were positively impacted through the use of these tools, specifically in the biology department. An upper-division cell and molecular biology course was revised to utilize active-learning computational activities that endow students with functional knowledge of a selection of biological databases and computational methods for analyzing and visualizing molecular biology data. In the process, the students acquired a high-level understanding of key biological processes, such as signal transduction.

Faculty incorporated many CRT principles into these biology courses: (1) explicitly eliciting and valuing students' contributions to discussions, (2) emphasizing peer-to-peer interactions, and (3) group work. Biology faculty also selected examples from students' lived experiences, identified notable African American scientists, and discussed their contributions. Another aspect of culturally responsive pedagogy is the use of both cooperative and collaborative learning, which fosters empowered learning communities and social construction of knowledge (CST principle 4). Collaborative learning was incorporated through group lab work and group-generated reports, even though students ultimately submitted individual reports for grading. This approach developed the interpersonal skills necessary for students to build a positive learning community and increased students' capacity for working in teams. At the same time it emphasized the role of individual responsibility.

Evaluation Question (2) for Goal (1): How are STEM and Non-STEM faculty implementing computational and data sciences tools, techniques, and strategies into their courses? In addition to understanding what CDS tools were being infused in their courses, we wanted to know how they were being used. Specifically, it was important to understand how faculty from various disciplines were interpreting "computational data sciences infusion" and how this interpretation translated into their course planning and classroom practices. Observational and faculty survey data revealed that faculty were integrating more "computation," "computational thinking," and "computer literacy" in their courses, with some increased focus on the uses of "big data" in their fields. We observed that faculty implemented activities that required students to use various computational strategies. These strategies were generally focused on showing students how to compute values and interpret their results. On the other hand, when faculty integrated computational thinking, they used strategies related to problem-solving using data and focused on the thinking required to address a problem as opposed to simply interpreting computational results. Computer literacy was perceived as the need to help students understand the various forms of technology that existed to support the analysis of big data. In these cases, faculty were focused on making their students aware of technology, and how it could be used. In all cases, faculty wanted to show how computation, computational thinking, and computational literacy could be used to solving real-world problems students would encounter in their fields, as well as to support the development of students' computational skills for addressing those problems.

Faculty use of computational and data sciences ranged from "using more computers in the classroom" to "analyzing big data using sophisticated computational tools and techniques." Several faculty members commented that they would like to use computational sciences in more sophisticated ways; however, their students "need more of the basics" and there is a need for more resources to do this effectively. Despite these challenges, there was an overwhelming agreement that student's increased awareness of computational data sciences is important in their careers. A computer science faculty member commented:

> I have used various computational data sciences tools in my COSC 150 course. This is an entry-level course that exposes students to computational data sciences and (incorporating CDS in lower level courses) provided an opportunity for our majors and other majors, as well, to understand the importance of these tools (early in their studies). Many students think that CDS is the same as computer science and it is not. Students are now more aware that CDS is a different field than computer science with lots of opportunities available in various fields.

Faculty from non-STEM departments also noted that students' increased awareness of computational sciences tools and techniques helped them to better understand the benefits of these tools to their future careers.

Evaluation Question (1) for Goal 2: What were faculty's initial perceptions of CDS and CRT infusion in their courses? Data from various sources indicated that the initial perceptions of faculty regarding computational sciences and culturally responsive teaching were positive. Many faculty members had participated in other projects focused on instructional improvement by using active-learning strategies in their classrooms and were therefore very open to improving their teaching in ways that would help students succeed. In addition, as faculty members at an HBCU, they were very familiar with equity-focused teaching practices. Hence, faculty were generally open to incorporating CRT and CDS because they believed that it would help their classes be more engaging and promote active learning. When asked why they participated in the project, faculty members stated that they felt that the goals of the project supported the needs and goals of their courses. Faculty responded that they participated in the project because "I wanted to improve my class performance," "I wanted to provide students with a more relevant curriculum," and "I have some courses which require students to develop ability and skills on computation." Faculty who participated in the project continued to hold positive perceptions and attitudes about infusing CDS and CRT in their courses. Faculty also noted a commitment to improving their pedagogical skills, building positive relationships with their students, enhancing students' interest in STEM, and increasing students' awareness and competencies in computational sciences. Many faculty members commented that they were attracted to the program because it allowed them to build interdisciplinary collaborations. As one faculty member expressed, "This program would significantly help our students to become better/stronger STEM students overall and also allow faculty to foster relationships between engineering and many other STEM departments across our campus."

These positive perceptions and attitudes remained constant throughout faculty members' participation in the project. Although faculty members stated that they would still need ongoing support to integrate CDS and CRT in their courses - because they felt that their participation in the project had an overall positive impact on themselves and their instruction - they were committed to continuing to engage in this work once the project was complete. Data from the final faculty survey revealed that faculty are becoming more comfortable with the implementation of culturally responsive teaching in their classrooms.

Evaluation Question (2) for Goal 2: What were STEM and non-STEM faculty's experiences in MTIDES activities and professional development activities? Analysis of the data revealed that faculty had an overall positive experience from the MTIDES meetings, activities, and workshops. Specifically, they discussed how the XSEDE workshops were critical to their ability to infuse computation data sciences principles and tools in their practice. In addition, many of the interdisciplinary activities and modules created by the faculty incorporated the XSEDE tools used in the workshops.

Twenty-seven faculty members participated in the two professional development activities in Year 3 (fall and summer PD workshops). Data collected from these professional development workshops indicated that faculty have positive attitudes and perceptions about infusing computational data sciences and culturally responsive teaching in their classes. For example, when asked to report on her experiences with incorporating CRT and CDS in her class, an Information Science and Systems (INSS) faculty member reported,

> Overall, I found the cultural sensitivity teaching protocols to have been received positively by my students. At first, I was skeptical about how students would receive this new instructional approach. Although the addition of NodeXL was not received favorably in my class, the concepts related to social networks, social media, and the NodeXL program are great ways to wrap up the semester and were received favorably. In my opinion, the addition in INSS 141 serves as a beacon to open up students to learning more about computers and technology. I look forward to trying this again in my Fall 2016 INSS 141 class.

Other faculty members reported similar sentiments. In survey data following an MTIDES professional development workshop, 82% of the faculty surveyed noted that their participation in the MTIDES workshop improved not only their understanding of CDS and CRT but helped them understand how to apply these concepts and principles in their class. In addition, faculty reported that this new understanding of these tools helped to minimize some of the anxiety they had regarding how to integrate CDS tools and CRT strategies in their classrooms.

Faculty data revealed that the content of these workshops was helpful to them in meeting the goals of their courses and programs. As one faculty member commented:

> I think bringing more attention to the area of computational sciences and teaching for diversity helps make students more interested in exploring these types of fields and it has also helped me improve my skills as well.

Evaluation Question (3) for Goal 2: How has faculty participation in MTIDES activities shaped their perceptions, attitudes and instructional practices regarding the infusion of CDS and CRT in their courses? Overall, data collected from faculty suggest that faculty believed that implementation of CDS tools, activities, lessons, and modules would have a positive impact on student learning, engagement, and persistence in their courses. Specifically, data revealed that faculty improved their own understanding of computational data sciences tools and this helped them improve their overall teaching. Faculty noted that through their participation in this project, they not only gained a sufficient understanding of CDS, but they could see how applying CDS tools would benefit their students and enhance their instruction. Further, many faculty reported they were able to see how they could collaborate with other faculty to create learning experiences that would be engaging for students and expose them to skills that they may need for future jobs in their chosen fields of study. These cross-disciplinary collaborations were key to deepening faculty understanding and how to implement ideas that were used to develop activities, lessons, and modules in their respective STEM courses at MSU.

The following graphs depict how faculty perceived the impact of integrating CRT and CDS in their courses. The following graphs show faculty responses to the questions of whether they felt that pass rates had improved and whether they felt satisfied with the changes they made in their courses, integrating computational data science tools and culturally responsive teaching practices (Figures 1 and 2).

Fifty-percent of the faculty surveyed attributed increased pass rates in their courses to integrating CDS and CRT into their instructional practices (Figure 1).

In addition to reporting a positive impact on student pass rates, faculty strongly agreed that their participation in MTIDES activities had a positive impact on their instruction and empowered them to improve their courses. Overall, faculty reported that they were satisfied with the changes that they made to their courses through the infusion of CDS and CRT (Figure 2).

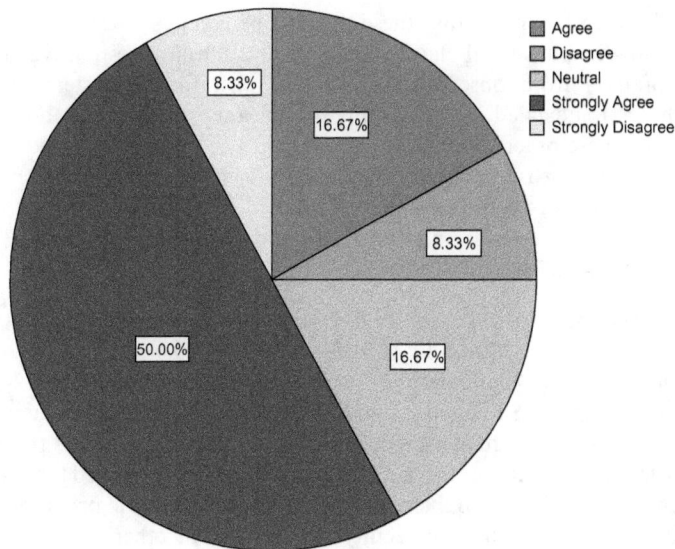

Figure 1: Faculty Response to the Question: "The Pass Rates for Your Class Improved Due to the Culturally Responsive Teaching and Bringing Computational Tools to Your Courses."

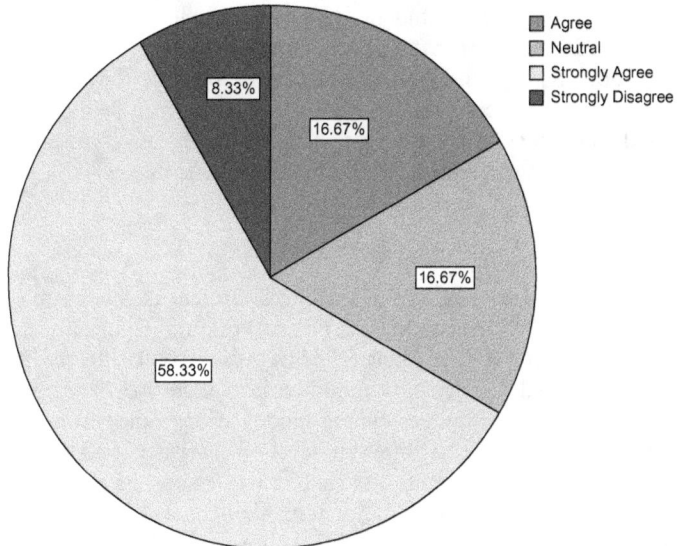

Figure 2: Faculty Response to the Question: "Overall, Are You Satisfied with the Changes to Your Course That Culturally Responsive Teaching and Computational Tools Brought to Your Course".

In addition to faculty noting these positive perceptions, attitudes, and practices toward computational data sciences and culturally responsive teaching, analysis of data from observations over the past four semesters (using the Wilcoxon test) indicated a statistically significant difference in how faculty implemented these practices in their classrooms. The findings revealed a statistically significant increase in the areas of culturally responsive lessons (p value = 0.02), more positive student: teacher−classroom interactions (p value < 0.01), and equitable access to computational resources in observed MTIDES classrooms (p value = 0.044).

Evaluation Question (3) for Goal 2: What aspects of the computational sciences certificate program appeal to STEM and non-STEM majors? Data also revealed information related to the appeal of the certificate program to STEM and non-STEM students. Most STEM and non-STEM students were initially unaware of the program. Of those students who were aware of the program, there was a desire to learn more about the CDS certificate program. Based on the needs assessment data, we began to increase student awareness of the program through advertising and the addition of faculty members from other disciplines to the project (in fact, one of the strengths of the project was faculty retention). Using a five-point Likert scale for responses, over 200 students were surveyed in a needs assessment to determine their awareness of and perspectives on the Computer Sciences certificate program. Analysis of the data revealed that the average score was near 4.0 for all questions on the survey, which indicated that both STEM and non-STEM students had a favorable perception of infusing computational data sciences in their courses. The computational data sciences appealed to both STEM and non-STEM majors because they could see how computational data sciences would be useful in their chosen fields. Student data also revealed that students felt that by participating in this certificate program they would be more marketable in their future career fields.

Discussion

The outcome of our work resulted in the empowerment of faculty to infuse the Computational and Data Sciences (CDS) framework and Culturally Responsive Teaching Principles (CRTP) in their STEM classrooms. Using the knowledge and techniques learned, faculty have modified several courses based on the CDS framework and CRTP techniques. These modifications range from a complete redesign of STEM courses to different levels of infusion and integration of appropriate modules, software tools, and other lessons into several existing STEM courses. Among the other major tangible benefits of the program is the development of a comprehensive and detailed proposal for the CDS certificate program for STEM and non-STEM majors. The result of extensive brainstorming sessions by an interdisciplinary team of faculty from academic departments across the MSU campus, the proposal includes the major goals and objectives of the certificate program and detailed course content (i.e., recommended instructional methods, instructional resources, and software tools).

To date, MTIDES faculty have presented their findings and results at several national conferences, and received awards and accolades at the department-, school-, and university-wide levels. In addition, faculty have received letters from students expressing appreciation for the efforts faculty took to facilitate their academic endeavors. The MTIDES faculty credit this appreciation for incorporating the techniques they learned at professional development workshops

We observed connections between what we accomplished in other STEM and non-STEM disciplines, and we can use these lessons learned to motivate, promote, enroll, and increase the graduation rates of students in additional STEM-related disciplines. Additionally, we would like to alleviate student apprehensions about Big Data and instill a culture that reflects what one MTIDES faculty aptly stated, "with the right tools for analysis, Big Data are just data to answer questions, solve problems, make decisions, and plan strategies […]"

An additional benefit of the program was expressed by one faculty member, who said, "the MTIDES Program has facilitated the engagement of multidisciplinary work among faculty with very diverse, both academic and cultural, backgrounds and will definitely foster more research."

Conclusion

There are several lessons learned from this project. As one senior administrator remarked, "[I am impressed] by the open-mindedness and commitment from the MTIDES team. The faculty and staff worked beyond expectations and supported the project without reservation." TIDES was transformative by increasing faculty members' understanding of culturally responsive and student-centered teaching in STEM. As one stakeholder remarked, "We now better understand how to blend this into lectures and modules that involve integrating more computation into homework, quizzes, and exams."

The Last Word

A senior MTIDES administrator fittingly sums up Morgan's TIDES experience as "Self-reflection is an antidote to implicit bias." Finally, diversity and inclusion begins with an intentional mindset and must always be intentional.

References

Bettinger, E. (2010). To be or not to be: Major choices in budding scientists. In C. T. Clotfelter (Ed.), *American Universities in a Global Market* (pp. 68–98). Chicago, IL: University of Chicago Press.

Brainard, S. G., & Carlin, L. (1998). A six-year longitudinal study of undergraduate women in engineering and science. *The Research Journal for Engineering Education, 87*(4), 369–375.

Chen, H. T. (2015a). *Practical Program Evaluation: Theory-Driven Evaluation and the Integrated Evaluation Perspective* (2nd ed.). Thousand Oakes, CA: SAGE Publications.

Chen, X. (2015b). STEM attrition among high-performing college students in the United States: Scope and potential causes. *Journal of Technology and Science Education*, 5(1), 41–59.

Cheryan, S., Master, A., & Meltzoff, A. N. (2015). Cultural stereotypes as gatekeepers: Increasing girls' interest in computer science and engineering by diversifying stereotypes. *Frontiers in Psychology*, 6, 49.

Coggins, P., Dupont, J. B., & Campbell, S. D. (2008). Using cultural competence to close the achievement gap. *The Journal of Pan African Studies*, 2(4), 44–59.

Cross, T. L., Bazron, B. J., Dennis, K. W., & Isaacs, M. R. (1989). *Towards a culturally competent system of care: A monograph on effective services for minority children who are severely emotionally disturbed* [Monograph]. Retrieved from https://eric.ed.gov/?id=ED330171

Extreme Science and Engineering Discovery Environment. (XSEDE). Retrieved from https://www.xsede.org/

Gay, G. (2010). *Culturally responsive teaching: Theory, research, and practice* (2nd ed.). New York, NY: Teachers College Press.

Guzdial, M. (2008). Education: Paving the way for computational thinking. *Communications of the ACM*, 51(8), 25–27.

Ladson-Billings, G. (1995). But that's just good teaching! The case for culturally relevant pedagogy. *Theory into Practice*, 34(3), 159–165.

Lee, I., Martin, F., & Apone, K. (2014). Integrating computational thinking across the K–8 curriculum. *ACM Inroads*, 5(4), 64–71.

Manyika, J., Chui, M., Brown, B., Bughin, J., Dobbs, R., Roxburgh, C., & Byers, A. H. (2011, May). Big data: The next frontier for innovation, competition, and productivity. Retrieved from https://www.mckinsey.com/business-functions/digital-mckinsey/our-insights/big-data-the-next-frontier-for-innovation

Moses, B. P., & Cobb, C. (2001). *Radical equations: Math literacy and civil rights.* Boston, MA: Beacon Press.

National Academies of Sciences, Engineering, and Medicine. (2017). *Building America's skilled technical workforce.* Washington, DC: The National Academies Press. Retrieved from https://doi.org/10.17226/23472

National Science Board. (2010). *Science and engineering indicators 2010.* Arlington, VA: National Science Foundation.

Noonan, R. (2017). *STEM jobs: 2017 update* (ESA Issue Brief No. 02–17). Retrieved from US Department of Commerce, Economics and Statistics Administration website http://www.esa.gov/sites/default/files/stem-jobs-2017-update.pdf

Ost, B. (2010). The role of peers and grades in determining major persistence in sciences. *Economics of Education Review*, 29(6), 923–934.

Packard, B. W., Gagnon, J. L., LaBelle, O., Jeffers, K., & Lynn, E. (2011). Women's experiences in the STEM community college transfer pathway. *Journal of Women and Minorities in Science and Engineering*, 17(2), 129–147.

President's Council of Advisors on Science and Technology. (2012). *Engage to excel: Producing one million additional college graduates with degrees in science, technology, engineering, and mathematics.* Retrieved from https://obamawhitehouse.archives.gov/sites/default/files/microsites/ostp/pcast-engage-to-excel-final_2-25-12.pdf

Rask, K. (2010). Attrition in STEM fields at a liberal arts college: The importance of grades and pre-collegiate preferences. *Economics of Education Review*, *29*(6), 892–900.

Sengupta, P., Kinnebrew, J. S., Basu, S., Biswas, G., & Clark, D. (2013). Integrating computational thinking with K-12 science education using agent-based computation: A theoretical framework. *Education and Information Technologies*, *18*(2), 351–380.

Seymour, E., & Hewitt, N. M. (1997). *Talking about leaving: Why undergraduates leave science*. Boulder, CO: Westview Press.

Sithole, A., Chiyaka, E. T., McCarthy, P., Mupinga, D. M., Bucklein, B. K., & Kibirige, K. (2017). Student attraction, persistence and retention in STEM Programs: Successes and continuing challenges. *Higher Education Studies*, *7*(1), 46–59.

Strenta, A. C., Elliott, R., Adair, R., Matier, M., & Scott, J. (1994). Choosing and leaving science in highly selective institutions. *Research in Higher Education*, *35*(5), 513–547.

Thomasian, J. (2011). *Building a science, technology, engineering and math education agenda: An update of state actions*. Retrieved from National Governors Association Center for Best Practices website https://www.nga.org/files/live/sites/NGA/files/pdf/1112STEMGUIDE.PDF

Wilensky, U., & Reisman, K. (2006). Thinking like a wolf, a sheep, or a firefly: Learning biology through constructing and testing computational theories—an embodied modeling approach. *Cognition and Instruction*, *24*(2), 171–209.

Yarbrough, D. B., Shulha, L. M., Hopson, R. K., & Caruthers, F. A. (2011). *The program evaluation standards: A guide for evaluators and evaluation users* (3rd ed.). Thousand Oaks, CA: SAGE.

Chapter 15

Strengthening Computer and Mathematical Sciences Engagement and Learning

Sambit Bhattacharya, Daniel Okunbor, Chekad Sarami, Perry Gillespie and Radoslav Nickolov

Reflections

Approximately one—two years before applying for the TIDES opportunity, faculty from the Department of Mathematics and Computer Science at Fayetteville State University (FSU) were engaged in workshops of the Integrated STEM Academic Success (ISAS) program funded by the National Science Foundation's Historically Black Colleges and Universities — undergraduate program (HBCU-UP). While there were several outcomes of these events, two significant threads of discussion would later mature into a focused effort to write our TIDES proposal. Faculty wanted to experiment with different pedagogical practices in their teaching, and they needed support to implement them. Another discussion was based on the observation that most faculty in the department were born and had spent their early lives in non-US countries. Most participants in these discussions agreed that this meant there were some real differences in cultural background between the foreign-born professors and their mostly US-born students. Anecdotal notes show professors reflecting back on their early years as traditional undergraduate students who were able to give maximum time to studies. This was different from what they were used to seeing in their FSU students, most of whom juggled families and part-time jobs while attending college. It was also difficult for our professors to appreciate the cultural backgrounds of FSU students and how it relates to their decisions to invest time and effort in activities that would distract them from their academic goal to succeed in STEM. It was apparent from our discussions that we needed to address issues beyond those already being addressed by the ISAS program.

A few months after our final ISAS workshops, we became aware of the AAC&U TIDES call for proposals. Culturally responsive teaching (CRT) was a term new to most of our faculty, but it seemed like an approach that could work to bridge the perceived and real differences in the cultural backgrounds of our faculty and students. Our TIDES project was inspired by these earlier discussions during faculty meetings.

Institutional Context

Fayetteville State University (FSU) was founded on November 29, 1867. Known at that time as the Howard School, it was responsible for educating children of color. Today, Fayetteville State University is the second-oldest state institution out of the 16 universities within the University of North Carolina (UNC) system. As of fall 2017, this comprehensive regional institution offers 33 Baccalaureate, 8 Masters, and 1 Doctorate. This historically black institution has a unique student population. Of the 6,226 students enrolled (5393 being undergraduates) in fall 2017, about 59% are African American, 20% are Caucasian, 7% are Hispanic, and 2% are American Indian and Asian. Another unique quality of the student population at FSU is that 47% are over the age of 24, 68% are female, and 76% are commuting students. This could be a result of FSU's close proximity to the largest military base on the East Coast.

At FSU, there are 29 Math and Computer Science faculty members. Only two are American born and the others are foreign-born with baccalaureate degrees from other countries. Prior to getting the TIDES grant, the STEM faculty indicated major challenges they were facing in the classroom in a STEM faculty retreat sponsored by ISAS. Some of these concerns were (1) language barriers, (2) civility in the classroom, and (3) understanding the culture of the students. Some faculty made efforts to improve their communication by practicing language skills daily, and others had chosen to use music as a universal language to connect with students. Another main concern voiced by the STEM faculty was the lack of responsibility and respect from some students as displayed in the classroom. The TIDES grant gave us an opportunity to develop STEM-faculty-driven workshops, which focused on implementing "cultural diversity" in the classroom. In these workshops, facilitators addressed the concerns mentioned earlier. We also invited students to participate in a few of the workshops. Through our TIDES project, one Computer Science faculty member introduced musical software to aid the students' programming abilities, while another used robotics.

Introduction and Background

Research has shown that students' persistence depends on three major tenets, namely (1) intellectual engagement and achievement, (2) motivation, and (3) identification with the STEM fields [9]. Intellectual engagement and achievement involve heavy doses of hands-on inquiry, problem-solving, and pursuit of scientific knowledge. Students are motivated when they know that their success in a course is somehow intrinsically guaranteed after they have put in their honest effort. It is important that students identify with STEM through well-coordinated active and collaborative learning.

Our TIDES project at Fayetteville State University, entitled "Strengthening Computer and Information Sciences Engagement and Learning (SCISEL)," was based on these tenets. The program was designed to (1) revamp courses in math and computer science – Introduction to Computer for Technical Majors (CSC 105), Introduction to Programming Methodology (CSC 120), Program Design and Implementation (CSC130), Computer Organization and Architecture I (CSC 201), Calculus I and II (MATH 142 and MATH 242) and Discrete Mathematics (MATH 150) to include CRT initiatives; (2) provide professional development for math and computer science faculty in the area of CRT through a summer boot camp in effective curriculum design, pedagogies, and faculty focus group meetings; and (3) improve self-efficacy of math and computer science students through engagement and STEM learning best practices.

In determining which strategies to utilize, we felt it imperative to glean the perspective of students. We interviewed an African American traditional male student who was in his sophomore year in computer science. The student grew up in two households, raised as the only child by both his grandparents and father in Fayetteville, NC. Although he lived with his mother out of state until the age of four, he has spent the majority of his life in Fayetteville. The student is a second-generation college student; his aunts and uncles have all obtained college degrees. His father finished college as an art major and has been the most influential person in his life. The student had planned to go into the military after graduating from high school; however, with the encouragement of his father, he enrolled fulltime in college. According to him, working with computers was a delight and his ability to tinker with computer hardware and play computer games ultimately motivated him to choose computer science as a major. In his first year, he completed CS105, CSC120, MATH129 (Pre-calculus), MATH130 (Trigonometry), and MATH 142 (Calculus I), receiving B's and C's. According to him, he dropped AP Calculus class in high school because he was not connecting culturally with his mathematics instructor. He indicated not liking mathematics classes at the college/university level. As opposed to his high-school mathematics courses, where content was taught based on formulas and shortcuts, he was easily bored with the lengthy explanations and rigor of college mathematics. The student was overwhelmed by the amount of information and having to filter that information through the heavy accents of some of the foreign professors during math sessions. It was quicker and more effective for him to watch videos on YouTube or Khan Academy related to the concepts that he struggled to understand during class times. The student believed that a personal connection with faculty based on sharing background information about each other would help with cultural/language barriers. Preparing handouts for the students in advance and more efficient use of the class whiteboard would enhance the communication and remove the cross-cultural barriers.

Cross-cultural barriers would also be addressed with implemented mandatory office hours with faculty.

This anecdote of support for CRT from the student and education research community prompted the selection of strategies for the SCISEL program including:

(1) Electronic Portfolio (E-portfolio): Electronic portfolios are a unique assessment regime that can serve as a valid way to document student progress, encourage student involvement, showcase student work samples, and provide a method of student-learning outcomes and curriculum evaluation.
(2) Algorithm-generated Multimedia with Cultural Context: Ethno-computing broadens participation in computing and helps all students understand the relevance of education to social justice. It also enhances the inclusiveness of educational practice in a multicultural, democratic society.
(3) Physical Computing and Personified Feedback: Physical computing (e.g., educational robots) provides a tangible context that heightens student motivation, allowing them to experience the embodiment of the programs they create.
(4) Redesign Using Games Programming: Games programming approaches are used to teach digital logic and computer organization with extensions to adaptive and interactive online curriculum.
(5) Using EarSketch for Promoting Learning in SCISEL Courses: EarSketch is a National Science Foundation-funded initiative that was created to motivate students to consider further study and careers in computer science.

Implementation

CRT has three functional dimensions: (1) The institutional dimension, (2) personal dimension, and (3) the instructional dimension. Personal dimension refers to the process by which instructors learn to become culturally responsive. We have updated and added course content to reflect CRT in our SCISEL courses. The instructional dimension refers to the practices and challenges associated with implementing CRT in classroom. Classroom management refers to those activities of classroom teachers that create a positive classroom climate within which effective teaching and learning can occur [12]. Classroom management certainly is a key to successful implementation of CRT. Not unique to FSU, we have in our CS classes underprepared students, non-traditional students, IT issues, and computer/cell phone distractions, etc. The nature of CRT enables us to treat our students just like our children. As it takes a village to raise a child, the faculty in the Mathematics and Computer science department at FSU collaborated and worked closely together to implement CRT. In the end, implementing CRT helped us to address these issues and has led to a more positive classroom climate. In our course revisions and teaching, we have addressed several other aspects of teaching at HBCUs: (1) Non-traditional students' class attendance, (2) female students in STEM, (3) mentoring and co-teaching, and

(4) diversity of course content. Additionally, our approach incorporated the following modern pedagogy:

(1) Encouraging students and faculty to be creative and to be willing to try new ways and methods.
(2) Promoting students' social interaction via team-based learning, cooperative learning, and peer assessment assignment. Students also showcase their project, peer-evaluate one another's work, and are individually and privately provided with the instructor's final comments and grade.
(3) Teaching students how to use WordPress or iPython to embed their code and multimedia contents.

Universities and colleges have traditionally separated science and music. This is in contrast to ancient times when science and music were thought of as from the same fields. We are arguing that knowledge of both art and technology not only makes the learning fun, but also stimulates students to study the subjects in more depth. It also later enables them to better collaborate in their workplaces. In the following sections, we describe our main activities in more detail.

To that end, we have introduced the use of music in one of the sophomore classes – CSC 220 – Data Structures and Algorithms. We have applied the use of data structures in the process of creating music. We use JEM (Jython Environment for Music) [13] to give students an easy way to manipulate musical notes (using the Python programming language), and then introduce an assignment that requires the use of a stack data structure to "songify" a text document into a piece of music.

Faculty Development

We had several workshops to help faculty to infuse their courses with CRT. Our workshops covered topics such as team-based and cooperative learning, sharing tools (i.e., GitHub, [1]bitBucket, GDrive), incorporating semester-long projects into CS 1 and CS 2 courses, teamwork models and culture, and challenges in teaching Computer Science Topics online and offline. We also gave three in-depth workshops on teaching introductory programming courses using EarSketch.

Hands-on, Music-related Classroom Activities in CS1

The EarSketch Python library was created as a novel approach to teaching STEM where music provides the cultural context in which students learn computing. EarSketch offers an appealing mix of flexibility and simplicity since its programs can be run both in a standalone Python IDE and directly within web browsers. Although originally offered for high-school students, EarSketch modules have sufficiently advanced to the point where a massive open online course (MOOC) titled, "Survey of Music Technology," has been recently offered on Coursera. This course assumes no technical or musical prerequisites from students and teaches a wide range of topics from acoustics and psychoacoustics to algorithmic composition and music information retrieval. Another recent advancement is the publication of a textbook [2], which provides a hands-on introduction to the field of music technology as a creative pursuit at the intersection of technology and arts. This textbook is more suitable for traditional, face-to-face course offerings at the undergraduate level. In our CSC 105 courses, we posed EarSketch programming projects in which students were competing in teams with each other. They shared their resulting compositions via EarSketch Social media and liked, tagged, and commented on their work.

One of the other cultural elements that we targeted was images and controllers, the latter of which is widespread via computer/video games. We used EarSketch in a project to do Sinification with their favorite images. We also introduced a JythonMusic Environment for students, which enables students to write Jython programs that can manipulate or create music in the formats of MIDI or WAV files and do creative programming. In one of the projects to introduce students to the microcontroller, we used OscIn and OscOut objects of the JythonMusic environment to create graphical arts and music at the same time using smartphones. Students are also assigned projects that require them to songify a piece of text with the help of a stack data structure.

Graphing Techniques Using Transformation and Sound Transformation

One of the important skills in the pre-calculus course is knowledge of how to graph non-basic functions. We made a connection between graph transformations and sound transformations through the lesson. Any audio signal is mainly a function of time[1]. In this particular lesson, students see, side by side, the effect of the translation of the graph on the sound (as the function being translated) using Mathematica. The following table (Table 1) shows the relation.

Robotics

A common perception is that computation produces artifacts that are not tangible since it is mainly about operations that occur in software. With an enhanced understanding of computation, students or other interested persons may relate the operations of software to events that affect the physical world (e.g., sound playing on a computer, or an image composed of colored pixels shown on a screen). Robotics is a form of physical computing where the strong links between computation, sensing, and actuation provide benefits to a wide range of real-world applications.

For several years, faculty from our department have worked on pedagogical applications of robotics to teach Computer Science [5,6]. In these applications, students were instructed to write software programs to control single robots to do tasks like traversing a maze or sensing light and reacting (e.g., to avoid bright

---

[1]The digital sound is a discrete function, where the sound is sampled at different times.

Table 1: Transformations of Graphs vs Recordings.

Transformations of graphs	Audible effect or audio application.
Horizontal shifting	Delay/progression when played with the original.
Vertical shifts	This result is DC offset, which can sometimes cause audible clicks, especially if it is amplified.
Vertical stretching and shrinking	Vertical stretch results in amplifying the recording and vertical shrinking softens the recording.
Horizontal stretching and shrinking	Speeding or slowing the recording (note the pitch does not remain constant).
Reflections about the axis	Phase inversion. The student will see how they can do voice cancellation.

light). During our TIDES-supported workshops on culturally responsive pedagogy, we discussed other forms of physical computing which could leverage the natural curiosity of our students and relate the learning content to more personal and social experiences. During our discussions, while looking at various options, one of the co-authors, Sambit Bhattacharya, applied for entry into the NASA Swarmathon competition [7]. This competition is inspired by swarm intelligence for robots, which, in turn, is inspired by observation of how homogenous collections of animals behave in nature to find food and avoid predators [8,11,12]. Swarm robots usually lack the centralized control to determine each robot's individual behavior; however, global behaviors can emerge through many local interactions, which are simple in nature. Studies show that simple rules executed on the individual robot can explain complex group behaviors, and it is sufficient to support only local sensing and communication. The advantages of swarm intelligence are robustness at the level of the group where individual failure is not a significant problem; individual behaviors are easy to implement; and the approaches are scalable since the control mechanisms do not depend on the number of individuals in the swarm. Since the 1980s, swarm robotics has become a large research field. As it becomes more developed, the advantages of using a swarm robotics solution are more clear. Swarm robots offer a cheaper solution because each agent only needs to be able to do a specific task [12]. Additionally, swarm behavior in general can be a useful approximation for how human society operates, which has the previously mentioned benefits of parallelism, robustness, and scalability. Utilizing a swarm approach, we get additional features such as:

- parallelism, which allows robots to divide tasks;
- robustness – if one robot or many fail, progress can still continue; and
- scalability – as the number of swarm robots increase, problems are solved faster.

The NASA Swarmathon competition was well aligned with TIDES objectives since it has a strong teamwork component. One condition for participation in the competition was that our students do outreach to local high schools. It was interesting to observe our students, who had spent considerable time and effort to develop swarm robotics software, chose to explain the technology to high-school students with the help of analogies, namely societal and human cooperation – mirroring our own TIDES teaching approach. The FSU team won first place in the physical championship category of the competition in 2016, and has participated every year since then.

Results

Overall, the SCISEL program had a positive impact on students, faculty, and our department. The program benefitted computer science and mathematics students in several ways. The redesigned computer science and mathematics courses that included best practices and CRT pedagogies led to almost immediate improvement of students' achievements in these courses as measured by the percentage of final grades of A, B, or C. For example, this percentage increased from 59% to 68% in CSC 105, from 64% to 69% in CSC 120, and from 72% to 82% in MATH 251 (Linear Algebra) between academic years 2013-14 and 2014-15, respectively. Various program activities gave students opportunities to interact with their computer science and mathematics professors outside the classroom and to exchange cultural information with them on educational backgrounds, pedagogy, and goal settings in STEM. Students also had opportunities to showcase their work to TIDES leaders and institution coaches, as well as to university administrators.

Over a period of two academic years, faculty were given the excellent opportunity to become familiar with and implement CRT in their work to improve student learning. The numerous faculty development activities enabled them to creatively redesign courses, to incorporate effective modern pedagogy approaches, and to be appreciative and mindful in everything they do of their students' and their colleagues' cultural differences.

TIDES provided CRT as a strategy for achieving various outcomes of goals set in the Department of Mathematics and Computer Science's annual Operational Plan and Assessment Record. One such outcome is student satisfaction with instruction, as measured by the average score on the combined students' evaluations of faculty instruction for the courses taught by the department's faculty during the academic year. For the two academic years of the SCISEL program, 2014–2015 and 2015–2016, the average score was 4.45 and 4.47 on a scale of 0–5; 5 being the highest), respectively. These are the highest scores the department has had to date. For comparison, the average score was 4.33 in 2013–2014, and 4.43 in 2016–2017. While we recognize that many factors influence these scores, we do believe that CRT played a role since all faculty in the department were actively and enthusiastically involved in the SCISEL program's faculty development activities.

Conclusion

Our TIDES project has had a significant impact on recruitment, retention, progression, and graduation rates of underrepresented minorities and women in Computer Science and Mathematics at our university. The university faculty, especially faculty within our STEM departments, believe that providing opportunities for students to incorporate learned knowledge using project-based learning methods and culturally responsive pedagogical practices will continue to support learning and enhance retention, persistence, and graduation rates well beyond the expiry of the TIDES grant.

Our TIDES-supported program continues to serve as a model for all STEM and non-STEM academic programs here at FSU and at other colleges and universities with a significant number of women and members of underrepresented groups. Our university leaders are aware of the necessity for CRT in a culturally diverse environment such as FSU and have committed to relevant institutional activities focused on CRT. Faculty participants continue to serve as facilitators for professional development for faculty across the campus, and are available to assist other colleges and institutions.

Last Word

Since our faculty started this project, we realize that innovative pedagogical approaches must be combined with the power of CRT; we have come a long way because of it. The culture shift in our department seems to have been fundamental and long-lasting as a result of our participation in TIDES. Our meetings frequently include discussions of cultural differences and dynamics in the classroom within diverse university settings and how it helps to be explicitly aware of these.

References

1. Retrieved from https://earsketch.gatech.edu/
2. Manaris, B., & Brown, A. (2014, May). Making Music with Computers: Creative Programming in Python, Chapman & Hall/CRC Textbooks in Computing.
3. Freeman, J., Magerko, B., McKlin, T., Reilly, M., Permar, J., Summers, C., & Fruchter, E. (2014). Engaging underrepresented groups in high school introductory computing through computational remixing with EarSketch. In *Proceedings of the 45th ACM technical symposium on Computer science education* (pp. 85–90). New York, NY: ACM
4. Eglash, R., et al. (2006). Culturally situated design tools: Ethnocomputing from field site to classroom. *American Anthropologist, 108*(2), 347–362.
5. Bhattacharya, S., & Czejdo, B. D. (2010). A state diagram creation and code generation tool for robot programming. *Journal of Computing Sciences in Colleges, 25*(3), 120–127.

6. Czejdo, B. D., & Bhattacharya, S. (2009). Programming robots with state diagrams. *Journal of Computing Sciences in Colleges, 24*(5), 19–26.
7. Retrieved from nasaswarmathon.com
8. Brownlee, J. (2011). Clever Algorithms: Nature Inspired Programming Recipes. "Swarm Algorithms" CC/Non-commercial, pp. 237–274.
9. Hecker, J. (2015). *"Swarmie User Manual", Quick Start Guide for Physical Robots*. University of New Mexico. Retrieved from Github.com
10. O'Kane, J. M. (2014). *A gentle introduction to ROS*. Columbia, SC: Department of Computer Science and Engineering.
11. Quigley, M., Gerkey, B., & Smart, W. (2015). *Programming robots with ROS*. Sebastopol, CA: O'Reilly Media, Inc.
12. Yogeswaran, M., & Ponnambalam, S. G. (2010). *Swarm robotics: An extensive research review*. Selangor: School of Engineering, Monash University, Sunway Campus.
13. Eglash, R., Gilbert, J. E., & Foster, E. (2013). Toward culturally responsive computing education. *Communications of the ACM, 56*(7), 33–36.
14. McCoid, S., et al. (2013). EarSketch: An integrated approach to teaching introductory computer music. *Organised Sound, 18*(02), 146–160.
15. Lee, M. J., & Ko, A. J. (2011). Personifying programming tool feedback improves novice programmers' learning. In *Proceedings of the seventh international workshop on Computing educationresearch* (pp. 109–116). Providence, RI: ACM.
16. Joint, A. (2013). *Joint Task Force on Computing Curricula, Association for Computing Machinery (ACM) and IEEE Computer Society*. Computer Science Curricula 2013: Curriculum Guidelines for Undergraduate Degree Programs in Computer Science. Retrieved from http://dx.doi.org/10.1145/2534860
17. Jui-Feng, W., Shian-Shyong, T., & Tsung-Ju, L. (2010). Teaching Boolean Logic through Game Rule Tuning. *Learning Technologies, IEEE Transactions on, 3*(4), 319–328.
18. Topping, K. J. (1996). The effectiveness of peer tutoring in further and higher education: A typology and review of the literature. In S. Goodlad (Ed.), *Mentoring and Tutoring by Students* (pp. 49–69). London: Kogan Page.
19. Damon, W., & Phelps, E. (1989b). Strategic Uses of Peer Learning inChildren's Education. In T. Berndt & G. Ladd (Eds.), *Peer Relationships in Child Development* (pp. 135–157). New York, NY: John Wiley & Sons.
20. President's Council of Advisors on Science and Technology. (2012). *Engage to Excel: Producing 1million additional college graduates with degrees in STEM*. Retrieved from http://www.whitehouse.gov/sites/default/files/microsites/ostp/pcast-engage-to-excel-final_2-25-12.pdf
21. Buzzetto-More, N. (2006). Using Electronic Portfolios to Build Information Literacy. *Global Digital Business Review, 1*(1), 6–11.
22. Popper, E. (2005). Learning goals: The foundation of curriculum development and assessment. In K. Martell & T. Calderon, *Assessment of student learning in business schools: Best practices each step of the way,* 1(2), pp. 1–23. Tallahassee, Florida: Association for Institutional Research.
23. Martin, J., & Sugarman, J. (1993). *Models of classroom management: Principles, applications, and critical perspectives*. Calgary, Temeron Books Inc.
24. Retrieved from https://jythonmusic.me

Chapter 16

Measurement and Assessment

Kate Winter and Gabriele Haynes

Overview

Kate Winter Evaluation (KWE) provided external evaluation services for the TIDES initiative. In partnership with the TIDES PI and stakeholders, KWE collaboratively developed the logic model, various data collection instruments, and the evaluation design narrative. KWE collected data annually from the TIDES project staff and statistically analyzed the findings for significant changes in outcomes and other indicators. In addition, KWE offered conclusions and recommendations for implementation. This chapter highlights the evaluation framework guiding the monitoring and assessment; the metrics used for each of the intended outcomes of TIDES; the data collection instruments and analysis strategies, and the outputs, outcomes; and evaluative findings as well as limitations and recommendations for future program cycles.

The mixed methods evaluation design for PKAL's TIDES initiative assesses both program fidelity and impact. Collection and analyses of qualitative and quantitative data support the determination of the extent to which the initiative met its objectives. Additionally, KWE compiled benchmark data to examine longitudinal trends and provided continuous feedback to the PI. As noted earlier in this monograph, the overarching goal of the TIDES project was to broaden participation in the computer/information sciences through professional development that empowers faculty to implement culturally responsive pedagogies. There were eight goals associated with this, and each project selected which goals they planned to pursue directly and indirectly through program activities. Figure 2 of Chapter 1 illustrates each of the eight program goals and the number of institutions pursuing them directly, indirectly, or not at all, while Table 1 below maps these goals to the data needed to measure them. The long-term TIDES goals were sustained behavior change in STEM teaching, increased diverted and equity in STEM, and evidence-based professional development model for STEM faculty.

Table 1: Project Goals and Data Needed.

Goal	Data Needed to Measure Change
(1) Computer science curriculum/ courses (re)designed to be culturally responsive	Project reports, observation rubrics completed by coaches
(2) Increases in faculty utilization of culturally competent pedagogy	Project reports, observation rubrics completed by coaches
(3) Increases in faculty self-reported awareness of why and how to be culturally responsive and self-reported confidence in implementing culturally competent pedagogy	Pre- to post-faculty survey of TIDES participants; supplemental faculty surveys from project-level activities
(4) Student-specific (long-term) outcomes:	
• Increases in students' sense of belonging in STEM, perception of the relevance of STEM, and/or self-efficacy in STEM, particularly for traditionally underrepresented students	Pre- to post-scores on student surveys
• Increases in pass rates (higher course scores), particularly for traditionally underrepresented students	Course scores from department/college: Baseline is the year prior to intervention implementation
• Increases in retention rates (term to term, year to year), particularly for traditionally underrepresented students	Retention data from department/college: Baseline is the year prior to intervention implementation
• Increases in graduation rates, particularly for traditionally underrepresented students	Graduation data from department/college: Baseline is the year prior to intervention implementation
• Increases in representation of traditionally underrepresented groups in STEM	Student demographic data from department/college (at course level, minor, major): Baseline is the year prior to intervention implementation

Project Fidelity

Descriptive information on project implementation was collected to assess the degree to which activities occurred as proposed. Activities included the competition (call for proposals, proposal selection), the summer institutes and annual fall STEM conference, and the development of an instrument to measure efficacy in culturally responsive pedagogy. Administrative data including attendance rosters from the PKAL introductory webinars, letters of intent to apply for the program, and actual proposals submitted were used to assess if the target population was effectively recruited and if there was a perceived need for this kind of faculty support. Program documentation, including competition materials, event agendas, institutional project materials and evaluation reports, and interviews with project staff were used to assess the fidelity of the implementation. In collaboration between KWE, TIDES leadership, stakeholders, and participants, the efficacy instrument was developed. TIDES was implemented with high fidelity.

Evaluation Framework and Structure

The evaluation framework combined elements from developmental evaluation (Gamble, 2008) to support assessment of iterative attempts at solutions to shifting and emergent problems, elements from utilization-focused evaluation (Patton, 2011) to ensure that evaluation activities and findings were meeting the needs of the project, and realistic evaluation (Pawson & Tilley, 1997) to ground the evaluation activities in the real-world context of the problems the project sought to remedy. Each approach informed the kinds of data that was collected, the timing of data collection, the analysis strategies, and how formative and summative evaluation findings were shared with project participants and stakeholders.

The formative evaluation of TIDES monitored the implementation of program activities in real time and used preliminary and qualitative data including administrative logistics, participant feedback, and quantitative survey findings to make recommendations for mid-course corrections to ensure that the program was as effective as possible when the time arose to assess the impacts of the program. Developmental evaluation, as described by Gamble (2008), seeks to solve problems by using innovation within the organizations that are seeking solutions. He describes the linear path to problem-solving and its inability to solve complex and moving problems that shift with human experience and environmental exposure. Developmental evaluation allows for the exploration of problems (in an organizational context) as the framing of them shifts and the solutions are adapted in the process of designing and implementing program activities. This is relevant to a program like TIDES where the main goals are shared, but the path to solutions is not linear and there are many moving parts to the problems and the potential solutions. Using this approach, the data collected and types of analyses conducted were ever-shifting to reflect lessons learned, successes, and failures. This method of evaluation blends well with utilization-focused (Patton, 2011) and realistic (Pawson & Tilley, 1997) frameworks that were applied to the entire evaluation process.

Utilization-focused evaluation seeks to include the stakeholders in the design of evaluative questions, data collection and analyses-approach to ensure that the findings meet the needs of the stakeholders. It also seeks to promote the actual utilization of the results in the creation of policies and programs to address social injustices (Patton, 2011). The TIDES evaluators regularly communicated with stakeholders and the principal investigator to design and execute this evaluation. The program theory of change, represented in the logic model shown in Chapter 1, for the TIDES program was designed in collaboration with the principal investigator, and the types of data collected and analyzed were decided upon collaboratively with stakeholders and the evaluators. The program logic model includes the inputs, activities, outputs, and outcomes/impacts planned as part of the program and illustrates the way in which the program activities will lead to the intended change. By having stakeholders involved in creating the program theory and designing the evaluation, the needs of the program become a priority in the evaluation, which promotes the utilization of the findings for future program cycles or to promote activities that are likely to lead to long-term impacts/lasting change.

Finally, the entire evaluation was framed with a realistic lens (Pawson & Tilley, 1997), wherein the evaluation was designed and conducted within a realistic paradigm that recognized and accommodated the "real-life" context in which the problems existed. In the case of the TIDES program, that meant acknowledgment and accommodation for the complexities of the real-world setting in which the program sought to make a change (i.e., unwelcoming "chilly" climate for some students and faculty in STEM, faculty lack of self-efficacy in culturally responsive pedagogy, issues of departmental culture, personal obstacles of students and faculty due to racism/sexism/classism, etc.). By using this framework, the evaluation could accommodate the needs of the program (meeting goals, making an impact) with the needs of the evaluation (gathering/analyzing data, reporting findings) so that the findings are applicable in the real-life context where the problems exist and so that the findings are useful for future iterations of program activities seeking to meet similar objectives.

Methods and Data

The project was structured such that there was evaluation taking place of the project overall (i.e., the portfolio of all TIDES efforts) as well as at the local, individual campus project level. Each campus-based project was required to have their own evaluation, but the depth and breadth of these evaluations varied widely. To accommodate this variation while supporting the overall portfolio assessment, each project was required to provide a specific set of data, utilizing an Excel template and narrative prompts comprising an annual report. The TIDES project evaluators collected and analyzed data directly at the portfolio level from faculty and administrative participants, in addition to a meta-analysis of the campus-project-level data and findings.

Mixed methods data collection and analysis provided formative and summative evidence of program outputs and outcomes. Data were collected directly at the portfolio level, as well as from the project-level evaluations. Data collection instruments and analysis are discussed by each level below.

TIDES-level Metrics Collected Directly (Portfolio Level, Primary Analysis)

An original survey was designed for this project to address CS faculty self-efficacy related to culturally responsive pedagogy (Winter & Mack, 2018), based on psychometrically sound scales (Bandura, 2005; Yoon & Lafayette, 2012), but modified for the domain of culturally responsive pedagogy in STEM. Final psychometric testing is underway, and we should release the instrument soon (Winter & Mack, 2018). The survey comprises three scales that address faculty perceptions of self-efficacy engaging in culturally responsive pedagogy (CRP), perceptions of the group efficacy of their department/college, and the outcomes expected from engaging in CRP in STEM. It was administered prior to and after the professional development phases each year of the project. Demographic and career information collected includes gender, race/ethnicity, native discipline, academic rank/title, and institutional type and characteristic.

Institutional data were collected from each campus using a template to ensure that all campuses submitted the same data points. These data included student demographics (gender and race) in the department major, department minor, college, and institution (depending on which major a particular campus was choosing to implement TIDES within and whether they had both college- and institution-level data) and were collected annually from 2014 through 2017, which was a no-cost extension year. Student data were explored for frequencies of distributions by demographic for graduation and retention. These data allowed for monitoring of changes in frequencies at the campus and portfolio level. Not every campus was able to provide all data points, but the majority shared gender and race demographics for department majors, which is the most relevant for TIDES activities, while having and exploring the distribution of demographics at the institution level provided a contextual picture for comparison to assess the impact of TIDES activities.

Participant feedback was gathered in the form of short surveys of all participating faculty at the annual summer institutes. The survey asked about the usefulness of and likelihood of using content from the various sessions, as well as satisfaction with the allocation of time to various activities. Analysis of these data indicated that faculty perception of the value of the sessions was high and that participants planned to make use of much of what they learned. Faculty feedback was used to refine the summer institute format to incorporate additional time for campus teams to meet with one another without scripted content.

Interviews and focus groups were also conducted to assess and improve these meetings. These took place face to face during the summer institutes and the annual AAC&U STEM Conference, as well as by phone. Interviews and focus groups were audio-recorded, transcribed, and coded for analysis using open and axial coding approaches (Saldaña, 2012). Participants were asked open-ended questions about their perceptions of the utility of the TIDES content and activities, as well as to provide their perceptions on whether TIDES was influencing their readiness to engage all students in their CS classrooms.

Additionally, participation counts were collected to monitor who was attending each year and to give context to the scale of these meetings. In addition to the TIDES project staff, advisory board, and institutional coaches, there were 40 faculty and administrators from the TIDES campuses at the summer institute in 2014, 65 in 2015, 63 in 2016, and 44 in 2017.

TIDES-level Metrics Collected Indirectly (Campus-level, Secondary Analysis)

Student surveys were administered variably throughout the life of the project and across the campuses involved. An original survey was designed for the TIDES project to assess student perceptions of belonging, self-efficacy, and climate in STEM. A couple of campuses used the instrument, while some modified it, and others administered their own. Based on data from the projects that used the same questions (from the instrument provided) across time, analyses were attempted but data were too limited to show useful and/or valid findings as further discussed in the limitations section.

Many campuses conducted focus groups of their student participants. Campus-level project evaluators conducted the focus groups, transcribed and coded the data, and provided briefs of the findings to both the project and the TIDES evaluators. Due to the wide scope and scale of the TIDES project, these data were only analyzed at the campus level but provided useful information as part of formative evaluation efforts and allow for mid-course corrections to better serve the TIDES program goals.

Analysis

Descriptive statistical analyses, including calculation of frequencies, mean, and standard deviation, were conducted on quantitative data. Appropriate inferential and non-inferential statistics tested pre-post data to determine whether there was a significant effect over time for participants or their students. Content analysis (Hsieh & Shannon, 2005; Saldaña, 2012) was used to analyze the qualitative data, including interviews, focus group discussions, program documentation, and open-ended items from the instruments. KWE established baseline self-efficacy scores and explored differences by demographic and/or career details, controlling for confounding variables. Bivariate correlations between variables and faculty self-efficacy explored target variables for inclusion in multiple regression analysis to explore the unique contribution of each variable on self-efficacy level, as well as relationships between all variables in the model. In a couple of project years, women participants scored higher on the measure for expected outcomes, but there were no significant differences in other scales, or by race, or institution type. Additionally, matched-comparison t-tests were conducted to explore the significance of changes in individual self-efficacy scores from pre- to post-test. Finally, scores for changes in self-efficacy were computed and explored for differences by faculty and institutional characteristics, finding that only on one subscale did responses differ by gender (women scored higher on the second self-efficacy subscale at the 0.05 level). Because change scores did not differ by race, first-generation status, race, STEM discipline category, or the number of summer institutes attended, no further analysis was conducted to regarding unique contributions of factors.

Outputs, Outcomes, and Evaluative Findings

Overall, TIDES was effective in attaining all of its short and long-term goals. Table 2 maps the goals to their status as of Fall 2016 for goals 1–4, and as of Summer 2018 for 5–8.

From the kick-off at the TIDES Institute in 2014 through the Fall data collection prior to the 2017 summer institute, TIDES impacted 276,229 students, more than doubling its goal of 100,000. The first year was largely spent planning and developing, with only three campuses offering new or redesigned courses in the 2014–2015 academic year. By the 2015–2016 academic year, all campuses had TIDES courses offered. Figure 1 shows the demographic distributions by gender and representation status (i.e., white or underrepresented minority,

Table 2: Project Goals and Their Status.

Goal	Status
(1) Computer science curriculum/ courses (re)designed to be culturally responsive	About 26 new courses taught, 140 redesigned courses taught, and 83 modules created
(2) Increases in faculty utilization of culturally competent pedagogy	All projects reported on faculty utilization of CRP and described student impacts
(3) Increases in faculty self-reported awareness of why and how to be culturally responsive and self-reported confidence in implementing culturally competent pedagogy	Discussed later – statistically significant changes with large effect sizes on all efficacy measures
(4) Student-specific (long-term) outcomes:	
• Increases in students' sense of belonging in STEM, perception of the relevance of STEM, and/or self-efficacy in STEM, particularly for traditionally underrepresented students	Six campuses reported gains in student scores on surveys measuring sense of belonging, eight in perception of STEM relevance, and seven in student self-efficacy in STEM
• Increases in pass rates (higher course scores), particularly for traditionally underrepresented students	Six campuses reported higher scores for students in TIDES courses, noting particular improvement among white and URM women and URM men
• Increases in retention rates (term to term, year to year), particularly for traditionally underrepresented students	Six campuses reported increases in student retention (in major)

Table 2: (*Continued*)

Goal	Status
• Increases in graduation rates, particularly for traditionally underrepresented students	Three campuses reported increases in student graduation
• Increases in representation of traditionally underrepresented groups in STEM	Five campuses demonstrated success recruiting white and URM women and URM men
(5) Sustained behavior change in STEM teaching	Through the process of drafting this monograph, it became clear how deeply ingrained the new TIDES approaches to participants' teaching philosophy are
(6) Increased diverted and equity in STEM	Institutional data over time were showing trends for increased representation of white and URM women and URM men
(7) Evidence-based professional development model for STEM faculty	This monograph, prior chapters, conference presentations, and papers demonstrate the efficacy of the TIDES program for broadening participation in the computer/ information sciences through empowering faculty to implement culturally responsive pedagogies

URM) of the students exposed to TIDES activities through participation in a TIDES course or a course offered by a faculty member engaged in TIDES through Fall 2016.

TIDES partners published their successes, sought and obtained additional funding opportunities, saw students receive awards, and offered and participated in workshops, events, and other training mechanisms to promote the program's shared goals of improving the experience and the outcomes for diverse students in STEM higher education. Because each campus focused on slightly different program goals, they achieved a wide array of intended and unintended outcomes that promote diversity in STEM. Over the life of the TIDES project and across the portfolio, there were 26 new courses taught, 140 redesigned courses taught, and 83 modules created.

A particularly significant outcome of TIDES can be seen in the change scores from before to after participation (Figure 2). These data were collected through the *TIDES Efficacy Scales for Culturally Responsive Pedagogy in STEM* (Winter & Mack, 2018). It must be noted that these data represent only the

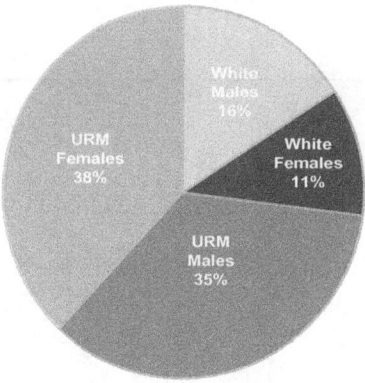

Figure 1: Demographic Distributions by Race and Gender of Students Impacted by TIDES.

42 participants who completed a dual (retrospective pre- and post-) version of the instrument immediately prior to the 2017 summer institute. The instrument went to all prior TIDES summer institute participants and asked them to critically assess where they were when they started participating in TIDES and then to critically assess where they were in summer 2017. Some of the respondents started in 2014, but others joined in 2015 or 2016. New participants in 2017 were administered the "pre" test only and are excluded from this analysis.

The *TIDES Efficacy Scales for Culturally Responsive Pedagogy in STEM* comprise four scales, three of which have subscales. The group efficacy scale contains nine items focused on perceptions of departmental or "group efficacy" at engaging diverse student in STEM, with a "general practices" subscale with six items related to supporting students in general and a "cultural responsiveness" subscale with three items about cultural differences between students and higher education. "Welcoming environment" is a composite of three items about perceptions of how welcoming the department climate is for diverse students, staff, and faculty. The "self-efficacy" scale comprises 15 items related to engaging in culturally responsive teaching practices, with the "preparing to implement" subscale including eight items related to diverse cultural awareness and responsiveness, an "implementing" subscale with four items more generally focused on student-centered teaching, and a "reflection and student connection" subscale with three items related to reflecting on and using feedback to improve one's teaching. "Expected outcomes" comprises 12 items related to the expected outcomes of engaging in various culturally responsive teaching practices.

Each scale and subscale demonstrates a statistically significant change in score at the 0.001 level, and each has a large effect size, which is a more useful measure of change than the p value (Sullivan & Feinn, 2012). As shown in Figure 2, the largest effect size was in the self-efficacy scale (1.53 standard deviations), with its subscales varying from a high of 1.6 SD for the "preparing to implement" CRP, to a low of 0.9 SD for "reflection and student connections," with "implementing

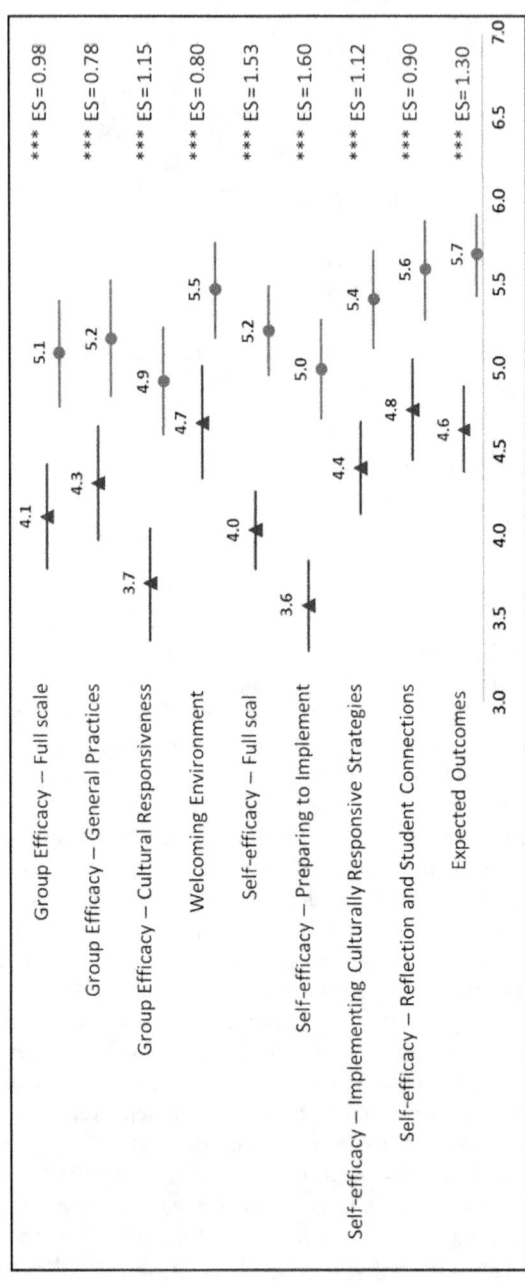

Figure 2: Pre- and Post-scores on the Measures of Efficacy in CRP in STEM.

CRP" in the middle at 1.12 SD. Given the focus of the TIDES content and opportunities for practice through the campus-based projects, it could be argued that these outcomes reflect the structure of TIDES. There was more time allocated to preparing participants to implement CRP than there was to the specifics that would have given participants more confidence in their readiness to implement them and to engage with students. This is a solid foundation for continuous improvement and an exciting finding for the project.

Additionally, single-item measures on the instrument solicited feedback about how various feelings of satisfaction, perceptions of preparation and institutional diversity goals, and opinions regarding institutional support for CRP (Figure 3). Data from the 42 respondents in 2017 who completed the combined retrospective pre-test and the post-test demonstrate statistically significant changes in scores at the 0.001 level and moderate to high effect sizes. The largest effect size is on the item asking about preparation to teach diverse students (1.4 SD).

By way of annual gatherings of TIDES stakeholders, a community/network was formed with the shared goals of achieving lasting impacts through TIDES activities. This networked community is being further evaluated through Cultural Historical Activity Theory (CHAT) (Hummelbrunner & Williams, 2011), in an ongoing effort to explore *why* the TIDES program worked (Mack & Winter, 2018). As noted previously, feedback surveys from TIDES events showed that faculty and stakeholders found the gatherings useful for learning about culturally responsive practices, how to incorporate them into syllabi and apply them in their classrooms, and for promoting TIDES activities in their work. The events also fostered a strong sense of community and the "safe, brave space" needed to affect the change TIDES intended (Ali, 2017; Arao & Clemens, 2013). Additionally, the STEM Central platform supported the sharing of resources and materials and virtual engagement – both synchronous and asynchronous. This added layer of connectivity supported the spirit of community and sustained it between in-person events.

Evaluation Limitations

The evaluative data analyses were limited by the variance in reporting, data collection/submission, and variation across institution-specific goals. Over the course of the program, institutions drifted toward "what works" for each of them, which supported goal attainment but hindered our ability to aggregate results. Program "mapped goals" were incorporated into the design too late for all institutions to adopt them, and they were not directly addressed by every participating institution. Additionally, data collection and submission and annual reporting were not standardized early enough to collect comparable data over time. This impeded our ability to track changes over time, but it supported formative analysis of all projects and therefore their ability to enact refinements to programs. The student survey administration is an example of this hurdle, as most projects modified the provided instrument. The variation in administered items both precluded our ability to aggregate the data for composite analysis

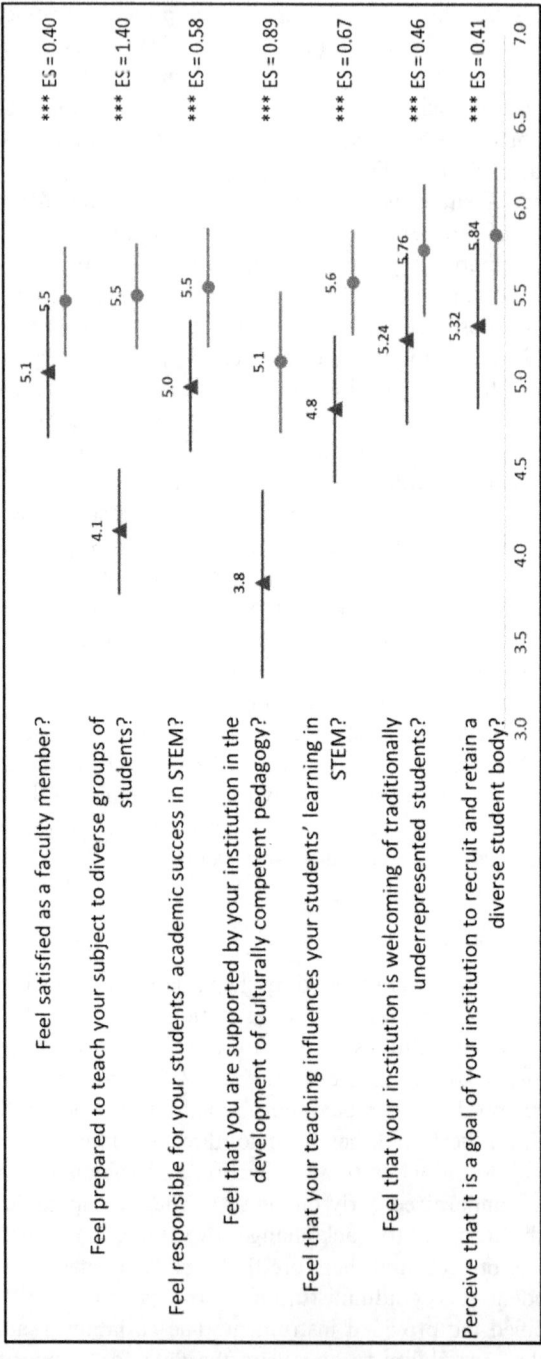

Figure 3: Pre- and Post-mean Scores, Confidence Intervals, and Effect Sizes.

and undermined the possibility of tracking changes in students over time, as some campuses did not offer the same instrument version more than once. Having a standard instrument, common administration cycle, and a reliable way to match scores from pre- to post-test would have provided a more useful dataset for analyses of student perceptions/experiences in STEM and through TIDES activities. Likewise, even at the portfolio level, the tracking IDs generated and provided to participants in 2014 failed horribly, as in 2015 whole projects completed the instrument using the same code. For this reason, we were unable to track changes within individuals over time and resorted to administering the combined retrospective pre- and post-instrument in 2017. There are numerous supporters (Pratt, McGuigan, & Katzev, 2000; Rockwell & Kohn, 1989; Skeff, Stratos, & Bergen, 1992) of this approach, and given the relationship we had developed with the participants and our direct plea for them to not artificially deflate their pre-scores or inflate their post scores, we are confident we have reliable data. It should be noted that the snapshot data each year, when removing newcomers (who were flagged as "baseline"), the scores were increasing significantly in many scales from year to year.

Conclusion

External evaluation of the TIDES program monitored and assessed project outputs and outcomes from the development of the competition through the no-cost extension year. The data collected and analyzed demonstrated that TIDES had a significant impact on its faculty and administrator participants, and that the participants, in turn, are having an impact in their classrooms and departments. While standardizing the data collected and shared through campus-level project evaluation, efforts would certainly facilitate the evaluation at the portfolio level, attempting to "shoehorn" diverse projects into pre-packaged assessment instruments, and metrics would likely diminish the impact of the program. In fact, it has been posited that reform frameworks that focus heavily on common data procedures frequently ignore the voice and needs of the community being served (Wolff, 2016). This is why the evaluation of TIDES was grounded in meeting the stakeholders' needs (i.e., combining a mixed-methods design with a utilization-focused evaluation framework). This was accomplished through the annual gatherings and regular communication with stakeholders and program staff, ensuring the voice of the community was kept in the forefront throughout this project.

Even with the limitations discussed here, the findings are quite positive, especially with the size and scale of this project and the fact that it was a pilot. The data do not signal a need to modify aspects of the TIDES structure or curriculum. The goals of the TIDES program remain crucial in the current climate of U.S. STEM higher education. The TIDES experience and evaluation demonstrate that this is an effective model for broadening participation in the computer/information sciences through empowering faculty to implement culturally responsive pedagogies.

References

Ali, D. (2017). Safe spaces and brave spaces. *NASPA Research and Policy Institute*, (2), 1–13.

Arao, B., & Clemens, K. (2013). From safe spaces to brave spaces: A new way to frame dialogue around diversity and social justice. In L. M. Landreman (Ed.), *The art of effective facilitation: Reflections from social justice educators* (pp. 135–150). Sterling, VA: Stylus Publishing, LLC. Retrieved from http://culturalcollectivekc.org/files/BraveSpaceAraoClemens.pdf

Bandura, A. (2005). Guide for constructing self-efficacy scales. In T. Urdan & F. Pajares (Eds.), *Self-efficacy beliefs of adolescents* (Adolescenc, pp. 307–337). Greenwich, CT: Information Age Publishing. Retrieved from http://www.uky.edu/~eushe2/BanduraPubs/BanduraGuide2006.pdf

Gamble, J. A. A. (2008). *A Developmental Evaluation Primer*. Canada: The J.W. McConnell Family Foundation. Retrieved from http://50.87.232.11/wp-content/uploads/2015/08/wrappingup_evaluateyourproject_resources_developmental_evaluation_primer.pdf

Hsieh, H. F., & Shannon, S. E. (2005). Three Approaches to Qualitative Content Analysis. *Qualitative Health Research*, *15*(9), 1277–1288.

Hummelbrunner, R., & Williams, B. (2011). Cultural historical activity theory. In *Systems Concepts in Action: A Practitioner's Toolkit* (pp. 434–454).

Mack, K. M., & Winter, K. (2018). Teaching to Increase Diversity and Equity in STEM (TIDES): Assessing Effectiveness using Cultural-Historical Activity Theory (CHAT). *Paper Presented at the American Education Research Association Annual Meeting*. New York, NY.

Patton, M. Q. (2011). *Essentials of Utilization-Focused Evaluation*. London: Sage.

Pawson, R., & Tilley, N. (1997). *Realistic evaluation*. Thousand Oaks, CA: Sage.

Pratt, C. C., McGuigan, W. M., & Katzev, A. R. (2000). Measuring Program Outcomes: Using Retrospective Pretest Methodology. *American Journal of Evaluation*, *21*(3), 341–349.

Rockwell, S. K., & Kohn, H. (1989). Post-then-pre Evaluation. *Journal of Extension*, *27*(2).

Saldaña, J. (2012). *The coding manual for qualitative researchers*. London: Sage.

Skeff, K. M., Stratos, G. A., & Bergen, M. R. (1992). Evaluation of a Medical Faculty Development Program. *Evaluation & the Health Professions*, *15*(3), 350–366.

Sullivan, G. M., & Feinn, R. (2012). Using Effect Size – or Why the P Value Is Not Enough. *Journal of Graduate Medical Education*, *4*(3), 279–282.

Winter, K., & Mack, K. M. (2018). The TIDES Efficacy Scales for Culturally Responsive Pedagogy in STEM: An Outcome of the Teaching to Increase Diversity and Equity in STEM Project, Manuscript in preparation.

Wolff, T. (2016). Ten Places Where Collective Impact Gets It Wrong. *Global Journal of Community Psychology Practice*, *7*(1).

Yoon, S. Y., & Lafayette, W. (2012). Development of the Teaching Engineering Self-Efficacy Scale (TESS) for K-12 Teachers. *American Society for Engineering Education*, *25*(2), 466.

Index

Academic achievement, 22
Academic and social deficiencies, 3–4
Academic honesty, 207
Academic STEM practitioners, 28
Acculturation, 44
ACL. *See* active-collaborative learning (ACL)
Active-collaborative learning (ACL), 213
Active-learning computational activities, 239
Active-learning Day, 39
Activity structure, 191
Administrative policy, 175
African American communities, 23
African American telecommunication, 103–104
Afrodescendiente, 41
Agent-based models, 40
Aggressions, 34
Algorithm-generated multimedia with cultural context, 252
American Chemical Society, 38
American educational systems, 16
American Society for Microbiology, 38
Android phones, 192
Animations, 64–65
Annotation, 142–143
Annotators, 142
Anti-religious sentiments, 55
Apostolic communities, 55
Aptitude, 191–192

Architecture, 251
Arduino micro controllers, 78–79
Artificial Intelligence (AI), 78
Arts and humanities, 2
ASCII beep character, 217
Asian American and Native American Pacific Islander Serving Institution (AANAPISI), 74
Association of American Colleges and Universities (AAC&U), 2, 229
　TIDES Institutes, 106
　TIDES program, 219
Association of Technology and Social Sciences, 148
Attitudes, 191–192
Authenticity, 89–90

Balanced teaching pedagogy, 24
Batch-processing capabilities, 144
Beat Creator, 222
Big Data, 230–231, 239
Binary number system and computational methods, 104
Biology–CS learning community, 194
BitBucket, 253
BitPim, 104–105
Bivariate correlations, 264
Black Lives Matter, 116
Black, mixed-race spectrum, 41
Black Puerto Ricans, 34
Blended teaching and learning approach, 119–120

Blues, 220
Borough, 74
Breakpoint, 121
'Bro-gramming', 60
Bystander effect, 100

Calculus, 251
California State University, Northridge (CSUN), 218
   COMP, 110, 218–219
   culturally responsive content development, 220–223
   gender gap, 224
   minority-serving institution (MSI) status, 218
   peer mentors, 225
   underrepresented minority women campus, 218
   YouSpeak, 224–225
Campus-based professional development, 67
Campus-based project, 262
Campus initiative goals and boundaries, 27
Campus leadership, 137
Campus-project-level data, 262
Campus-wide teaching symposium, 213
Caring, CRT, 162–163
Catholic cultural expectation, 55–56
C. elegans, quantitative analysis, 143–145
CGP. *See* Cybernetic Girls Can Be Pinky (CGP)
Challenging introductory courses, 103
Challenging us to change
   changes in students' computer attitudes, 197
   CS results across institutions, 195–196
   learning community background, 188–189
   partner institutions, 193
   process oriented guided inquiry learning (POGIL), 189–190
   TIDES community, 187
   Westminster, 190–192
   Westminster College, 187–188
   Westminster results, 194–195
CHEM, 111, 192, 194
Chemistry–CS learning community, 192
CienciaPR, 41
Class enrollment, 107
Classification accuracy, 144–145
Class-restricted pathways, 17
Classroom
   discussions, 139
   facilitation, 190–191
   management, 252
   management software, 205–206
   pedagogy, 64
Classroom-based research experience (CRE), 138–139
Closing the Achievement Gap Task Force (CAGTF), 155
CMPT, 140, 192
CMSC, 203, 163
Codecademy, 179
Coding, 78
   experiences, 25
Collaborative learning into classroom, 61
Collectivism, 24
Color-blind racial attitudes, 42
Colorism, 41
Combined online and classroom teaching, 119
Commitment, 74–75
Common Academic Program, 54

Common Academic Program (CAP), 58–60
Communalism, 25
Community, 59
 service learning, 223
Community co-learning, 9
"Components of Academic Mindset" model, 156
COMP110 TIDES@CSUN course, 225
Computation, 239
Computational art history module implementation, 140–142
Computational Data Science (CDS), 230
 certificate program, 233–234
 tools, 229, 237, 240
Computational notebook, 120
Computational sciences (CS), 36–37
Computational Studies of Speech Production and Perception, 80
Computational thinking, 239
Computer analysis module, 139
Computer and mathematical sciences engagement
 faculty development, 253
 graphing techniques, 254
 hands-on, music-related classroom activities in CS1, 253–254
 implementation, 252–253
 institutional context, 250
 introduction and background, 250–252
 reflections, 249–250
 robotics, 254–256
Computer Attitude Questionnaire, 195–196
Computer for Technical Majors, 251

Computer literacy, 239
 course, 41
Computer Organization, 251
Computers and the Human Mind, 80
Computer science
 baccalaureates, 3
 enrollment, 58
 faculty, 139
Computer Science Department, 88
Computer Science Freshmen (CASF), 195–196
Computer Science I (CS I) course, 202
Computer Science on Florham Campus, 108
Computer Sciences certificate program, 244
Computers role in science and medicine, 192
Computing, 78
Conceptualization, 26
Contemporary US educational strategies, 15–18
Content delivery, 69
Content development, culturally responsive, 220–223
Context information, 121
Controlling registration, 80–81
"Cookbook" experiments, 137
Co-principal investigators, 175
Core curriculum, 137
CPS, 150, 65–66
CPS, 151, 66
C4Q (Coalition for Queens), 87
Craps, 220
CRE. *See* classroom-based research experience (CRE)
"Creative Media Applications", 64
Critical consciousness, 22

Critical evaluation of our times, 59
Critical intelligence, 159
Critically conscious learners, 22–23
Critical thinking, 36
CRT. *See* culturally responsive teaching (CRT)
CS35, 179
CS4ALL, 87
CSCI, 100, 89–90
   grade distributions for, 84
CSCI 1205, 103, 105, 107
CSCI 2215, 103–104, 107
CS0 courses, 196
CS education, 91
CS for Insight (CS35), 179
CS-interdisciplinary psychology module, 142
CS POGIL activities, 191
CS results across institutions, 195–196
Cultural change, 70
   in classroom, 62
Cultural competence, 66, 165, 230
Cultural congruity, 44
Cultural constructs, 44
Cultural diversity, 221, 250
Cultural hegemony, 17
"Cultural iceberg" model, 156
Culturally competent learners, 22–23
Culturally congruent approach, 25
Culturally responsive approach, 147
Culturally responsive computational science
   art history, quantitative analysis, 139–142
   biology and computer science module, 143–145
   evaluation method, 145–146
   evaluation results, 146
   implementation, 138–139
   participants, 145
   psychology and computer science module, 142–143
Culturally responsive pedagogy (CRP), 4, 18–20, 263
   centers, 20
   characteristics, 20–21
   diverse learners, 22
   faculty members view, 23
   faculty role, 21–22
   power of, 21
Culturally responsive strategies, addressing recruitment, 115–117
   background, 119–120
   computation, 118
   computational modules, 120–123, 126
   faculty workshops, 123–127
   participant feedback, 128
   TIDES activities, participation in, 118
Culturally responsive teaching (CRT), 66, 68–69, 230, 250
   accessible, 158–159
   application, 159–160
   background and significance, 155–156
   concept of culture, 156
   conceptualization, 154
   cultural factors, 154
   cultural sensitivity and responsiveness, 154
   impact on faculty, 161–162
   impact on students, 162–164
   implementation deltas, 160–161
   implementation/methodology, 156–157
   implementation pluses, 160
   operational definition, 155–156

relevant, 157
results, 161
scholarly influence, 156
TIDES journey, 165–166
Culturally responsive teaching principles (CRTP), 237, 244
Culturally sensitive content, 147
Culturally sensitive pedagogies, 77
Cultural makeup, 158
Cultural responsiveness, 7, 11, 157
Cultural symbols, 33–34
Cultural variation, 69
Culture, 25
and musical traditions, 221
CUNY, 76, 87
CUNY-Cornell Tech-Verizon initiative, 87
Curriculum
community property, 66–67
redesign, 205–206
Cyberlink Brain Body Interface, 104
Cybernetic Girls Can Be Pinky (CGP)
activities, 37
curriculum revamping, 40–41
faculty development activities, 41–42
gender inequities, 38
implementation/methodology, 37–39
programming workshops in different languages, 40
quantitative analysis and critical thinking, 39
science interests and perceptions survey, 39–40
student empowering program outcomes, 42–44
Women in Science undergraduate course, 40
Cybernetic Girls Program (CGP), 36

Data collection instruments, 262
Deficit model, 61
Deflection, 42
Design-Make-Play, 89
Developmental evaluation, 261
Digital divide in society, 192
Disaggregating data power, 90
Discover–Adjust–Assess process, 155, 158–161
Discussion leaders, 125
Diversity, 59
in computer science, 136
and inclusion, 55
"Dysfunctional illusions of rigor", 124

EarSketch for Promoting Learning in SCISEL Courses, 252–253
EarSketch Python library, 253–254
Ecology, 40
Ecology Society of America, 38
Educational pursuits, 55
Education curriculum, 75–76
Effective responses, 191
Electronic Portfolio (E-portfolio), 252
ELITE, 160
Employed culturally responsive pedagogies, 16–17
E-portfolio, 122
Equity through access to computer science learning
background and significance, 177–178
ethnic and racial backgrounds, 176
faculty believe, 176
implementation/methodology, 178–179

MECHANISM program, 182–183
results, 179
Ethnic and racial groups, 75
Ethnic identity, 44
Ethnicity, 76
Ethnographer, 159
Eurocentric cultural mores and thoughts, 16
Eurocentric epistemology, 18
Evidence-based professional development, 259
Evidence-based rational approach, 91
Evidence-based strategy, 61
Exercises, 121–122
Experienced faculty, 125
Experienced teacher-scholars, 60
Experience, social-professional cohesion, 66
Extreme Science and Engineering Discovery Environment (XSEDE), 230–231, 235, 237

Facebook status updates, 142
Face-to-face classroom instruction, 119
Facilitators, 125
Faculty, 60
  development, 41–42, 252–253
  focus groups, 67
  indifference, 4
Faculty culture, changing
  background and significance, 58–62
  implementation and methodology, 62–67
  institutional challenges and responses, 56–58
  mission and catholic identity, 54–56
  results, 67–68
Fairleigh Dickinson University (FDU), 97
Faith traditions, 59
Fayetteville State University (FSU), 249–250, 252
Feedback
  from students, 67
  on workshop, 127
Feelings of isolation, 2
Festival of Computer Science, 220, 225–226
"Fishbowl" exercise, 116
Fixed mind-set, 124
Fixing the student, 61
Fostering an environment for all students to succeed
  background and significance, 102–103
  class enrollment, 107
  CS concepts and real-world systems, 111
  female and minority students percentage, 108
  grades, 110–111
  graduation rates, 109–110
  inherent learning difficulties, 112
  TIDES course enrollment, 108–109
  underrepresented minority (URM) students, 111
  women and minority students, 111
Frequent lowstakes assessments, 112
Freshman Year Initiative (FYI) program, 79–80
FSU. See Fayetteville State University (FSU)
Full-time faculty member, 189

GDrive, 253
Geek culture, 136
Gender, 76
   gap and music, 223–224
   imbalance, 60
   inequities, 40
General Chemistry/Computer Science learning community, 189
Generation computing, 219
Geographical information systems (GIS), 40
Girls Who Code and Black Girls Code, 87
GitHub, 253
Global knowledge economy, 16
Grades, 110–111
Graduation data assess, 62
Graduation rates, 109–110, 135
Graphics-based lab projects, 66
Graphing techniques, 254
GraphPad QuickCalcs, 143
Graphs *vs.* recordings, 255
Greco-Roman philosophy, 17
Grit and self-efficacy, 102
Growth mind-set, 124
Guess the Genre, 222
Guess the Note, 222
Guided inquiry materials, 189–190

Hands-on, music-related classroom activities in CS1, 253–254
Harvey Mudd College, 179
Hidden but accessible truths
   accessible truths, 89–90
   background and significance, 76–79
   course recruitment, pedagogy, and outcomes, 79–82
   ethnicity estimates for populations, 75
   evangelizing, 86–88
   group work, 83
   implementation, 79
   learning focus, 82
   projects, 83–84
   student feedback, 82–83
   TIDES community of practice, 88–89
   TIDES continue to Ebb and flow, 84–86
High-frequency low-impact testing, 207–208
Hip-hop, 220
Hispanic Serving Institution (HSI), 35, 74, 218
Historically Black College and University (HBCU), 229, 233
Historically Black Colleges and Universities — undergraduate program (HBCU-UP), 249
Homogeneousness, 34
Horizontal aggressions, 34
"The Hub", 160–161
Human–computer interaction, 102, 104
Human Genetics/Computer Science learning community, 188
Humanities, 148
   courses, 137–139
   faculty, 139
Huynh, Virginia, 223
Hybrid learning, 119

Implicit bias, 34, 174
Impostor Syndrome, 34–35, 124, 204
Improving facilitation, 191

In-class activities, 206
In-classroom/active learning approaches, 201–202
In-class social cohesion, 64
Inclusive teaching, 118
Indio, 41
Individual introspection, 9
Industry Standard Architecture (ISA) systems, 122–123
Information and intelligence students, 83
Information manipulation, 78
Information Science and Systems (INSS), 241
Information theory, 78
Inherent learning difficulties, 112
Inquiry-based pedagogy, 61
Inquiry learning, 112
Institutional readiness, 6–7
Instructional congruency, 24
Instruction modules, culturally responsive, 223
Instructor as facilitator, 189
Integrated STEM Academic Success (ISAS) program, 249
Integrated *vs.* individualized cultural framework, 24
Intellectual capabilities, 20
Intellectual property messages, 207
Interests, 191–192
"Investigative computing" skills, 179
Invisibility, 2
IrfanView, 144

Joint Committee on Standards for Educational Evaluation, 236

"JupyterDayPhilly: Transformative Teaching with the Jupyter Notebook", 120
JythonMusic Environment, 254

K-12, 17, 87
school settings, 41
Kate Winter Evaluation (KWE), 259
KEEN network, 60
Khan Academy, 251

Lack of belongingness, 2
Latino stuff, 33–34
Lawrence Technological University, 136–137
Leadership
capabilities, 40
support, 68
Learning, 174
communities, 191
community background, 188–189
community pairings, 188
cycle approach, 189
environments, 62
objectives, 191
teams, 189–190
Learning Teaching Center (LTC), 68
Liberal education, 2–3
Liberty indoctrination, 16
Life flexibility, 36–37
Linear algebra, 256
Low-stakes assessments, 105
Lyrics Processing, 222

Machine learning system, 144–145
"Machista", 44
Macro-aggressions, 34

Male-oriented stereotypes, 78
Male registrants, 80
Marginalization, 2
Marianist, 54–55
  education, 59
Matched-comparison *t*-tests, 264
Math, 251
Measurement and assessment, 259–260
  analysis, 264
  evaluation framework and structure, 261–262
  evaluation limitations, 269–271
  methods and data, 262
  outputs, outcomes, and evaluative findings, 265–269
  project fidelity, 260–261
  TIDES-level metrics collected directly, 262–263
  TIDES-level metrics collected indirectly, 264
Mediators, 21–22
Mentors Enable, Connect, Help, Advocate, Nurture, Intervene, Sustain, and Motivate (MECHANISM), 182–183
Me Too movements, 116
Mexican music, 220
Microaggressions, 34, 118, 174
Middle-class cultural values, 19
Minimization, 42
Minority and non-minority students, 56
Minority-serving institution (MSI), 218
Mission and catholic identity, faculty culture, 54–56
Mission-level commitments, 3
Mixed-race spectrum, 41
Model minority, 174

Montgomery College (MC), 154–155
Morgan faculty, 229
Morgan State University (MSU), 229, 233–235
Morgan TIDES Program (MTIDES), 229–231, 233
  activities, 242
  data collection methods, 236–237
  faculty, 245
  workshop, 242
Mulato, 41
Multiple programming languages, 207
Multi-racial students, 179
Multi-year retention, 62
Music in programming
  content development, culturally responsive, 220–223
  Festival of Computer Science, 220, 225–226
  gender gap, 223–224
  implementation/methodology, 219–220
  institutional context, 218–219
  instruction modules, culturally responsive, 223
  introduction/background and significance, 219
  peer mentors, 225
  reflection, 217–218
  YouSpeak classroom interaction system, 218, 220, 224–225

Nanotechnology and its applications, 104
NASA Swarmathon competition, 255–256

National Academies Summer Institute for Scientific Teaching (NASIST), 232
National Council for Women & Information Technology (NCWIT), 113
Pacesetter School, 198
National Science Foundation (NSF), 68
Scholarships, 174
National Society of Black Engineers (NSBE), 220
National Treasure by the National Trust for Historic Preservation, 233
Near-peer mentor program, 220
NodeXL, 241
Non-STEM faculty, 236
Non-White individuals, 42
North Carolina State University (NCSU), 202, 205
Number crunching, 78

Office of Enrollment Management, 57
Office of Institutional Research and Effectiveness (OIRE), 163
One-on-one research, 98
Online statistical calculators, 143
Open-source platform, 120
Open-source programs, 140
Open-source technology, 120
Orchestrators, 22
Organizational context, 2–3
Organizers, 21
Orientation sessions, 80
OscIn and OscOut objects, 254
Out-of-class lectures, 209
Out-of-class outings, 80
Out-of-class time, 204–205

Parallelism, 255
Parallel R, 230
Participant feedback, 128
Partner institutions, 193
Pattern recognition algorithms, 140
Peer mentors, 225
Peer mentorship, 227
Peer-to-peer interactions, 239
Personal and cultural strengths, 20
PHYLIP, 144
Physical computing and personified feedback, 252
Pitzer College
administrators, 178–179
CS courses, 178
faculty thought, 176
individual perspective and approach, 175–176
intercultural understanding, 176
lower division computer science courses, 181
multi-racial students, 179
students ethnic and racial backgrounds, 176
theory of social justice, 176–177
upper division computer science courses, 181
Pivotal Moments, 182
POGIL. *See* process oriented guided inquiry learning (POGIL)
5-point Likert scale, 145
Polling, 191
Power and privilege, 7
Practical wisdom, 59
Pre-college education, 17–18
Predator/prey relationships, 43
Pre/post qualitative attitude surveys, 210

President's Council of Advisors on
    Science and Technology
    (PCAST), 234
Primarily white institution (PWI),
    33
Prior accomplishments, 20
Problem-based learning, 103, 112,
    137
Problem-solving skills, 65, 261
Process oriented guided inquiry
    learning (POGIL),
    189–191, 198
Process skills development, 189
Pro-equity, 43–44
Pro-female, 43
Program Design and
    Implementation, 251
Program Evaluation Standards,
    236
Programming, 78
  assignments, 66
  language, 77
  modules with programming
    concepts, 222
Programming Methodology, 251
Project-based learning, 64,
    66, 88
Project-based teaching, 21
Project goals, 265–266
Project Kaleidoscope (PKAL), 3,
    38
Project Kaleidoscope Regional
    Network meetings, 36
Project-oriented environment, 137
Project-related activities, 213
Pro-women, 43–44
Prussian system in America,
    15–16
Pseudonyms, 42
Puerto Rican ethnicity, 34
Python programming language,
    120–121

QC Office of General Counsel, 80
Quarter-based curriculum, 201
Queens College (QC), 74

R, 230
Racial and ethnic groups, cultural
    heritages of, 20
Racial and structural inequities, 4
Racist practices, 42
Random Music, 222
Random number generation, 220
Rationalization, 42
Recruitment and retention of
    underrepresented minority
    groups
  implementation/methodology,
    236–238
  institutional context, 233–234
  introduction/background and
    significance, 234–235
  reflection, 229–232
  results, 238–244
Redesign using games
    programming, 252
Reflection, 12
  prompts, 122
Religious identity, 55
Research assistantship, 137–138
Retention rates, 102
Reverse discrimination, 42
Rhythm, 220
Rhythmic-movement
    expressiveness, 25
Robotics, 254–256
  with EZ-robots, 104
Robotics Clubs, 38, 42
Robustness, 255

Salsa, 220
Sankey diagram, 85–86
Scalability, 255
Scale of Words, 222

Scales, 220
SCALE-UP/Active-Learning teaching, 213
SCALE-UP approach, 202–205
Scholarship, 59
Science, Technology, Engineering, and Mathematics (STEM) program, 174
  classrooms, 1–2
  education initiatives, 89
  employment, 234
  faculty, 259
  fields, 219–220, 250
  and non-STEM majors, 244
Scientific skepticism, 8
Scientist profile, 121
Second-language program, 155
Secure copy (SCP), open-source tools, 140
Secure shell (SSH), open-source tools, 140
Seeds for Success Workshops, 42
Self-affirmation, 99
  theory, 204
Self-assessment and reflection, 214
Self-efficacy, 7, 99, 164, 267
Self-managed learning teams, 189
Self-paced learning, 119
Self-reflection, 7, 69
Semester-based academic calendars, 201
Sensor network optimization, 136
Similarity matrix, 145
Sinclair Community College, 57
"Sink-or-swim" mentality, 199
Skin-color hierarchy, 41–42
Social media, studying patterns in, 142–143
Social-professional cohesion, 66
Social responsibility for individual privileges, 25
Societal baggage, 77
Society for Toxicology, 38
Society of Hispanic Professional Engineers (SHPE), 220
Society of Women Engineering (SWE), 220
Sociology/Computer Science learning community, 189
Sociology–CS learning community, 192, 194
Sophomore-level labs, 126
Sound Recorder, 222
Specialized recruitment, 80
"Spinoff" professional development events, 161
SSPT, 60–61
S-STEM initiative grant, 182
Staff facilitators, 125
Statistical computing, 238
STEM-literate citizenry, 16
STEM-oriented mindset, 148
STEM-related skills, 76
Stereotype threat, 118
Strengthening Computer and Information Sciences Engagement and Learning (SCISEL), 251
Strings To Beats, 222
Student-Centered Active Learning Environment, 202
Student-centered learning approach, 189
Student-centered teaching, 267
Student–faculty relationships, 22
Student learning
  outcomes, 59
  and retention, 68
Students'
  computer attitudes, 197
  confidentiality, 42
  cultural factors, 158
  engagement, 57, 61

mastery, 69
underperformance, 19–20
Student Success and Persistence Team (SSPT), 56
Student–teacher relationships, 23
Student teaching assistants, 56
Survey of Music Technology, 253
Systemic marginalization, 3–4
Systems thinking, 184
   and project conceptualization, 26–27
SYSTEMS VIEW of Program Evaluation, 236

Tablets, 192
Teacher–classroom interactions, 244
Teacher–student relationship, 156
Teaching introductory programming courses, 101
Teaching scientific knowledge and skills, 36
"Teaching to Diversity in CS" workshop, 193
Teaching to Increase Diversity and Equity in STEM (TIDES), 4, 15, 229, 256–257, 262–263, 271
   campus-based projects in, 18
   community of practice, 28
   contemporary US educational strategies, 15–18
   faculty teams, 25
   institutions, 5
   journey into the deep, 9–10
   journey into the unknown, 7–9
   journey into the world, 10–11
   professional development program, 6–7
   program-level objectives, 6
   race and gender of students impacted by, 267

re-conceptualization, 4
STEM faculty professional development domain, 4
"Teaching Toolkit", 160–161
Teamwork skills, 139
Tech Talent Pipeline (TTP), 87–88
Term project, 122
Text to Melody, 222
Theorized learning, 20
"Think-pair-share" approach, 83
Thought-provoking sessions, 175
TIDES
   community, 187
   Community of Practice, 88–89
   conference, 100
   learning communities, 187, 194
TIDES courses
   enrollment, 108–109
   interest in STEM, 146
   thematic focuses, 145
TIDES@CSUN, 217, 220
   modules, 222
TIDES Tribunal, 29
Tiny Earth initiative, 40
Tones, 220
"Toolkit" of teaching ideas, 160
Traditional educational tribalism, 18
Traditional interpretation of students, 157
Tribunal model, 29
Tri-college community, 119
Tri-College workshop, 126–127
Trigueño, 41
T-test score, 143, 264

UD. *See* University of Dayton (UD)
Undergraduate research, 137
Undergraduate STEM programs, 36

Underperformance, 19–20
Underrepresented groups, 204
Underrepresented minority groups, recruitment and retention of
  implementation/methodology, 236–238
  institutional context, 233–234
  introduction/background and significance, 234–235
  reflection, 229–232
  results, 238–244
Underrepresented minority (URM) students, 111
Underserved minority (URM), 218
Universal Design for Learning (UDL), 121
University of Dayton (UD), 63
  base funding for targeted programs, 55
  curriculum changes at, 59
  faculty development, 66
  initiative, 60
  mission and catholic identity, 54–56
  problems at, 56
  religious identity, 55
  in STEM fields, 57–58
  teaching and learning importance, 54
University of North Carolina (UNC) system, 250
University of Puerto Rico in Humacao (UPRH), 33
University of Puerto Rico (UPR) system, 35
Unofficial CRT principles, 157
Unstructured Data Analysis Tool (UDAT) text classifier, 142–143
Upper-level physics courses, 126

Upside-down pedagogies, 202
Utilization-focused evaluation, 261

Version 3.5c of PHYLIP, 140
Vibrant technology community, 75–76
Victimization, 42
Virtual reality and mental health, 104
Visual art, automatic analysis, 140
Vocation, 59

Wearable electronics, 83–84
Westminster College, 188
  learning community background, 188–189
  partner institutions, 193
  POGIL activities, 190
  results, 194–195
  TIDES project, 188, 190–192
White fragility, 34
White privilege, 34
WiTNY, 87
WNDCHRM, 140, 144
'Women and Science', course, 39
Women in Technology and Entrepreneurship in NY, 76
Women in Technology New York (WiTNY), 87
Workforce development, 87
Workload
  among students, 64
  policies, 59
Workshop to Increase Diversity and Equity, 129
World Music Drum Machine, 222
Wright State Computer Science and Engineering Department (WSU-CSE), 202

Wright State University
    active learning classrooms, 212
    active learning engagement, 211
    "computer scientist" identity, 212
    control group, 211
    experimental group, 211
    implementation/methodology, 204–208
    in-classroom activities, 211
    methods and motivation, 203–204
    non-URM students, 212
    progression rates, 211
    results, 208–210

XSEDE. *See* Extreme Science and Engineering Discovery Environment (XSEDE)

Yellow Ribbon Program, 104
YouSpeak classroom interaction system, 218, 220, 224–225
YouTube, 221, 251